ISRAEL, DIASPORA, AND THE ROUTES OF NATIONAL BELONGING

Many diasporic Jews have strong ties to Israel, but what does diasporic nationalism mean, and is it necessarily tied to territory? Over the course of four years, Jasmin Habib was a participant observer on tours of Israel organized for diaspora Jews as well as at North American community events focusing on Israel and Israel–diaspora relations. During this time, Habib conducted extensive interviews with tourists and community members. The result is a startlingly honest, theoretically rich, and detailed analysis of official tour narratives and tourist interactions at a range of Israeli archaeological, historical, and military sites.

In this first ethnographic account of North American diaspora Jews imagining and experiencing Israel, Habib blends anthropological, historical, and cultural studies theories together in an analysis of diaspora nationalism that has broad implications. Reflecting on her personal history as a peace activist of mixed Jewish and Palestinian parentage, she looks at community events in North America that celebrate the attachment and sense of obligation to Israel and Israeli Jews, and presents community members' various exchanges on the conflict between Israel and Palestine. What emerges from this compassionate exploration is Habib's provocative contention that much of the existing literature about North American Jews and their relationship to Israel ignores their diverse reactions to official narratives and perpetuates an 'official silence' surrounding the destructive aspects of nationalist sentiments. As a result of this silence, Habib argues, Jewish studies has been unable to assert disciplinary autonomy from Zionist theory, and modernism, nation building, and national territory have not been interrogated as analytical categories in these new geopolitical contexts.

(Cultural Spaces)

JASMIN HABIB is an assistant professor in the Global Studies Program at Wilfrid Laurier University.

JASMIN HABIB

Israel, Diaspora, and the Routes of National Belonging

UNIVERSITY OF TORONTO PRESS
Toronto Buffalo London

ISBN 0-8020-3702-X (cloth)
ISBN 0-8020-8510-5 (paper)

Printed on acid-free paper

National Library of Canada Cataloguing in Publication

Habib, Jasmin, 1964–
  Israel, diaspora and the routes of national belonging / Jasmin Habib.

  (Cultural Spaces)
  Includes bibliographical references and index.
  ISBN 0-8020-3702-X (bound)   ISBN 0-8020-8510-5 (pbk.)

  1. Jews, American – Travel – Israel.   2. Jews – United States –
  Attitudes toward Israel.   2. Jews – Identity.   4. Israel and the diaspora.
  I. Title.

  DS132.H22 2004   305.892'4073   C2004-901525-7

All photographs are courtesy of the author.

University of Toronto Press acknowledges the financial assistance to its
publishing program of the Canada Council and the Ontario Arts Council.

This book has been published with the help of a grant from the Canadian
Federation for the Humanities and Social Sciences, through the Aid to
Scholarly Publications Programme, using funds provided by the Social
Sciences and Humanities Research Council of Canada.

University of Toronto Press acknowledges the financial support for its
publishing activities of the Government of Canada through the Book
Publishing Industry Development Program (BPIDP).

For Amit and Na'aman Habib

In Memoriam

Eliezer (Lushi) and Zillah (Bitcover) Iram
John and Marushka Novak

Contents

ACKNOWLEDGMENTS ix

Introduction 3

1 Zionism, Diaspora, and Israel 27

2 Touring Israel 37

3 Celebrating Return: One Nation, One Land 42

4 Development and Democracy 65

5 Settling the Nation, Defending the State 84

6 The Politics of Securing Peace 107

7 Representing Israel 119

8 Identifying (with) Israel: Zionism and the State 123

9 Identifying (with) Israel after Zionism 139

10 Narrating Relations for Diaspora 165

11 Longings 167

12 A Home Away from Home 192

13 Routes to Belonging 213

14 Fielding Questions of Identity 242

15 Diaspora Belonging 255

APPENDIX: INTERVIEW QUESTIONS/GUIDELINE 269
NOTES 271
BIBLIOGRAPHY 285
INDEX 303

Illustrations follow page 132

Acknowledgments

It is with great pleasure at the completion of this process that I acknowledge the support of family, friends, teachers, and colleagues. They have enriched this project and deepened the challenges as well as the rewards.

Although I am unable to name them here, I want to express my deepest gratitude to the participants and those who facilitated their participation. All of them contributed by inviting me into their lives. Without their generosity, this book would not exist.

My PhD supervisory committee in anthropology at McMaster University – Harvey Feit, Louis Greenspan, and Ellen Badone – and later in the reading stages, Richard Preston and Gerard Vallee, offered insights that are reflected here.

Harvey was the model of supervisory patience and care. As a scholar who has shown that research can be shared with activist commitments for the long term, he has been an inspiration to me. Louis Greenspan was especially crucial to the day-to-day planning and execution of the research project, discussing it with me at all stages, not only in his office but also at early bagel breakfasts and over lunchtime noodle soups.

Not least of the pleasures of being in academia is the opportunity to place myself in conversation with others. Special thanks to Joseph Buttigieg for sharing his warm intelligence and giving me enthusiastic guidance, from the time I was at the University of Notre Dame, and to Will Coleman, whose experience and friendship guided me through and beyond the postdoctoral stage at the Institute on Globalization and the Human Condition at McMaster University. In the summer of 2000, the School of Literary Criticism at Cornell University provided me the opportunity to engage with Peter Novick on the merits of this project as well as to learn about the place of Holocaust history in American culture. As they shared their work in progress, Etienne Balibar, David Carroll, and Dominick LaCapra contributed to my working through a range of questions about texts, narratives, and the social. For their professional guidance in my journey through the first stages beyond my postdoctoral fellowships, my thanks to Alan Harrison, former dean of the Faculty of Social Sciences at McMaster University, and Robert Campbell, dean of the Faculty of Arts at Wilfrid Laurier University.

For the gifts of their friendship throughout this writing process, I thank Nahla and Sami Abdo, Virginia Aksan, Linda Axford, Daniel Coleman, Davina Bhandar, Mario Blaser, Mark Behr, Stephen Cain, Mazen Chouaib, Judy Clarke, Matt Cooper, Maria di Cenzo, Jody Decker, Lise Feit, Len Friesen, Nora Gold, Atif Kubursi, Eudene Luther, Andy and Harriet Lyons, Mike Ma, Eva Mackey, Graeme MacQueen, Ruchama Marton, Theresa McCarthy, Fath McCord, George McLauchlan, Ora Markstein, Dawn Martin-Hill, Mary Millen, Tom Miller, Rick Monture, Susie O'Brien, Adele Reinhartz, Joanna Santa Barbara, Sheyfali Saujani, Dana Sawchuk, Terry Schevciw, Imre Szeman, Patricia Seymour, Michael Small, George and Leonore Sorger, Charlotte Waddell, Kathryn Wardropper, Peter Widdicombe, Christl Verduyn, and Mark Vorobej.

Thanks to Mike Evans for discouraging me from going to law school and suggesting I consider instead anthropology. He has been a great source of motivation, and I especially value his continuing friendship and support.

My gratitude goes to my editor at the University of Toronto Press, Siobhan McMenemy, who provided enthusiasm, support, perspective, and insight from the first day I discussed the manuscript with her. Her keen editorial suggestions are reflected throughout. Matthew Kudelka carefully copy edited the text, which made it clearer and more readable. Frances Mundy skilfully shepherded the manuscript through production, and Meagan Heath cheerfully assisted me with proofreading and indexing. I am also grateful to the anonymous readers at UTP and the ASPP for their suggestions.

My family has been wonderfully supportive of my reading, writing, and travelling habits. A warm thank you to Geries, Haya, and Husna Habib, to my Tandler family members, Eda and Yoel, Gila, Amos, Maya, Tamar, and Yael, and to Yaron, Rachel, Sivan, Noy, and Gal – for their nurturing love and for providing me with a home away from home.

A warm thank you to my brother Rami for his mindful and ever-supportive protectiveness.

It is to my parents that this book is dedicated. They are my home in the world and have made everything that I accomplish possible.

My lifeline throughout this process has been Jim Novak. He was drawn into reading and commenting on many drafts of this text. It was he who helped me find my voice. I am grateful for his love, patience, and great wit.

The last stage of writing this book was marked by the passing of Edward Said. It was his life-long commitment and example that paved the way for young activists and scholars to approach the Israel–Palestine conflict with critical and confident insight.

This project was funded, in part, by doctoral and postdoctoral research fellowships from the Social Sciences and Humanities Research Council of Canada; the Centennial Scholarship from the Department of Anthropology at McMaster University; research grants from the School of Graduate Studies at McMaster University; a postdoctoral Research and teaching fellowship from the Dean of Social Sciences at McMaster University; the United Nations Association–Hamilton Community Foundation Award; the Aid to Scholarly Publications from the Social Sciences and Humanities Research Council of Canada.

ISRAEL, DIASPORA, AND THE ROUTES OF NATIONAL
BELONGING

Introduction

A Great Miracle Happened Here [Israel]
A Great Miracle Happened There [Canada]

To allegorize my approach to this project, I begin with a toy that signifies the spirit of Hanukkah – a four-sided top called a *dreidl* in Yiddish, a *sevivon* in Hebrew. During Hanukkah a popular game is played with this top. On each of the four sides is a letter standing for one word of the phrase 'a great miracle happened there.' But if you happen to be playing the game in Israel, the last letter stands for 'here' (a great miracle happened *here*). Thus the words on the top change from *there* to *here* depending on where Jews find themselves – an interesting representation of the identity of contemporary diaspora Jews. The top's spinning mass imparts movement and stability. In the same way, the identities of diaspora Jews resonate in contexts that destabilize traditional notions of belonging, notions fixed to one particular place; these identities oscillate between narratives of belonging *there* and those of belonging *here*. I am seeking to understand how people live as a diaspora, how they use the national terms of identity to place themselves in relation to a community they define as their nation (Jews), a territorial space they claim as their ancestral homeland (*Eretz Israel*), and its modern manifestation as a nation-state, Israel.

In this book I examine diaspora Jews' cultural practices: specifically, I consider how they produce history, nation, identity, culture, and claims to ancestral territory. I consider narratives that identify Israel as the Jews' homeland; I also consider various multicultural and multinational identifications of North American Jews that encompass and subvert these narratives. Many scholars writing on nationalism have discussed how the concepts of place, home, and nation are abstract ideas that can be materialized as they are territorialized.[1] But how do people forge ties to a nation-state in which they do not live? And how is this nation-state transformed from a geopolitical space with boundaries and borders, passports and military institutions, into a cultural space with parallel holidays, myths, and heroes? I am less interested in contributing a new ethnography of the North American Jewish community than I am in understanding the relationships to Israel developed by Jews in North America. These relationships constitute forms of what I call diaspora nationalism. This research question leads to a different kind of analysis of the multiple locations of cultures than one that is ethnographically focused on one community's everyday habits or one that simply assumes, or naturalizes, North American Jews' relationship to Israel. For Jews in such transnational and transborder networks, national attachments are multiply recast even as they are simultaneously resituated.

At this political conjuncture it is important to explore diverse perspectives on nation, homeland, and diaspora. I hope to provide insight into first, the role played by structural and institutional forms, and second, the cultural meanings produced by people who locate their identity in relation to a place other than the one in which they reside. With the globalization of theory and the postmodern turn against essentialism, identity is now conceived as multifaceted. Many academics have shifted their theoretical focus from issues raised by notions of purity and authenticity to those raised by hybridity; from nationalism to multiculturalism; and from homeland to diaspora; less, however, is known about whether any of these theoretical debates reflects coincident hybrid and multicultural identifications and practices.

My underlying objective in this book is to consider ways of thinking outside of – and perhaps even beyond – the dominant paradigms that link identity to territorial nationalism. Zionist and Jewish nationalist ideas about identity were long ago reframed in multicultural and international settings – in what I call diaspora nationalism – and they should be recognized as authentic forms of identification to nation, homeland, and nation-state. My main concern is how belonging and national subjectivity are produced; my secondary focus is on how cultural subjects position themselves vis-à-vis a zone that is deeply enmeshed in nationalist and territorial conflict.

The research subjects are Jews living in Canada and the United

States whose practices are diasporic: they identify Israel as their home-land and nation-state yet they live outside its territory. Although Zion-ism – which is essentially the nationalist movement to found a state for the Jews – informs their practices and understandings, their locations vis-à-vis Israel cannot simply be described as Zionist.

There are two nationalities that identify Israel-Palestine as their homeland: the Jews and the Palestinians. By virtue of their locations – be these within the state, or outside the state, or as a diaspora or, for most Palestinians, in exile – and also by virtue of their histories, thus two nationalities take very different approaches to imagining the nation and their place in the world in relation to it. All Palestinians claim a direct genealogical, historical, and territorial relationship to what was once Palestine and is now Israel and the occupied military zones of the West Bank and Gaza. All were directly affected by the founding of Israel in 1948. Most were displaced around 1948 or 1967, and many have lived under direct Israeli military control or gover-nance, or in refugee camps in the surrounding states. On the other hand, most of the world's Jews – some of whom have a spiritual con-nection to Jerusalem – are unable to claim a direct territorial or kin con-nection to the land that predates the founding of Israel in 1948.

It is not surprising, then, that the literature describing Israel and Pal-estine presents polarized perspectives on identity, homeland, history, and conflict in the region.

The position most often described as pro-Israel goes something like this: Israel is the culmination of biblically decreed prophecies. Ever since the rise of Christianity, and especially in Christian lands, the Jews as a people have suffered a particularly virulent form of racism – called anti-Semitism – and this has led to their humiliation and harass-ment, to *pogroms*, expulsion, and death. Zionism emerged in Europe as a nationalist movement in response to the 'Jewish problem.' Seeking to liberate the Jews, it called for the establishment of a Jewish state. The Second World War and the Holocaust proved, more than any other events in history, that the Jews would never be safe until they had a refuge in the form of their own state. Israel was established as a mod-ern, European state with Zionist ideology as its guiding principle. The Arabs were offered a state alongside the Jewish one, but they refused it, and all land acquisitions since that time have been a result of defen-sive wars conducted by Israel. Israel is the jewel in a rough crown: it is a democratic, Western-oriented state in a region dominated by pre-modern, antidemocratic sensibilities and by monarchial and dictatorial regimes, all of which to some degree hate both the West and the Jews. This explains the ongoing danger for Jews living in the Middle East and the need for a strong Israeli military presence. It is the right of any Jew to return to his or her ancestral homeland, because it is the only state where Jews have sovereignty.[2]

The Palestinian and Arab perspectives are strikingly similar to the Zionist one. Israel is a settler state that arose out of a distinctly European colonial nationalism called Zionism. Since being forcibly displaced in 1948, the Palestinians – and all other Arabs in the region – have suffered under what they call *al nakba*, or the catastrophe. Three reasons can be given for this situation: oil, Western guilt over the Holocaust, and the essentially settler-colonial nature of Zionism. Because the West did not prevent the Holocaust, it felt obligated to establish a place of refuge for the Jews. The Palestinians have paid the price for this. The West's unquenchable thirst for oil has meant that monarchs and dictators in the region receive support from western Europe and the United States despite the oppressive nature of their regimes. All of this has distorted not only the political but also the economic systems of the region. As a settler-colonial and thus expansionist state, Israel never intended to share the land with its indigenous inhabitants. Thus it has, since 1947, forcibly displaced Palestinians from their homes, expropriated their lands, and destroyed their economy. Israel's profoundly militaristic stance has undermined all alliances in the region and endangered all of its neighbours. If the Jews can return to their ancestral lands after a three-thousand-year absence, then so too should the Palestinians be allowed to return after only a half-century's absence.[3]

These perspectives form the core of almost any discussion about Israel, the Jews, and the Palestinians. The problem is not that there is no single truth or that every writer or interpreter takes a position or entertains one or another version of one of these perspectives. Rather, the problem is that researchers have rarely made the effort to cross over – that is, to be sensitive to or mindful of other perspectives. It is as though every writer or researcher has chosen a side and having done so, simply staked a claim to it.

When it comes to these issues, I have had both the privilege and the distinct advantage of having grown up in a family that is deeply committed to a peaceful and just reconciliation of the Israel-Palestine conflict. My family's history, and my own continued activism for just such a reconciliation, have informed my interpretations of what people in each of these communities consider critical for the other to understand.

I was born in Israel to a Jewish mother and a Palestinian father. My father immigrated to Canada in 1969; my mother, my brother, and I followed in 1970.[4] My maternal grandparents escaped the horrors of the Holocaust by settling in the city of Haifa, in northern Israel, in the early 1930s. Some members of my maternal grandmother's family perished in Europe; others were able to escape to France and to Israel. My maternal grandfather's family was rescued by my grandfather and his brother and brought to Israel. My mother and her sister were born in Mandate British Palestine before the Declaration of the State of Israel.

My father was born in Palestine. As a result of the UN Partition Plan of 1947, he and his immediate family were removed from their home in Beisan, now also known by its Israeli or Hebrew name as Beit She'an. They became internal refugees in the northern Galilee district of the new State of Israel. Their home and property in Beisan were declared off-limits for security reasons, and although they became Israeli citizens, they have never been allowed to reclaim it. Members of his mother's family, who had been living in Haifa, became refugees in Lebanon during the same period. Some, though not all, have since left Lebanon for Cyprus, England, Canada and Australia. As far as I know, none of my father's family have ever been allowed to return to claim their property in Haifa or Beisan or to gain citizenship since their escape and expulsion.

This, then, is part of the background to my entrée into this field of research.

In developing this ethnography, I was seeking to discover how people who have no direct family or personal experiences in Israel develop a relationship to the state. However, I do not mean to suggest that their relationship is somehow less authentic. Rather, my desire was to explore just what the basis of this relationship is, how it develops, and how it endures. Although our relationships to Israel are different, none is more legitimate than all the others. While my visits to Israel are similar to those of many immigrants to their first home, the tours organized for North American Jews also constitute a sort of homecoming.

What interests me are the individual and collective practices that tie some North American Jews to Israel and that lead them to identify Israel as their homeland and refuge. Anthropological and cultural studies approaches to investigating these processes of identity-making frame my questions and this research.

Once I started this research, I began to realize that there was a perspective I had never been exposed to in my personal experiences: the perspectives of North American Jews committed to Israel. Hannah

Arendt's words spoke to my goal when I first set out to conduct this research. She writes:

> Political thought is representative. I form an opinion by considering a given issue from different viewpoints, by making present to my mind the standpoints of those who are absent; that is, I represent them. This process of representation does not blindly adopt the actual views of those who stand somewhere else, and hence look upon the world from a different perspective; this is a question neither of empathy, as though I tried to be or to feel like somebody else, nor of counting noses and joining a majority but of being and thinking in my identity where actually I am not. The more people's standpoints I have present in my mind while I am pondering a given issue and the better I can imagine how I would feel and think if I were in their place, the stronger will be my capacity for representative thinking and the more valid my final conclusions, my opinion.
>
> Culture and politics ... belong together because it is not knowledge or truth which is at stake, but rather judgment and decision, the judicious exchange of opinion about the sphere of public life and common world, and the decision what manner of action is to be taken in it, as well as how it is to look henceforth, what kind of things are to appear in it.[5]

The positions that I had little understanding or appreciation of or exposure to, and about which so little ethnographic work had been done, became my ethnographic subject. While conducting research in these communities, I knew that I was both an outsider and an insider: I am a Jew and a Palestinian; a Canadian and an Israeli; a peace activist and an anthropologist. I say this not to suggest that one part of me was in or out, but rather to point out where I stood and, at the same time, how that stance constantly shifted.

With all this in mind, I decided to try to understand what Jews in North America are being told about Israel and how they come to understand their relationships to Israel – how they judge Israeli politics, culture, and history in general and the Israeli–Palestine conflict in particular. And what, if anything, defines their diaspora lives – that is, in the most simple terms, their lives as Jews living in a relationship to Israel as their home away from home.

I decided that besides poring over the literature, I would need to do at least two other things: participate and observe Jewish community events, especially those where Israel is the focus; and participate and observe organized tours to Israel that are designed for Jews living in

North America. My hope was that in following this methodology I would see how Israel is represented to North American Jews while they are in their home communities, as well as how Israel is represented to North American Jews while they are in Israel. To this end, it would be vital for me to listen to the official narratives about Israel and Jewish identity presented to North American Jews, and then to try to understand how and when individuals took up these narratives. I am investigating how national meanings are created through public and popular cultural events and through the social and political links between those events.

There is a vast literature on Jewish identity, history, and practices in North America. In general, North American Jews are presented as socio-economically successful and as active in local and national politics. They have built strong and effective community development organizations, which help support community institutions such as Jewish community centres, temples and synagogues, geriatric residences, day schools, and Jewish Studies programs in universities.

Sociologists and demographers measuring Jewish identity have pointed to rates of travel to and support for Israel as important variables.[6] As anthropologist Jack Kugelmass has pointed out, these aspects of identity 'are some of the areas that need to be considered in an ethnography of American Jewry.'[7] I agree with this critical assessment and have taken up the challenge of exploring these relationships and practices.

In many ways, then, my project is about the politics of location: the location of diaspora Jews, the location of Jews in Israel, the location of the presentation of narratives, and the location of the listeners to and readers of those narratives. But 'location' has more than a geographical meaning here. Following feminist writer Adrienne Rich,[8] location is the place into which we are set, the place in which we find ourselves and through which every person's perspective on the world is made. One is located not only by one's perspective on or interpretation of the world but also by context, history, and politics. Location is also about how one's perspective can be multiply cast and creatively emergent while also being framed by one's social and historical context. Although often associated with feminist theorists, Rich's work has far more nuance because it is not essentialist – it promises movement, not stasis. As I read her, Rich would suggest that although one may be born a woman and one is set into the world as such, one has the opportunity to redefine what *woman* is. Thus, recognizing one's location may also mean learning how to take another route and thus finding your way to another place.

I want to suggest, as well, that anthropologists rethink their practice of naming people by locating them geographically – that is, of naming people as living in diaspora or in diaspora cultures or communities because they do not live in their original territories. I contend that diaspora must be understood as a location in Rich's terms – that is, not as a geographical location but rather as a practised relationship to homeland. It is because of these practices of identification with Israel that the Jews with whom I travelled, and whom I joined in community events, could be defined as living as a diaspora and as participating in diaspora nationalism. Following this argument, then, Jews who do not feel any attachment to Israel, or who do not participate in Israel-centred events, should not be defined as diaspora Jews since they do not at all locate themselves as such. In fact, they may not identify themselves mainly as Jews and may simply describe themselves as Canadians or Americans or Torontonians or New Yorkers. Israel may not matter to them very much at all. While I have not done research with this latter group, I believe these issues are important when it comes to understanding the positioning of those who do have attachments to Israel.

One of my goals is to give readers an awareness of what is at stake in the many debates on Israel, Palestine, Jewish identity, and the Arab–Israeli conflict. Developing this ethnography enabled me to get at a far greater range of views about nationalist identities than those furnished by scholars and, as problematically, by the political players of this troubled region. There is more at stake than recounting the history of Zionism or delineating its political ideology. People make sense of their lives in very complicated and often unanticipated ways despite the rigid ideologies to which they are exposed.

I began my fieldwork 'officially' in the spring of 1994 and continued it without break into to the summer of 1998. However, I was attending community events and making contacts with people in the two Canadian communities[9] where I planned to do research as early as the fall of 1993. For the first year of research I was living in a major urban centre with an estimated population of 175,000 Jews; then I moved to a nearby smaller community with an estimated population of 5,000 Jews for the rest of the research period. While living in these cities, I observed and participated in many public events in community centres, synagogues, libraries, and schools. While I was living in the smaller city, I often travelled to the larger one to attend community events and meet with people. The metropolitan region in which I conducted the research has one of the largest populations of Jews in Canada, so it has many well-established Jewish community institutions and annual events, including book, film, and music festivals. All in all, I had many opportunities to develop relationships with people. I attended at least one public event a week over the course of the research period, and often two and three a week between October and May, when there tended to be a higher number of activities. Thus, I attended more than two hundred events over the course of the research period.

I attended community events that were about Israel, or about Israel-Palestine relations, or that presented Israeli personalities or celebrities – musicians, filmmakers, authors, and the like. These public and popular narratives, most of which were presented, practised, and performed by Jews, for Jews, and about Jews, were the focus of a good deal of my research. They included public lectures, conferences, and book readings sponsored by community institutions (e.g., Jewish community centres and synagogues); fundraising and lobbying efforts by organizations (e.g., the United Jewish/Israel Appeal, the Jewish National Fund, the New Israel Fund, Peace Now, Friends of Bar Ilan University [Israel], Friends of the Hebrew University [Israel]); and university programs (e.g., Jewish Studies and Middle Eastern Studies). Israeli and North American Jewish politicians, academics, and writers as well as prominent leaders and activists spoke at these events. Celebrations of Jerusalem's three-thousandth birthday in 1995, Zionism's hundredth anniversary in 1997, and Israel's fiftieth birthday in 1998, involved festivals, concerts, and parades and marches. These were often sponsored by important organizations such as the United Jewish Appeal and Jewish community centres.

There were also annual book, film, and cultural festivals (e.g., Ashkenaz, a Yiddish revival festival), as well as educational events (e.g., Holocaust Education Week). When invited, I also attended the board meetings of some of the communities' Jewish organizations involved in lobbying and fundraising for Israeli projects.

Besides spending time in communities and attending community events, I chose to participate on tours of Israel in order to experience Israel with diaspora Jews. I chose tours of a type popular in the communities with which I was engaged.[10] Almost everyone I met had travelled to Israel on one of these tours in the past, especially on their first trip to Israel; or they planned to do so sometime in the future; or they knew others who had already been on such tours. So I was able to discuss the experiences of these tours even with people who had never been on one.

I asked for permission to go on tour from each of the sponsoring organizations. I sent each organization a letter of request, a copy of my proposal, and consent forms to be signed by those tourists who were willing to participate in the research. In one case this process seemed no more than a formality, and nothing of significance was discussed with the sponsoring agents. In another case, members of a board of directors of the sponsoring organization were involved in my tour planning. With the last tour, not only did I have permission, but I was also introduced to the group in a welcoming letter sent to the tourists, each of whom was informed about my background as well as my research interests. As in the other cases, not everyone agreed to participate, but it was with this group that I enjoyed the most opportunities for conversation.

People's perspectives on Israel became clear through the questions they raised on tour and at lectures they attended in their own communities. To extend these findings, I conducted a series of formal interviews with those whom I met in the community and on tour. These interviews form the third and most important part of my field research. Of the over one hundred people whom I met and with whom I discussed Israel and its place in their lives, quite a number became close friends or at least acquaintances. Some I only came to know on tour, and did not meet again later. Everyone I personally invited to an interview agreed to participate.

All but one of the families I met was Ashkenazi – that is, of European background. Their traditional language was Yiddish, although many of the present generation had never spoken it. In the course of the research, I met only one Palestinian Jewish family. They had lived in the Galilee area before Israel was founded in 1948. As Jews from Arab lands whose traditional language is Arabic, these people are referred to as 'Oriental' Jews. I did not meet any Sephardim – Jews whose families were expelled in the seventeenth century from Spain (*Sfarad* in Hebrew) to countries such as Morocco and Algeria and whose traditional language is Ladino (a dialect of Spanish written in Hebrew script). Many but not all of my respondents were Conservative or Reform Jews. Some were Modern Orthodox, others Reconstructionists.[11] Those whom I met ranged in age from early twenties to early nineties; those with whom I had the most contact were middle-aged (late thirties to mid-sixties) and older (mid-seventies to nineties). Almost all of those I met had children and grandchildren. Among the middle-aged group, there was a good deal of active support for Jewish community organizations and their activities, especially in Israel. Some sat on the boards of Jewish organizations that support Israel; others were leaders or fundraisers for similar institutions, either as employees or as volunteers. Most of those with whom I interacted were professionals – teachers, lawyers, professors, social workers, or businessmen. Many were very wealthy or at least upper- or upper-middle-class. Many were comfortably retired but still active – avid golfers, artists, travellers, political or community volunteers. Quite a number of them had contributed many years of community service to cultural and social agencies.

I first became involved in the research just after the signing of the Declaration of Principles (DOP),[12] better known as the Oslo Accords, between the State of Israel and the Palestine Authority in 1993. It was a moment of creative dialogue between and among Jews and Palestinians in North America. People crossed one another's paths in ways that they had not previously done. Although in essence the peace accords recognized the right of Israeli Jews to a secure Israel in the Middle East, and the right of Palestinians living in the West Bank and Gaza to live free of Israeli military occupation, the question of the Palestinians' right to return to their homes of 1948 and the question of Jerusalem's status were left to later stages. A little more than a year after the accords were signed, an Israeli Orthodox Jew assassinated one of the essential participants in the process, Israeli Prime Minister Yitzhak Rabin. This marked the beginning of the end of an era. Today the accords and the optimism they inspired have vanished, although the question of Palestine remains. This book provides a glimpse of the kinds of debates that were raging in the community at the time; it also hints at the kinds of issues that will have to be resolved if there is to be peace in the future.

Extended discussions with those who became my friends helped me develop a richer sense of just what is at stake for those many Jews who have made Israeli politics and culture an important feature of their lives. Though we often disagreed, it was through these discussions that I learned a great deal about North American Jews' deep attachment to Israel. Though these friendships I came to see the possibilities and the risks that those in the Israeli and Palestinian communities face as they struggle to transform the Israel–Palestine conflict.

On the State of Ideological Affairs

History is a significant element in nationalist as well as diaspora practices, so it is important to understand how nations officially represent their past in public culture. Theories of representations of the past

guided my examination of the narratives of nation as they were presented on tours and at community events. I consider these theories
specifically in the context of the insights I drew from them for understanding my research findings.

Writing on diasporas, anthropologist James Clifford in his book
Routes[13] warns against using ideal types and modelled paradigms of
diaspora and suggests that researchers remain open to a variety
of diaspora situations and practices. That said, a number of definitions
of diaspora have been quite useful for understanding the practices of
place, of living diaspora lives. An important example relates to the criteria for defining diaspora established by historian Gerard Chaliand
and geographer Jean Pierre Rageau in their *Penguin Atlas of Diasporas*.
According to Chaliand and Rageau, many criteria define diaspora,
including the dispersion of a community due to political or natural
disasters, and the memorialization of the dispersion; but 'what charac-
terizes a diaspora, as much as its spatial dispersion, is the will to survive
as a minority by transmitting a heritage.'[14]

'Dispersion,' 'history,' 'collective memory,' 'the transmission of heritage,' and 'survival' constitute the key terms for this definition of
diaspora. Fundamental to this description is the emphasis on cultural
practices rather than on place or geographical location in the world.
The focus here is on the need for the collective to 'transmit its history,'
to 'preserve its identity,' while adapting to circumstances after its dispersion – in other words, on survival as a community.

This emphasis contrasts with the definitions that a number of
anthropologists (though not all) have been using. In the 1990s, anthropologists and other social scientists began to take interest in groups
described as exiles, tourists, migrants, immigrants, and diasporas –
peoples seemingly defined by their location outside the bounds of
nations, cultures, and ethnic or minority communities. Much of the
theoretical interest in these groups seemed to be based on unease with
older definitions and problems, which, it was argued, were simply
reproducing epistemological and static models of nation, culture, and
community. In addition, feminist, postcolonial, literary, and postmodern theories had deconstructed modernism's epistemological givens of
female/male, self/other, Orient/West, and tribe/state and created
new epistemological terms for consideration and debate. Through
efforts to escape static and bounded notions of culture and place, new
concepts such as travel, ethnoscapes, diaspora, exile, geography, cre-
olization, space, place, and border cultures emerged; the purpose of

these terms was to describe a globalizing world and cultures no longer bound by the parameters of modernist anthropology.[15] With these shifts came an interest in non-territorial locations. For example, anthropologists Smadar Lavie and Ted Swedenburg write that '...the phenomena of diasporas calls for reimagined "areas" of area studies and developments of analysis that enables us to understand the dynamics of transnational cultural and economic processes as well as to challenge the conceptual limits imposed by national and ethnic/racial boundaries.'[16]

What is not explicit, however, is just what those conceptual limits are. For example, what is the fundamental difference between those living in a 'transnational cultural and economic process' and those who live in a capitalist world? Are 'diaspora' and 'exile community' simply new terms for defining immigrant, ethnic, or minority communities? Is diaspora a matter of geography or culture? It seems that nothing distinguishes a diaspora from any other community except the assumption that some members of that community may have a relationship to another place that its members either came from or long for. But coming from another place is a very different practice from longing for another place, and implies very different experiences.

In his celebration of 'travelling' cultures, which seem to both recognize and seek roots and routes, Clifford apparently rejoices in the 'invocations of diaspora theories, [and] diasporic discourses,'[17] though without specifying why. Geographers Neil Smith and Cindi Katz argue that although Clifford's notions of 'location' (and I would add his ideas about 'diaspora' and 'traveling culture') reach for 'a dynamic rather than a static conception of location ... [his] series of locations' and 'diverse, but limited spaces' suggest a multiplication of absolute spaces rather than a radical rethinking of spatial concepts.[18] In a similar vein, anthropologist Arjun Appadurai's concerns about the past privileging of the local and the representational in Western analyses of 'native' people have drawn him toward a celebration of deterritorialization. This is evident in his discussion of 'disjuncture and difference' in the new cultural mediascapes of late capitalism. In 'Global Ethnoscapes: Notes and Queries for a Transnational Anthropology,' Appadurai writes:

> There are some brute facts about the world of the twentieth century that any ethnography must confront. Central among these facts is the changing social, territorial, and cultural reproduction of group identity. As groups migrate, regroup in new locations, reconstruct their histories, and

reconfigure their ethnic 'projects,' the ethno in ethnography takes on a slippery, non-localized quality, to which the descriptive practices of anthropology will have to respond. The landscapes of group identity – the ethnoscapes – around the world are no longer familiar anthropological objects, insofar as groups are no longer tightly territorialized, spatially bounded, historically unselfconscious, or culturally homogeneous.[19]

While I am sympathetic to the postmodern project, such theories provide little direction for understanding diaspora practices. It seems that anthropologists interested in the epistemological potential of the term *diaspora* have scarely begun to analyse what I call 'practices in place' – That is, those creative practices that people meaningfully engage in so as to locate themselves in relationship to a place, be that place a home or an envisioned homeland.

It is not simply that some anthropologists are using abstract definitions of diaspora. However delinked these definitions may be from the chains of a nation-state or from modernist notions of place, there are serious problems inherent in defining or describing a 'diaspora' as a thing rather than as a process or a relationship. The inherent suggestion is that some people, and some communities, are somehow out of place. For this reason, some anthropologists have responded to the deconstructionism of the 1980s by placing the paradigm before the people. As a result they have assumed rather than illustrated that communities of interest – exiles, immigrants, and migrants – continue to have a relationship to another place or that they feel they belong elsewhere.[20]

Thus, anthropological diasporas have included communities of exiles, migrants, and refugees. The only common denominator for these is the status of their members – in a world where people's 'official' identities can only be defined in terms of nation-state or territorial boundaries – as deterritorialized or displaced subjects. In this way, some anthropologists have stopped mapping identities and cultures onto communities in such a way as to define them in relation to nation-states; instead, they simply define communities by their dislocation from the same static nation-state. Not much has changed. Why describe people who live away from a place once or presently defined as their historical, traditional, or indigenous homeland as a diaspora unless and until it has been established that the community members have maintained a relationship to home, define their present identities in relation to their past home, or would return home given the chance? To do so would be to neglect to historicize people's locations and to again map a homeland onto their identities and destinies when that homeland may or may not be a significant part of their self-identification. I would ask: What is the advantage of placing people living away from a homeland or an ancestral home in one category? Furthermore, will people who claim to belong to a nation that claims as its homeland another geographic place forever be defined as people out of place? What can home mean? Do we not return to the age-old dichotomy foreigner/friend, self/other, when we define communities in this way? Is it not more dangerous to resituate difference on the basis of one's ability to possess or maintain territorial and geographical dominance, and is such difference not reinforced by these notions of diaspora? Has a new essentialism located in territoriality emerged in the search for hybrid relations? It is also quite troubling when anthropologists, whose science is in 'the local,' bring together such vastly different experiences of place as those of exiles, refugees, and migrants under the category *diaspora*. All of this is to suggest that we need to be critical not only of our definitions and classifications of people based on their geographical location, but also in our assumptions about the meanings of home and homeland. We must pay special attention to the degree to which these new categories have been informed by and reproduce dominant cultural models based on nation-state politics and priorities.

Moreover, in those investigations of diaspora which are more discriminating (i.e., where the diaspora under investigation excludes people who are refugees or exiles), much of what emerges relates to the survival of tradition and the persistence of communal and collective identities among those whose experiences were at least in part defined by a relationship to what had been historically, ritually, or administratively defined as their homeland.[21] In an academic world that has sought to rupture these very concepts,[22] anthropologists are talking diaspora while still examining the invention of culture[23] in ever-emergent communities and the relationships people develop in, among, and across imagined communities.[24] In other words, the terms for 'practices in place' – of collective memory, community, and tradition – are being examined in much the same way as they have been in the past. Only the terms used for identifying these supposedly new identities – for example as deterritorialized – seem to have changed.

Many scholars are writing about lives lived in a home away from homeland; however, they are not writing about the very practices that define this continuing relationship to homeland. This is what interests me here. Celebrations of hybridity within displaced communities are the interest of scholars like Paul Gilroy and Jacqueline Nassy Brown; in contrast, my emphasis in this text is on an emplaced community's relationships to a homeland.

This excursion through the literature on diaspora leads me back to the literature on nationalism, on the role of history and national identity; and the role of public culture. Theories of the creation, presentation, and performativity of the nation provide rich descriptions of how the narratives of the past create and territorialize national histories and create national places. This alerts us to how diaspora Jews respond to and to varying degrees subvert nationalist narratives of belonging in and to Israel.

It is important to recognize that theorists of nationalism always assume community relations to the state, rather than out-of-state or diasporic identifications. Despite this gap, and because they are dealing with nations, much of what they have to say is relevant to identifications of the sort made by diaspora nationalists.

In his study of the historical origins of nationalism, *Imagined Communities*, Benedict Anderson makes a useful attempt at a conceptual definition of the nation. Anderson defines the nation as an 'imagined political community': 'It is imagined because members of even the smallest nation will never know most of their fellow-members, meet them, or even hear of them, yet in the minds of each lives the image of their communion.'[25] This idea may seem fairly obvious, but Anderson is careful to point out that his is not an essay on invention or falseness (in contrast to Hobsbawm and Ranger's work on the 'invention of tradition,'[26] for example). Rather, it is an articulation of the imaginative and creative production of community. The virtue of Anderson's approach is that he understands that people think beyond the immediate presence of others in order to conceive, identify with, and form relationships with others. He writes that 'the nation is always conceived as a deep, horizontal comradeship.' And just as every individual imagines belonging with others in their community, Anderson understands the appeal to national identification 'in a world in which the national state is the overwhelming norm.'[27]

Another virtue of Anderson's approach is that it describes how nationhood and a sense of national identity are liable to be experienced by people as representations of belonging – that is, nationalism is highly socially mediated. As such it must be examined as a social practice (like religion and kinship) rather than as a political or ideological formation (like liberalism or socialism). This points to the need to understand nationalism in interpretive rather than simply spatialized and territorialized political terms. This helps us avoid the logic of 'this people lives on this land' and, thus, all things within this territory must be of national significance. Furthermore, thinking about national identity in this way complicates the simple view that national identities are cultural belongings rooted either in deep quasi-natural attachments to a homeland or in blood ties. In fact, they are complex cultural constructions that emerge out of specific historical conditions. Since national subjects are not necessarily in direct communal solidarity, the imaginings of national communities are lived through representations. Cultural theorist John Thompson points out a paradox in all this: institutions that some anthropologists and other social scientists see as having a globalizing effect – for example, the mass media – Anderson sees as fostering communal identifications. The creation of and support for the Israel Broadcasting Corporation would be an example of this politics of national imagination.

Anderson's scholarship provides a corrective to the scholarly work that had been done on nationalism prior to the mid-1980s; but he does not examine the qualities of nationalist representations with which people creatively engage as they form a relationship to, or identify themselves as, members of a nation. As many scholars have pointed out, national culture and national identity require concepts such as national heritage and traditions. Their main argument is that such representations of a people's past are set in terms that define these traditions and communal practices as not only authentic but, more importantly, as stable, and that as such, they present an invariant history. Scholars writing about such inventions do so with varying degrees of sensitivity to people's power to create and recreate their own histories: some contend that tradition is created by and against elites;[28] others focus on tradition as a practice rather than an ideological construct.[29] Because the field is so wide-ranging, and I have limited goals in mind, I examine only a few writers who discuss the construction of the past and the role of public culture events that temporally mark the emergence of and identification with the nation.

With respect to the past and its constructedness my interest in the past focuses on what cultural theorist Roland Barthes called 'mythologies.' In

Mythologies,[30] Barthes examines myths as discursive forms that naturalize realities instead of historicizing them: 'Myth has the task of giving an
historical intention a natural justification ... What the world supplies to
myth is an historical reality, defined ... by the way in which men have
produced or used it; and what myth gives in return is a natural image of
this reality.'[31] Myth is not false so much as it is a reworking of 'historical
reality.' And it is this reworking that is part of what Barthes suggests is
a 'dialectical relation ... between human actions.'[32] Moreover:

> Myth does not deny things, on the contrary, its function is to talk about
> them; simply, it purifies them, it makes them innocent, it gives them a
> natural and eternal justification, it gives them a clarity which is not that of
> an explanation but of a statement of fact ... In passing from history to
> nature, myth acts economically: it abolishes the complexity of human
> acts, it gives them the simplicity of essences, it does away with all dialec-
> tics, with any going back beyond what is immediately visible, it organises
> a world which is without contradictions because it is without depth, a
> world wide open and wallowing in the evident, it establishes a blissful
> clarity: things appear to mean something by themselves.[33]

In other words, it is the iteration of history that is important, and
myths are creative productions of history. Barthes is not suggesting that
what is being represented is either true or false so much as he is asking
us to recognize that myth-making is necessary in order to 'organize a
world,' so that 'things appear to mean something by themselves.' In
order for us to understand the role that nationalist narratives perform,
we must first understand the potential for history to be 'organized,'
'naturalized,' 'essentialized,' and depoliticized.[34]

In her examination of the 're-presentations of the past' in Mexico,
anthropologist Ana Maria Alonso argues that although Anderson's
Imagined Communities has made a contribution to analyses of identities,
the 'centrality of histories to national imaginings ... remains at the edges
of his argument.'[35] She chooses to focus on how such histories are
shaped and remade: 'Historical chronologies solder a multiplicity of
personal, local and regional historicities and transform them into a unitary, national time. They link the experiences of day to day life to events
which are categorised as "national" and in so doing, they reinforce the
solidarities of nationality.'[36]

Alonso is arguing here that history is not only 'naturalized' (as in
Barthes) but also nationalized. Those who are empowered to make his-

tory – or what she calls 'hegemonic ideologies' – creatively 'transform popular histories' into national stories by naturalizing, departicularizing and idealizing them: 'Naturalisation disguises the transformations effected on subordinated histories by turning re-presentations into "raw facts" which cannot be contested. Framing, voice, [and] narrative structure are all manipulated to conceal the work of reinterpretation in which power and knowledge are intimately linked. The effects of truth render invisible the effects of power.'[37]

Alonso echoes much of Barthes's argument in *Mythologies*, but then she adds two important points that lead to a richer understanding of the 'representation of the past.' First, the processes of 'framing, voice and narrative structure' add an element of living representation to Barthes's model, which seems more object-oriented. Second, these representations are 'effects of power,' the implication being not only that those with power make history, but also that the context in which these representations are articulated is also important.

Next, Alonso describes how historical discourses and practices are 'departicularized' – that is, how they 'are emptied of the meanings which tie them to concrete contexts, to definite localities' so that 'the signs of subordinated and regional histories are appropriated and revalued, invested with new meanings which reproduce a hegemonic national ideology and the relations of domination it configures and legitimates.'[38] In other words, local or regional histories disappear in the face of nationalizing discourses. In this way a singular history is created where there were many histories. Again, it is power that determines whose history gets told.

Finally, Alonso describes the process of 'idealization' whereby 'the past is cleaned up, rendered palatable and made the embodiment of nationalist values ... Pasts which cannot be incorporated are excluded by national history.'[39] In other words, the histories or stories of those who cannot be embodied within a nation's imagining of itself are made to disappear through the processes of 'idealization.' Alonso here is suggesting that national histories are stripped of the histories of others while a unitary, single history of the nation is being created. Note as well that she is not assuming that only monolithic histories are created; rather, 'popular and official memory exist in relation to each other' and are constantly being negotiated as such. Questions of how such representations develop are indeed also important.

Anthropologist Don Handelman goes a step beyond all this by considering how histories are experienced, especially as public cultural events. He contends that events may be organized to 'encode' a nation's history, with 'important consequences for national cosmology.'[40] Events 'are devices of praxis that merge horizons of the ideal and the real, to bring into close conjunction ideology and practice, attitude and action.'[41] They are also 'structures' with 'relatively high degrees of replicability.'[42] Handelman is interested in the design of these performances and in how they embed their audiences in the story of the nation. The organizers set up a particular history through commemoration; they also temporalize the audience's experiences. He explains the roles of national narratives in this way:

> First the narratives encoded by ceremonial can telescope into and out of one another with little contradictions ... Second, together these planes encode narrative through various modalities of time – linear, oscillating and cyclical. Together, resonance and modality enable the multidirectional cross-indexing and cross-referencing of lengthily separated period and events. The result is a complex temporal grid of the mastery of time, a blueprint that helps shape the meanings of national history and that interprets ongoing, national existence through the perception of such temporal processes.[43]

For example, Israel sequences national days of commemoration, such as Holocaust Remembrance Day and Independence Day, in an order that evokes and 'reflects the importance accorded to the encoding of cultural time in [the nation].'[44] In this example, the themes of catastrophe and rebirth are played out narratives and commemorative practices: 'It is in part through temporal rhythms that national history is generated, and it is within this ethno-history that this nation-state is legitimated in large measure to itself. This hegemony of ethno-history constitutes a moral economy of time, one keyed to innumerable injunctions to remember, and so to re-member.'[45] For Handelman, the opportunity to *perform the nation* is not simply about time-out-of-the-ordinary or ceremonial time; it is also 'primarily "expressive" in its emphasis on the mutuality, reflectiveness, and solidarity of togetherness.'[46]

Anthropologist Robert Paine considers the 'ontological issues' involved in the formation of national identifications. In an effort to understand 'Jewish identity and competition over "tradition" in Israel,' he considers the interpretations of time and place as they are differently experienced by nationalist-territorialist Jews (e.g., the settlers in the Occupied Territories). He writes that in Israel 'there are groups who enact their lives as though they are living in different Israel's from one another. Each group, each "Israel" is an attempt to constitute Jewish identity in Israel.'[47] Paine articulates the differences between Jewish identifications with Israel by situating those differences in ideological terms – terms, however, that are complicated by notions of time and place. Moreover, he suggests that we study 'Zionism as a Jewish quest about meaning and means of redemption,'[48] and he writes that 'one should expect dialectically arranged forces at play around Zionism and Judaism and "being Jewish" today, and also expect them to be embedded in historiography.'[49] In very much the same vein, many tour sites and community events in Israel are designed to evoke periodizations and temporalizations of the national that, as Paine suggests, can only be interpreted through particular understandings of Zionism and Judaism. Often the sites are experienced and the narratives are performed so as to position the participants in the context of a memorialized event.

In all of these discussions, and in many debates on national identity and nationalism, there is a tendency to assume that individuals do not 'talk back,' or articulate oppositions, or interpret and imagine the national, in ways at variance with official and institutionalized representations and narratives of nation. Ironically, then, although theories of nationalism and national identity describe people's activities as creatively imagined, a great deal has been written about how representations of the nation are imaginatively created and produced, and relatively little about how imaginative national subjects are in interpreting these representations.

National imaginaries are formed within a real world of ideas and practices, and they are bound within a range of narratives that carry with them some determinant of national identity, of what a nation *is*. But for us to understand the constraints placed on audiences to imagine national identities and the national community and their freedom to do so, we must fully contextualize these imaginings. Official narratives of the nation influence individual actions, but we must not interpret such ideologies of official imaginings as inevitably totalizing. We must examine and analyse them in context.

I am interested not only in how nationalist narratives of Israel are represented to diaspora audiences but also in how these audiences interpret such narratives. Thus, I turn to cultural theorist Michel de Certeau. His theories of practices in everyday life help explain how people select ('poach' in his terms) official and ideological narratives and play an active role in making them personally meaningful. Those who write on nationalism and representations of the past typically emphasize the political meanings of narratives and how intentions cannot be isolated from their institutional narrators and producers; in contrast, de Certeau emphasizes the critical potential of everyday readers and consumers of culture to make sense of their world. Interpretations of narratives can be ideological or institutional; that said, they can also mark a break with accepted practices and common understandings.

·Like other postmodernists, de Certeau[50] emphasizes people's critical potential to wrest and co-opt narratives. According to him, an emphasis on consumption, or on reception and interpretation, need not involve rejecting a general historical context or the character of the narrative's cultural field of production, although his main focus is on the local event. In order to recognize what he calls 'resistance' to narratives, we need to understand the dominant or culturally sanctioned meanings of events, narratives, and other performances. De Certeau urges us to examine the performances of power, the point being to understand the production, limits, and specificity of what becomes commonly accepted as knowledge. By examining 'resistance,' we challenge our assumptions about dominant and ideological forms, and we force ourselves to think differently about how those ideological forms are consumed or interpreted. De Certeau offers his own work as a counterweight to Foucault's, as a theory of those tactics which can resist, subvert, and make use of dominant or 'foregrounded' power structures:

> A society is thus composed of certain foregrounded practices organizing its normative institutions and of innumerable other practices that remain 'minor,' always there but not organising discourses and preserving the beginnings or remains of different (institutional, scientific) hypotheses for that society or for others. It is this multifarious and silent 'reserve' of procedures that we should look for 'consumer' practices having the double characteristic, pointed out by Foucault, of being able to organise both spaces and language, whether on a minute or a vast scale.[51]

De Certeau's model suggests that we not only uncover and describe dominant discourses or narratives; furthermore, it suggests that in order to understand their effects, we must also examine the contexts and interpretative practices engaged in by the consumers or audiences of those discourses or narratives.[52]

Theories of nationalism locate the effects of a narrative on a whole polity; de Certeau's theory of tactics shifts the analysis to the interpretations made by those subjects for whom these national narratives are intended. His 'theory of practice' enables us to consider not only the political effects of a narrative but also the position of the reader. When theory is applied to the narratives in this way, anything like a single, totalizing ideology collapses, because audience members are then capable of interpreting the narratives in a number of ways, and because the narrative itself is reconceptualized as a site of 'play,' with the interpreter redefined as an engaged, active, and creative subject. Following de Certeau, then, I begin my analysis with the assumption that consumers of nationalism are able to contest a dominant order of representation and that context, community, and the intentions of the narratives' producers cannot control the function of those narratives.

De Certeau contends that audience members are capable of poaching, or making alternative interpretations; yet his theory is not simply a celebration of individual imagination. Like Adrienne Rich, he recognizes that interpreters or consumers are always located on a field of social forces and that because these fields are dynamic and shifting, the possibilities for consumption and interpretation are multiple. However, de Certeau's theories also accept that every audience relies on what is 'available' – that is, no one can transcend the cultural and material context of his or her life. Audience members cannot escape these social forces, but they can, by poaching from a range of sources or experiences, subvert or reinterpret the conventions of particular interpretive practices.

Anderson, Barthes, Alonso, Handelman, Paine, and de Certeau have all contributed to my theorizing on diaspora nationalism and diaspora Jews' practices of place. Diaspora Jews live in the multicultural milieu that is North America, and they creatively imagine their relations to Israel by poaching, consuming, and interpreting the national narratives of Israel presented to them during tours and at cultural and community events. Although they do not live within the geographic borders of Israel, the narratives of that nation-state have become their narratives of belonging as a nation (as Jews). This form of diaspora nationalism is based on a sense of obligation and responsibility to preserve the collective, in memory, tradition, and practice.

De Certeau's is a theory of interpretation. Cultural theorist Henry Giroux also signals a way into the discussion of such popular texts as those presented during tours and at community and cultural events. His sensibilities are far more critically minded than those of de Certeau, whose imaginings of strategies and tactics are more individual than collective, more subjective than political. Giroux allows his interpretive lens to include communities beyond those in conflict. The politics of Israel and Palestine are defined not only within these two diverse communities, but across their national and political realms and in the imaginations of others. Conceptions of what a Jew is, or what an Arab is, or what a Palestinian is, and where each community belongs, are not limited to those national communities. It is to a much wider public that I would like to speak, for texts of belonging and nationalist narratives circulate much more widely and thus must be interpreted as dialectically affecting other politics in other places. Following Giroux's observations on public pedagogies, this text, 'attempt[s] to bridge the gap between private and public discourses simultaneously putting into play particular ideologies and values that resonate with broader public conversations regarding how a society views itself and the world of power, events, and politics.'[53] As a consequence of some of the most heinous political and military violence in this and the past century, millions around the world have been displaced from their lands. Unfortunately, Jews, Israelis, and Palestinians are not the only communities that have to confront questions of territoriality and belonging. Their experiences may contribute to a greater understanding of some of these issues.

1

Zionism, Diaspora, and Israel

In the beginning, there was the Land of Israel, and then there was exile, and the Jews lived as a nation without a land. Until they had a land of their own, there would always be a 'Jewish problem.' So goes the Zionist narrative. Zionism promised freedom, redemption, revolution, liberation, and normalization, and it was to form the ideological basis for the founding of Israel as the Jewish state.

On tours of Israel and at community events, key Zionist tropes are presented as part of the narrative of nation. More recently, however, post-Zionists have begun to question some of Israel's founding narratives, especially those informed by Zionist interpretations of history. Although no explicitly post-Zionist narratives were presented on tours or at community events, some diaspora Jews that I met had formed what I would describe as post-Zionist relationships with Israel.

Although diaspora Jews contribute both moral and financial support to Israel, disputes at the organizational level over whether to make *aliyah* (i.e., migrate to Israel) or continue to live in North America have lost some of their intensity. Among North American Jews, the general assumption nowadays is that even those who feel some attachment to Israel will remain in North America. This has had implications for how Jewish identity is analysed and measured by social scientists interested in differences and similarities between Israeli Jews and the Jews of North America.

As a political movement, Zionism began to take root in the late 1800s as a response to the rise of nationalist movements throughout Europe, and also, in no small measure, as a response to the conditions in which Jews had been forced to live in Europe – especially eastern Europe.

Thus, Zionism was a national movement created both in and against exile.

All Zionists agreed that the Jews were a cultural-historical entity, or a religious-national entity, or a race, or a people, or a nation, or a combination of these. While different branches of Zionism had different ideas about how to revive or rescue the Jews and Jewish identity, they all declared that all Jews had an equal right to a national home. Most Zionist writings at the turn of the century historicized the Jews' condition, suggesting that Jews had always been in constant conflict with gentiles (or non-Jews) and that Jews would continue to live alienated and insecure lives until they had a nation-state and territory to call their own. These calls resonated for European Jews. In Russia, for example, anti-Semitism was pervasive and state policies restricted the Jews' freedom of movement and conscripted male Jews into armies for longer than normal terms. Central to the Zionist project was the idea that life for Jews outside of a territory they could call their own was always going to be difficult, insecure, and dangerous.

Every Zionist's program included an assessment of the steps that would have to be taken to liberate the Jews. These programs also presented the conditions from which Jews needed to escape. Some Zionists focused on the role of anti-Semitism, attributing it in part to the Jews' abnormal status among nations. They called on the Jews to gain the self-determining status that the French of France and the Germans of Germany could claim – this was 'political Zionism.'[2] Other Zionists attributed the Jews' condition to their alienated relationship to land. This argument, which arose out of the peasant-centred ideologies of the time, went that because Jews could not own or did not own farmland, they were alienated from the labour necessary to become members of a *Volk* or a people. These thinkers mirrored the socialist movements around them and thus developed 'socialist Zionism.'[3] Still other Zionists believed that a 'return' to Israel was part of a messianic calling – this was 'religious Zionism.'[4] This last was a nationalist religious project that sought to restore the 'chosen people' to their Holy Land. Always, the assumption was that with the founding of a nation-state for the Jews, the diaspora would disappear and with it the abnormal and insecure condition in which all Jews lived. This is sometimes referred to as the 'negation of the diaspora.'[5]

Some Zionists wanted to establish a cultural centre for Jewry in Palestine, and did not expect that all Jews would return to the Holy Land. The most important proponent of this 'cultural (or spiritual) Zionism'

was Asher Zvi Ginsberg, better known as Ahad Ha'am.[6] Born in 1856
to an aristocratic Russian Ukrainian family, he became a Jewish scholar
and philosopher. Late in life he made *aliyah* to Palestine, where he died
in 1927, before the state was founded. Ahad Ha'am's concerns for the
Jews in diaspora were rooted in his fear that the Jews would assimilate
and thus lose their identification with their greater purpose. He
believed that from the 'restoration of the Land' would emerge a kind
of 'Hebrew renaissance' that would strengthen the resolve of those
Jews living in diaspora to preserve their Jewishness.[7] Ahad Ha'am's
Zionism assumed a continued relationship between the Jewish state
and its diaspora. His understanding of the history of the Jews living in
diaspora, among other peoples, away from their spiritual centre –
Israel – was as bleak as that of his Zionist contemporaries. Unlike
them, however, he did not believe that the Jews would return to the
Holy Land even when it became possible. He was interested in the
revival and survival of Jewish culture outside and beyond the spiritual
centre of Israel; he assumed that this centre would gain great significance for Jews living elsewhere.

For its first fifty years, Zionism was not a mass social movement in
Europe. Few European Jews made *aliyah* during this time; most Jews
who left Europe went to the United States.[8] After the Second World
War and the Holocaust, Europe's Jews found that almost all gates to
North America were closed to them.[9] At this point their need for ref-
uge took on a new urgency.

The Zionists who had moved to Palestine before the Second World
War had built and created political, security, and social institutions
such as the Jewish Agency. Through diplomatic contacts, they had persuaded the Ottoman Turkish rulers (who occupied the region until
1917) to allow them to buy land in Palestine from absentee landlords. In
1917, after Ottoman rule had ended, they persuaded the British, who
had a mandate over Palestine, to declare the region a Jewish homeland
(this was the Balfour Declaration). They founded communal settlements, *kibbutzim* and *moshavim*, in the Galilee and on the Negev Desert.
They developed a presence in the cities and founded Tel Aviv. They
established schools, political institutions, and social service agencies.
And they built a number of national institutions such as the Hebrew
University in Jerusalem.[10]

There are many competing narratives[11] of what followed all of this. I
provide only a sketch to serve as a foundation for later chapters. After
the Second World War and with the end of British rule in 1947, the UN

declared the Partition of Palestine, the purpose of which was to accommodate what had been defined as the two interested parties, the Arabs of Palestine and the Jews. Throughout 1947 and 1948, the Arab countries that surrounded Palestine, including Jordan, Egypt, and Syria, engaged with Zionist forces and turned Palestine into a military battle ground. Around this time, many Palestinians became refugees forced to live in the surrounding states. On 14 May 1948, Palestine's Jewish leaders declared an independent State of Israel.

The founding documents of the State of Israel were bound to reflect both the hardships of life for Jews outside Palestine and the triumph associated with the founding of the new state. Below is an excerpt from the Israeli Declaration of Independence.

In the Land of Israel the Jewish people came into being. In this Land was shaped their spiritual, religious, and national character. Here they lived in sovereign independence. Here they created a culture of national and universal import, and gave to the world the eternal Book of Books.

Exiled by force, still the Jewish people kept their faith with their Land in all the countries of their dispersion, steadfast in their prayer and hope to return and here revive their political freedom.

Fired by this attachment of history and tradition, the Jews in every generation strove to renew their roots in the ancient homeland, and in recent generations they came home in their multitudes.

Veteran pioneers and defenders, and newcomers braving blockade, they made the wilderness bloom, revived their Hebrew tongue, and built villages and towns. They founded a thriving society of its own economy and culture, pursuing peace but able to defend itself, bringing the blessing of progress to all the inhabitants of the Land, dedicated to the attainment of sovereign independence.

The Holocaust that in our time destroyed millions of Jews in Europe again proved beyond doubt the compelling need to solve the problem of Jewish homelessness and dependence by the renewal of the Jewish state in the Land of Israel, which would open wide the gates of the homeland to every Jew and endow the Jewish people with the status of a nation with equality of rights within the family of nations.

Despite every hardship, hindrance and peril, the remnant that survived the grim Nazi slaughter in Europe, together with Jews from other countries, pressed on with their exodus to the Land of Israel and continued to assert their right to a life of dignity, freedom, and honest toil in the homeland of their people ...

It is the natural right of the Jewish people, like any other people to control their own destiny in their sovereign state ...

The state of Israel will be open to Jewish immigration and the ingather-
ing of the exiles. It will devote itself to developing the Land for the good
of all its inhabitants ...

Even amidst the violent attacks launched against us for months past,
we call upon the sons of the Arab people dwelling in Israel to keep the
peace and to play their part in building the state on the basis of full and
equal citizenship and due representation in all its institutions, provisional
and permanent ...

We extend the hand of peace and good-neighbourliness to all the states
around us and to their people, and we call upon them to cooperate in
mutual helpfulness with the independent Jewish nation in its Land. The
state of Israel is prepared to make its contributions in a concerted effort
for the advancement of the entire Middle East.

We call upon the Jewish people throughout the diaspora to join forces
with us in immigration and construction, and to be at our right hand in the
great endeavour to fulfill the age-old longing for the redemption of Israel.[12]

Embedded in this document are many important Zionist markers.
The same ones are often encountered in the national narratives of
belonging that are presented on tours of Israel and at Jewish community events in North America. These themes and tropes, and their narrations, can be framed as follows:

- Jews, while not all born in Israel can return to it because it is the site
  of their nation's birth. They are the chosen people and it is their
  chosen land.
- The Jews have yearned for return ever since their initial exile.
- The land the Jews came to was nothing but a 'wilderness.' The Jews
  'returned' and created a 'thriving society' as if none had existed
  there before. They are dedicated to 'bringing the blessing of
  progress' not only to the inhabitants but also to the entire Middle
  East.
- The Jews have 'returned' to their home. They have restored it, reclaimed it, reconstituted it, and redeemed it. All of this identifies them
  as organic to the land; non-Jews are simply the land's inhabitants.
- The Holocaust proved that the Jews' 'abnormal' situation of 'homelessness and dependence' could be resolved only by granting them
  the 'status of a nation' among the 'family of nations.'

- The 'newcomers' to Palestine – and, later, Israel – were 'pioneers and defenders.'
- Arabs are perpetrators. They use violence to attack Jews, who thus must always be on the defensive.
- Arabs simply 'dwell' on or 'inhabit' the land, though they have been 'granted' citizenship in the Jewish nation-state.
- Jews around the world are called on to fulfil 'the dream of generations' through immigration or support for Israel.

A few years after the Declaration of Independence, and in lieu of a constitution, a number of Basic Laws were drawn up, the most significant of which was the Basic Law of Return. Formulated in 1950, this law granted 'every Jew, wherever he may be, the right to come to Israel as an *oleh*[13] [a Jew immigrating to Israel] and become an Israeli citizen.'[14]

Many studies of Israeli identity highlight these and other Zionist themes. They focus on how Israeli history is 'officially' represented in museums, at archaeological sites, and during public and cultural events.[15] They all locate Zionism in the text and have been useful in my analyses of the narratives presented to diaspora Jews.

But Israel's history has been marked by much more than the liberationist historiography of Zionism; it has also been marked by militarism. Israel has fought wars in every decade of its existence.[16] The following are among the most significant battles (as they are called by Israelis):[17]

- The 1948 War of Independence: a war with Israel's neighbouring states, including Egypt, Jordan and Syria. It led to the end of British rule in the region and to the expansion of Israel's borders to include some of what had been designated as the Arab state in the 1947 UN Partition Plan.
- The Six Day War of 1967: a pre-emptive war with Israel's neighbouring states, including Egypt, Jordan, and Syria. It resulted in the reunification of Jerusalem and the occupation of the Sinai, the Golan Heights, and the rest of Palestine (the West Bank and Gaza Strip).
- The Yom Kippur War in 1973: a bold military attack by Egypt on Israel's high holiday surprised Israel's military establishment and led to a transformation of security apparatuses and practices.
- The Operation Peace for Galilee in 1982: a war with Lebanon ostensibly aimed at destroying the terrorist bases of the Palestinian Liberation Organization, then located around Beirut.

- Desert Storm (Persian Gulf War in 1990–1): a war aimed at removing Iraq from Kuwait. Iraq targeted Israel in an attempt to undermine a coalition of Arab and Western states, which included the United States, United Kingdom, and Canada.

Israel's recent history has also been marked by a series of peace agreements. The most important agreements include the following:

- The Camp David Accords, signed with Egypt in 1982, which returned the Sinai to the Egyptians.
- The Declaration of Principles (DOP) – more commonly known as the Oslo Accords – signed by the Israelis and the Palestinians in 1993. This led to a partial withdrawal of Israeli forces from much of the West Bank and Gaza Strip. This led, as well, to the signing of peace agreements with other Arab states, most importantly with Jordan.[18]

Although they were never fully implemented, the Oslo Accords marked the first time in the region's history that an official peace between Israel and its neighbours seemed on the horizon. For some Palestinians and Israelis, both Jews and Arabs, the accords inspired considerable hope for a just peace; unfortunately, this optimism faded at the close of the millennium, when a new cycle of violence erupted. Still, the basis for any agreement remains the same: the recognition that two nations claim a land that was once Palestine and is now Israel.

Israeli Zionism and North American 'Pro-Israelism'

While the State of Israel was being established, debates about the place of the Jews that had begun during the formation of the Zionist movement continued, especially between North American Jews and Israelis. Each side seemed to be defining and redefining Zionism to suit its own political purposes. Israel had invited all Jews to return to Israel, and North American Jews on the whole supported Zionism and Israel; even so, very few Jews from North America chose to relocate to Israel. The mission statements of Jewish institutional organizations reflected all of this: calls to make *aliyah* became less and less strident, but at the same time, North American Jews steadily increased their financial and political support for the new Jewish state.[19] According to Israeli political scientist Gabriel Sheffer, 'It is known that in the late 1980s and early 1990s, Israel's annual income from donations raised in the U.S. amounted to some $300 million, investments in Israel [from abroad] amounted to about $600 million, and the amounts transferred from all other Jewish diaspora communities have amounted to about $200 million annually.'[20]

In the late 1970s and 1980s, a number of social scientists began examining the differences between Jews living in the North America and those living in Israel, and found that Zionist issues remained central.[21] The studies cited most often include Steven Cohen's *Modernity and Jewish Identity* and Charles Liebman and Steven Cohen's *Two Worlds of Judaism*.[22] Cohen and other researchers conducted similar studies for the Canadian Jewish community.[23] Two interesting issues can be extracted from these studies. First, rates of 'pro-Israelism' are used to measure North American Jews' levels of commitment to Israel. Cohen contends that 'pro-Israelism' is a more useful term for discussing American Jews' attachment to Israel because Jews living in the United States do not express classical Zionist perspectives on what it means to live away from Israel. 'Zionists' in the United States lack 'any distinctive analysis of Jewish life' outside of Israel.[24] That is, American Jews show little or no understanding of Zionism's classical emphasis on *galut*[25] or exile. Thus, *aliyah* is not as significant to them as it is to those who follow classical Zionist ideology or, as importantly, to Israeli Zionists.

Second, Cohen in his quantitative analyses of Jewish identity includes the rate of attachment Jews have formed to Israel.[26] He explains that his 'analysis of pro-Israel activity *per se* is confined to travel to the Jewish State' and to 'attitudinal components of support for Israel' distinguished along the lines of 'orientation to the classical tenets of Zionism, concern for Israel, and support for her government's international policies.' In the *Two Worlds of Judaism*, Liebman and Cohen summarized some of the results of their quantitative analyses of American Jews' relationships to Israel: 'About one-third are relatively indifferent to Israel, another third are moderately pro-Israel, and a third are passionately pro-Israel.' Furthermore,

> Among the two-thirds of American Jews who are pro-Israel, almost half respond affirmatively to a more stringent set of questions. They have visited Israel, they claim to have had personal contact with an Israeli during the preceding twelve months, they want their children to spend a year in Israel, they plan to visit Israel in the next three years, and they call themselves Zionists. To be sure even among this more passionately involved segment of the population only a fraction would qualify as Zionists by the typical Israeli's criterion, which emphasizes commitment to *aliyah*, [mean-

ing] resettlement. Only 15 percent of American Jews say they have given some thought to settling in Israel, and an even smaller number say they could 'live a fuller Jewish life in Israel than the United States.'[27]

Liebman and Cohen are constrained by the limitations inherent in quantitative research methods. That said, it is important to point out a few other weaknesses in their approach as they relate to their definitions. Most significantly, they leave undeveloped many questions about just *how* Jews might identify with or relate to Israel. For example, the term 'pro-Israelism' suggests a favourable attitude toward the State of Israel as a political entity. But do people who are attached to Israel automatically support its policies? Or is some other relationship being described here? Moreover, responses to the sentence, 'If Israel were destroyed, I would feel as if I had suffered one of the greatest tragedies of my life,' do not reveal just what meanings Israel might have for people or what is embodied in such a relationship that its end could be considered a catastrophe. Finally, in this analysis, as in others, Israelis and North American Jews are located in terms of Zionist politics. That is, it is Zionist ideology that defines Jews who live outside of Israel as a diaspora community. As some anthropologists do, sociologists like Cohen and Liebman assume and naturalize a relationship between the North American Jewish community and an ancestral and newly claimed territory. As a consequence, they do not explore what these relationships might involve.

In this book I examine how Zionism continues to inform current public cultural events designed by, for, and about Jews living outside of Israel. I also examine how these polarized identity categories fail to account for the rich and complicated meanings and practices of many diaspora Jews in North America. Many of these relationships could in fact be characterized as post-Zionist.

Post-Zionist narratives deconstruct the classical Zionist narratives and call for a rethinking of what Israel represents and even a redrawing of its territory. Israel's 'new historians,' who include Ilan Pappé, Tom Segev, Avi Shlaim, and Zvi Sternhall, best represent these issues, although there is scholarship from other fields. This historiography questions the representation of Israel as an embattled state in the Middle East – in particular, its treatment of the Palestinians before, during and since 1947.[28] It also questions the role that Israel played during the Holocaust[29] and the discrimination encountered by Oriental and Sephardic Jews within an Ashkenzic Jewish state.[30] All of the post-

Zionists are critical of conventional Zionist wisdom, but they also vary in their predictions about Israel's future. Some maintain a Zionist outlook (e.g., they believe that Israel should remain a Jewish state), but most propose that Israel become a state of its citizens rather than primarily 'the Jews' state.[31]

2
Touring Israel

Nations are imagined, represented, and performed for their national audiences. A key component in any understanding of the meaning of Israel is that it is the nation and state of the Jews. What happens on tour – what tourists are told about Israel and the Jews' identity – is an important focus of this research.

The tours[1] I accompanied were quite typical of their kind. They were study tours, and they were organized by Jewish agencies that fund projects in Israel – projects ranging from reforestation to democratization. They were designed to forge links between diaspora Jews and Israeli Jews, and between diaspora Jews and the State of Israel. On these tours, we were taken to places where – so we were told – financial contributions from diaspora Jews had changed Israeli lives. The funded projects included community centres, municipal parks, water reservoirs, and social programs for inner-city teens, new immigrants, and battered women and children. These projects were run not by state agencies (although many had overlapping responsibilities with the state), but rather by non-governmental organizations designated worthy of support by the fund's board of directors.

How, then, did tour guides present and represent Israel to an audience of Jews from North America?

Every organization that arranges tours has its own orientation (more on this below). That said, the guides assigned to the tours were extremely important because they performed, narrated, and produced the many nationalist narratives of Jewish belonging. All tour guides in Israel must complete a tourism course and be licensed by the Israeli government. Their job is to provide information about Israel's history, geography, and people. Each organization was assigned an Israeli tour guide; each of these guides was accompanied by at least one other Israeli and by one North American representative from the sponsoring agency. On top of this, there were often also site-specific guides. So, for example, a member of the *kibbutz* would guide us on the *kibbutz* tour.

The North American representatives of the funding organizations who accompanied each tour were there to 'make sure everybody is happy,' as one put it. They were there to ensure that the tourists were satisfied with the organization's itinerary, accommodations, and planning, and also to promote, highlight, and provide information about their agency's good works. While we were riding the tour bus between destinations, these representatives were sometimes asked to contribute their perspectives or knowledge about Israeli politics or culture. But all agency representatives participated on an intermittent basis; thus, in the end, it was the Israeli guides who were crucial to the experience.

The tours I accompanied were arranged by the Israeli and North American professional staff of three sponsoring organizations. I will call them the Israel Land Fund tour, the Israel Civil Society Fund tour, and the Israel Development Fund tour. The price quoted for each tour included return economy airfare; prepaid four- or five-star accommodations, most meals included; bus transportation to all tour sites; and entrance fees to those sites, as necessary. The tours averaged ten days. Two big agencies that I travelled with arranged tours for hundreds of participants every year. Once in Israel, these larger groups were divided into smaller ones of twenty-five to forty. Groups were usually arranged so that Torontonians travelled with other Torontonians, New Yorkers with other New Yorkers, and so on.

A general outline of the itinerary was always available, but the details usually were not known until around two weeks before departure. Almost every tour included visits to Tel Aviv; West Jerusalem, the Old City, and the Jewish, Christian, and Armenian quarters; a *kibbutz*; an archaeological site; the Golan Heights, Galilee, the Jordan Valley, and the Negev Desert. At least one dignitary or government official, such as a mayor or cabinet minister, would welcome the participants, sometimes making a long speech outlining his or her position on a particular political or social issue.

Each tour also had a theme:

- The Israel Land Fund tour (1995) celebrated Jerusalem's three-thousandth anniversary.
- The Israel Civil Society Fund tour (1996) highlighted and celebrated

regional peace agreements emerging from the Oslo Accords and Israel's democratic future.

* The Israel Development tour (1998) marked Israel's fiftieth anniversary.

The Israel Land Fund (ILF) raises funds for land and water development projects. From the ILF's 'Participant's Guide':

Among the main features of our program is a first-hand look at some of the outstanding achievements of [ILF] in beautifying the land, protecting the environment and enhancing the quality of life for all to enjoy ... We are very proud of the fruits of [many decades] of effort and energy which [ILF] has devoted to the state of Israel on behalf of the entire Jewish people. From our beginning ... when a group of committed, dynamic and visionary Zionist leaders created [ILF], to the present time in which [ILF] plays a pivotal role in the absorption of a massive wave of *Aliyah* throughout Israel, the ability to turn dreams into reality has given vital proof of the meaningful role of [ILF] for Jewish people the world over. As a participant on this tour you have an integral role in these accomplishments, and in the work of the years to come.

The Israel Civil Society Fund (ICSF)'s 'Itinerary Guide' claimed:

[ICSF] has been at the forefront of the movement to build a society dedicated to tolerance, justice and pluralism. Now, its efforts are even more imperative to create a civil society in which the rights of each and every citizen are respected ... The Study Tour you are joining offers you the opportunity to gain first-hand knowledge of the issues that [ICSF] deals with on a daily basis. You will also have a chance to see the political and social contexts in which varied citizens' initiatives operate.

The Israel Development Fund (IDF) directs the funds it raises toward a wide range of social services, both in Israel and around the world. The IDF's 'Resource Book,' which was a part of our tour package, stated:

We have had the opportunity to visit Israel on many occasions and it was always said that we were visiting in 'Historic Times.' Once again we will have the opportunity as we celebrate the 50th Anniversary of the state of Israel ... We all take pride in the many accomplishments and growth of the state of Israel. We, in the diaspora, play our role in the collective responsibility of *Aliyah* and *Klitah* ([meaning] immigration and absorption). Supporting [IDF] ensures Jews suffering from oppression will have an opportunity to live and express themselves freely in a democratic open society.

The participants were strongly engaged by the materials provided for them, and most participants carried their tour packets with them for the first few days, to read during meals, on the bus, and during breaks. I learned soon enough that the orientation provided generally matched the political and social interests of the participants. More often than not, however, after the first few days they would consult their packets only to learn about the day's itinerary.

Whatever the organization's political or social orientation, all of the sites chosen by organizers as well as the narratives presented at those sites seemed to have been arranged in such a way as to place Jews, their histories, and the survival of their traditions in the territory and body politic of contemporary Israel. At their core, these narratives were Zionist; they represented the Jews as a nation belonging in and to Israel, and they showed the Jews as a threatened population surrounded by chaotic and undemocratic populations. It was always emphasized that the Jews, *all* Jews, must secure their survival as a nation by supporting Israel as their nation-state.

Israel and the Jews' identity were linked through what I call 'narratives of belonging': In ancient, biblical, and recent historical times, Jews longed for Israel; this longing, and the subsequent settlement and development of the nation-state, are evidence of their belonging. The narratives locate the Jews' return to Israel as part of a modernizing and democratizing trajectory. Tropes of return and redemption infuse the descriptions of modernization, especially in and around the Negev Desert, which suggests that not only the Negev but also non-European Jews were developed or civilized by Israel. The main evidence for Israel's democratic nature is that the state recognizes non-Jews living within the state and protects their places of worship.

Tour presentations focused on the need to defend and secure a tiny nation-state surrounded by dangerous and forceful enemies. The presentations about the War of Independence, the Six Day War, and the conflicts with Lebanon and Syria all highlighted these themes. New settlements, often referred to as neighbourhoods, were presented as necessary for the nation's security – as corridors built to defend Jerusalem, the Jordan Valley, and the Upper Galilee from military as well as demographic intrusions.

Many tour participants resisted the interpretations of history and the explanations for current social conditions presented to them by their hosts. In doing so, they were displaying a high level of engagement and indicating the extent to which these were meaning-making performances for both the tour guides and the tourists.[2] That is, in making sense of the narratives, the participants were selecting and deciding what was meaningful and locating themselves politically, socially, and in the context of their own personal histories.

On each of these tours, I visited a vast number of sites and listened to many discussions. I have decided, however, to focus on only some of those sites – the ones that seem to have mattered most to North American Jews. These sites were the focus of many conversations in hotel rooms, at meal times, on the bus, and later (after the tourists returned to North America) in discussions at community events and during the interviews.

When preparing accounts of these narratives, I reviewed all written texts (guidebooks and materials provided to tourists by the organizing institution, often including Israeli government documents), video and audiotapes, and my field notes. Any tourist I travelled with – and any who travelled to Israel in the same time period – would find them familiar.

3
Celebrating Return: One Nation, One Land

Common to all the tours were narratives that linked the Jews to the Land of Israel in such a way that the territory became exclusively associated with the Jews' struggle and historical and teleological mission. Jews are embedded in the Land and the Land is in turn embedded in the Jews' history. Biblical and archaeological sites were made significant by being presented as evidence of the Jews' long-term longing for and belonging to the land. But more recent historical events were also reinterpreted in Israel, especially with respect to the Holocaust. In pointing to the nationalist resonance of these narratives, I recognize that there are counter-narratives and counter-histories; although I do not present them here, I have tried to signal (sometimes in the notes) where I know they exist.

Chronologies are crucial for understanding the historical narratives of a nation, and participants often asked their guides for clarifications and illustrations. As we passed ancient sites, participants seemed especially confused. On the Israel Civil Society Fund (ICSF) tour, in response to a tourist's request for an explanation, the guide, Sivan, provided what she described as a 'child's understanding' of history. She stretched out her arms and explained that her head represented the year zero, her one hand the year 2000 BCE, or the period of Abraham, and her elbow the period of the Patriarchs, David, and the Second Temple. The shoulder of her other arm represented the destruction of the Temple in 70 CE, her elbow the 'return from exile' in 1948, and her hand the year 2000 CE. This description seemed to satisfy most of the participants, who later during the tour referred to this performance several times.

On the Israel Development Fund (IDF) tour, after a bit of prompting by some tourists, Arnie, the guide, explained the terms he had been using:

I've been throwing out time periods and I'll try to do [a] simple [explanation] ... [We begin with the] Canaanite period. They were the original inhabitants of the land ... They were inside the land from 3300 years BCE. Notice the dates: I'm talking now about Jewish historical sites. BCE, which is 'before common era' ... [With the] conquest of the Israelites in 1250 ... the Canaanite [period ended]. [The] Israelite period, Kings of Israel [begins] from that time period, 1000 BCE, up until the destruction of the ... First Temple. [Then the] Babylonians [in] 586. Second Temple period up until ... 70 CE ... And from then on, friends, it's simple: It's Romans, it's Roman Byzantine, it's Muslim, Crusaders, Mamaluks, Turks, Brits, and we're on to the present.

References were also made to archaeological sites. The findings at these sites were presented as proof that there had been Hebrew or Israelite tribes in the area. While travelling through Galilee, in the north of Israel, Sivan told us:

There were several huge cities when the first [Hebrew] tribes entered that part of the land ... This is something that can be proved [sic] archaeologically ... There were Canaanite kingdoms, 'city kingdoms' they were called, and there you can see the penetration of a different set of tools, of pottery and then of writing. And then you can see how the Hebrews are penetrating the land over the layers of the Canaanite [period] ... This is very, very obvious because they found here something that looks like a palace and a very, very big gate [built in] a very different style [from] the Canaanite [style], and this is what we call today the Solomonic Gate, [or] the Solomonic Palaces, simply because it comes together with the Hebrew period or the Israelite period of the Kings in Jerusalem. This is quite an incredibly big site. It is one of the biggest city kingdoms that ever was in this area.

Sivan, like Arnie, dated the region in terms of a Jewish or Israeli-Jewish historiography. According to them, history in the region began with the Canaanites and moved through the Israelite, Roman, Roman Byzantine, Crusader, Mamaluk, Ottoman and British eras. Except for the Israelite Period, the guides represented these eras in terms which suggested that the land had been merely 'occupied' until the return of the Jews. Palestinians, Muslims, and Arabs were not described as part of the region's history. This particular referencing system enabled the guides to basically ignore people who had lived continuously in the area, who at best were referred to as 'occupiers.'[1] This chronology of the region's inhabitants served to erase entire histories and communities; it located only the Jews, and it suggested that other people occupied but did not *inhabit* the land while the Jews were in diaspora. This distinction is important, for it contrasts the integral and organic relationship that the Jews have to the land with a distant and inauthentic relationship that others have to it. Others' histories were being hidden by the dominant discourse, which situated Jewish and biblical history in the region.

Some cultural theorists argue that the Jews' relationship to Israel has been defined by a deterritorialized rather than a territorial diasporicism, yet they also maintain that the Jews have an ongoing indigenous relationship to that same land.[2] A close reading of the popular and public national narratives does not suggest indigenousness; rather, it suggests that even though it is possible that the Jews were not there first, the land is still theirs because it was chosen for them and they were chosen to live on it. In more secular terms, they are the land's oldest living survivors. This suggests that if the Canaanites and their traditions had survived, they might have had some claim to the land today. This in turn may explain the need to delegitimize and 'disappear' others' histories; it may also explain why in general, narratives of survival resonate for Jews in Israel and around the world.

This strategy obliterates local histories and helps frame what people see as they tour the country. When Sivan referred to an archaeological find in northern Galilee as the Solomonic Gates, she was placing this find in a Jewish historical frame of reference to Solomon. Arnie claimed that the agricultural terracing we saw came 'right out of the Bible. This [is the] Judean mountains and all of our agricultural festivals and laws come out of this land.' Here, he neglected to point out that the Palestinians in the area also built terraces and continue to do so. Yet the Palestinians have been made to disappear. Naming the area Judea also locates it in a Jewish historical geography.

On all the tours, references were repeatedly made to biblical and ancient periods. These narratives highlighted the Jews' long-term presence in the region and also legitimized their return to it. On the Israel Land Fund (ILF) tour, we were taken to a garden and park called Neot

Kedumim. One of park guides, Laurie, introduced herself as an American Jew who had made *aliyah* years earlier. She explained that in Hebrew, *neot kedumim* means 'biblical gardens': '*Neot* means ... oasis and *kedumim* ... means ancient; but ... many Hebrew words have opposite meanings and though it means ancient it also means going forward, so [*Neot Kedumim* means] [in order] to go forward we build on our meanings of the past.'

We followed Laurie along a stony path through the gardens to a sheltered and slightly raised seating area, from which we could look over the rest of the gardens. It was a warm, sunny day and we were enjoying the opportunity to be outdoors. Laurie spoke again:

> We are looking at a very long tradition which goes back to the very beginning of the Bible ... just like the Garden of Eden ... And when we look at the setting of the Bible what we're looking at is a society where people are farmers. That's why we have traditions that are about farming ... [But] not all of us have grown up on a farm and to try to understand why we do what we do ... [and] why we have certain traditions, we have to go back in our imagination. That's why we have this place, to help us understand ... So we've created here something that is disappearing from the world. But in some ways, we have a connection because no matter how many roads, or how many malls, or how many cities or how many buildings you build, if you plant a fig tree if you plant an olive tree it's going to grow exactly the same way it did two thousand years ago. So some things never change. Okay. So that's why we're here.

Never deviating from the biblical sources, Laurie associated the cultivation of the land with the Jews' past traditions and practices. She then referred to important Jewish and national holidays – Passover, Lag B'Omer, Sukkot – describing each in terms of their importance to agricultural communities. When explaining the importance of wild plants such as hyssop, and the effects of inclement weather on wheat fields and olive trees, she placed these things in the context of the Jews' traditional or ritual processes on this land:

> A lot of the plants that grow here became symbols of something in the Bible and the hyssop became a symbol of monarchy ... For example, the Exodus: when the Israelites, our ancestors, left Egypt, they were told to slaughter a lamb and take some blood and paint the door posts so that the plague would pass over us and our houses, and what they were supposed

to do it with was with a bunch of hyssop, and one of the interpretations is that they were supposed to remain honest and humble; not too easy for the Jews, maybe.

This last remark prompted laughter and nods of agreement among the tourists. Only another Jew could have made an in-joke like this, and it highlighted, as such jokes do, the insider status of the participants as well as their guides.

A short time later, a tourist asked Laurie if the garden had been 'public land.' She replied simply that the land for the garden had been 'allotted by the Israeli government in 1965' and that 'nobody wanted it.' She was implying here and in an earlier comment ('there was nothing here') that the land had been empty when Jews created the garden. At no time did she mention that hyssop, figs, almonds, wheat, and especially olives grew in this garden before it was planted. It is ironic that before the State of Israel was founded, this garden's crops formed the basis of the Palestinian peasant economy.[3]

Near the end of our visit to the garden, Laurie commented on the 'unusual qualities of the olive tree' and its symbolic meaning for the Jews. In the Jewish tradition, she told us, olive oil is used to light the *menorah* and to anoint high priests and kings.

If you're an olive farmer and you want to plant new olive trees, you don't plant the pits because it takes too long. You take one of these little shoots that comes out of the base of the trunk and this is your next generation of olive trees ... You cut the shoot, it will stay fresh even for a few days, and you put it in the earth and it will start growing. That is the special quality of the olive tree – that it reproduces through these shoots ... So this is the image of the shoots that are the next generation of the olive tree. There is a very nice verse in ... Psalm 128 that says 'Your children are like olive trees around your table.' This is the next generation of the olive tree. Your next generation is sitting around your table. And the end of that Psalm says: 'You should see that the children of your children have peace on Israel.' This is the wish, the hope, for everybody: the continuity of the generations, [and] peace on Israel. This is what we wish and hope for everybody, and that is the wish that I would like to leave us all with. Joy and family and peace on Israel, Amen.

To this statement, many of the tourists responded, 'Amen.' Laurie's comments also prompted retired Reform Rabbi Leopold – a tour partic-

ipant who had remained attentive during Laurie's scriptural presentations – to rise from his seat to say 'There are many homilies on the olive
and one interesting one: just as the olive has to be beaten before the oil
rises to the top, so the Jewish people suffer persecution but ultimately,
despite everything ... we rise to the top, to which I can only say, *Alevi*.'
Laurie and many of the tourists seem thrilled with this interjection,
which reinforced much of what Laurie had been telling us. This tour of
the garden had begun with stories about beginnings – about Adam and
Eve, Israelite settlement and planting practices. Now it was ending
with an exaltation: a long-suffering people had returned to their land.

Masada, in the Negev Desert near the Dead Sea, is an archaeological
site and popular tourist destination. It has long been associated with
the myth of Israel and Zionism.[5] On the IDF tour we were taken to
Masada. After a long drive out of Jerusalem, we rode a newly built
funicular to the mountain's top. Some tourists seemed quite nervous as
the vehicle shook and swayed in the strong wind. Still, their excitement was palpable, and once we reached the top, many began to wan-
der around, looking at the many excavated sites and reconstructed
walls. Our guide, Arnie, gathered us under an awning to keep us out
of a cool rain that had begun to fall, and began by telling us that Masada 'simply means small fortress.' He skipped through the Chalcolithic
and Macabbean eras until he came to the Romans. He explained that
Herod the Great – a 'Roman puppet leader,' a 'king,' a 'paranoid,' a
'strange fellow,' and a 'great builder' – built Masada as a possible refuge. Then,

> in the year 66 CE ... Herod is long gone [and] the Jews revolt against the
> Romans, and for four years there's a Jewish revolt, [from] 66 up to 70 ...
> [Then there is the] destruction of the Temple in Jerusalem ... In 70, the
> revolt theoretically is over, but it's not over, because here at Masada there
> was a group of zealots ... One [part of this group was] called the Sikari.
> They were knife-wielding assassins – [who] also kill[ed] Jews, they ...
> didn't [just] kill Romans. Any Jew who [was] opposed to [the] revolt,
> they'd stick him ... And so, banded together, they were raiding Roman
> supply lines in the mountains. They would get water and goods at En
> Gedi [the oasis nearby] ... For three years the zealots were on top of
> Masada with their families, with sheep and goats and donkeys ... they
> lived up here. And in the final battle scene, the mass killing.

Most of the tourists were listening intently, sometimes whispering quietly among themselves. At one point, someone whispered the word 'suicide.' To this, Arnie immediately responded: 'Who said "suicide"? [It was a] mass death and killing at Masada.' Arnie asked us to be patient, that in time we would understand why he insisted on this interpretation and why he felt he had to make this intervention. He then asked us to follow him for a short walk toward a site marked 'Synagogue' (see photo 1).

As we stood inside the reconstructed walls of the synagogue, Arnie told us he had something very important to share:

> A few years ago my son had his Bar Mitzvah ... here ... [But when] he read his Torah ... he was rubbing elbows with those Jews from Masada. They were wearing Phylacteries ... They were wearing prayer shawls two thousand years ago. And I said to him: 'Son, you decide what you want to do with your life, as [to] what definition [you choose] as a Jew. But today you take one commitment: that you pass on the Torah, the word, to the next generation.' The minute the link is broken we're finished, just like the Edomites, the Moabites and everyone else. We'll just simply disappear. That's part of the meaning of Masada. They were people who believed in the Jewish lifestyle. They may have been extremists but they went to the end believing that there was only one way to live and that was the way of a Jew, and things haven't changed all that much.

To this, many of the participants nodded agreement. By associating every ordinary Jew's sacred experiences and practices with those of Jews of the past, and by doing so within the walls of an ancient synagogue, Arnie was combining the forces of the past with a present-day messianic calling. He was summoning every Jew to continue practicing his or her own tradition, to ensure that the Jews did not 'simply disappear.'

After moving through the Roman baths, storerooms, and other excavated and reconstructed sites at Masada, Arnie took us to the edge of a fortress wall to tell us what we had all been waiting to hear: why he defined the last days of the zealots as a 'murder' and not as a suicide:

> In the first attempt by the Romans [to break into the fortress] ... the leader of the zealots, named Elizar Ben Yair, gathers all the last soldiers and their families together ... And he says to them simply: 'It doesn't look good. The Romans are getting close. The ramp [up the mountain] is complete. The wall [we've built] is going to be collapsed very soon. They've already

made a break. We blocked it up with timber and we're going to have to
decide what our destiny will be.' And he tells them: 'We were born free.
We are free Jews. Slavery is not for us. The children will be abused. The
women will be abused. The old people will have their bones broken and
... be carried away. A slave is nothing. [It] is not the way for a free Jew.'

According to Arnie, the Jews of Masada were not pleased to hear
that they would all have to die rather than become Roman slaves. But
as time passed and they began to lose their battle against the Romans,
their leaders made the decision. At this point, Arnie explained why he
insisted there had been no suicide atop Masada:

Here and, in their last breath, they died as free Jews. The bottom line here
... [is that it was] not suicide. The bottom line here is not murder. It is the
desire to resist a larger empire forcing their will upon you. They wanted
to die as free Jews ... [Suicide?] That's not it. [It was] resistance: the small
against the large [and] the just against the wicked. It happens in many
places. These were people that took their lives based upon that understanding of who they were. Born as Jews, [they] died as Jews. For that reason we used to – not so much today – swear in our armoured division
here ... [to] tell [the soldiers] that they are the continuation of the last
defenders of Masada. They were the end of the Second Commonwealth.
We are the new independent state. They are defending the state as those
zealots died here on Masada. That's the connection. We say 'Masada shall
not fall again.' It's a little Jewish paranoia because things haven't changed
much. We're still the minority in a very tough neighbourhood. We have
large countries around us. We have Saddam Hussein who, in one day,
can tip the world this way or the other way, just like that. One person in a
tough neighbourhood can turn awful. Everything that's going on around
us changes all of our lives. So things have not changed all that much. As a
strong, small country we can exist. We must be spiritually strong, like the
zealots, and also be able to defend ourselves, like the soldiers who are
sworn into the army, here at Masada and at different places in the country. Resistance, that's the word, not suicide.

In this way, Arnie was linking the Jews' past struggles with their
present condition: rebellion and resistance had always marked the
Jews' quest for autonomy and freedom. He was presenting one of many
controversial interpretations of the Masada myth. His was significant
because it referred to, and framed, what he saw as the danger facing

modern Israel. 'We're still the minority in a very tough neighbour-hood,' he told us. 'Things haven't changed that much.' Most impor-tantly, 'We must be spiritually strong, like the zealots, and also be able to defend ourselves.'

Themes of siege and self-defence dominated all the narratives of mil-itary struggle, whatever era they referenced. Jews were always pre-sented as defending their communities against ever-present enemies. Ultimately, it was the Jews' vision of liberation and redemption that sustained them, their traditions, and their nation.

On the ILF tour, while we were driving through the Valley of Aya-lon on our way to a tree-planting ceremony in the Negev, our guide, Talia, presented us with the biblical tale of Joshua. Linking biblical and ancient stories to more contemporary examples of the Jews' struggle, she drew our attention to the area's history as a battleground:

> We are now in the ... Valley of Ayalon. [Do you] remember when Joshua
> was fighting the Cannibals, and he was losing time ... and [he cried out to
> God]: 'Will you please help me?' and God said, 'Why not?' and he said,
> 'Let the sun and the moon stop their course above the Valley of Ayalon.'
> This is why Joshua ended the battle successfully and then God let them
> go their way ... The Valley of Ayalon, as a matter of fact, is the place of lots
> and lots of blood ... We know, [in the] second century BCE, when Judah
> Macabbee was on his way to Jerusalem to fight the Assyrians, [that] he
> had to fight his way through the Valley of Ayalon, because it is on the
> way to Jerusalem ... In recent times, in 1917, it was General Allenby, the
> British General Allenby ... who had to fight the Turks here in the Battle of
> Ayalon ... And during the War of Independence there were four battles
> that took place here ... They all failed and this is why the Valley of Ayalon
> was a package that was not part of Israel. It was part of no man's land,
> and we could not go through the Valley of Ayalon until 1967.

By naming biblical, ancient, and recent heroes of the Jews – Joshua, Judah Macabbee and General Allenby – and by setting each of them into this landscape, Talia was describing the Valley of Ayalon only in relation to the Jews' struggle for autonomy. She emphasized the Jews' heroic struggle and the decisiveness of their military victories. But she left out how all of this changed in 1967. The area we were travelling through was outside the Green Line (the internationally recognized boundaries of Israel); in other words, we were in territories that had been under Israeli military occupation since the Six Day War of 1967.

More than any other place, Jerusalem is crucial to any understanding the Jews' connection to Israel. Jerusalem's history was presented as metonymic of the Jews' past exile and subsequent return.

Every tour itinerary included modern West Jerusalem[6] and the walled Old City. West Jerusalem is the site of modern Israeli institutions (the Knesset, the Supreme Court, the Israel Museum, and the Hebrew University); modern communities (French Hill, Gilo, Talpiot); gentrified communities (the German Colony, the Russian Compound, Beka'a, Yemin Moshe); and old and new markets, restaurants, and cafés (Ben Yehuda Street, King David Street, and Nahalot). We were also taken to many sites that memorialized military victories. On no tours were we shown East Jerusalem, where most of the city's Palestinians live and work and where there are few Jewish institutions.

Every tour presented the Jews' relationship to Jerusalem as unique. The guides told us that the Jews had a historical claim to the city that no other religious, cultural, or social community could assert. While we were driving into Jerusalem for the first time on the IDF tour, Arnie described the importance of the city for Jews in this way:

> Now many other people hold Jerusalem sacred. For the Christians it is [about] the last week in the life of Jesus in Jerusalem. However, they have Bethlehem, Nazareth, [and] for many Catholics, Rome and other shrines all around the world. The Muslims hold Jerusalem sacred because of Mohammed's night journey ... They also have Medina and Mecca in Saudi Arabia as holy cities. But when it comes to the Jews ... there's only one holy city, and that is Jerusalem. And unlike many people around the world, we took Jerusalem with us. We couldn't physically visit; we couldn't get there ... so around the Passover *seder*, at the end of the *seder* ... every Jew, whether they live, in Sweden, Poland, Morocco, Kurdistan, or in Yemen, they ended the Passover, the exile story, the slavery story, with freedom in Jerusalem. That was the wish of the Jewish people. There are very few cultures in the world, or people, that take cities with them.

Jerusalem was idealized, romanticized, and presented as uniquely important for the Jewish faith and culture. When other faiths were presented as having other sites of importance, their deeply spiritual and historical ties to the city were effectively dismissed in favour of those of the Jews.

Later, Arnie explained why the final prayer in the Passover *seder* – 'Next year in Jerusalem,' – had been altered in Israel to 'Next year in the rebuilt Jerusalem.' He attributed this change to the fact that the Jews were now in Israel:

> The Wall around us, the buildings around us, the kids in the street, the schools, Ben Yehuda Street – This is Jerusalem. As the Prophet Isaiah prophesised: After destruction, after dispersion, we will hear the children's voices in the streets once again and that is what it is all about.

In presentations like this one, the city's non-Jewish residents were given no legitimacy. It is as if Jerusalem existed only to be returned to the Jews, who were the only group with a rightful claim to it. Non-Jews residing in the area were made to disappear from the city's history, including its role in world history. They were presented as lacking the same rights to the area as the Jews. Having emphasized all of this and having linked Jerusalem to all Jews' identity and history, Arnie further explained the importance of Jerusalem:

> It is our national capital. It is the capital of a people that are dispersed throughout the world. [Jews have] only one city and that is Jerusalem. It's amazing to think that our biblical writers in the Book of Psalms foretold the future of the Jewish people and said if Jerusalem should ever be forsaken, then I should forget exactly who I am ... These words should be embedded in your memory. Jews, unlike many other people, have a communal memory ... I ask you: where are the Moabites, where are the Edomites, where are the Philistines, where are the Canaanites, where are the Romans today, where are the Babylonians, where are the Assyrians ... and where are we? We are back in our ancestral biblical homeland. They have disappeared. Why? Number one, they never wrote down their laws and passed them on to the next generation, and number two, they had no communal memory, and as Jews we pass these things on. The words are short but they're very clear from Psalms 137: 'If I forget thee, O Jerusalem, may my right hand forget its cunning. May my tongue cleave to the roof of my mouth; if I do not set Jerusalem above my highest joy' ... So in many ways that ascent is not only physical, it is spiritual.

Just as Arnie was finishing, we reached the lookout point at Mount Scopus in Jerusalem. We all climbed out of the bus, and as we looked over the city, Arnie led a toast:

> I want you to just take one moment. Think of your immediate family or possibly those who are not here with you right now – maybe your chil-

dren, maybe your parents – who are not here with you right now ... [They are] spiritually here with you. And remember the defenders of the Jewish people, whether they fought in the ghettos in Europe, whether they fought in the camps, whether they fought in the Israeli Army [or the] ... [Israeli Defence Force] pilots ... If they'd been around fifty years ago, maybe history would have been written in a completely different way. We are one family. We are one people. This is one city. This is ours ... together.

With this pledge, Arnie was connecting the Jews of the past to those of the present and connecting all Jews together as a people. The Jews were to be celebrated as fighters and defenders, and they would have to continue to protect Israel militarily. In this way, claims to Jerusalem were presented as sacred and secular, and its defense as necessarily military.

On the ILF tour we were extended a special opportunity to celebrate Jerusalem's three-thousandth birthday. Surprisingly, this celebration was not held at the top of Mount Scopus or on the sacred site of the First Temple or in the Jewish Quarter of the Old City or even in the Knesset. Rather, it took place on Ammunition Hill, a memorial park commemorating Israel's victory in the Six-Day War. Around the park, plaques marked the sites of what had been Jordanian bunkers.

On the night of the celebration, we were taken to the site in the early evening and led to an area where hundreds of seats had been arranged in a half-circle in front of a stage, which was dramatically lit by tall torches. Israeli folk songs and dances were performed, interrupted briefly by speakers, who included dignitaries and government officials, including the deputy mayor of Jerusalem. One of the last speakers that night was the Israel Defense Forces Chief of Staff, who had this to say to us:

We the Israelis celebrate today a holiday ... [This is] a holiday of the reunification of Jerusalem for twenty-nine years. But what is twenty-nine years in the history of this city? This city, a city of peace ... It is a true love story with the Jewish people and Jerusalem. This is the only city that Jews never left. In the whole history of the Jewish people, Jews were living here, remembering Jerusalem, not only here but wherever they were. And I believe that many of you are with us today only because of one reason: because Jerusalem is the beating heart of the Jewish [people]. It's a city of happiness and a city of sorrow. It's a city that witnessed, in its streets, kingdoms [rising] and falling ... But it is the city that was always the capital of the Jewish people ... My generation was lucky to liberate Jerusalem.

Twenty-nine years ago ... young people thought to liberate Jerusalem ...
All Israelis, remember the song [*Jerusalem of Gold*], and whenever we
heard it on the radio during the war I believe that all of us had tears in
[our] eyes. We should remember [the soldiers] making it possible for us to
be here in the united Jerusalem and remember them every day, not only
today. And we ... promise to keep Jerusalem and to keep it safe.

Thus, Jerusalem's reunification and liberation were cast as metonymic
of all that the Jews have endured, and of all that they desire as a nation.

It was always the Old City that tour participants were the most
excited to visit, especially if they were seeing Jerusalem for the first
time. The Old City tours always followed the same route: from the
Armenian Quarter through the Jewish Quarter, then through the Chris-
tian Quarter and along the periphery of the Muslim Quarter. In the
Armenian Quarter we were presented with the history of the Armenian
Christian institutions and told of the Turkish massacre of the Armenians in the 1920s. We were taken into small gift shops and shown the
Armenians' distinctive blue-and-white pottery. The Christian Quarter
tour included a walk along part of the Via Dolorosa, the route of
Christ's Crucifixion, as well as a brief tour of the Church of the Holy
Sepulchre. We walked through only a part of the market area, and only
along the border of the Muslim Quarter, and we were never taken to
the holiest Muslim sites in Jerusalem – the Dome of the Rock and the Al
Aqsa Mosque in the plaza area known as *Al Haram al Sharif* (or Noble
Sanctuary) and the Temple Mount. On no tour were we ever given an
opportunity to encounter Arabs, explore their districts, or experience
the military occupation as the Palestinians do. Except as past and
potential enemies of the state, non-Jews were not part of any presentation of life in Jerusalem.

Most thrilling for the participants were the tours of the Jewish Quarter, in the southeastern section of the Old City. Most of the original
buildings and shops in the area were either demolished and rebuilt or
modernized during the massive reconstruction and restoration of the
area that followed Israel's 1967 victory over Jordan (see photos 2–6). The
area contrasts sharply with the Muslim, Christian, and Armenian quarters which are older and more crowded and where nothing in the way
of beautification has been done. The Jewish Quarter is entirely Jewish[7]
and includes shops, homes, archaeological sites, *yeshivot* (religious sem-
inaries), and the holiest site of all, the Western or Wailing Wall.

On every tour, we were led through the residential areas of the Jewish

Quarter. We stopped at several excavated sites labelled 'First Temple Period' (see photo 5) and 'Second Temple Period,' as well as at synagogues that, we were told, had been destroyed by the Jordanian Legion during the war of 1948 but that had been partly rebuilt since 1967, when Israel 'reclaimed' the area. These synagogues now functioned as outdoor museums and memorials: the before-and-after photographs and narrations served as reminders of the War of Independence (1948). It seemed they were intended to highlight the ever-present dangers for Jews living under Arab rule. At these sites, guides always commented on the differences between Arabs and Jews: Arab leaders allowed Jewish institutions to be destroyed; in contrast, Israeli leaders protected all religious institutions – churches and mosques – that were within their borders and under their control. We were also led along 'the Cardo,' an excavated main street from the Byzantine era, which had been transformed into a boulevard lined with reconstructed Byzantine columns (see photo 4).

Every tour included a visit to the Wailing or Western Wall, called in Hebrew the *Kotel*. This is one of Judaism's sacred sites. According to Jewish tradition, this is the Wall of the Second Temple. It is where Jews have always come to pray and to lament the destruction of the First and Second Temples. The tour participants always approached the Wall if they had the chance. Some placed handwritten notes in its crevices. Yet discussions of the plaza's importance were kept to a minimum and were not deeply religious or ritualized. On the IDF tour the guide read poetry, not scripture, as we stood in the plaza in front of the Wall. On the ILF tour, a long Jerusalem Day march through the modern city marking Jerusalem's three-thousandth anniversary culminated at the Wall. Instead of waiting for sundown, when Israel's Chief Rabbinate and other dignitaries were to present their welcoming remarks, most of the tour participants returned to the hotel to prepare for the Sabbath dinner.

On the ICSF tour, we spent very little time at the Wall, and we were given only a very brief history of the importance of Jerusalem for Jews' worship. However, it was on this tour that we were taken to the Western Wall tunnels. These tunnels form a narrow corridor from the plaza along the Muslim Quarter's walls and into the Muslim Quarter (see photo 7). This corridor divides the Jewish Quarter from the Muslim Quarter. Some Jews recognize it as a sacred site, claiming that the wall along the tunnel is the wall of the Second Temple Mount. But the Western Wall tunnel is a controversial site, because it also runs under the

Muslim Quarter. The Muslims claim that excavations in the area are structurally weakening the Muslim holy sites above the tunnels.[8] Interestingly, along the Western Wall tunnels, the plaques for the various sites are not drawn from Jewish religious writings or traditions; there are no psalms or rabbinical statements. Rather, the plaques are very simple, for example, ENTRANCE GATE TO THE TEMPLE MOUNT, AND MEDIEVAL BASEMENT.

The controversy surrounding the Western Wall tunnels was reflected in the different ways that the tour guides discussed their importance. On the ICSF tour – which was sponsored by a group associated with Israel's peace camp – the guide asked us to turn around and retrace our steps back to the tunnel entrance instead of walking right through to the Muslim Quarter. The Muslims and Palestinians were opposed to this foot traffic, mainly because settlers had been using the tunnels to get to their homes in areas that according to international law had been illegally occupied and settled by the Israelis.

The guides had many opportunities to talk about the sacred nature of these sites, yet they rarely did so. Rather, they highlighted their significance to the *nation*. Even though they repeatedly described Jerusalem as the Jews' spiritual home their discourses focused mainly on the city's social and political importance to Israel and the Jews. That is, national rather than spiritual importance was accorded to the sites visited. At the time, some of the most contentious debates in Israel and in North American Jewish communities focused on the role played by Israel's Orthodox rabbis in the 'Who is a Jew?' debate. This may explain why the guides were reluctant to emphasize religious matters. Most North American Jews do not follow Orthodox practices and most Israelis are secular, so perhaps it was proper for the guides not to emphasize these matters. Jerusalem, then, was presented as the nation's ancestral and traditional centre, if not as its religious capital as well.

Various sites in the Old City presented opportunities to reflect on the nation's distant past. The more recent past was remembered atop Jerusalem's Mount Herzl. Here, the Holocaust was memorialized and the nation's survival was commemorated.

On every tour of the memorial sites, both the guides and the sites' own interpreters emphasized the heroism of the Jews and of those non-Jews who risked their lives to help them. The destruction of the European Jews was downplayed, and emphasis was placed on the Jews' resistance, and ultimately their survival. This trope of redemption linked the foundation and legitimacy of the State of Israel to the European and diasporic or exilic eras in the history of the Jews.

In 1953, Israel established Yad Vashem, the Museum of the Holocaust and Heroism. Talia, the ILF tour guide, explained the meaning of Yad Vashem: 'Yad [in Hebrew] is hand. It is also a memorial ... It comes from the prophet Isaiah, and he simply said, "I will put on my home, I will put on my cities, and walls, a place and a name that shall never be forsaken, that you should never forget."'

The IDF guide, Arnie, described the site in this way:

> Yad Vashem is called the Hill of Remembrance ... To the north we have our defenders of the modern State of Israel. On the top is the tomb of the visionary Dr Theodore Herzl. And to the south is the Yad Vashem. Memorial Hill is all one mountain. It's physically connected. It is symbolically connected and this is what we're going to be dealing with ... at the memorial site or complex ... This is not a museum. We'll be making that distinction as we go through Yad Vashem before we have our ceremony at the Valley of the Destroyed Communities. Yad Vashem is our national memorial site for the Holocaust victims and heroes. It is called the Museum of Holocaust and Heroism. Unlike many Holocaust museums ... Yad Vashem is a dynamic experience ... The personal part, the personal connections to the Holocaust, makes everything important. We can say six million, we can say eight million, we can say twelve million [died]. The numbers are cold. They are things that are difficult to relate to ... Yad Vashem is not a museum. The museum is only a small part of this complex.

The complex is part of what is called Remembrance Hill. This is the site not only of the Museum of the Holocaust and Heroism but also of Israel's National Cemetery and the tomb of the father of Israeli Zionism, Theodor Herzl. The memorial complex includes the Avenue of the Righteous Gentiles, the Warsaw Ghetto Plaza, the Valley of the Destroyed Communities, and the Children's Memorial. As the tour guide noted, Mount Herzl and Remembrance Hill are all 'physically [and] symbolically connected.'

The tour presentations focused on the heroism of those who resisted the Nazis and of those who founded the Jewish State after the devastation of many of their communities in Europe. Often it was implied that this celebration of heroism could only be fully appreciated in Israel, where Jews now form the majority, and where their very existence in their own state speaks to their continued survival. On one tour, we stood on the path leading to the Warsaw Ghetto Plaza, and Arnie – the guide who immigrated to Israel in his twenties from the United States – explained:

Unlike many Holocaust museums that we have in Washington, Los Angeles, Miami and maybe several in Canada, [this one] has a different outlook ... It is the only place in the world where it is the Jewish people telling the story of what happened to the Jewish people from the Jewish standpoint. It is not a museum in a country where Jews are not the majority.

Clearly informed by Zionist understandings of the diaspora, Arnie was implying that Holocaust museums outside the State of Israel could not but focus on the victimization of the Jews in Europe rather than on their survival and resistance. He went on: 'This is not a graveyard ... This is a memorial made to respect the victims and honour the heroes ... Poland [and Auschwitz in particular] is a cemetery and a graveyard.'

In interpreting the sites for us, Arnie emphasized the resistance by Jews and non-Jews during the Holocaust, as well as, the need for Israel, a nascent state in the 1950s, to create its own heroes.[10] For example, at the Warsaw Ghetto Plaza, he pointed to two frescoes set into a wall. He explained that one of the frescos represents a 'weak period' in the Jews':

[There's] nothing really honourable about it. Their heads [are] down and that was [the] Israel of the 1950s. [It represents] the survivors themselves, who were still in mental shock from everything they [had undergone, and] the younger generation who didn't know anything about their parents from that time period. [This was all] in a young country looking for new heroes.

The other fresco in the same plaza, with its strong, rounded faces framed by long, flowing hair, represented the Jews of the Warsaw Ghetto Uprising. Arnie explained that this fresco was built for the new state, for an Israel that had a 'Jewish army looking for new myths' in the 1950s.[11]

Farther along the path, we stopped in front of a tall stone column in a small courtyard that overlooked Jerusalem, just in front of the Children's Memorial. Arnie described its significance:

This is the pillar of heroism. I told you this is Israel. The heroes are important to a young Jewish nation. They still are important to those who escaped from the camps, those who fought in the ghettos, those who blew up crematoriums in the camps at Auschwitz-Birkenau ... And this pillar, straight up, represents strength ... Again [this is for] a young country. This is a memorial to our heroes from that time period.

At Yad Vashem, the heroes of the period include non-Jews. Along the Avenue of the Righteous Gentiles, there are more than 6,000 dedication plaques and carob trees planted, including one for the famous Oscar Schindler. Why carob trees? Our guide explained: 'You cut them down, take out the roots, they grow back. You can't get rid of a carob tree. It [represents] courage. It [represents] strength.'

On the IDF tour, one of the participants, Ozzie, a man in his fifties, led us to a tree dedicated to the Righteous Gentile who had secured his family's safety in Europe. He began his story of rescue and survival by expressing his deep love and respect for the man who had rescued him and his family. The visit to the Avenue of the Righteous Gentiles was taken up as another occasion to celebrate the strength of the human spirit – and of non-Jewish heroes. It was not a moment to remember the destruction or victimization of the community.

Although Jews' and non-Jews' heroism was the focus of the narratives, the Jews were presented as a people uniquely targeted by the Nazis.[12] Arnie contended that the word 'Holocaust' only referred to what had happened to the Jews:

> [The word] 'Holocaust' ... is sort of thrown around. [There is a] Cambodian Holocaust, a Rwandan Holocaust, ecological Holocaust. Friends, 'Holocaust' is a set period of time. Holocaust was only [targeted at] one people that were written down for a final death solution. [There was] only one. There were gypsies who were killed, and I've heard of homosexuals, and other people ... who said, 'Listen, *these* people were killed.' True, I'm not playing that down at all, but only one people [and] only one ethnic group had a stamp of death [and] of annihilation and ... that was the Jews ... I don't want to cry about it. People say, 'Well, he's crying, [what about] the gypsies? You don't hear about them.' [And, 'What about the] twelve million Russians [who] died in the Second World War?' That's not the point. Only the Jews were put on an industrialised death machine, from the minute that [they] were fingered or taken out as a Jew, right up to those last moments. [The] Holocaust happened to the Jews and when you mix it in with tribal warfare, [or] with ethnic cleansing – which are catastrophes and horrible – it loses [the meaning of] that particular time period and what happened to our people.

The guides did not emphasize the victimization of the Jews; they did, however, emphasize the uniqueness of the Jews' experience as a people. In the case of the Holocaust, it was the Jews who were targeted for annihilation in a way that no other human group had ever been.

This representation of the exceptional nature of the Jewish genocide reinforces the community's unique place in history – its chosen-ness, if you will – and resonates with popular representations of Jewish history, such as Deborah Lucy S. Dawidowicz's *The War against the Jews*. Holocaust historians are themselves divided over these questions.[13] Some focus on the deeply ingrained anti-Semitism of European and especially German society,[14] others on the modern and bureaucratic rationality of the era.[15]

None of the guides gave a comprehensive account of the background to the Second World War, such as the rise of the Nazi Party in Germany, and few provided any details about the Jews' displacement and transfer into labour and death camps. On one tour, however, just as we were about to enter Yad Vashem's Children's Memorial, the guide stopped to tell us about Treblinka:

In [one] camp ... because the children were holding up the lines into the industrialized death machine, they were taken into a Red Cross building, [which] was a façade. There were nurses outside. There were flags hanging. [It] looked like a beautiful structure ... They were taken behind the building. As the lines went toward the gas chambers ... [the children] were immediately killed and buried in large trenches. They were just holding up the production line.

The murder of the Jews was presented as premeditated and as designed to ruthlessly target the most vulnerable members of any community, its children. Descriptions of Jewish children's experiences of the Holocaust, especially in the camps, were the only ones that emphasized the victimization and suffering of the Jews.

The path leading to Yad Vashem's Children's Memorial is lined with broken stone pillars, which we were told had been cut short in order to symbolize the fact that no child honoured here ever reached adulthood. The Children's Memorial is the one place at Yad Vashem that was designed to be experienced. It is the site for remembrance, not heroism. It does not present information or history, and there is little to see or hear. It is as if all of the silences of this space could only be filled with the chaos and noise of war. After my first visit to the site, I wrote these field notes:

We all walked towards the Memorial, and as we neared the entrance of the Memorial, a quietness and stillness hung over the group. It was the first time that I noticed silence; only the sound of shoes shuffling over the coarse stones. Until this moment, tour participants have been chattering one among the other, asking the tour guide about the flowers that lined the walking paths, wondering aloud where the cafeteria might be and how long before we would be returned to the hotel. The silence was just barely broken by the sound of a woman's voice emerging from within the memorial. We enter the memorial in a line, grasping the cold, black metal railing on our right, set to guide us one by one into and through the dark room. Soon there is darkness and small flickering lights and the woman's voice becomes audible. The walls of the small room are covered in mirrors that create the illusion that we are surrounded by thousands of tiny, white flickering candles. It is strangely angelic. The woman's voice calls out a child's name, his/her age and where s/he was from, in English, Hebrew and Yiddish. Dedicated to the estimated one and a half million children listed as victims of the Nazis, we are later told that it takes this tape, running from 8 a.m. to 5 p.m., 22 months [on another tour I was told it takes seven years] to complete its cycle of naming. It takes us less than a minute to walk through the memorial, but long after leaving the room, the voice and images haunt me. And I am not alone. Around me, tourists are overcome. Rather than enter into the next building, the Museum, they choose to walk back to sit at the Warsaw Ghetto Plaza for a time before returning to walk through the Museum. Many choose never to enter the darkness of the Museum, preferring to remain in the sunny plaza and walk among the flowers.

After this visit, I walked to the plaza, sat for a short while with the others, and then returned to the entrance to the main museum, where I met up with some of the other participants.

Just inside the Museum of Holocaust and Heroism there is a large fresco, which was designed by Israeli artist Naftali Bezen. All of the guides interpreted it in similar ways. Talia's interpretation:

I think [the first panel] is a premonition that something horrible is about to happen and that thing happened in the second picture in which everything is so abnormal ... Everything is completely decapitated, desecrated, everything is totally wrong, like hell itself. Fire here and here. Everything is on fire. [Like Jacob's ladder]. Jacob is in despair. He does not let go of hope and hope here is in the symbol of the ladder. [Do] you remember Jacob's dream? That angels went up and down the ladder, so he did not let go of that tiny bit of hope. And the third picture you see that something good is happening. Now the fish. The fish tell us something in the way of the boat. In the boat we see a figure that can be either a person or a lion, a Lion of Judah. It may be a symbol of strength, courage. Direction sign, very definitely to a direction, pointing to the east. And there we see symbols of life in the way of the working tools – the wheels, people are moving. And the last picture is new life, new life completely. We see the lion here is rowing, strong Lion of Judah. We see the candlesticks coming from that ladder and now the candlesticks are bright and shiny and beautiful and yet ... new generations, new life.

Themes of destruction, survival, and redemption are crucial to any understanding of this site and its importance to the Jews.

The Holocaust Museum itself houses a permanent exhibit, mainly of photographs and documents from the camps and from Germany during the 1930s and 1940s. These chronicle the rise of the Nazis and the resulting carnage. There are also photographs taken by a German soldier who served in the Warsaw Ghetto. The exhibit includes photos of begging, starving, dying, and dead ghetto inhabitants. Although the sign at the entrance to the exhibit, WARNING AND WITNESS, hints at the ambience inside, what is immediately striking is how much it diverges from the narratives of heroism and resistance that were presented to visitors before they entered the museum itself.

In the museum, the victimization of the Jews during the Holocaust is unambiguous. The museum is very darkly lit. All of its photographs are black and white, their labels are stark and plain. There are pictures of the dead being carried out of the ghettoes ... Nazi posters ... Nazi marches ... the aftermath of Kristallnacht ... Once in the museum, the tour participants were left on their own, without a guide. Most visitors walked around, taking different directions, reading some of the captions, speaking to one another in hushed tones. It seemed that little captured the visitors' attention for more than a few minutes. These photographs, these posters, these slogans seemed so familiar. Indeed many of us had seen them before.

On the ILF tour, a group of visitors followed Reform Rabbi Leopold, a tour participant, into a building adjoining the museum. In the dark room, lit only by flames that rose from small pits in the floor, each labelled with the name of a camp and commemorating those who died there, the Rabbi began to recite the *Kaddish*, the Jewish prayer for the dead.

All visits to Yad Vashem ended with a visit to the Valley of the

Destroyed Communities. In a courtyard, the tour organizers held a ceremony that included the *Kaddish* as well as prayers, spiritual readings, and sombre music. In the Valley of the Destroyed Communities, huge sections of Jerusalem stone have been excavated to form a maze of 107 chambers with twenty-five to thirty foot walls. Each chamber is engraved with the name of a region or country, and each wall is engraved with the names of the Jewish communities destroyed during the Holocaust (see photo 8). Most of the walls are covered from top to bottom with the names of the communities. Visitors to this site are encouraged to search for the communities of their families; many are astonished to see the names of so many communities engraved on the stones.

This site is most impressive for its evocation of what Israeli anthropologists Handelman and Shamgar-Handelman call the 'presence of absence.'[16] Here, as each of us stood looking at these walls engraved with list after list of villages, towns, and cities, we could remember the images of the past as well as experience the inability to fully represent them. That is, to imbue those stones with meaning, each visitor had to remember the past, to piece it together with the stories of loss, with the images of the past as told in the museum, as told to us by family and friends, and as told to us through formal history and in popular culture. One could never again know or see the communities that had disappeared. This experiential reconstruction of history in effect placed the Holocaust in Israel. Though we were standing in Israel, thousands of miles away from many of the sites of destruction, we were overwhelmed by the representation of Europe's disappearance of the Jews. The memorial placed the sites of the Holocaust within the territory of the State of Israel, the Jews' newly reconstructed community.

Not all of the tours included a visit to Yad Vashem but Holocaust memorialization was possible at other sites. On the ICSF tour, as part of a visit to the Diaspora Museum in Tel Aviv, we were taken into a room simply marked, 'Remember.' Sivan, our guide, explained that 'without understanding the need for such commemorations as Holocaust Remembrance Day, Israelis cannot understand what they are doing here.' The room she led us into had enormous columns of black iron hanging from its ceiling. These were referred to as 'memorial columns.' Sivan led us under the columns, and we looked up and into them. These massive black structures represented industrial ingenuity while at the same time evoking overwhelming danger. There were no photographs or other documents in the room. Our guide asked a young female participant to read the only plaque on the wall:

In the year one thousand nine hundred and thirty three of the Christian era, Adolph Hitler came to power in Germany. In his time the Germans and their accomplices murdered six million Jews, among them a million-and-a-half Jewish children. Imprisoned in ghettos, the victims fought desperately for their lives while the world stood by in silence.

The young woman broke down, and others began to weep openly. Our guide explained that the last sentence in that inscription was the only condemnation of any kind found in the entire museum. 'This is not a second Yad Vashem,' she said, and went on to explain that the memorial columns and the other exhibits in the museum were ultimately about a 'nation fighting for its life.' In other words, the nation's history was one of resistance and revival. Victimization was not to be emphasized or remembered as such.

All of the tourists reacted emotionally. However, I want to point out that most of the tour participants were Ashkenazi, – that is, they were the Jews most affected by the Holocaust. These sites resonated for them in a way that other sites – for example, the Israeli war memorials – did not. But for these participants, these sites had other important elements, as I was to learn during the formal interviews.

At biblical, ancient and historical sites throughout Israel, time, place, and history are linked to the tropes of reclamation and redemption. These tropes reappear in the nation-building and settlement narratives that have established Israel's modern, Western, and democratic status as a nation among nations.

4

Development and Democracy

The infamous statement that Israel was founded for 'a people without a land' in 'a land without people' was most clearly articulated during the visits to the Negev Desert. The guides described the desert's emptiness and barrenness prior to the Jews' arrival (more often referring to it as the 'return'). The story of the Negev's development is essential to any understanding of Israeli and diaspora nationalism.

Narratives of the Negev must be examined for two reasons. First, from the perspective of urban and suburban dwellers – the majority of tour participants – there are few implications to colonizing a desert, especially one that is popularly represented as desolate and unpopulated. Second, narratives about settling the desert naturalized the Jews' relationship to the land, in much the same way as the Jerusalem narratives naturalized Jews' relationship to that city. The Negev's economic and agricultural development was described during the tours as Israel's miracle. A rich and productive land had become a wasteland after the Jews left it. Since their return, the Negev had become a site of creative production, not only of agricultural produce but also, notably, of a new model for civilization – socialism in the form of the region's many *kibbutzim* and *moshavim*, a way of life 'invented' by returning Jews.

On the Israel Land Fund (ILF) tour, we spent a long, busy day in the Negev. We left Jerusalem early in the morning, and as we descended from the mountains into the desert, our guide, Talia, presented our day's itinerary. The tour participants listened eagerly. She began by telling us that 'the Negev is two-thirds of the territory of Israel. The larger part of the Negev, which is the northern part of the Negev, is no longer a desert ... You will see, we made it into a flowering garden.' At this point, an elderly tourist interrupted Talia: 'Is all the territory we see here Israel?' Talia replied: 'Definitely, definitely, the whole Negev is Israel. Who else would want the desert?' The tourist responded: 'Sure, they get the oil and we get the desert!' A few minutes later, Talia ended the word volley that this tourist had begun by saying: 'You know, Moses took us to the desert for forty years and brought us to the only place in the Middle East where there is no oil!' Laughter rocked the bus. This useful understanding of the Jews' predicament set the tone for the Negev narrative and introduced its themes: a people who had wandered the earth, and who had done God's bidding, had been assigned a place in the world seemingly bereft of resources; its people had to toil endlessly and creatively in order to survive. These themes were to recur on all the tours.

In fascinating ways, the tour guides temporalized the Negev in nationalist terms: BCE or 'before common era' and CE or 'common era' were often replaced in the narratives by 'before Zionism' or 'after Zionism' (see photos 11 and 12).

In her examination of *kibbutz* museums in Israel, Tamar Katriel found that the narratives told by the 'pioneers' and settlers who had founded the *kibbutzim* typically began with their experiences of anti-Semitism in Europe or with their ideological reasons for participating in the *kibbutzim*. They described how, once in Israel, they had found redemption by working on the land *as their nation's land*.[2]

According to all of the guides, this redemption of the land and its people was the lifelong dream of Israel's first prime minister, David Ben-Gurion. With the Jews' return, the barren Negev was improved; it became a nurtured and nurturing site, bearing fruit and other hallmarks of civilization. By settling the land, the Jews redeemed it, and now it has become a garden again. On the Israel Development Fund (IDF) tour, the guide, Arnie described the Negev and its importance:

The British Mandatory Period sent a group of surveyors to the Arava Valley here in the early 1940s [to] check out the water sources, check the soils, and tell us what we can do down there, and the bottom line was 'uninhabitable, uninhabitable.' And until David Ben-Gurion and the greening of the Negev, there was no one here. That's the mid-forties, and nothing [was] here on this road, nothing whatsoever, and you're going to see what's in front of you in two minutes ... *This* is what is called 'uninhabitable': these are hot houses, you don't have to heat them, [you] just need the sun down here. [There are] flowers, vegetables, wall-to-wall agricultural production with computerized Israeli ... water systems made in Tel Aviv. They're even exported all over the world. Desert. Sand. *This* is what can be done!

Furthermore,

> David Ben-Gurion ... was the first one that saw the potential of the Negev.[1] He said now the true Zionism is to resettle in the Negev, and he himself said, 'I'm going to be an example,' and he came all the way down here, and it's really far down south in the Negev, to a really young and small *kibbutz*, Sde Boker. And ... they accepted him and he had here a wooden shack where he lived and from here they dragged him back to government, but this was his home ... The house of Ben-Gurion, it's ... just a wooden shack ... And today it's a place to visit and you can see he lived in sheer simplicity surrounded by his roots.

Clearly, the narratives of the Negev were about more than making the desert bloom. They were also about remaking the Jew. Key to this process was the Jews' identification with the land and their response to this identification. This is how Arnie, an American-born Jew who had made *aliyah*, described his own awakening in the desert:

> I got off the bus in 1972, in December, right here. There was nothing around [and] I didn't know where I was going. I walked with a backpack down this road right here into a small farming community, knocked on the door of a family ... who spoke very little English, and I had an awakening, a spiritual awakening, not ... in synagogue or in Hebrew school but here in the Arava [Valley]. I [gained] a little bit of [a] deeper understanding [of] what it is to be a Jew in the Land of Israel, not necessarily from a religious aspect, but being Israeli and a Jew put together is probably the main reason why I'm standing here in front of you today. If the first experience is positive and meaningful, then it's a long-lasting effect. This is really home for me, which is all like desert to you. But I see ... just so many fantastic people here living in the middle of nowhere [with that] pioneering spirit, helping one another ... It's the Israel that I first saw and met here that sort of gave me that little push that decided if I was already Jewish I may as well do it here.

In this way, Arnie was connecting the processes of remaking the desert and remaking the Jew. The Jews succeeded in transforming the desert into a habitable place, and this, for them, was evidence of a special link between the Jews as a people and the land of Israel.

The guides also made explicit references to progress and economic development. They presented both culture (skills, technology, modern knowledge) and agriculture as having been brought to the land by the

Jews, as evidence of Jews' modernity, productivity, and creativity. They contrasted Jewish technology, culture, production, and agriculture against the more primitive farming practices of its former inhabitants:

The main idea is to make agriculture into an industry. It's not going to be an unskilled farmer that goes out to the field and plants what he wants. It will not be seasonal, it will be an industry that works all year round and creates the right environment so that they can hire people for permanent jobs all year round and will get results every month of the year. The Negev is 60 per cent of Israel, and the potential here is agriculture. (Talia, ILF)

The whole Arava Valley is one plastic greenhouse growing hot house tomatoes, green peppers, cucumbers, eggplants, 90 per cent for export, not even [just] for the local farmers. [And the] flowers! You've got to fly over this area to understand what's going on here – the latest in agricultural technology, hydraulics, the works! (Arnie, IDF)

Here is a *kibbutz* which [has only been] here since the seventies and you will see the beautiful thing of having green fields where the [technology has been developed so that the] sandy and salt water is being poured with a lot of fresh, sweet water that pushes the salt level down in the ground and then you can put in all sorts of seed and grow watermelons, melons, and even grapes ... There are vineyards here also. (Sivan, ICSF)

The Negev's newest colonists use all the latest technologies, including biotechnology and bio-engineering, to build and maintain desalination plants, irrigation projects, greenhouses, fish farms, and water reservoirs. Science is now civilizing the desert.

On the ILF tour we were taken to an experimental greenhouse in the Negev. Dr Dov Kirschner, a scientist who works on a number of research projects, was assigned as our guide. He presented us with the latest technologies and discussed their commercial worth, not only for the local *kibbutzim* but also for Israel's international trade. In his presentation he highlighted the Israelis' creativity and their commercial successes.

This agricultural revolution has done more than feed the people; it has generated an enormous food surplus that can be exported. Kirschner exclaimed: 'Now Israel has plenty of products, much more than it needs, and of course we are exporting whatever we can. Anything from citrus, high-quality olive oil, bananas, avocado, and more and more.' The desert has been 'redesigned' so that it produces not only necessary foodstuffs but beautiful flowers as well. All of this requires highly sophisticated knowledge, research, and development.

Later on the same day we were taken to what was described to us as a site 'reclamation.' Near the town of Ofakim northeast of Beer Sheva, we were introduced to a forestry expert, Ori Dan. After a brief welcome, Ori told us that there is very little rainfall in the area. He then proceeded to describe the tree-planting project at the site. I looked around and saw that we were on a flat surrounded by steep, undulating sand hills. There were no trees anywhere in sight. I waited for an explanation and soon realized that this was an exercise in imagining a future, a future of the desert in bloom. The forester pointed us in the direction of Tel Aviv and told us that although in the north of Israel, 'flat areas' with 'deep soil' can be cultivated and irrigated with treated sewage, where we were standing, the steep slopes, gulleys, and shallow soil made this almost impossible. 'Two thousand years ago,' he told us, 'there were farmers in this area [who] used the local resources for agriculture [but] in the seventh century, when the nomads invaded this area, they destroyed the famous old agriculture and they caused desertification ... They changed the natural vegetation by overgrazing.' He described the park we were standing in as comparable to the many other parklands scattered around Beer Sheva and other Negev settlements. He and his fellow scientists were trying to improve the land, trying to rehabilitate it by improving its value for grazing and for tourism. When asked, Ori identified the little vegetation we could see. He explained that the process of rehabilitating the land partly involved 'managed grazing' – that is, 'bringing herds [sic] of Bedouins to this area.'

Despite what we had been led to believe, this was not a tree-planting ceremony. Rather, it was a lesson in how people in the past had destroyed the land and how the Jews had returned to reclaim and improve it. Implied here was that the Israelites – who by all guides' accounts had inhabited the region some two thousand years before – had farmed the land with great care. After they were expelled, nomads had overgrazed and mistreated the land, turning it into a desert. Having reclaimed the land, the Jews were now using their knowledge and expertise to revive and rehabilitate it. At the time, it seemed ironic to me that on the one hand, nomads were being blamed for the area's desertification, and on the other hand, Jews were now returning the nomadic Bedouins – albeit under managed conditions – to revive the area's flora.

The Jews' organic relationship to Israel was being linked to the revival of a barren land. Other narratives focussed on the collection and utilization of water to ensure a productive future. On the ILF tour we were taken to an installation in the desert that resembled an oil refinery: pipes traversed deep natural and artificial valleys, carrying precious rainwater from the mountains to huge metal tanks. The tour participants were impressed with the massive structures and with the planners' estimates of how much water would be collected at these stations. Talia, the ILF guide, told us that 240 million cubic metres of water were being collected. Of that, only 44 per cent would be used as drinking water:

> The plan is that within five years they will add 30 million more cubic metres and then another 50 million cubic metres ... By that time, we are going to have enough reservoirs that they can enlarge and develop the [amount used for] agriculture ... One goal will be to catch and collect the floodwater ... In a good year you can have between 100 and 200 million cubic metres a year.

These overwhelming statistics highlighted the resourcefulness and technological astuteness of the Jews; they also described a process capable of transforming the desert into practically a flood zone.

The idea of redeeming the Jews lay at the core of all these narratives, and this project was to be realized through a new relationship that the Jews brought to the land. That said, is seems that civilizing others was also part of the mission. Israeli agricultural expertise – that is, Jews' scientific knowledge of the land – was set in stark contrast to the simplicity of non-Jews' premodern relationship to the land. For example, Sivan, the guide for the Israel Civil Society Fund (ICSF) tour, told us that the Palestinians of the town of Jericho were not productive farmers; rather, they were beneficiaries of the good fortune of living in an oasis:

> Now, we're going into the Jericho area. If you look to the right and forward then you see already the greenery of Jericho ... famous throughout many periods for different types of crops, mainly for bananas, for oranges, for grapefruits ... But Jericho is in an oasis. It is not a desert. It's true its climate is very hot. It's true that there is hardly any rain throughout the winters. But it is an oasis. The waters that come down on the mountains went into the ground level, trickled through the layers of lime-

stone and then come out in the Jericho Valley ... This was one of the oldest
cities or towns in the world. There have been found remnants of Neolithic
man there. That is way back, eight thousand years before the common
era.

Note as well that Sivan was describing past cultures in archaeological (Neolithic man) rather than cultural terms. Once again, this served
to delete the histories of other peoples who had settled in the region
many centuries ago. Furthermore, Sivan presented Palestinian labourers and even another country, Jordan, as having benefited from the
Jews' Green Revolution:

Palestinians would come from ... all the villages around. They depended
on that [work] as a source of living. More and more you could see trucks
coming and unloading ... I've seen it even in California with the Mexicans
being unloaded from buses and then picked up by the end of the day.
[And] this is how it functioned and everybody profited from that. In a
way, even the Jordanians profited from having these beautiful settlements here [in the Jordan Valley]. Do you know why? Something in geography – which is called geographical diffusion. Even if we [didn't] have
formal contacts with Jordan, the dripping system, something that was
invented in Israel ... [which] moved to the other side ... It is very interesting to see because if you look at maps, aerial maps of Jordan and this part
[of the Jordan Valley] before 1967 and after '67, you will see a great
change.

Even in an oasis, peasants must have farming skills and knowledge
about rainfall and irrigation. But this fact was being denied in favour
of the assertion that Palestinians' productive labour in Israel and
beyond was the result of Israeli initiatives. The displacement of the
Palestinians, who for years after the founding of Israel had formed a
large migrant labour pool, and who were forced after 1967 to get permission to cross the border in order to work, was also ignored. The
focus was shifted instead to the benefits accrued by the Jordanians.

Even non-European Jews, the Sephardim and Oriental Jews – who
had immigrated to Israel from Arab and African countries such as
Morocco, Iraq, Yemen, and Algeria – were repeatedly framed as unskilled workers who had been moved into new settlement towns in the
Negev[3] in the 1950s. While we were driving past a 'development town'
in the Negev, Talia had this to tell us:

The absorption of new immigrants was always a huge problem. You never knew if you were doing the right thing, especially in the beginning. At the beginning, people were coming from all over ... 600,000 Jews left their Arab countries [and] they were engaged in a war of survival ... They had [to learn] to live ... They had no idea. And a lot of mistakes were made, a lot ... Again, there were people from Iraq, or Yemen, or North Africa, that immigrated here ... In each village they put Israeli-born youngsters who were experts in agriculture, they put them in charge. They were ... the teacher, and the brother, and the babysitter, and the instructor; they were everything. The people were given tools, but not as a present, just as a loan. They were given a few animals, like cows, like mules, and they were taught from A to Z how to do things that were professionally agricultural ... to teach them [the professional way] to do it.

On the IDF tour, similar stories were told. One development town that we visited had been transformed into a very beautiful *kibbutz* town due in no small part to the development funding provided by the IDF, the sponsoring agency of our tour. So we were told. As we drove out of the town, Arnie gave the reasons for the community's past poverty:

Fifty years ago with the waves of immigrants from Morocco and from Romania, Israel did not have the tools to put up the housing that they have today, to get the jobs that we have today, to have the social programming ... Many of the new immigrants emigrated from [places] where they didn't have the skills, they came from places where they did not have running water and electricity, and [this *kibbutz*] simply turned into a backwater ... The goal was not necessarily to turn [this place] into a nice middle-class community – it happened that way. The goal was to teach the local people to run their own lives, to give them that type of training, and to help them along, to make a connection.

So although a single category – *Jew* – defines the national collective, in these narratives a cultural distinction was being made between different kinds of Jews. Ashkenazim are western European Jews who come to Israel from modern countries. It is assumed that they arrive with a wealth of knowledge and skills. Non-European Jews, including the Sephardim and the Oriental Jews, are perceived as 'undeveloped,' as the products of premodern or primitive understandings of work, the land, and state development. From this Eurocentric perspective – one that has always dominated Israeli politics – those belonging to these groups must be moved into communal structures, such as those set up in development towns, in order that they might become more civilized and develop the proper skills needed to help modernize Israel.

Thus, the tour descriptions constructed several important national myths. Two in particular: that of the visionary leaders, pioneers and scientists who brought the desert back to life after centuries of neglect; and that of the desert giving rise to new Jews. The precise nature of the relationships between the people and the land, the colonizer and the colonized, the newcomer and the native, was never explained or questioned. Instead, the presentations created a linear national historical narrative: from desert to garden, from a neglected past to a decidedly Jewish future.

In sum, through the Negev narratives the Jews were inscribed with an organic link to the land. Thus, only the Jews could have revived the desert and recovered its potential. This myth subordinated other histories of the land – and as importantly, other *people* on the land – and made those histories and those peoples disappear. The presentations naturalized this economic, political, and cultural dominance in ways that inextricably linked the Negev's recovery to the establishment of the Jewish state.

Moreover, the tours represented Israel as a fair and tolerant state. This was emphasized in accounts of the Arabs, who were often described as living 'alongside' the Jews in Israel.

On each of the tours, the guides took great pains to explain that although some Arabs lived in Israel, clear distinctions had to be made among them. There were the Druze, and there were the Bedouin, and there were others referred to as Palestinians. They were categorized mainly in terms of how friendly they were toward Israel. The Druze and the Bedouin have rights that the Palestinians cannot and do not enjoy. In large part this is because Palestinians do not serve in the Israeli Defense Forces. The Druze and the Bedouin do serve, the former as conscripts, the latter as volunteers. Nevertheless, tour presentations about the Bedouin and the Druze revolved less around their commitment to the Israeli state and more around their traditional (i.e., primitive) ways of life.[4] Thus, although the Bedouin and the Druze were depicted as clearly 'on side,' the descriptions of them were presented with some distance.

On the IDF tour, while we were driving through the Galilee in northern Israel, Arnie described the area and the Arabs who live in Israel:

Now I want to make this clear distinction. Up here in the Galilee ... we have Arabs [who] call themselves Palestinians [or] Israeli Arab citizens [who] call themselves Palestinians, and also we have Bedouin villages up here in the north. The Bedouins of the north, some 80,000 of them, have a little different standing [from the Palestinians]. [From] some of these villages here, the Bedouins volunteer for the Israeli Defense Forces ... the Israeli army. We just went by a village [where] almost all the Bedouins ... finish high school. They're no longer Bedouins. They don't roam around anymore in tents. They're living in homes. They built villages. They serve in the Israeli Defense forces. They are Muslims and they volunteer for the army ... They are part of the Galilean population of close to 500,000 Arabs, Palestinians, [and] non-Jews living in Galilee ... A lot of people are not aware of the fact that there are large segments of the Bedouin population in the north [who] do volunteer for the Israeli army. They are not drafted ... They volunteer for units depending on what religion, [and] depending on what extended family they belong to, and many of them are doing duty in service inside of Lebanon today ... Another reason why they can build these homes [is that] after they finish the army or stay in the army ... they get special housing loans just like Jewish families or Jewish soldiers, and this is one of the reasons why they can buy these or put up these private homes. I want to again just let you know that twenty or thirty years ago, these people were living in tents and corrugated ... tin metal huts on the top of this hill ... [This village is one] big extended family ... I think if you look in the phone book in this area you may find that there are three or four thousand of them, and there are no street signs in the village [so] you just ask. This is the part of the world where you ask 'Do you know ... someone' and everyone knows who they are and they'll send you there.

The northern Bedouin were represented as benefiting greatly from their relationship to Israel. They had become modern. They were no longer nomadic, their children were finishing high school, and they had abandoned their tents for permanent housing. But the tour guides also reminded us that these Arabs were holding on to some traditional practices; for example, they lived in clan-based communities where everyone knew all about everyone else. Arnie also made a strong distinction between the northern and southern Bedouin:

The word Bedouin comes from Arabic *Bedou*. *Bedou* is a man in the desert, a people of the desert. The Bedouins who are living ... in the Judean Desert are no longer nomadic, like the traditional Bedouins who wandered from oasis to oasis with their tents and goats and their sheep. They are here all the time. They are squatters. They do not own the land at all. They don't pay taxes. They live in their tents and huts out here and they have tractors where they have the water tankers. They go to the government wells, fill them up and have running water next to their tents. A great majority of them now have cell phones [because with cell phones] you don't have to put in telephone lines. [They have] battery-operated television sets inside the tents and mostly Subaru front-wheel-drive vehicles. They traded the camels for the Subaru.

Many but not all southern Bedouin had committed themselves to the Israeli state and were slowly becoming 'modern' in the sense of acquiring cell phones, TV sets, and utility vehicles. Arnie described them as 'no longer nomadic' and as people who simply squatted on the land, who owned no land and paid no taxes. But he offered no reasons why they now lived this way. In fact, their ancient migration routes had been shut down by security borders between the region's states. Furthermore, some of their villages still had not been recognized by the Israeli government; thus they had no access to electricity, sanitation, and piped water. These issues were never raised during the ILF tour. Only on the ICSF tour were some of these issues taken up, though not in any direct or critical manner – the 'greater good' was always modernization. That the Bedouin might choose to remain nomadic, or that they might conceive their relationship to the land as different from that of other Israelis, was never seriously discussed.

On one occasion, Arnie noted that the Bedouin were being put to good use by the Israeli army. In the desert, especially around the Dead Sea, they were being used to track down Palestinians and their arms caches. However, the emphasis was almost always on the need to modernize the Bedouin for their own good.

On the ICSF tour, we were taken to a home in a Bedouin village, where we met a Bedouin activist whom I will call Jenan. Jenan's father had allowed her to attend a high school in Haifa – a privilege usually reserved for boys, since generally speaking, Bedouin girls are not supposed to live away from their communities until they marry. In her twenties, Jenan was a social worker at the local high school. She and some other villagers had formed a woman's organization five years earlier. She spoke to us about a number of difficulties her community faced. These included the need for immediate government funding for a village daycare and a village high school. Until recently, the government had refused to build a high school in the village, fearing it would become 'another Bir Zeit' (a Palestinian University in the West Bank that was often closed down due to the activism of its faculty and students). Jenan also talked about the biases built into Israeli educational programs, especially those designed for female students. For example, places in social work programs are reserved for women of twenty or older. According to Jenan, this assumes that a woman has served two years in the military before entering university, because most girls complete high school by the time they are eighteen. For Bedouin women, the rule often means having to wait out the two years, and more often than not getting married instead.

With these issues before them, the first questions the tour participants asked Jenan were 'Why did your family support you in a way that was so unusual?' and 'Are there many differences among the tribes' treatment of women?' Jenan replied that she was one of five children, of whom only one was a son, and that as a young girl she noticed how well her brother was treated – as if his life was special relative to hers and her sisters. She yearned for the respect that in her community was usually reserved for men. When she was fourteen, she approached her father about going to high school outside her region, and he supported her in this, although he 'suffered' for his decision because it was such an unusual one for a father to take in her community. She believed that her father was different because he had worked in the 'Jewish sector' and had seen how Jewish fathers treated their daughters. Thus, he was more open to the possibility that his daughter might want something different for herself.

The most insensitive questions posed to Jenan by a tour participant concerned the availability of sex education, access to birth control, and the openness of the community to issues of sexuality. This question reminded me how indelicate this visit was. I felt only compassion for Jenan and for the other Bedouin women with her, all of whom would have considered such discussions shameful in public, and especially so when there were men in the room. Jenan, by answering in terms of women's health in general, handled the questions well.

When asked about how the new land agreements had affected the village, Jenan explained that the government had bought up 80 per cent of the land owned by the Bedouin and left the Bedouin only 20 per cent to build on. Many Bedouin had refused to be bought out; however, the two families in her village who had agreed to the deal had become very rich. She noted that all of the new houses we could see in her village were no more than three years old (see photo 10).

Jenan talked about how difficult life is for the Bedouin and how dependent they had become on government support, especially since their resettlement. She also presented the Israelis as having modernized the community, in particular with respect to women's rights.

Nonetheless, the tour guides took a patronizing attitude toward the Bedouin and their villages. On one occasion we were told a little more about how the Bedouin had been affected by the Israeli government's land and settlement policies, especially its policies toward 'unrecognized villages.' These villages did not enjoy the rights that had been extended to recognized villages such as Jenan's. When discussing the policy to resettle the Bedouin, Heidi, who represented an ICSF-funded NGO, noted the Israeli government's insensitivity to the Bedouin. In one case, the Bedouin were moved into a housing settlement. They promptly took the roofs off their new homes, moved their cattle inside, and set their tents up outside. The tourists were much amused by this tale; even so, they continued to listen intently as Heidi explained that one of the goals of her organization was to get people to 'think differently' about the Bedouin, though this could not but be 'especially difficult.' Bedouin practices were too often explained as merely primitive and as largely untenable in a modern world; thus, it was the duty of Israeli and Jewish organizations, in modernizing these people, to show sensitivity to their traditional ways.

On the ILF tour, Talia told us that the Bedouin still lived 'in a clanlike formation,' 'as tribes,' and by the 'rules of the desert,' which included a 'great sense of hospitality' as well as the 'law of blood revenge.'

In many ways, then, the Bedouin were represented as Israel's noble savages. They had been useful to the modern Israeli state, but they were still perceived as 'primitive' because they had preserved their premodern and traditional mores.

On all of the tours, very similar representations were made about the Druze, and although one of the tours included a visit to a Druze village, it consisted of only a half-hour stop at a bazaar.

On the ILF tour, while we were driving toward a Druze village in northern Israel, Talia described the Druze as Muslims. However, they were not Sunni or Shi'ite Muslims, like most in the Middle East. According to Talia, the Druze followed a secret religion to which only a few elite scholars in the community had full access. She told us that they were 'very much like the Jews' because they were 'close-knit,' and lived 'conservative lives,' though they had 'no formal observance of religion' and 'their mother is just like the Jewish mother.' Finally, she declared that: 'the Druze are always loyal to the Jews. They are brothers.' In the army, they were 'tough soldiers' though 'never officers.' Furthermore, 'they know the mentality of the Palestinians [and] they are very tough, so they usually get assigned to Palestinian towns and border patrols.'

On the IDF tour, Arnie presented the tourists with a very similar description as we drove through the Golan Heights:

> Druze men are drafted by law, since [in] 1948 the Druze ... made a Covenant with the state of Israel. They originally ... were fighting with Palestinians, [until] they went over to the Israelis' side, to the Jewish side. They have a very traditional kind of society. [This is about the majority of] the Druze in Israel ... [There are] eighty thousand [Druze] inside of Israel drafted into the army and to the security forces. [They are] very important in the security forces [because] they're Arabic speakers, their Arabic mentality, culture, and they were very, very important [in the Israeli] secret police force ... Druze are an ethnic group. They are a group of people that live in the Middle East. They live in Lebanon, Israel, Syria ... They're not Muslims, [rather] they have a secret religion. They follow the Egyptian Prophet Hakeem. In the eleventh century they were a breakaway from the Islamic religion. And Druze have something very, very special about them. They are loyal to every country that they live in. They have no national aspirations. They're sometimes more Israeli than the Israelis. They're drafted in the army. They're in the Parliament. They're in all walks of life. [They are] very, very Israeli.

Clearly, both Talia and Arnie wanted us to understand that the Druze were very much a part of Israeli society. As Arabs, they were highly useful to the Israelis because they could infiltrate and police Palestinian areas in Israel and in the West Bank and Gaza. The Druze had no 'national aspirations' of their own, and this differentiated them from the Palestinians – it made them 'safe' Arabs.

But the Druze of the Golan Heights had not been party to the 1948 Israeli-Druze pact; thus, their experiences with and resistance to Israel needed to be explained in other terms. These Druze had refused[5] to accept Israeli citizenship, and as a result, they were, in Arnie's terms, 'caught in the middle.' Arnie described the Druze of the Golan:

> Now on the Golan Heights the Druze are in a little bit of a different situation. They were in Syria until 1967 [and] loyal Syrians, and now they're under Israeli administration. Israel has annexed the Golan Heights [and] they're [under] Israeli law here. [They have] Israeli licence plates, Israeli

identification cards. The Druze were given the option to take [Israeli] IDs [and] citizenship. [In] four [of these villages] the Druze are in a vacuum ... They are enjoying Israeli administration. They are prosperous. These are all new fields [of] cherry trees, apples – everything is newly planted. And you'll see that the houses [display] a lot of prosperity. However this is still the Middle East and a lot of them are still very loyal to the Syrian government and to Syria. [They have] families living right across the fence on the other side in several Druze villages ... They're just caught in the middle.

Arnie's tone made clear his profound contempt for this group. They were enjoying all the benefits of being a part of Israel, yet they were refusing to participate fully (i.e., accept Israeli citizenship). That they had been part of a forced annexation by the Israelis was downplayed; from Arnie's perspective, the benefits of occupation should have taken precedence over everything else.

In what seems to me an irony, Israel's Palestinians were discussed almost exclusively in terms of their citizenship rights, including their right to vote and their access to government services. Thus, in the tour guides' discourses, they were transformed, by virtue of not being Bedouin or Druze (i.e., not being traditional and friendly), into a group of citizens. The Palestinians living in the State of Israel were hardly ever discussed on the IDF and ILF tours, except in terms of what made them different from the Bedouin and the Druze. When we passed by an Arab village, this fact was pointed out. The most important point made was that the Arabs, 'including the Palestinians,' have the privilege of voting in Israeli elections and even have their own political parties.

Little or no mention was made of the structural inequalities that the Palestinians have to endure in Israel. For example, they suffer higher rates of unemployment, underemployment, and poverty; they were used as cheap labour and do not receive employment benefits from the state; and they are forbidden to enter some professions and to buy or rent land in certain areas.[6] It was not mentioned that the Palestinians have long been resisting the expropriation of their lands, and that the State of Israel denies them building permits and blocks their access to housing.[7] Rather, the presentations were almost exclusively about the Palestinians' desire to participate more fully in an Israeli state. The narratives focused mainly on the Palestinians' political participation rather than economic and social self-determination.

It was the ICSF tour organizers who took the most care to discuss the fact that although Palestinians do have democratic rights as citizens of

the state, they also face some disadvantages. But in these presentations, the Palestinians who spoke to us – and these people were all
involved in projects funded by the ICSF – rarely had the opportunity
to tell us about their experiences of inequality; instead, they focused on
their projects and on their financial needs.

In fact, when the inequalities between Israeli Jews and Palestinians
in Israel were discussed during these sessions, some tour participants –
and some tour organizers – seemed very uncomfortable. At one presentation in Nazareth, we were told just how little money the Israeli
government was making available for Arabs' education. The Palestinian education expert highlighted the cultural aspects of these disadvantages and suggested that a separate but equal school system might
promote cultural pride among Palestinian students and perhaps lead
to higher graduation rates for those students. When they heard this
proposal, many ICSF tourists reflected on it in terms of past segrega-
tion policies in the United States, and expressed their dissatisfaction
with the idea. Some tour participants, unable to understand that this
educator's proposal amounted to an affirmative-action plan (similar to
ones in the United States), countered that as citizens of the State of
Israel, Palestinians should learn under Israeli educational guidelines
and authority. The presenter explained that the Palestinians did not
want to teach their children the history of Palestine from an Israeli perspective – that they had their own interpretations of that history. At
this, the participants grew silent and the focus of the discussion shifted
to education funding in Arab villages. In this way, obvious social inequalities and the cultural differences were dismissed, and attention
was diverted to a less contentious subject.

After we left this session, we met a group of Palestinian women who
were participating in an economic development project that was partly
funded by the ICSF. The tour participants asked questions about the
kinds of resources and services available to Arab women in Israel; they
completely ignored the cultural aspects of their status as second-class
citizens.

At the end of the day, on our way back to Tel Aviv, Karla, the North
American ICSF staff member, decided to provide some context to what
we had heard earlier in the day:

> Traditionally in Israel, the Arab sector – Arab communities – would get
> one dollar worth of resources and services for every three dollars that
> went into Jewish community groups. It's a long conversation about why

that was the case, but that was the case for many years. And even under ...
the previous Likud Government everyone agreed ... that simply wasn't
fair. It wasn't a question of official policy – that was the reality ... In addition ... things like preschools that were not funded by the government
were funded in the Jewish sector by the Jewish community, by money we
all gave in the United States, Canada, Britain, and so on ... particularly
starting from before statehood until now, that went only to Jewish communities. For a variety of reasons, Arab communities had no sources that
they could get ... comparable money from. So the economic situation in
Arab communities was really very dismal. Now at least over the last ten
or twelve years ... everyone agreed this was not fair and it was not
healthy, [and] it was not right. [But] nobody ever has enough resources
and it wasn't a high enough priority and so they didn't do anything about
it. Under the Labour Government ... they finally made a change, and they
improved the situation so that for every dollar that went into the Arab
communities, every dollar in resources and services, two dollars went
into the Jewish ... It sounds weird to present it that way. The [ratio]
changed from one to three to one to two [compared to] how much money
the Jewish communities would get. No, there was no justification for it.
There's an explanation for it, but nobody could possibly justify it.

A woman in her forties who was on her first tour to Israel asked
Karla just why the Jews were supporting Arab communities and why
Arabs were not expected to provide support for their own communities. To this, Karla responded: 'First of all, lack of interest.' Then,
almost as if she knew that she needed to correct what she had just said,
she began again:

To begin with, it was illegal [for Arabs to divert monies to the Arab sec-
tor]. It's very hard to do it when it's illegal. Because the government was
concerned about subversion or whatever ... I'm trying to be fair. So it was
illegal. On top of it, the truth is there wasn't that much. You know the
Jewish community is really unusual. People organize, we organize to take
care of our own for reasons ... Historically, if we don't take care of our
own, who's going to take care of us? The Arab community doesn't have
that same tradition to the same extent. There are lots of needs in the Arab
world. The Arab world was angry at the Palestinians that stayed here and
didn't leave. You know, there are a whole bunch of [reasons].

In response to Karla's statement, another tour participant – a man in his early sixties who was a prominent lawyer and Karla's friend – attempted to correct her version, telling us that in fact billions of dollars had been raised by what he called the 'Palestinian diaspora.' She corrected him, pointing out that these funds had been raised for the 'territories' (meaning the West Bank and Gaza Strip) and that 'we're talking about in Israel proper. People didn't ... want to strengthen the Arab sector in Israel. There was resentment, [and] there wasn't the same tradition.' The 'people' Karla was referring to were, of course, Israeli Jews. In this way, she managed to back away from explaining the Israeli government's policies vis-à-vis any transfer of funds between Palestinians in diaspora and those in the State of Israel and in the Occupied Territories. Instead she reproduced a common myth that simply blamed the victims. According to Karla, Palestinians had no tradition of giving to their own communities and the Arab nations had political reasons for denying the Palestinians any support. The ICSF had opened the door to a discussion of differences and inequalities, as well as to a possible critique of the ethnonationalism that underpins Israeli laws which limit Palestinians' access to land and social programs and which deny them full equality. However, the presentations perpetuated deeply held racist assumptions about the victims of these policies. According to this framing of the problem, the Palestinians were incapable of fending for themselves and could not count on their Arab brethren for support.

No less problematic was that Palestinians were often represented as thieves. On the ICSF tour, this happened twice. During a presentation of the hardships facing Jewish settlements in the Jericho district, Sivan described how the Palestinians had been stealing agricultural tools, equipment, and even cars, which added to the struggles of their 'pioneering' Jewish neighbours:

> As a matter of fact they have enormous problems now along the Autonomy [borders] and the other areas where the police, Palestinian police, are in charge, and that is the theft of agricultural tools. Most of these villages deal with agriculture and there's a problem that is not yet solved, just like the plague of stealing cars. In the area of Jericho that is not as problematic, simply because this is such a caged area, more easy to handle than other areas in Judea and Samaria.

With so much attention focused on the petty crimes committed by Palestinians, two facts were sidelined: Palestinians had been living under Israeli military occupation; and they constituted a pool of cheap agricultural labour for the very same *kibbutzim* they were now accused of stealing from.

On another occasion, a local guide, Yacov Itamar, was assigned to drive our group to a site on the Golan Heights. He told us that the local Arabs were a problem because they were stealing fresh produce to take home to their families. As a result, local farmers were beginning rely on foreign labourers. Some tour participants were shocked that foreign workers were being brought 'this far,' as one put it. They had assumed that foreign workers had jobs in the factories of Israeli towns and cities and not on *kibbutzim* – the institutions most often identified with Jewish self-sufficiency.

The representations of Israel's Arabs were contradicted in many ways. They were a problem for those who considered Israel a modern, democratic, and tolerant state. How could one account for the social and economic discrepancies between Arab and Jew? Also, did the Jews have a right to declare that the *kibbutzim* and *moshavim* were self-suffi-cient, as the cherished myth had always claimed? It seems that in fact these institutions relied heavily on cheap Palestinians labour and, more recently, the labour of foreign 'guests.' While these issues were never fully articulated in the above terms, it seemed that the other problems (closure of the territories, theft) that were discussed created a disjuncture that few of the tour participants missed in their interpreta-tions of what Israel had become.

Furthermore, when discussion shifted from modernity (develop-ment and democracy) to the security of state, there was a dramatic change in the representations of the place of the Palestinians and other Arabs.

5
Settling the Nation, Defending the State

Israel's military conflicts with neighbour states and the Israel–Palestine conflict were of great interest to both guides and tour participants. In fact, the tourists seemed to be most interested in battlefields and other military sites, and at times the guides and presenters were taken aback by their knowledge and by their divergent perspectives. Israel's military history was not my main interest; even so, I found it interesting how the guides discussed the Arab and Palestinian presence in Israeli society in terms of the debate about Israel's security. Inevitably, Israel was presented as beseiged and as dangerously outnumbered by its enemies. For example, the Arab and Palestinian responses to the UN Partition Plan of 1947 and the Declaration of State in 1948 were represented as no more than a series of strong military offensives taken against the Jews and their state. Any movement toward a defusing of the military threats that Israel faces must take into account the Jews' perennial belief that they have always been the target of others – Romans in the Roman era, Christians in the era of exile, and Arabs in the present day – and that only Jews can be entrusted with the security of the nation. Although it could easily be argued that Israel's military strength is unmatched, these narratives of siege and insecurity recurred in representations of the War of Independence (1947–8), the Six Day War (1967), The Yom Kippur War (1973), and the Operation Peace for Galilee War (1982). Throughout these presentations, the Jews' security was always linked to their need to settle the land.

On all tours, the guides pointed to a number of 'experimental stations' that had been settled 'practically overnight' in the prestate period. These *kibbutzim* served as the heroic core of the narrative of the new Israelis' pioneering efforts in the Negev. When we arrived at these sites, many of us expected to see pioneer villages or living history museums and were surprised to find that they were identified mainly as military outposts. Revivim was the very first of these, as well as the southernmost. When we arrived there we were taken first to a large hall, where we watched a short film. The film began:

> Back in the 1930s and 1940s you had to have a vision to believe that some day there'd be something here ... Preindependence Jewish leaders recognized the importance of the area in terms of defense and development of the agricultural sector and research into the needs of settlements into the far reaches of the Negev.

This Genesis-like introduction helped sustain one of Israel's founding myths: that the land was empty and that it was the Jews' vision to reclaim and revive the Negev. It also asserted that the site was not only for research but also for defence. We also learned that the 'Jewish Agency [the official World Zionist Organization's institution in Palestine] bought land for Jewish settlement,' even though 'the British, who ruled the country at the time, issued their White Paper [prohibiting] the establishment of Jewish settlements.' In the film, Jews committed to settling the Negev were presented as a hardy band of pioneers who simply wanted to explore and settle the land and develop a loving relationship with it. Thus, living in 'a cave which had been used as a cistern in Byzantine times ... the new settlers ... studied water sources, climatic effect and potential crops,' all the while experiencing 'loneliness, seclusion and isolation.' They also 'chart[ed] potential roadways with Haganah patrols.' Jewish 'self-defence' units know collectively as the Haganah were the military branch of the Jewish Agency. Soon enough, 'pioneers at the outpost had shown that Jewish settlement in the Negev was possible,' and 'new settlements were established.'

The film's narrator told us that as a result of Revivim's success, eleven new agricultural outposts were settled in 1946 and 'an 1,100 additional settlers were brought to the Negev Desert in accordance with the master plan for Jewish settlement and defence.' The film presented Revivim as the impetus for the UN's decision to include the Negev in the proposal for a Jewish state. 'It was the first such recommendation by an international forum.' The 'heroic' component in all this was that the settlements had been developed as a means to subvert and bypass the British White Paper of 1939, the purpose of which had been to prevent European Jews from settling more land in Palestine until all parties – Jews and Arabs – had reached some agreement on the future of Palestine.

Having established Revivim's importance in the 'master plan to settle the Negev,' the film's narrator explained that 'in December of 1947, Bedouin neighbours [and] agitators from Hebron' ambushed a group of pioneers, inflicting some casualties. 'Eventually Revivim formed a single fighting unit' and, with other settlements being established in the area, 'was sent to action.'

In May 1948, soon after the British left Palestine, Revivim began preparing for an attack by the 'Muslim Brotherhood,' which was supported by an 'Egyptian invasion force.' The 'attack on Revivim' began in July 1948 and ended in December, when Air Force reinforcements arrived and the 'Egyptian offensive in the area collapsed.' In this narrative, the military importance of the site was downplayed; once again, the Arabs were presented as the attackers, their target in this case being a small, fortified agricultural *kibbutz*. By admitting that Revivim was an important military outpost, the narrator would have been implying that the settlers themselves had invaded the Negev. In this presentation, the settlers' activities were trivialized; instead, they were described as agronomists.

While the film downplayed the military importance of the site, the walking tour that followed the film highlighted that importance. Our *kibbutz* guide, Stephanie, who had immigrated to Israel from the United States fourteen years earlier, began by reminding us that 'in 1943, there's nothing here; not even the bunkers, not even the barbed wires. All that was here is the dead grass, the weeds, one or two small, small, small trees, and nothing else, nothing.' Again we were being presented with the story that the desert was empty until the Jews settled it. The land had been 'bought by the Jewish Agency' from 'a few Bedouin' and 'Arabs who didn't live in the country anymore.' Interestingly, Stephanie almost immediately acknowledged that in the 1940s, this site served mainly as a 'guard post.'

Soon after, we were taken to Revivim's historical museum. We came to a large tower and were told that it was a replica of the water towers that had been used to 'establish a fact, a presence on the ground.' According to both local tradition and Ottoman Turkish law, any group could stake a claim to the land by building a structure on it.[1] For 'experimental stations,' water towers were built as the first structures. Soon after, we were led into a cave-like structure. 'This first cave is not the original cave that [the pioneers] lived in,' we were told, 'but it's a bunker that they dug out for a command post for the army ... [in] 1948.' Inside we saw replicas of the communications and military equipment that had been used. At one point, a tour participant asked Talia, the Israel Land Fund (ILF) guide, to translate a label from the Hebrew; Talia explained that it was the pledge of allegiance taken by the *kibbutz* fighters at the time: 'I swear allegiance with this gun ... as assigned to me by the Haganah organization in *Eretz Israel*. I will fight ... the enemy of my people for my country with no surrender, with no fear, and ... giving myself to do anything ... necessary.'

What struck me most at the time was that we were never taken to any of the gardens and never shown any of the agricultural or 'experimental' successes of this particular research station. We were being presented mainly with an account of the military defence of this and the other early *kibbutzim* in the area.[2] It was never clear to me whether this was intentional. At Revivim and other cities, it was nearly impossible to separate settlement issues from security ones.

The narratives of siege and defence were encountered everywhere in Israel, not only at the *kibbutzim* but also at sites defined mainly in terms of their military importance to Israel. This was reflected in the tour itineraries for Castel and Ammunition Hill, which told us that we could expect to see 'how Jerusalem was secured in 1948' and 'how Jerusalem was united in 1967.'

On the Israel Development Fund (IDF) tour, after a short drive through Jerusalem, we got off at Castel and began climbing a barren and eerily quiet hill, the site of a pivotal battle in the 1947–8 war. Our guide, Arnie, led us along a dusty path toward the hilltop, stopping sometimes to translate and explain the large blue plaques.

At the first one, he pointed to a map of the Mandate of Palestine. He told us that the story of the Battle of Castel and the War of Independence began in April 1947 when the UN recommended the partition of Palestine. He framed the affected communities' responses in this way: '[The] Arabs don't want it. The Jews say, "Okay, we've got nothing to lose."' Without explaining why the Arabs might have rejected such a plan, he described the battles that began soon after the Declaration of Independence:

The battle started in the cities [and] on the roads [with people] attacking buses ... You [would] drive through an Arab village, put down the windows and wait to see what happened. [The bus] had guards over the wheels around it so it wouldn't take any bullets and it had a little scoop in front and a place to put barbed wire and nails that would take off the tires of the bus. [Taking the bus was] like driving in a fortified vehicle.

The Jews were presented as having done nothing more than accept an internationally sanctioned solution to a conflict over land, and as being threatened for doing so by those who stubbornly (and, it was strongly suggested, illegitimately) opposed their settlement. According to Arnie, after some loss of life a decision was made to carry out a plan called the 'D Plan' – in Hebrew, *Tochnit Dalet* – a strategy that meant 'captur[ing] the high points, sending the people out ... Now we take the offensive, [we] don't wait to be hit.' Arnie described this action as an 'offensive' measure, yet in the same breath he framed it in the context of the need to develop better measures to protect the Jews.

As we walked up the hill from plaque to plaque, the tour participants seemed riveted by the presentation. At the midway point Arnie told us:

[There were] hundreds of [Arab] fighters to defend the Castel here. The battle lasted five days and the Arabs had a light artillery and sharpshooters in very ... rainy ... weather ... The Jewish forces had few reinforcements and no supplies ... The Arabs have the mountaintop, the hilltop, they have the weapons, they have the advantage that held off five attacks already.

According to this description, the Jews were the underdogs and had to hope for a miracle. At a point nearer the top of the hill, Arnie explained how the battle ended:

On the Castel, the commander of the Arab forces, ... Abed Kadir El Husseini is killed, and that night the Arab defenders take his body and they abandon the site for his funeral. The next day in Jerusalem, in the morning attack, the [Jewish] fighters who couldn't take the hill ... come up. [There was] no opposition whatsoever. The Castel is in Hebrew, in Jewish hands.

Was this a miracle or simply a lucky break? We were left to ponder this as we continued toward the hilltop. Once there, a number of us had questions about the surrounding area but were told to wait. Arnie thought it important to tell us about one other important battle that took place in the Jerusalem area.

Using the topographic model at the site, Arnie described the Battle of the Burma Road. Again the narrative focused on the immense suffering of the Jews, especially those 'under siege' in Jerusalem in the summer of 1948. The Burma Road was a vital supply route for the city's Jews. Arnie explained gravely that 'Jerusalem was almost lost' but 'this was a modern miracle for the Jewish people. The world had written off the modern State of Israel. In 1948, [Israel was] written off. So this is what the Castel's all about.' The Jews survived as a nation because of their heroism in the defence of Jerusalem.

While I do not want to represent the alternative history of this battle, it is worth pointing out that in histories of this era, no distinction is ever made between the Palestinians who were resisting displacement and the colonization of their land and the Arab states who joined the war 'from outside.' During the tours, it was never mentioned that the Palestinians had any justification for opposing the new settlers. In fact, the Palestinian cause was never represented in any way. It was suggested that Arabs simply 'didn't want' the partition of Palestine; the Jews were then presented as living under a state of siege. All of this implies that only non-indigenous military forces – the Egyptians and the Jordanians – were involved in battles against Jewish settlers; it also ignores the Palestinian experience of this partition and their reasons for resisting it. Arnie's narrative emphasized the Jews' experiences of siege and focused solely on their need to defend themselves against *outsiders*. Despite this emphasis, some tour participants posed very difficult questions for Arnie at this site. These questions seem to have arisen directly from Arnie's approach to framing these issues. Not all of the participants accepted his interpretation of this war, and some inserted the Palestinians back into the narrative.

On the ILF tour as well, we were told about the many battles for Jerusalem. But instead of taking us to any particular site, Talia asked us all to 'try to imagine, when you look [all around] you. During the War of Independence, they were shelling Jerusalem from that place [just above the road we are driving along] ... Jerusalem was tiny then ... and [the Arabs] had the advantage.' Imagining this space in these terms reinforced the most important facets of the siege narrative. As we drove along these roads we were surrounded by hills and valleys, which were described to us as beautiful but also dangerous, for they were also places that were used (and, it was implied, could *again* be used) to hide attackers. Talia also explained that during the War of Independence the Jewish community was 'besieged by the Muslim community of Jerusalem' and that a 'survival plan' had to be drawn up to rescue the Jews. As we drove along this route, she pointed to a number of old trucks set along the narrow ridge of the roadway. We were told that they were models of the vehicles used to save the Jews during the siege of Jerusalem. Talia asked us to look out our bus windows again:

> When you look at the trucks, you can see how small they were, how outdated [they were]. I mean we're talking about 1948 and still they were outdated even then. They tried to put on some [armour] plates to [stop the] bullets but it didn't help them very much. Now these trucks were very heavy because they put water tanks on them, a lot of supplies, a lot of medical supplies, and they had some soldiers on [them] and they sent them in convoy to Jerusalem. And along the way they [met] a few obstacles. One of them was here. Now take a look ... Even today with this modern road, it is so easy to ambush the road ... Then there was no way to turn. Each truck was small, heavy, loaded and as soon as they started to throw stones from the hills – and the villagers did that – the convoy had to stop and they were engaged in a battle that was always bloody, always.

Arab villages were thus sites of 'ambush,' 'shelling,' and danger. Significantly, the villagers were the aggressors. The simple methods the Jews used in fighting for their survival were emphasized. This was a people against whom the odds were stacked. Underscored here were the efforts of a small group of people, mostly farmers, to defend themselves using the simplest of tools – hand tools, outdated trucks, and the like. Highlighted were the Jews' ingenuity and their collective efforts to battle a well-organized and heavily armed Muslim majority. In light of all of the difficulties they faced, the Jews' victory was nothing less than miraculous.

These interpretations of the war also emphasized the illegitimate role of the external Arab forces, although there was little effort to explain just how these forces were a factor. On the Israel Civil Society Fund (ICSF) tour, we were told about the siege of a *kibbutz* that was attacked by the Egyptians during the 1948 war. In this presentation, Sivan, our guide, emphasized that the enemies of the nation were close even when they seemed far away. She told us that the Egyptian forces had crossed the 'entire Negev Desert' in their efforts to reach Jerusalem. The suggestion was that no Israeli city could ever really be safe from any Arab state that wanted to attack it.

Bravery, boldness, and courage characterized all of Israel's military endeavours, and its victories told the tale of a nation that was surviving against all odds. By all tour accounts, one of the most important of Israel's victories was the Six Day War of 1967. This war was a turning point for Israel: by winning it, it was able to reunify Jerusalem as the nation's capital. This war also secured for Israel a presence in the region and confirmed that it was a powerful military force.

On a 1995 tour celebrating Jerusalem's three-thousandth anniversary, the mayor of Jerusalem and other Israeli leaders called on the tour participants to recognize a 'united Jerusalem' and the 'heroes' who had united the city. In almost every way, this tour of Jerusalem was more a celebration of the 1967 war's 'accomplishments' than a celebration of Jerusalem's role in modern Israeli society or Jewish culture.

On the IDF tour, we were taken to Ammunition Hill State Memorial Site and Museum, which is housed in a reconstructed bunker and trench system and is 'dedicated to the reunification of Jerusalem during the Six Day War, 1967.' From 1948 to 1967, this area served as Jordan's command post and armoury.

At this site, the 1967 war was represented as a colossal victory for Israel's political and military leaders. After walking around the trenches, we were taken into a small auditorium and shown a film about the war. The film's narrator characterized the battle as a national one to defend all Jews. In all of the narratives, the Arab forces – the Egyptians and Jordanians in particular – were represented as the aggressors. Israel was represented as being forced to 'defend itself' and eventually to 'counter-attack.'

The film presented one soldier's experience of the war. He talked about his call to duty and about three of his fellow comrades in arms, two of whom died in the battle. Each stage of the battle was described in detail:

We're about to enter the Jewish Quarter. Before me is the Dung Gate. Breathe deep, we're about to realize a dream to return to the Old City. In those moments I felt that I could digest everything: all the sights of war, the wounded, the smoke. I had built for myself a sort of protective wall ... We were moving under the walls, and for a moment my sense blurred. Sounds of shooting brought me back to reality, we continued defending ... the Old City ...

Descending the steps to the Western Wall, I'm not a religious man, never have been, but I am touching the stones of the Western Wall ... The battles had ended. I stood weeping. Letting out all the tension, all the fear, the worry, the pain that had accumulated the last few days.

Artillery fire and the sounds of battle filled the auditorium as dark, hazy slide photos of the battle were shown on the large white screen. The narrator's slow, gentle voice was highly compelling. Although he was a soldier, he did not speak in military language; seemingly, he represented an ordinary man's responses to the chaos of war. The soldier described the heroic efforts in battle, emphasizing how even as a secular Jew, he understood the spiritual significance of the battle. Jerusalem's reunification was presented as a national victory, and the battle was described in such a way as to suggest that victory was inevitable – it was the Jews' national mission to reunify the city.

In all Israeli military narratives, no reference was made to the non-Jews who lost their lives or their land as a result of these battles. For example, we were never told about the disappearance and destruction of more than four hundred Palestinian villages during the 1947–8 period. Nor were we told about the hundreds of thousands of Palestinians who have been displaced from their homes since 1967.

Jerusalem's capture was the key moment in the 1967 war; however, Syria was also involved in the war as well as in the Yom Kippur War of 1973–4. Syria's Golan Heights were occupied by Israel in the 1967 war; parts of those heights were later (illegally) annexed by Israel in December 1981.

On the ICSF tour we were taken to the Galilee region, just south of the Golan Heights. We visited a *kibbutz* on a hill overlooking the Galilee. Small, simply decorated rooms have been provided to accommodate Israeli and international tourists, in an area separated from the settlement's residential area. After a peaceful night, we were given a short tour of the *kibbutz* by one of its original founders; after that, we were divided into small groups and directed to a line of jeeps at the *kibbutz* gate. Each jeep had a driver, who would show us the Golan Heights.

We drove through lush hills along dusty roads, passing orchards, DANGER: MINES signs, and military bases. The tourists asked the driver to describe the local residents and their *kibbutzim*. When one tourist asked about the military importance of these places, the driver asked us to wait until we met another local resident, who would discuss these things with us.

Twenty minutes later, we got out of the jeeps. We were high above the Hula Valley, at the site of an old Syrian bunker (see photo 9). A local resident, Pinhas, greeted us. A fit man in his thirties, dressed in civilian clothes but with a gun on his hip, he began to tell us about the Golan, noting that he wanted to do so 'without getting inside politics.' He told us that we had come to the area at a critical moment 'because right now, no one really knows nothing. Maybe next year we'll need passports here or maybe not!' With this, he suggested that Israelis – and presumably Israeli Jews rather than Israeli Druze or Bedouin – in the region were living with the fear of the unknown. According to him, the peoples of the Golan had got along well until the mid-1950s. Until that time, 'simple farmers [lived on the Western slopes and] they even used to trade with the Israelis down below, selling horses, wheat, cows, whatever they got.' It was not until 'the Syrian Army started to arrive and they took most of their civilians that used to live here, pushed them deep inside Syria and to the area of Kuneitra, Damascus … and … just started to build a closed-off military area.' From that point on, according to Pinhas, there began 'shooting and shelling mostly with Russian artillery, Russian cannons, once a week, twice a week on different Israeli *kibbutzim* and *moshavim*.' Between 1964 and 1967, Israeli families in the region were forced to live 'inside the bomb shelters.' He then asked us all to 'just imagine yourself [as] one of the Israeli farmers who use[d] to go out to farm his land and, of course, this was also a good target for the Syrian cannons. They see one of the Israeli tractors outside [and] they start to shoot.'

According to Pinhas, 'all those problems continued until '67.' He then explained why Israel chose to enter into a war with Syria. He said that 'at the beginning, there was no plan to climb the Golan Heights' because it seemed an impossible task to 'climb the mountain under fire and to capture the Syrian bunkers on top,' and also because the estimated risk to Israeli lives was too great. Syria was a dangerous nuisance, but it was not enough of a military threat that Israel would willingly go to war against it. Only when 'a small mission, a small group of people' from the northern *kibbutzim* met with Levi Eshkol, the Israeli prime minister at the time, did a discussion begin, and it was 'because of a lot of pressure that came from those Israelis and also a lot of pressure that came from the Israeli Minister of Defense Moshe Dayan and the Israeli Chief of Staff, Yitzhak Rabin – [that] finally Eshkol decides [and he] starts giving orders to bring up troops.' Thus, according to Pinhas, it was only as a result of a local populist movement that Israel entered into a war with Syria. Israel here was being presented as a country on the offensive, but it was also being presented as a reluctant participant. The resulting victory was nothing short of miraculous. On the fifth day of the Six Day War, despite a shortage of military resources – 'the Air Force was not so big' and was 'busy down south' – Israel gained the upperhand:

> Step by step, ... we started very early in the morning [using] big bulldoz-ers [with] metal shields of course, tanks, and infantry units. [It was] only in the afternoon [that] the first Israeli soldier arrived [at] the first line of Syrian bunkers, almost the same place we are standing [in] right now.

According to Pinhas, only after the Golan Heights were captured did one of the *kibbutz* fighters realize 'what a big threat we got from the Syrian Army.' In other words, it was a defensive war after all.

At this point, our guide shifted the discussion from the miraculous victory of 1967 to an interpretation of the contemporary situation:

> You must understand the big argument in Israel today is not about giving back the land. We are not talking about the land. And also it's not about bringing back those people that are living in the thirty-two Israeli settle-ments on the Golan Heights ... The only argument in Israel today is if we can trust the Syrians. This is the argument.

Pinhas was framing the issue in terms of security rather than in terms of Israeli or military occupation of the land. According to him, Israel did not want or need the land, and it was only because Israel is not very good at media relations that the Syrian-Israeli conflict was being misrepresented to the world: 'They always say ... the land ... the Israelis "captured" or "took away" from Syria.' He suggested that the real issues were 'if we can trust Syrians' and 'who wants to be respon-sible for this decision.' Even so, Pinhas admitted that Israel too was a threat for the Syrians: 'Imagine yourself [as a Syrian, and] the Israeli tanks are sitting two hours ride from the Syrian capital city, from Dam-ascus and, of course, it's also a big threat to [Syrian President] Asad.' And yet it was Israel that wanted the peace, and it was the Israelis who were 'tired from giving three years in the army. All of us are tired from giving one month in the reserve until the age of forty five or fifty. All of us wants peace.' He added this warning:

> Now another thing you must understand: Asad's youngest brother ... he's the one in charge of ... law and, by the way, also in charge of raising the

drugs inside of Lebanon, in the Bakka Valley, [including] opium, hashish, marijuana, [and] all those wonderful things ... [With] this money ... they support the Syrian economy and they also support some terrorist organizations, like Hezbollah. But again, they say to those terrorists, you are not allowed to be active through ... the Syrian territory. You are only allowed to be active through the Lebanese territory. Then they can say it's not Syria [that's behind these actions].

This representation of the enemy as dangerous, and as relying on terrorism and an illegal economy, did not end Pinhas's presentation. He had one more 'amusing' story 'just for ending' to tell. Pointing to the bunker site, he told us:

There were three or four places like this all over the Golan Heights. This was like a small place for vacation to the Syrian officers. [There was] water ... coming from a natural ... underground spring. They built a small swimming pool ... This was a small club, [with] dressing rooms ... and even a small canteen ... They used to sell cold drinks and everything and [there] were very fancy toilets and showers ... Now there is another wonderful story that the Israelis [talk about] in ... different *kibbutzim* and *moshavim* in this area ... The people [said that] every week there was only one day [of every week] that was quiet. [There was] no shooting, no shelling, no nothing. Usually this was every Thursday. Now this is why: Every Thursday afternoon, [a] red bus used to patrol the different Syrian bunkers. This was a big red bus loaded with women inside and, let's say in nice words, those womens [*sic*] were just for fun to the Syrian officers. Now the story is that every Thursday afternoon, when the Israelis [who] lived in *kibbutzim* and *moshavim* ... looked in their binoculars, [and they saw] the red bus ... patrol the Syrian bunkers, they start[ed] making telephones [to] each other: 'Tonight we don't need the bomb shelters, this is going to be a quiet night.'

While we stood overlooking the *kibbutzim* and looking up at the abandoned Syrian bunkers – shot up, marked with dark graffiti – Pinhas was presenting us with examples of Arab immorality and stupidity. The latter was contrasted with the cleverness of the *kibbutzniks*, who had quickly discovered that Thursday afternoons were impromptu ceasefires.

It is interesting that Pinhas backed away from discussing what many considered a key issue in the Golan: water. But very soon after when we returned to our bus, Sivan discussed the conflict in those very terms:

> When in the early sixties, Israel as a state decided to build a national water system [using the Golan Heights and natural gravity to bring the water down through the Jordan Valley] the Syrians objected bitterly ... At first they tried [to intervene] with the United Nations and then [when it] was recognized ... that Israel is entitled to use the water, so then [the Syrians] started [to shoot us] with artillery. These were heavy, heavy fights ... at the place where the pumping station should have been ... As a result, the pumping station could not be built and it has moved down to the Sea of Galilee ... Now [the] '67 War was also called the 'War over the Water.' Some of you may remember that [in response to the water project that the Israelis had planned but failed to build], the Syrians invented the idea of diverting the water into a canal that would start at the sources of the Jordan River, at Banias ... They started the canal with the financial aid of many Arab countries. They had all the money and they started [building] the canal. [This] meant that the Jordan River water would stop coming down to the Sea of Galilee but [would] rather ... end up in Jordan and that was a very major threat to Israel. When [the Israelis reached] the Golan in '67, the canal was found. It was almost completely built.

All of this served as further justification for Israel's fear that Syria might control the area. By occupying the Golan Heights, the Israelis were defending their northern border as well as much-needed water resources.

Military narratives about the Golan were presented on other tours as well. At a site overlooking the Syrian village of Kuneitra, now abandoned, Arnie (IDF tour) explained the importance of this site. They described a surprise attack by the Syrians in 1973 on Yom Kippur – one of the Jews' holiest days – and the heroism of the Israeli officers who fought back. Israelis remember the Yom Kippur War as one that induced widespread national panic: it was the first time the Israelis had ever been caught off-guard and ill-prepared. Arnie described the period:

> In 1973, on Yom Kippur morning ... the Syrians [and] Egyptians opened fire on the Suez Canal and the Syrians, in a joint military action, massed fifteen hundred tanks on the front line of the Golan Heights. That is the largest concentration of armour in the history of modern warfare. There

wasn't one battle in World War II that [involved] fifteen hundred tanks ... And the Syrians massed the tanks and came across the Golan Heights. The Syrians, within a matter of hours, completely destroyed the over one hundred thirty [Israeli] tanks ... on the southern flank. Not one tank was mobile after the initial attack. On the northern flank, just on the other side of this dirt road ... going up the hill there, there's a Valley called the Valley of Tears, and one unit held off the northern attack and assault by the Syrians. It was led by a Yemenite Jewish officer, Victor Kahalani, who is now Minister of Police and Internal Security in the government. And he stood there with thirteen tanks, six of them ... immobile, seven ... going up and down the same ramp and shooting at the Syrians, [and] they held out into ... the early evenings. The Syrian paratroopers ... commandos ... captured the Hermon Mountains. They took the Israeli position on top of the mountain and started their way down. They ... knocked out our artillery units, [and] the entire front line fell except for one spot at this Valley of Tears. At night, [the Israeli brigade led by] their commander, Victor Kahalani ... were shooting at tanks that they didn't see. All they saw were the shots, the flame ... burst of a gun. They'd shoot for it. They didn't [even] see the tank in the dark. They held out until ... midday next day till there was reinforcements on the northern [flank]. The Syrian generals rolled right across the Golan Heights ... within a number of hours. [It] takes our reserve units forty-eight hours to get organized [for the] counter-attack, [and to] push back to Kuneitra ... Kissinger steps in, [with] Richard Nixon's [support], [and] they were sending in supplies. We ran out of ammunition in '73 war. A lot of people don't realize that. [Those were] hard times. [It was] bad news. [Then the] Americans get involved. Henry Kissinger flies in [and] says, 'OK, the Syrians – they're finished now. They're ready to come to the negotiating table. They've got nothing left.' [They want the] Israelis to head back to the Volcanic Ridge and then things will start rolling in the Golan Heights for negotiations. Israelis said no way. [Kissinger] landed right here ... It's a tank position. [He] took out the map and made a decision that we'd give back Kuneitra ... to the Syrians and keep the ridge. That's why we're here today in 1998. [That was] the situation [in the] last war [in] '73. There was a total intelligence failure. The Syrians and Egyptians were planning to attack. They surprised us and that won't happen again because here in the Golan Heights it's readiness all the time. It's more tanks and it's more soldiers.

Arnie was presenting the Yom Kippur War as a profoundly serious threat to Israel. As it turned out, Syria's fear that Israel would annex the heights was well founded. In 1981, over Syrian Druze resistance, Israel annexed the area, displacing the region's people yet again.

Soon after the annexation, in 1982, Israel became embroiled in another conflict, 'Operation Peace for Galilee.' More often, it is referred to as the Israeli-Lebanese conflict.

On the ILF tour, on our way to the Israel–Lebanon border, we passed Kiryat Shmona, a development town that in the 1990s had often been shelled from Lebanon. Talia had this to say about the town:

> These are some of the bomb shelters. It looks like a very peaceful town, which it is, unless it starts getting *katyusha* rockets ... Kiryat Shmona was not always like that. [It] was so far away from central Israel ... Broken up people ... in mind and body ... were placed ... here. And it was really far away for them, [far] from anywhere, [far] from anything. They were not equipped, not emotionally and not professionally, to be here, and it was very difficult for them. And then when Kiryat Shmona became a border town and it was hit constantly by terrorists from Lebanon, people here started to lose their courage. The town looked terrible. It was dirty. It was not being [rebuilt]. It was neglected. It was really terrible and the people here cried out to heaven, until the summer of '82. In the summer of 1982, Israel went into Lebanon. The street that we are on right now ... was an unbelievable [sight]. The women of Kiryat Shmona were standing ... along the road, with tables [with] all kinds of soft drinks and coffee and cakes for the soldiers. And the soldiers kept on coming. Trucks ... of soldiers and tanks were going into Lebanon ... And the war went on and the war was over and Kiryat Shmona went through a complete change. Something happened to the people. Suddenly their backs straightened up. They became very proud of themselves and their town. They started to take care of their town and this is why Kiryat Shmona looks so pretty and so colourful.

For a development town like Kiryat Shmona, the war against Lebanon proved to be a 'good' war. It strengthened the people's resolve, it raised their self-esteem, and it gave them meaning and pride.[3]

Soon after passing through Kiryat Shmona, we arrived at a park and canteen area. We walked along a neat path to the international border, which was marked 'the Good Fence.' Once there, we gathered together and listened to Talia describe what was then an ongoing conflict with Lebanon. She had not been a soldier in the Lebanese war, but she thought it important for us to be exposed to an Israeli civilian's perspective. Avi, the retired brigadier general who was with us that day, would later provide the military perspective. Talia described the war:

> The story of this place starts quite a long time ago, about twenty-one years ago when a civil war ... ripped Lebanon apart. It was the south against the north ... As a result, the people who lived between the area of Beirut and Israel [were] caught in the middle. They [were] in [a] war against the North Lebanese, and of course they [were] sitting on the border with the Israelis. Israel [was] not an active enemy but it [was] still an enemy. There [was] nothing here, absolutely nothing. No trees, no buildings, not even a border ... The people of south Lebanon, just like [the people in] all of Lebanon ... are [from] many different religious [and] ethnic groups ... The fence was just a simple fence ... Inside south Lebanon you have military [personnel], you have villagers, you [have] Christians who are Christian Maronites, you have Sunni Muslims, you have Shi'a Muslims [and] you have Druze. You have many different groups that are not doing very well with each other. But you see people [in the south] are cut off from the north. They don't get supplies ... they don't get their mail, they don't get medical supplies [or] medical help. They are cut off. And then one day a patrol car goes along the fence and [the soldiers] observe that one of the girls that went along the fields stepped on a mine. She [lay] there and everyone [was] afraid to get to her to get some help [and] afraid to step on another mine. So Israeli soldiers crossed over and they helped her out and they [took] her out and [flew] her [by] helicopter to the Ram Bam hospital. [There] she stayed [and] was being treated. And just a side story, [she was] treated by a male nurse, a [Christian] Maronite male nurse, and he married her.

In response to this comment, the tourists laughed and applauded. Talia then continued, telling us this was a 'very meaningful incident' for it

> showed the farmers of south Lebanon that the villain is really not Israel [and that] Israelis are not really villains. And it takes a while but little by little, they [came] in for help ... And they began to trade ... And they start getting a day's permission to come to work for a day ... You have all kinds of facilities that help out the farmers of southern Lebanon. Now Israel realized [this was] an opportunity to start working with the south Lebanese militia. So they [train] them. They [give] them military clothing, they [give] them military vehicles, and there are a lot of connections between the two.

Israeli actions in the area were represented as necessary assistance to a population caught in a civil war. The Lebanese militia was represented as if it stood for the entire population in south Lebanon and as if its requests for military aid were legitimate. Yet it was a militia, and therefore weaker than an army both legally and politically:

> As a result [of the continuing 'chaos' in Lebanon], different terrorists start[ed] to infiltrate into the villages and start[ed] to shoot toward the border and toward the different Israeli settlements along the border. The situation is getting worse and worse [and the] militia cannot prevent them from infiltrating into the villages and the situation is growing gradually worse. The south Lebanese start to rely on Israel and they pressure Israel into helping them out. In the meantime, Kiryat Shmona and all the *kibbutzim* along the border also pressure Israel, and that results [in] Israel entering Lebanon in 1982.

Israel's military actions in Lebanon were represented as a response to the defensive needs of Israeli's border population and to Lebanese solicitation. But Talia also had to explain why Israel continued to occupy the area long after the civil war's end. She told us that Israel needed to create a security zone where the south Lebanese militia could be trained. They had become better at managing the local population, but they still could not secure the area without Israeli support.

After we returned to the bus, Avi, the ILF's North American representative, who had been assisting Talia on the tour, rose to tell us about the war from a military perspective. Avi was a tall, fit man in his mid-fifties. Now retired, he had served in Lebanon for two years and was the last commander in the Beirut area before Israel's withdrawal from Lebanon. His description of the conflict follows:

> The conflict with Lebanon started after the Six Day War ... Until the Six Day War it was a quiet border between Israel and Lebanon ... After the conflict with King Hussein [of Jordan] with the Palestinians, most of the Palestinian organizations moved from Jordan to Lebanon. From '68 until today ... every day [there was] another problem with [Lebanon] and we tried to do anything with Lebanon. I can remind you we [were] inside Beirut, the capital of Lebanon. This was the Peace for [Galilee] War and we stopped ... this war with the big idea [that] maybe we can change the government in Lebanon and ... create a new Lebanon with a good relationship with Israel. But in Lebanon, as you know, live Christian, Muslim,

Shia, Druzim, Sunnim, and all of them are Lebanese citizens. The civilian war in Lebanon started in '58 ... and from this time until today, every other month they have another conflict between the groups, especially between the religious groups, [i.e.,] between the Muslim Shia and the Christian. [It is the] same [as the] situation in Yugoslavia.

In other words, because Lebanon is a multiethnic country with many religions, it is bound to have civil strife. The country was in chaos long before Israel's military engagement. Avi was painting a picture of Lebanon as a chaotic and ungovernable country and one where Israeli intervention was legitimate. Note that by using the official name for the war, 'Operation Peace for Galilee,' Avi was shifting the emphasis from the defence of Lebanon (as Talia had described the war) to the defence of the Galilee area of Israel. Finally, Avi came to what he considered the crux of the matter. It was not just the Palestinians who had moved their terrorist organizations to Lebanon from Jordan who were the problem:

The problem in Lebanon today [is this]: Lebanon [is] controlled by the Syrians, and we think, and we hope, and many people in Israel believe, we can get a peace with Lebanon after the peace with Syria ... First of all, we need [to] finish the conflict with Syria, and after that maybe we can do [a] deal with Lebanon. We have [no] problems with the civilian people ... in the south of Lebanon.

Two questions were asked during these presentations. The first was from a middle-aged Canadian doctor: 'When was this war? What were you doing fighting this war?' Avi responded '1982!' His inflection, however, said much more. He was unmistakably taken aback. Both he and Talia had methodically chronicled the history of the war in Lebanon. Both of them had asserted that they were not taking political positions in their representations but simply telling it like it is. Yet it was clear to many of us that they were not presenting the peace movement's perspective on the war. Thinking back to those moments, I wonder whether the guides had assumed that the participants held antiwar positions and that it was their duty to enlighten them. For the Israel–Lebanon conflict had divided Jewish communities both inside and outside Israel, and it was largely in response to this war that Peace Now, Israel's largest peace movement, had been formed. This was also the war that led to the notorious massacre of Palestinians in the Sabra and

Shatilla refugee camps carried out by Lebanese Maronite Christians. That massacre led to an Israeli government inquiry, the Kahan Committee, which forced Israel's then–Minister of Defense, Ariel Sharon, to resign because of his 'indirect responsibility.' When the Canadian physician asked his question, I initially thought to myself that perhaps he was confused, because the guides had used the military names to describe the conflict: 'Peace for Galilee' rather than the Israeli–Lebanese War.

Yet no one challenged Avi or Talia's interpretation of the events that led to the invasion and occupation of Lebanon. Avi argued that the Israelis had invaded Lebanon because Palestinian groups had set up their terrorist organizations there and Israel needed to secure its borders against them. Talia's slightly different version was interesting only because she never once spoke of the Palestinians but rather highlighted Lebanon's need for Israeli intervention. She also seemed to be suggesting that the Lebanese both needed and wanted the modern amenities made available to them through their relationship with Israel.

On all the tours, the conflict with Lebanon was linked to the conflict with Syria. Israel was never described as illegally occupying southern Lebanon. Instead, the focus was on the 'peaceful' relations Israel enjoys with some of the south Lebanese. Why Hezbollah – 'terrorists' in Avi and Talia's accounts – continued to fight in southern Lebanon and was targeting sites in northern Israel was never explained in terms of Hezbollah's belief that it had a right to resist the Israeli occupation of southern Lebanon. Furthermore, Hezbollah and other resistance groups were never described as indigenous to region. Rather, the focus was on the support that they were receiving from Iran and Syria. The implication was that it was external rather than internal issues that engaged them. The need for an Israeli-controlled militarized zone followed this logic. In this way, the Lebanon–Israel conflict was linked directly to the Israel–Syria conflict, and so was the need for a continued Israeli military presence in the area.

To fully appreciate the military narratives, one has to accept Israel's perspective: it is the Jews who are in their rightful place. It is the Jews who, because they are surrounded by multiethnic, multireligious, premodern, chaotic, dangerous, and ungovernable others, are living under a state of siege. It is the Jews who belong, and it is their place that must be militarily secured lest all that is associated with it – modern development, democracy, tolerance, and a Western ethos – be lost.

The Israeli military play a key role in securing the state – or in Israeli terms, defending it. However, the urgency to secure the nation has not always been framed in militaristic terms. Many modern Israelis believe that by settling the land, they are securing it against any threat of future displacement in negotiations with the Arabs, mainly with the Palestinians. In this sense, Israel's struggle is also demographic. To secure their place in the region, Jews must claim the land by settling on it. Part of this strategy involves establishing 'security corridors' in the Jordan Valley, Greater Jerusalem, and the Galilee.

Although there had been an unofficial peace between Jordan and Israel for some time before those two countries signed their peace agreement in the 1990s, the need for Israeli-Jewish settlements in the Jordan Valley continues to be tied to Israeli security concerns. On the ICSF tour through Israel, Sivan warned: 'Behind Jordan there is Iraq. [We] calculate[d] that it takes thirty hours for the Iraqi army from its farthest place to get to Jerusalem, or to the mountains up here. Thirty hours is [nothing].' The implication is that Israel must create settlements in this mountainous region so as to control the high ground and enable the surveillance of the Jordanian side of the Jordan Valley. Furthermore, 'conquering the land' – that is, settling the land – is necessary not only to prevent Scuds and other missiles from reaching these sites, but also because a 'country or state is not conquered ... unless [and until] you have the troops going on the ground, bringing [in a] supply of food, bringing people in, [and] inhabiting the conquered land.' Another guide explained that by settling the area and creating 'facts on the ground,' Israelis would be able to ensure that even if a land settlement was eventually reached with the Palestinians, Israelis would never '[allow] these mountains [to] be owned by Palestinians.'

In this way then, Israeli security policy helped explain Israeli settlement policy. Israel can only be secure if it can move its ground forces into any area quickly; in order for this to be possible, Israeli Jews must settle the land. The land is only secure if it is inhabited, a process that follows conquest. This in effect collapses the distinctions between military and civilian security.

Israel's need to continuously surveille Jordanian and Palestinian territories assumes that land – any land, even where Palestinians live – can and must be used for security purposes. Thus, the tour participants were made to understand the lands captured during the Six Day War not as militarily 'occupied territories' but rather as Israeli 'security corridors.' And even though Israel had signed peace agreements with neighbouring Arab states, there was an ever-present fear of the Arabs. If not explicitly stated, it was implied that Arabs were not to be trusted. In this way was justified the policy of setting the land – doing so secured Israel from Arab states, even ones that did not share a border with Israel. From every perspective, Israel's security was paramount, no matter what the effects might be on others in the region.

Security was also presented as the reason for expropriating and settling broad swaths of land in and around Jerusalem.

On the ILF tour, Talia explained that soon after the 1967 war, municipal and state leaders decided to annex East Jerusalem. In doing so, they drew new boundaries for 'a bigger Jerusalem, a greater Jerusalem.'

On the IDF tour, while we were driving through hills overlooking a small Palestinian village, Arnie explained the 'concept' of Greater Jerusalem:

> The concept is that, okay, we had Israel and [West] Jerusalem [and there was always] a possibility to expand to the West. So we're not concerned with this. We are concerned with the future war or future situation of dividing ... or giving back parts of Jerusalem. And so we have to secure Jerusalem by building new neighbourhoods to the south, to the east, to the north [and] to the northwest ... It's not a matter of we've been here or not before. We're just going to secure a big [area] leading to the north ... Politically the understanding is that we should not create a Palestinian succession of the urban centres. We must stop that. [For example], there's [the Palestinian city of] Bethlehem ... If we don't have [the Jewish settlements of] Gilo and Talpiot [blocking the space between Bethlehem and Jerusalem] one day, [the Palestinian centres will] grow out and meet with that part of Jerusalem ... So, by doing that, you actually secure the separation of Muslim areas or Palestinian areas from this side [Israel].

In other words, if not for the development of new Israeli settlements, Palestinians might one day, by virtue of natural population growth, surround the city. Israeli Jews must therefore settle the areas in order to prevent the Palestinians from forming a contiguous territory and claiming a majority in the area.

Even areas outside Greater Jerusalem are claimed as part of Israel. For example, Ma'ale Adumim, home to 30,000 to 45,000 Jews, has been declared 'by consensus' and 'by the Labour Government' a part of Greater Jerusalem. Arnie explained: 'Because Jerusalem is one ... it is not to be divided and its character should be Jewish. There may be Palestinian residents in it, but we must ensure the fact that it's going to be very, very Israeli and not any other type [of settlement].' Through the claim that Ma'ale Adumim is part of Greater Jerusalem, the settlement has become a 'non-negotiable' site in any future 'land for peace' deal because Israeli policy states that Jerusalem will always be the undivided capital of Israel and the Jews. Furthermore, Ma'ale Adumim provides a route in and out of an area that the Israelis see as part of an eventual Palestinian autonomous zone. In Ma'ale Adumim is thus a settlement within the autonomous zone and the Israeli government is using this fact to legitimate its construction of 'bypass' roads – that is, roads which bypass the Palestinian urban centres and provide routes to and from the Jewish settlements within the Occupied Territories as well as in and out of Israel. We were told that the contiguity of Jerusalem with areas settled by Jews in the rest of these territories is of great importance to the Israelis. This concern is important for understanding Israel's settlement options and policies. Jerusalem must remain 'fortified' by 'Jewish settlers or Jewish inhabitants.' The guides discussed this demographic contest without any hesitation or embarrassment.[4]

But an external 'other' was not the only threat to the Jewish state. On all of the tours, we were told that more and more non-Jews were living in Israel, and that Jewish settlements were having to be established as a counter-measure. For example, a policy of Judaizing or Hebrewizing the Galilee was being fully implemented by the 1970s.[5] All the tour guides described this policy as we toured in the region; each, however, emphasized a different element of this practice. Nevertheless, all acknowledged that this pattern of settlement was meant to create a Jewish majority in an area that previously had an Arab majority and still might have one in the future. Arnie explained:

[There was] a process of bringing as many Jewish people to the Galilee, a process that started in the seventies mainly. Ben-Gurion [Israel's first prime minister] had this idea first. [The process was a matter of] dispersing the Jewish population in the Negev. But then at some point the Galilee seemed to be too scary, because the Arab population was the vast majority, and since we are dealing sometimes with the question of where you have an Arab majority ... that is land that may be negotiated in the future ... To take out that opportunity the Israelis started in the sixties, and then mainly in the seventies, a program to bring those settlements up to the top of the mountains. They don't occupy valleys down below where there are terraces and fields but rather sit up above ... And so there are many,

many settlements like this further around the Galilee. Some call it the Judaization, Hebrewization [or] Israelization of the Galilee ... This is really the term that was used [to mean] just to disperse Jewish population [in the areas] so that at no point [in the future would these areas] be negotiable, either. It's not the territories [of the West Bank]. It is not a contested area ... The majority of Israeli Arabs live in the Galilee and not elsewhere.

On another tour, participants were presented with a very similar version of this practice, but they were also told that this policy 'was very successful. There's now a Jewish majority in the Galilee.' The need to create and then maintain a Jewish majority in areas around Israel was talked of as a given. How land might have come to be owned by the Israeli Jews, or what happened in order to prevent the Palestinian population from expanding its land base was never revealed. Implied was that such settlements were established in uninhabited areas – as if for example, land not terraced might not also be owned or inhabited by local Palestinians. No reference was ever made to continued Palestinian resistance or to the many political and legal battles over these policies, including the annual Day of the Land demonstrations in the Galilee. Excluding such details is misleading in all cases and implies that this is a benign process, similar to the way that the 'pioneers' settled the Negev in the 1940s.

6

The Politics of Securing Peace

The first Declaration of Principles, more commonly known as the Oslo Accords, was signed in 1993 between the State of Israel, led by Prime Minister Yitzhak Rabin, and the Palestine Liberation Organization (PLO), led by Yasir Arafat. The basic contours of the signed agreement were: the phased withdrawal of the Israeli military from the territories occupied by Israel in the Six Day War of 1967; the creation of a new entity superseding the PLO, to be called the Palestine National Authority, to administer those areas; and continued negotiations over such outstanding issues as the fate of the Palestinian refugees living outside the State of Israel (e.g., in the Occupied Territories), and the rights to and boundaries of Jerusalem.[1] The political fault lines at the time ran between those who believed that peace would come only after Israel felt secure and those who believed that peace would come only after the Israelis withdrew to the 1967 borders and returned the land to the Palestinians. The latter was commonly known as the 'land for peace' position. These divisions represented a well-known and perhaps even classical dichotomy: peace through strength versus peace through justice.

Notwithstanding that many saw the Oslo Accords as the first steps toward peace, the agreement was barely discussed during the tours. In fact, Israel's conflict with the Palestinians was paid far less attention than the other conflicts in the region, and certainly far less direct attention than was paid the conflicts with Lebanon and Syria. On only one tour were we taken into an area referred to as Palestinian and that had been declared autonomous under the Oslo Accords.[2] At no other point on any other tour were we explicitly told when we were travelling in the 'disputed' or occupied areas or along Israeli bypass roads. Guides

sometimes referred to the Green Line of Israel, but most tour participants had little sense of its significance as the internationally recognized border so telling them we had crossed it or that it was to our left
or right did not register as significant.

More surprising, on the Israel Land Fund (ILF) tour the Oslo Accords
were represented as making Israelis even less secure. The first time the
Oslo Accords were discussed on the tour, it was in the context of a
famous Tel Aviv shopping district that had been the site of a suicide
bombing. Talia, our guide, told us:

> Unfortunately, many of these places may ring a bell for people not
> because it is a large shopping centre but during the peace negotiations
> with the Palestinians beginning in Oslo, this is where we had our first
> walkable [sic] suicide bombers in Tel Aviv ... There was a rash of bomb-
> ings at that time and one of them was here at the Dizengoff Centre. I only
> say that to just remind you that we carry on [with] our lives ... You're in
> downtown Tel Aviv now. People are at work right now. People are out at
> the cafes ... If we were to stop, or not carry on our normal life here after
> these incidents, the country would eventually empty out. You have to
> continue on. Things get cleaned up. We remember those who were killed,
> injured, maimed, but the quickest answer to those acts of terrorism is [to]
> get back to business, try to deal with it, keep on going.

Talia pointed out other suicide-bombing sites whenever we passed
them, but she never discussed the Palestinians' responsibility for them,
and referred only to 'Oslo.' Thus, on this tour, Oslo was discussed
mainly in terms of how it made Israelis less secure, not in terms of
peace building. Always embedded in these narratives were descriptions of Israelis as heroic for taking these matters in stride. Israelis
were committed to Israel and were leading normal lives even in the
most dangerous circumstances. They were different from North American Jews because they lived in constant danger. This presentation sub-
tly but powerfully sets up the dichotomy of those lives that are
endangered but committed to life in Israel as against the safety and
security for diaspora Jews. Interestingly, this theme often arose in discussions in North America, especially when peace-camp Israelis confronted anti-Oslo diaspora Jews.

The Palestinian uprising in the occupied territories, commonly
known as the *intifada*, was never mentioned during the tours. Perhaps
this was to avoid any discussion of Palestinian resistance to military
occupation and expanded settlements; perhaps it was a way to dimin-

ish or even dismiss the importance of that resistance. In many ways, these popular (i.e., non-state) representations of the conflict closely reflected the official rendering and silencing of Palestinian concerns.

On the Israeli Development Fund (IDF) tour, the Israeli prime minister himself, Benjamin Netanyahu, gave us a talk about peace in the region. Before entering a large lecture hall in one of Jerusalem's luxury hotels, we endured a long security line-up and check. Security guards and national and international television crews ringed the hall's interior. Around two hundred tour participants, all of them from Canada, sat waiting, chattering with excitement. Friends and acquaintances kibitzed with one another, talking about their experiences in Israel so far.

It was 1998 and Iraq had been in a tug-of-war with the world over its weapons of mass destruction. The world was on edge: North Americans were being warned to avoid the Middle East, and the UN secretary general, Kofi Anan, was shuttling back and forth between New York and the Middle East in an effort to defuse the crisis. Israelis were being warned to prepare for war; gas masks distributed; reservists were waiting to be called up. In this political climate, Netanyahu had arranged to speak to us.

After a short wait and a brief introduction, the prime minister came out from behind a curtain, nodded and smiled to the audience, and stepped up to the microphone. He began: 'We've had a recent reminder of the quality of the neighbourhood in which we live in this recent crisis.' This 'neighbourhood' was one in which 'radical regimes ... foster terrorists or indeed are committed to espousing the great terror of the ballistic missiles and nuclear war.' Furthermore, the region was 'replete with dictatorships, replete with radicals, replete with ideological and religious zealotry that is aimed at removing us.' Although in 'the first nineteen years of the state, it seemed very likely and very possible' for these Arab neighbours 'to remove us' because 'we were [on] a narrow strip on the Mediterranean coast,' the Six Day War 'had made the physical conquest of Israel impossible.' Israel had enlarged its territory from 'roughly ten miles, or ten kilometres wide in some places, [to] all of a sudden an enormous country. [It is now] seventy kilometres wide, Greater Israel, more!' Facetious comments notwithstanding, Netanyahu emphasized the importance of victory in the Six Day War to Israeli security: Israel had gained 'strategic depth' as well as 'strategic height':

Between 70 to 80 per cent of Israel's population ... lives on that crowded coastline along the Mediterranean and any potential raid of Arab armies ... now [must face] a very large or rather a very high, very tall stone wall that is over a kilometre high, which is the mountains of Samaria and the mountains of Judea ... That is the fundamental change in Israel's position that makes peace possible. The Arabs could attack us, which they did subsequently, but they couldn't conquer us. And the minute physical conquest was removed as an option, the peace option came to light.

Israeli victory and strength had made possible the peace agreements with Egypt and even with the Palestinians. The latter process 'still has to be completed.' Israel wished to 'complete the circle of peace [but we] cannot sacrifice the bulwarks of our security in the process.' If Israel returned to her 'pre-'67 boundaries,' it would 'unravel all the progress that we have made ... because if Israel again becomes an indefensible and vulnerable country the peace [agreement] may be put on a piece of paper but it won't hold in the real world.' Netanyahu warned that 'peace agreements, treaties, international contracts in this part of the world hold only as long as you have the power to enforce them' because 'what distinguishes this part of the world [are] dictatorships and undemocratic regimes that are not accountable to their people.' Netanyahu offered what he called 'the central lesson of the twentieth century': 'There are two kinds of peace. [There is] peace between democracies, which is self-enforcing and requires no deterrence, no security ... and peace opposite dictatorships, which requires security and deterrence [in order for it] to be maintained.'

Speaking then of the Nazi era, he said it 'produced the greatest calamity in the history of nations and the greatest calamity in the history of our nation, the Jewish nation.' He also characterized those who believed in peace in that era as those who had 'confused the two kinds of peace ... They [had] practised the peace of democracy, the peace of concession, the peace of appeasement' with a dictator, and much like any agreement with Iraq's Saddam Hussein, 'you cannot enforce or defend [these agreements and] they will not last.' In this way Netanyahu was associating all Arab regimes, which he had earlier defined as undemocratic, with the Nazi regime. He seemed also to be implying that Israeli Jews were facing similar circumstances to those faced by European Jews during the Holocaust.

He argued that the peace agreements with Egypt and Jordan were secure only because they were strategically defensible. Then he began to discuss the basis for any peace with the Palestinians:

The Palestinians happen to live on the protective wall of the mountains of Judea and Samaria. They want to be able to run their lives without us, which we accept. We want to be able to run our lives without being threatened by them. How do you resolve these two issues? Well, it's important to understand that one way not to resolve them is not to get off that wall, for the reasons I've said before.

The longer he spoke, the clearer his position became: The Palestinians, as Arabs, could not be trusted to sign a democratic peace, and therefore the only peace possible with them was one based on security. The lands the Palestinians lived on were also the lands that Israel needed to ensure its security; the population itself was not of strategic importance, and it no longer needed to be under military control:

> I don't know if you're aware of it, but there is no more Israeli occupation, it's finished! The Palestinians now control 98 per cent of the Palestinian population. Two per cent of the Palestinians live under Israeli jurisdiction. 98 per cent of the Palestinians now live under a Palestinian authority: 100 per cent in the Gaza district, 98 per cent in Judea [and] Samaria on the West Bank. They are no more governed by us. How did you not know that? Ninety-eight per cent of you don't know that 98 per cent of the Palestinians are living now under Palestinian rule!

It was true that most of the Palestinians living in what he called 'the West Bank, or Judea and Samaria' were living under some form of Palestinian administration; however, full sovereignty had not been transferred to the Palestine Authority. By framing the issue in this way, Netanyahu was redirecting everyone's attention from the withdrawal of the Israelis from Palestinian land to a withdrawal of Israeli military authority over the population. But Netanyahu knew that what was hotly disputed was precisely the withdrawal of Israel from Palestinian land. It was this condition of the Oslo Accords that his government was refusing to meet.

Netanyahu described the land itself simply as 'empty land, empty of Palestinians but essential for Israel's security':

> It is also land that we have a very deep attachment to because it is our ancestral homeland. It is Judea, where the word Jew comes from. It is the mountains surrounding Jerusalem, which we have some attachment to, and so on. But even if we didn't have that attachment, we have a clear security interest in maintaining those areas.

He was determined that the Palestinians would be allowed to 'fully determine their own fate, run their own affairs' only if 'certain powers' were 'curtailed or kept in Israel's hands':

> We want to wish [for] the best but we cannot base the future of Israel just on wishful thinking ... As you and I and all the friends of Israel and certainly the great Jewish people around the world – even those who live in this diminutive and small, constrained Canada – you surely will understand, I'm sure, that insistence on our part.

It was clear throughout Netanyahu's speech that the peace-camp and Labour Party's slogan 'land for peace' meant, under his leadership, 'land as security for peace.' Throughout, he made ominous references to past and current dictatorships and designated Israel's neighbours as dangerous because they were premodern and chaotic. Clearly, his priority was no more and no less than to secure the land for Israel. The land was important to the nation of Jews – that is, it was their ancestral land. Specifically, it was militarily and strategically important to the Jews' survival as a nation-state.

It is significant that these tour participants were not allowed to see or get an on-the-ground perspective of the implications of the Oslo Accords. A tour in and around the Palestinian autonomous areas – one that showed where Jews and Palestinians were living, where the bypass roads were being built, and what it was like to have to pass through security checkpoints – might have provided a better sense of what the military occupation and the accords meant for people living in the area.

Little time was devoted to the Oslo Accords on the tours; that said, it became clear over time that some tour participants had come to Israel with preconceived ideas about its peace and security needs.

On all of the tours, a number of participants challenged the guides' and lecturers' interpretations of Israel's predicament, especially with regard to the conflict with the Palestinians. These challenges were often more than mere differences of opinion; the tour participants were not always willing to accept the explanations provided to them. Often, their interventions were forceful enough that they imposed an alternative narrative to the one the guides were providing.

Many times, individual tourists provoked the guide or lecturer. I remember two occasions in particular. At the Castel – the site where in 1948 the Jews defeated the Arab Legion in the Jerusalem area – at least two tourists challenged the tour guide's representation of history and its implications for the present. Arnie, the IDF guide, had not presented the history of the 1948 war from the Palestinian perspective, and the tourists seemed aware of this. At the very first marker at Castel, Faye, a strong-willed woman in her forties, pointed to the 1948 map of Israel/Palestine that Arnie had been using and asked whether the blue dots represented Arab towns, cities, and villages and whether the yellow dots represented Jewish settlements. The guide replied that they did. Faye then said she was surprised by the number of blue dots and wondered aloud what happened to the people living in those places. Instead of answering her question, Arnie asked us to reserve all of our questions until he had finished telling us the story of Castel. When we reached the top of the hill, he turned to Faye and answered her question:

And before we leave here, 'cause I think it's a legitimate question, I think [Faye] asked about the people ... in the Arab villages. We have to keep in mind that the 1948 war was a war of survival. If we didn't win there was not going to be any continuation [of the State of Israel]. The Mufti of Jerusalem was very, very clear in all of his declarations. This will be a *jihad*. This will be a cleansing of the land. This will be ethnic cleansing. There will not be one Jew left in this part of the world. They will be pushed into the ocean. Which means the ones that didn't die here would eventually leave. That's the type of war it was in 1948. With all the pain and understanding of the refugee situation and these people['s] situation, I only say to them today look in one direction and that is their national leadership who believed and tried to convince them that it was going to take a few weeks, *bing bang boom*, we're finished, hunky dory, you can go back to [your village], [and] you can go back to [your town] and you can go back to ... a little village on the entrance to Jerusalem, and everything would be hunky dory. It's been fifty years now that they've lived in the situation that they live. No one has forgotten about them. They are still a part of the negotiations, eventual negotiations, that may take place some day but they will not be allowed to go back to villages where they lived because they made a big, big mistake. That's how I would look at their situation.

Faye responded: 'Okay, they made a big, big mistake [but] they are no longer that generation ...' But Arnie interrupted her:

Oh they still are. The Arabs and Palestinians have maintained a refugee mentality in the next generations. Jordan did not allow Palestinian refugees to leave the camps. They would lose their UN education, health and welfare benefits. The minute you left your camp, [you] didn't get it any-more. So they built a system maintaining refugees, and inside Palestinian communities some will proudly tell you that they are refugees even though they've never ever seen this village. They don't know where it is – well, they know where it is [but] they have maintained that for fifty years without any problem. [They think] they are still refugees.

Faye continued to press Arnie to answer her questions more directly and to deal with the dilemma she was placing before him:

What if there were, I mean hypothetically, what if there are ... the kids, [or] the grandchildren who say we'd like to go back. We have no ill feel-ing but we'd like to come back because this is where my grandparents and my great grandparents [lived] and we want to resettle in peace?

At this, a flash of anger crossed the guide's face. With a wave of his arms and hands, he stated vehemently:

Finished! I'll tell you why it's finished. Today in Israel I believe that the Arabs who stayed, and there were Arabs who couldn't get out, I don't want to make it all, you know, okay ... we want to live in peace [with them] ... These are Arabs who've lived in the Jewish state already for fifty years. No one is asking them to go anyplace. They are part of the popula-tion here. We believe that they're part of the democracy here. And anyone who came from any place else and said they want to come back, as far as our policy is concerned, this is a Jewish state. The right of return is for Jews and not for someone whose parents or grandparents left, for what-ever reason they wanted to. We do not have open immigration policies. As discriminatory as that sounds, the preference is for Jews in a Jewish country, even for the second or third generation of people who left ... these other villages.

He ended his lecture with a brief reference to the Canadian committee that was then responsible for examining what he called the 'refugee problem,' adding that the 'issue' would not have 'an overnight solution.'
Arnie was telling us that there was no possibility that the Palestinians would be allowed to return – that the descendants of those who had been displaced had no legitimate claims to the land because they had never seen it and because it was their fault that they were in this predic-

ament, since they had lost a war that their leaders had persuaded them to fight. It is ironic that Arnie resorted to the Law of Return to delegitimize the Palestinians' own claims: that law was based on the principle that the Jews had a right to return to a land they had longed for but not seen for two thousand years. Faye said as much when we walked back down the hill toward our bus: 'I imagine they would remember after fifty years what we remembered for two thousand.'

Right after Arnie finished responding to Faye, he was asked another question. This one was posed by Aaron, a fit-looking seventy-year-old who had last seen Israel in 1957. Aaron asked Arnie to point out where the controversial Jewish settlements were being built. Arnie pointed to various clusters of buildings and began to name some of the settlements. Aaron immediately questioned the matter-of-fact manner in which our guide was making his presentation: 'So why, he asked, 'wouldn't the Jewish settlements, instead of being beyond those trees, be down here in front of the trees where it's just got terraces?' In effect, Aaron was asking why the Israelis were building their new settlements beyond the Green Line rather than within it – that is, within the pre–Six Day War boundary of Israel. The question seemed to disturb Arnie. Till now he had been answering the tourists' questions calmly enough. He had shown a willingness to quietly debate these issues with the participants. But Aaron's question seemed to upset him, and he began to lecture us passionately:

Why? Because the 1967 border is gone, finished! As far as Israel is concerned, it's finished. Even moderates and left-wingers in Israel will agree with that. It was unlivable, unlivable. And around Jerusalem, there's areas now called Greater Jerusalem. It's Greater Jerusalem. Why? I'm not talking about the religious or historical standpoints now. I'm talking about the realistic standpoint 'cause I could give you all sorts of reasons why we could or why we should. There are people who would like to go [back] to the '67 border, let's just finish it, that's Palestine, this is Israel and finish it off. But that's not enough [for the Palestinians] and then they can ask well, why can't the people go back to [this village], why can't they go back to [that village]? Well it's obvious. If they went back, there'd be no Jewish country!

Having made this point, our guide seemed on the verge of convincing Aaron that there was a more realistic perspective, that he had been idealistic. The guide had revealed another political perspective on Jerusalem – that by forming 'Greater Jerusalem,' Israel had in effect annexed East Jerusalem, and therefore it was no longer necessary to negotiate over it. He had also presented Aaron with a number of classic slippery-slope, Israel-centred arguments against returning to the 1967 borders – namely, if Israeli Jews conceded to any Palestinian demands, they might have to give the Palestinians all they wanted in the future. Furthermore, if Palestinians were allowed to return to their villages, Israel would no longer be Jewish. Arnie resorted to this argument throughout the tour. Jews must stand strong on principles that protect them. If they drifted away from the national goal of a sovereign and powerful state, they would lose their place in history, both literally and figuratively. Jews were endangered and could easily disappear as a people.

But Aaron was not so easily convinced. He then asked Arnie to point out Har Homa, the site of a new settlement near the Palestinian village of Abu Ghoneim. The Israeli government under Netanyahu was claiming that this settlement was acceptable and perfectly within the spirit of the Oslo Accords because it was part of Greater Jerusalem. In this way Netanyahu was able to deny accusations that he was scuttling the formal peace negotiations with the Palestinians. The Palestinians and the Israeli peace camp fundamentally objected to the settlement for two reasons. First, although Palestinians were being refused housing permits and faced housing demolitions when they built without permits, new homes for Jews were always given the go-ahead. Second, this geographical area was considered part of Oslo's final status arrangements for Jerusalem, and Abu Ghoneim was the last of a ring of villages that encircled Jerusalem. In other words, allowing Har Homa to be built was going to create new 'facts on the ground' (as the Israelis liked to put it) prior to any final status arrangements and was therefore going to give the Israelis the advantage in any future claims over Jerusalem. In his response to Aaron, Arnie said only that this 'neighbourhood would block off any territorial continuity to East Jerusalem for the East Palestinians.' He described the village as a neighbourhood and implied that the settlement was necessary for Jerusalem's security. His position reflected Netanyahu's position on the situation. We never did see Har Homa on this or any other tour. Even so, it was clear to many of us that Aaron had asked the guide about Har Homa in a way which suggested that, according to some at least, building any settlements beyond the 1967 Green Line could not but cause problems.

Tour participants repeatedly challenged the interpretations presented to them by guides. Early on the Israel Civil Society Fund (ICSF) tour, we met with Victor Kahalani, who at the time was Israel's Minister of Security. Kahalani was introduced to us as a military hero. In 1974 he had been the military commander of the Golani Brigade, which had retaken the Golan Heights from the Syrians in what was presented as a bloody 'David and Goliath' battle. He was also the leader of a new political party in Israel named the 'Third Way.' This party was described to us as one that promoted peace with the Palestinians (e.g., the return of West Bank and Gaza Strip). However, central to its platform was strong opposition to the return of any Golani territory to Syria and of any Jordan Valley settlement areas to the Palestinians. It is interesting that an Israeli cabinet minister and decorated military hero was being challenged by diaspora Jews on matters of security and military pragmatism.

I will not recount all of the minister's lecture. Instead, I will discuss three questions that tour participants posed and the minister's response to the third one, mainly because I am interested in presenting the challenges, but also because the minister was to repeat critical themes of his lecture in his response. Wolfe, a man in his sixties who was very active with the Israeli-based peace movement, Peace Now, and who had travelled on alternative tours through Israel and the militarily occupied territories, first told the minister that he understood there was some debate among Israeli generals over how much of a threat the Palestinians actually posed to Israel, especially from the Golan and Jordan Valley, where Israel had electronic surveillance in place. Wolfe confidently stated that contrary to Kahalani's position, '75 per cent of generals say that settlements are not the way to go.' Second, he asked the minister, 'What do you think of the checkpoints?' Here he was referring to the Israeli government's controversial policy of closure, which had been set in place around this time and which was being used to prevent Palestinian labourers from crossing into Israel to get to work.

Another tourist, Gabriel, a soft-spoken businessman in his early fifties, also had some long-term engagement with Palestinian affairs. He asked: 'You made a statement that Israel should move out of Lebanon. Why don't you feel that the Jordan Valley could become another Lebanon?'

Visibly frustrated after the minister's lecture, Shelley, a woman in her early forties, asked Kahalani to discuss the possibilities for developing trusting relationships so that there could be 'protection' and 'defence' for both peoples.

The minister took all of these questions. He responded first by telling us that as a child, he had seen a cartoon: An Arab had drawn a map of the area with the Jews in the sea. The caption stated: 'This is your end.' When he saw this, he asked his father what it was all about, and from that day forward, he had 'to quit learning how to swim,' adding that 'none of my kids ... swim.' The minister said that he believed that some 'Arabs dream to push us out to sea. I don't trust them, any of them. Look what happened when we opened [the Western Wall] tunnels [in Jerusalem]. We have to be strong. I am not naive. I don't trust anyone in the world – just those who live here, [those] that must protect themselves.'

From the questions, it was clear that some of the participants linked security with human rights issues. They did not defer to the minister even though they knew he was a decorated hero and the highest-level government official we were to meet on that tour. If he considered the questions provocative, he showed no sign of it. He never raised his voice in his replies. However, he was extremely condescending and implied that the only Jews who could be trusted to make such decisions were his fellow Israelis.

Clearly, some tourists were troubled by Israeli militarism. It was fascinating to hear North American Jewish tourists suggest that the 1948 war might have sociological implications, and to listen to them suggest alternatives to Israel's settlement and security policies. It would be wrong to suggest that one challenger represented all tour participants, but it must also be noted that I never heard any tourist object to any of the challengers. Challenges were neither rare – especially with regard to issues of war and peace – nor were they unacceptable to the other participants. Everyone seemed to take these moments as one more part of what one participant called a 'steep learning curve.' All of this suggested that the participants were glad to expose themselves to more than one perspective across a range of complicated issues. It also signalled that many tourists were quite aware that both the past and the present could be read in multiple ways. Moreover, the participants showed no timidity at all when posing challenging questions to Israeli guides and hosts. The Israeli Minister of Security, a military hero, was addressed as if his views on military matters were no more legitimate than those of others; this was evidence of the diaspora Jews' strength and self-confidence. Many tour participants were very well off financially and constituted an elite. This undoubtedly accounted for some of their outspokenness. As I was to discover during my research, many North American Jews feel genuinely invulnerable, although many scholars of Zionism don't seem to appreciate this yet. What happens, then, when the locations of the narratives of nation shift from Israel to North America?

7

Representing Israel

For roughly four years I attended community events including lectures, book readings, film presentations, and community festivals. I can say with some confidence that the events I have chosen to examine represent the range of mainstream perspectives to which many Jews in a large North American community are exposed.[1] I explore the context of these narratives and the practices associated with attending the events or 'being there,' including the speaker/audience interactions that followed many of these talks in the next three chapters.

In this exploration of how Israel is represented to North American Jews, I limit myself to those narratives that were presented at public culture events. Excluded, then, are other kinds of representations, such as television broadcasts and newspaper and magazine articles – that is, 'private' representations.[2] Of course, in the discussions I had, people were not limited to public culture events. Many of them referred to articles they had read or to programs they had watched or listened to.

Though I attended many community events, there were too many for me to attend them all.[3] After some time in the field, I noticed that the best-attended events were the ones that featured Israeli lecturers – in particular, Israeli politicians, authors, and academics. Soon after I began the research, it also became clear that Jews in urban centres were concerned about many issues that had little or nothing to do with Israel. In fact, although Israel-centred events were heavily attended, Israel did not dominate the topics for public lectures and debates. For example, there were many lectures on such topics as the high rates of intermarriage among Jews in North America, and on the right of Holocaust victims and Jewish organizations to claim compensation for the monies transferred to Swiss banks during the Second World War.

Also, North American Jews celebrated their achievements and culture at Yiddish as well as Jewish film and book festivals. And during the annual Holocaust Education Week, films, lectures, and workshops were offered to educate the broader community. I attended as many events as I could in the hope of learning what these communities cared about most. The strong attendance at community events that had little to do with Israel supports the often-heard claim that North American Jews are active in a range of issues that are not tied mainly (or not tied at all) to Israel as the Jews' cultural, spiritual, and historical centre.[4] However, because my main concern was the relationship of North American Jews to Israel, I carefully examined only those events where Israel and Israel/diaspora relations were the dominant focus.

Generally speaking, many community members could be counted on to attend Israel-focused events. When attendance was free, the lecture rooms often filled quickly beyond capacity. Tickets often sold out well in advance. I did not attend many of the fundraising events held in the community, because the ticket prices for them were often well beyond my financial means. So it was only at the invitation and expense of others that I was sometimes able to attend these affairs.

I soon learned that community attendance was highest at temples, synagogues, and Jewish community centres.[5] Perhaps this high attendance simply reflected the community's affiliations and common meeting practices rather than their level of interest in the topic being presented. However, the passion and level of engagement I witnessed suggests that many audience members were there because they were strongly interested in the discussions that ensued. I often met people at community events whom I had met at previous events or in other contexts. These meetings often led to other invitations to attend upcoming events.

As far as I could discern, and from what I learned from others around me, the events in which I participated were all attended by mainstream Jews in the community; I did not attend religious services or events sponsored by ultra-Orthodox or nationalist extremists. Generally speaking, the people in attendance were neither ultra-nationalist nor ultra-Orthodox, nor were they especially activist in their orientations to Israel. These were public culture sessions for people who were interested in the issues facing Israeli society. Judging from their responses to the speakers, they were well versed in those issues.

In North American community settings, Israel was sometimes presented in ways that were semiofficial and state-sponsored. On occasion

I felt like I was on tour again. This happened at an exposition celebrating 'Israel at 50.' More often, however, there were diverse presentations that offered a range of views. These events sometimes evolved into emotionally explosive debates between lecturers and audiences. There were also many evenings during which presentations were offered on the almost arcane philosophies of Jewish-state relations. But the audiences were familiar with even these issues and showed an unexpected engagement with them.

These events in North American settings opened a window onto the responses of diaspora Jews to representations of Israel. As I showed earlier, tourists while in Israel often challenged their tour guides or lecturers. At the events I attended in North America, I learned soon enough which issues and debates engaged their audiences, who were well informed about the minutiae of Jewish history, philosophy, religion, and law. Whether they had been to Israel or not, their interest could not be questioned. Understanding Israel and the Jews obviously involved considerable intellectual and educational investment. But at the same time, it was clear from the public discussions that many in the audience were out of touch with daily life and politics in Israel – a point emphasized by some Israeli speakers. These audience members were on more familiar ground when discussing official representations of the past rather than the dilemmas facing modern Israel. When confronted with critiques of Israeli policies, some audience members adopted strongly conservative positions. To the frustration of some Israeli speakers, these positions often drew from images, ideas, and lessons of the past (similar to guides' presentations on the tours). As I will show in the profiles, these positions were not the whole story. Nevertheless, diaspora Jews often embraced as their own the very representations and assumptions presented by tour guides and by the 'official' lecturers in North America, and then used these views to think, talk, and argue about Israel and the Jews.

The range of views among community members was fascinating, and so was the passion with which people expressed those views, but more interesting still was the fact that although some events in the community had a strongly Zionist slant, others introduced post-Zionist and critical representations of Israel. The latter emphasized the 'normalization' of the Jews and the need to move away from concerns about the survival of the Jewish nation, with the goal of addressing the concerns of Israel as a modern nation-state like any other. Some Israelis visiting North America asserted that North American Jews owed them respect for living with all the discomforts of Israeli life, and declared that as Israelis they would not represent diaspora Jews' perspectives or desires unless they were also in the interest of Israelis. Some of these speakers also declared that the Jews' existential crisis was over: they now had a place to call their own. Taking up the issues raised by Rabin's assassination and the peace process with the Palestinians, Israeli Jews insisted that they were now living in a strong, secure, democratic, and modern state. From a position of strategic and moral strength, Israelis were now normalizing their relationships with other states in the region. These were not narratives of an Israel under siege or fearing its neighbours.

8

Identifying (with) Israel: Zionism and the State

At all the events where Israel was celebrated or discussed, there was never any question that Israel is the Jews' nation-state. Yet at the same time, these events raised questions about *which* Israel Jews in North America would want to identify with. I will try to highlight not only the taken-for-granted aspects of these presentations, but also, how they illustrated a much more multifaceted representation of Israel and Israelis than the narratives presented on the tours of Israel. Although some complex issues were raised on the tours, they were never fully addressed, and the overall impression was certainly not one of an already secure Israel. Even on the Israel Civil Society Fund (ICSF) tour, which emphasized democracy and peace, Zionist rather than post-Zionist narratives dominated. Moreover, the internal logic of how the tours were organized forced a balancing of perspectives: for every peace camp position, a more conservative or militaristic position was presented as well.

What is Israel in diaspora? And how are diaspora Jews asked to identify with these representations?

In 1998, many community events celebrated Israel's half-centenary. Although I attended many other Israel-centred celebrations – for example, Jerusalem's three-thousandth anniversary in 1995, and the Zionists's centennial in 1997 – the 'Israel at 50' events were among the most elaborate community events that I observed during my fieldwork.

The 'Israel at 50' pavilion at the fairground in the city where I conducted my research was, at 107,000 square feet, one of the largest and most expensive country pavilions ever exhibited in the region. It was sponsored by the Israeli Consulate and by 175 Jewish community organizations. More than one thousand volunteers worked in the pavilion for ten days, the duration of the fair.

This pavilion celebrated Israel's modern economy, and in particular its worldwide commercial success in computer- and engineering-based technologies. There were more than fifty vendor's booths displaying a range of Israeli goods, from summer sandals to non-alcoholic beer. Promotional literature was available by the basketful: investment prospectuses, vacation brochures, fundraising proposals for peace education, and so on. An art exhibit, 'Echoes of the Past – Visions of the Future' featured paintings, sculptures, and photographs. Some of these depicted everyday life and scenes from present-day Israel; others evoked the struggles and pain of the past. A large, colourful mural depicting '4000 years of Jewish history' covered one wall of the pavilion. The exhibit's centre stage had for a backdrop a reproduction of the Jerusalem cityscape. Here were offered fashion shows, musical performances, cooking demonstrations, lectures, and various entertainments.

In many significant ways, all of this corresponded closely with what was presented during the organized tours through Israel. Most impressive was the 12,000-square-foot Negev Desert display, which featured a small cabin labelled 'a *kibbutz*'; small greenhouses; two- and three-foot Roman columns surrounded by sand labelled 'Masada'; live camel rides for the children around a sandy desert; and a mosaic floor labelled an 'ancient synagogue floor.'

The Negev display presented the Jews' ancient past, Israel's pioneering spirit, and modern development practices. For example, in a simple, wood-panelled room, a *kibbutz* was described as 'a self-contained social and economic unit in which decisions are taken by the general assembly of its members and property and means of production are communally owned ... Traditionally the backbone of Israel's agriculture, *kibbutzim* are now also engaged in industry, tourism and services.' Nearby, flowers and vegetable plants were arranged inside a plastic-covered, four-foot-square wooden structure labeled 'greenhouse.' The growing method was described:

Protected agriculture ... another technique that conserves water because it reduces evaporation. In addition to providing over 90% of Israel's food, greenhouses throughout Israel grow many crops of high-quality fruits and vegetables which are exported to European and North American markets. As well, there is an enormous export market of flowers and ornamental plants.

The 'desert' showed a small bed of plants, with pipes snaking around them. This was marked 'irrigation system.' Labels explained how the search for water saving techniques has spurred the development of computer-controlled irrigation systems, including the drip method ... The drip method not only dramatically reduces the amount of water needed for irrigation, it also allows farmers to use poor quality water; the salts in brackish water do not damage the leaf canopy in the way that regular sprinkler irrigation would. Oranges, grapefruits, melons, avocados, wine from Israeli grown grapes and fresh flowers are among the products that have responded well to drip irrigation and now represent a significant export market.

This narrative was very similar to the one presented on the organized tour I had taken three years earlier. In another part of the Negev display, on a platform marked 'Masada,' were two Roman-style columns, one broken at the top and the other tilted slightly to one side. The label explained:

Masada is one of the most intriguing and popular sites in all of Israel. In 70 AD, after Jerusalem was destroyed, the Jewish Zealots fled to Masada, the best-fortified palace built by King Herod. They held out on top of Masada for three years battling the Romans, even though they were no more than 1,000 strong and surrounded by 15,000 Roman warriors. Through intricate water cistern and industrious farming methods, the Zealots sustained themselves for the three-year battle. In the year 73, anticipating imminent defeat, the entire group rather than surrender, committed suicide.

This was a different version of the Masada story than the one the tour guide presented on the Israel Development Fund (IDF) tour; it was also the more common version. In fact, the IDF guide had challenged one tourist for this very interpretation of the Masada myth: the guide had interpreted the end at Masada as mass murder; the tourist had characterized it as mass suicide.

In the centre of the Negev exhibit, young men wearing Bedouin head gear were taking children on camel rides. These rides followed a circular path around the other desert features. This troubling sight was the only live representation of Israel's Arab population in the entire building.

At the main entrance to the 'Synagogue Mosaic Floor' was a large plaque titled 'Revealing an Ancient Message.' It described how and when the mosaic had been unearthed and explained that Sepphoris, where the mosaic was found, is 'part of the Galilee not far from the city of Nazareth.' The plaque stated that the town was built in Roman times, around two thousand years ago, and prospered as a centre of Jewish life through the later Roman and Byzantine periods (third to seventh centuries CE). The plaque 'revealed' the significance of the mosaic:

> A story of promise and redemption that was central to Jewish belief. The first images that someone entering the synagogue would have seen depict the biblical story of Abraham and Isaac in which God promises to protect the descendants of Abraham and to make them into a great nation. Other scenes present images of the Temple of Jerusalem, which, though destroyed, still survived as a symbol of continuity which inspired hope for its restoration. A grand circle of the zodiac shows the organisation of the universe with the sun chariot at the centre symbolising the centrality and power of God. While this synagogue mosaic focuses on Jewish themes, some elements are common to the Christian art of the period. The Sacrifice of Isaac, the Angel's Visit to Abraham and Sarah, and the circle of the Zodiac can all be found in the art of Byzantine Churches.

All of the synagogue labels had been carefully written to depict the Jews' chosenness and history. Reference was made only to the Jews' place in history. For example, the description of the synagogue floor focused on 'the story of promise and redemption,' and offered no opportunity to discuss how it could be that 'some elements are common to the Christian art of the period.' Instead of conjecturing that the floor depicted the mingling of belief systems at the time,[1] the mosaic represented the 'story of promise and redemption ... central to Jewish belief.' Through this long-buried mosaic, the pavilion's organizers were highlighting the 'promise,' made in the past for the future survival of the nation.

The pavilion's exhibits were inspired by classical Zionist interpretations and idealizations of Israeli society. There was very little of the current culture, politics, or everyday life of Israelis. One could pick up information about diverse topics, but these were not part of the representation of Israel. So, for example, the Negev Bedouin were depoliticized, and exoticized as camel herders, and the Palestinians and the Druze were simply displayed on a platform at the entrance to the main stage area in an exhibit of life-sized figurines celebrating the Israeli cultural mosaic. Each figurine stereotypical. For example, a *kafiah* or head scarf covered the head of an Arab man; a woman dressed in a black embroidered dress carrying a basket on her head was a Palestinian woman; and tall men with long white beards, dressed in black suits and wide-brim hats, represented Orthodox Jewry. All were equally stereotyped in this display.

In North America, most popular entertainment events celebrating Israel presented a simplified, Disney-like version of Israel. However, some representations of Israel were more learned. These occasions were not entertaining in the same way; even so, they were clearly intended for the general and Jewish public rather than for an academic or specialized audience.

Of the many community events I attended, the most successful were those which took up the questions of Israel and the Jews' past in the region; Israel's desire to balance its religious and secular heritage and culture; and, of course, the Israel–Palestine conflict.

Imagining Israel's past as the Jews' past was a familiar theme. On the tours, Israel was represented as the cradle of the Jews' biblical and ancient history. It was interesting, though not surprising, to observe how similar efforts to construct Israel as the Jews' land and rightful place were made in North American settings.

At one event, an audience filled a large university lecture hall to warmly greet Dr Avraham Scheck, an American authority on the Dead Sea Scrolls. The lecture was the second of two and was open to the public and therefore broad in scope. According to the community member with whom I attended the event, Dr Scheck had described the sites and history of the Scrolls' discovery in the first lecture.

The purpose of the second lecture was to debunk the myth that the Dead Sea Scrolls were of significance only to those studying Christianity. It was also to demonstrate that the Scrolls held clues to understanding a key historical period in Judaism. Dr Scheck began by telling his audience that the Dead Sea Scrolls had been written at a time when major changes were taking place within Judaism – changes that would do much to establish some Jews' present-day practices. It would be unfortunate if the scrolls' research agenda were set only by New Testament and Christian scholars for, as Dr Scheck put it, 'a person who steals the Dead Sea Scrolls from the Jews effectively steals a part of Jewish heritage, especially if they are taken to be only a matter of Christian history.'

Dr Scheck acknowledged that the scrolls could also hold the key to understanding the rise of Christianity; even so, from his perspective the Dead Sea Scrolls documented grievances between Jews and were part of a common tradition that was to become the basis for contemporary Judaism. He explained that there were three sects of practising Jews during this era and that the scrolls reflected the *halakhic* or biblical basis for one of these sects, the Sadducees. He pointed out that although there had never been a time in Judaism when there was only one sect, the Sadducees were a breakaway group whose theological perspectives were to have a lasting effect on Jewish religious history. He described how the three sects were engaged in political disagreements over issues ranging from Jewish law to political action to theology. All of this was evidence of a rich culture that was to establish the terms of debates in Jewish theological history. Furthermore, although there had been peaceful debates among the Jews, the rise of Roman rule, the reign of Herod, the rise of Christianity, and the destruction of the Temple influenced the growth of a new Jewish messianism. Soon one group was talking revolution and provoking inter-Jewish political violence, including assassinations. Dr Scheck ended his discussion with the suggestion that such an understanding of the scrolls' history should lead to a consideration of the lessons for contemporary Jews' religious debates. He suggested that intergroup discussions needed to be protected lest they lead to radicalization, as they had in the past. The lesson of the scrolls was that debates among Jews could (and should) be peaceful, but they could also lead to violence.

For my purposes, the most interesting thing about Dr Scheck's lecture was that he presented a narrowly defined history of the scrolls' significance. His chronology was based on Israelite and biblical archaeological references; thus, he was situating the importance of the scrolls in Jewish history and outside the history of others. Moreover, the period to which he referred was not dated as 'Ancient Israel,' yet he succeeded in casting the term 'Israel' onto that past.

It is ironic that Dr Scheck was concerned that New Testament interests had dominated research into the Scrolls, yet he did not see that he was giving biblical and Israel-centred archaeology pride of place in the history of the Middle East in general.[2] Following the standard practice of those doing biblical archaeological research in the Middle East, he noted that the 'Qumran sect' was a 'group of people who separated off sometime after the Macabbean Revolt.' The Macabbees were a 'Hebrew tribe' who revolted against the Romans; they are often cited as important actors in the story of the Jews in the region. Dr Scheck used the contemporary name of the site where the scrolls were found, 'Qumran,' to name the 'sect'; he then linked the scrolls with the period of the 'Macabbean Revolt.' In this way he relocated the Jews' past and the scroll community into a present place, contemporary Israel. I am not suggesting that this scholar was involved in an idiosyncratic practice. Rather, this is the dominant historicizing discourse of the region. For Jewish audiences, his approach could only reinforce the claim that the history of Israel is exclusively, or predominantly, the history of the Jews.

Not surprisingly, then, in the question-and-answer session that followed his lecture, as many questions were raised about the present as about the past. With North American Jewish community leaders and members engaged in and enraged by the 'who is a Jew?' debate – mainly a debate about who has the authority to define who is a Jew in Israel – some audience members asked whether the divisions in the community could be compared to the past's 'sectarianism.' Indeed, the first question from the audience was: 'How do you compare the sects of the past to those of the present?' Dr Scheck replied that the 'movements of the past' were 'not about religious practices' *per se*, because 'everyone practised Judaism' and 'strictly adhered' to its religious laws. In contrast, 'modern disagreements' and 'religious movements' were defined by religious rather than political practices. In his answer, the scholar was able to avoid discussing the legitimacy of any one side's claims for the religious authority to perform conversions and ultimately, to define who is a Jew.

Dr Scheck was also asked whether the 'Zealots of Masada' had been 'members of the Essenes.' I had assumed that Masada would be invoked in this setting and I was not disappointed. After all, the story of a sect living in isolation and rebelling against a dominant political authority would sound highly familiar to anyone who had read or heard the Masada myth. Also, anything associated with the Dead Sea is typically linked to Masada. Dr Scheck quickly reiterated, as he had earlier in the talk, that the 'scrolls were found in a place very different' from Masada and that they had been 'written sometime before Roman rule' in the region. He explained that the 'Zealots were rebels against Roman rule,' and he distinguished them from 'Qumran sect,' whom he described as 'more peaceful.' However, he added that 'just about everyone rebelled against the Romans' except a very 'few aristocratic Jews' then living in 'the Galilee.'

Later, an audience member asked whether the 'differences among the groups in the past' could be compared to the differences between Orthodox, Conservative, Reform, and secular Israelis. The professor explained that although there are 'some similarities,' in the past '90 per cent of the population' lived a kind of 'common Judaism' and 'only 10 per cent of the population' practised in a 'learned' and 'ritual manner.' He added that 'the average Jew is Jesus ... He came from a small town, he read Torah, he knew Hebrew, he was an average guy in the Land of Israel.' And, the scholar repeated, the differences among Jews today are based on interpretations of religion, whereas in the past the disagreements were 'political.'

Still later in the evening, an exceptionally interested and knowledgeable audience member asked Dr Scheck how he could be sure that the documents he had referred to in his talk were dated prior to the Romans' arrival in the area if it was also clear that the scrolls included information about the Romans. Dr Scheck replied that everyone in the region knew that the Romans were coming and that a 'War Scroll' that the questioner was referring to indirectly (the questioner obviously knew his stuff) could be read as a warning to all to expect war. This position was consistent with his argument that the Qumran sect believed, and were announcing to all who would listen, that they were living the 'end of days.' He acknowledged that other scholars disagreed with him on this point, especially on his dating of the scrolls to before the Romans' arrival, but he believed that these people were misreading the scrolls.

I analyse this event to demonstrate how the audience members were linking the Jews' modern history with a common and ancient past. Dr Scheck, like the guides on the tours and like many other common representations available of Israel, had concentrated on locating the Jews in Israel and on showing the importance of the Qumran sites to the Jews alone. His lecture and others like it were open to non-Jewish audiences; that said, I am doubtful that non-Jews would have fully appreciated his talk. Unless they were interested in biblical archaeology or in Israeli history from a Jewish or Israeli-centred perspective, Dr Scheck's emphasis on a Jewish chronology – the Macabbean, Herodian, and Temple periods; his citation of certain ancient texts such as Josephus' *The Jewish Wars*; and his reference to prominent Israelis such as Yigal Yadin, Israel's most prominent nationalist archaeologist – would not have made much sense. He offered little information about non-Jewish communities of the time; overall, just as on the tours, the significance of archaeological finds was measured in biblical and Jewish-centred terms and as a background to current issues confronting Jewish communities.

At a fundraising event for an Israeli university, around one hundred people gathered in the auditorium of a Conservative synagogue. One of the synagogue's board members opened the evening by telling us that 'it is the remembrance of the past that makes this country [Israel] what it is.' We were told that the university for which funds were being raised had 'bridged Israel's past with its future' by bringing 'ancient prayers' to the present in the form of a computer disk holding 'three thousand years of knowledge.' The guest of honour, Yuval Bartock, was introduced to us as an archaeologist who had 'contributed to the biblical and spiritual knowledge of our beloved Land of Israel,' and who also served as one of Jerusalem's Western Wall tunnel tour guides. Mr Bartock had been invited to speak to us about the university's recent excavations in the Jerusalem area.

Mr Bartock, an Israeli Jew in his mid-fifties, began by telling us that 'Jerusalem has a variety of stories,' but that in order to understand the significance of his findings, we needed to keep in mind the historical dimensions as well as the geographical and topographical characteristics of excavated sites. He recommended that when conducting research on Jerusalem, scholars turn to historical texts such as the bible (for the First Temple and the New Testament periods) and Josephus (for the Second Temple period). His concern for careful research seemed questionable in light of his heavy reliance on biblical and classical texts for interpreting the excavations in which he was involved.

He admitted that his interpretation of the Jerusalem sites were contrary to those of other archaeologists working in the area; even so, he believed that what had been excavated in and around Jerusalem was evidence that the Temple Mount site was in fact 'Davidic' – that is, Jerusalem was indeed the 'City of David.' Having established the importance of this site for the Jews, he then argued that these findings served as justification for continuing to excavate in and around the Western Wall tunnels. He reflected on the 'euphoric swift victory' of Israel in 1967 and told us that for years since, there had 'been excavations of a tunnel along the Western Wall,' because neither 'rabbis nor Muslim sheikhs would allow the digging [of the] Temple Mount.' The Temple Mount has for centuries been known as the place where the First Temple was built, but it is also the Muslim site of Al Haram Al Sharif (i.e., the Noble Sanctuary). For these reasons, he explained, archaeologists had been compelled to dig along the wall, learning 'from the outside what was inside [the Temple Mount].' He explained that the three stone layers in Jerusalem represented periods in Jerusalem's history: (1) 'David's time or the First Temple Period'; (2) the 'time of the Church of the Holy Sepulchre' and the 'Second Temple Period'; and (3) the 'tunnel period and the period of the wall.'[3]

He then described how exciting it was to walk through the tunnel, which represented the interval from 'the Second Temple period to modern times' and also highlighted 'the centrality of the Temple Mount in the history of Jerusalem.' Here again, history meant Jewish history. This emphasis was even more emphatic than it had been on the organized tour. By Mr Bartock's account, even history since the Second Temple period – a span of time that included Mamaluke, Ottoman Turkish, and British occupation – disappeared into 'the tunnel period and the period of the Wall.'

He then told us that a group of archaeologists had recently decided to explore how the 'present Temple Mount is small compared' to the one 'in the *Mishnah* [a part of the Talmud that codified Jewish laws], [where] the Temple Mount is [described as] 500 by 500 cubic feet or 230 by 230 cubic meters.' Mr Bartock explained the significance of this: 'The Mishnah [refers not to] the present Temple Mount [but to the] one previous to the one [we call the Temple Mount] today ... It is exciting to believe that Herod went to build the Temple Mount based on the architecture of the Macabbean Temple Mount.'

And just in case we did not fully appreciate what this meant he added that 'Herod did not invent the site. He knew what was there before.' In other words, it was not the Romans' King Herod but rather the Macabbees, a Hebrew tribe, who were responsible for the Temple Mount structures. According to Mr Bartock, this research had established that the grand architectural design, which had for many years been attributed to the Romans (and to King Herod in particular), could now be claimed as the work of the Jews' kin, the Macabbees. Thus, future excavations in the area would be justified by the importance of the search for this 'expanded version of the Temple Mount.'

To end his lecture, he told us that every tourist in Jerusalem could now walk through the Jewish Quarter and appreciate the importance archaeological findings to the area's reconstruction. 'Because second-century Jerusalem was a Roman city ... we need to remove the Roman [layer] in order to reveal the Jewish structures, Jewish layers.' In effect, he was telling us it was appropriate to excavate Jerusalem in order to reach the buried history of the Jews. Layers could be exposed in order to reveal their history and traditions; the past was exclusively theirs. No other histories needed to be preserved since they were merely hiding essential Jewish structures.

1 Synagogue at Masada. The past is present. At this site, our tour guide tells us about his son's Bar Mitzvah, noting that the survival of the Jews is based in part on the continuity of such practices. Masada is a reminder of both the physical and the existential dangers that Jews face (photo from 1998).

2 Remainder/Reminder. On a tour of the Old City, we can't help but peer into the courtyard of a home that we are told is owned by a Palestinian family. It appears to stand next to the newly reconstructed yeshiva (foreground). Represented here are three faiths: the Wailing Wall Plaza is at the bottom right, Haram Al Sharif and Dome of the Rock and the Church of the Redeemer at the top and right (photo from 1998).

3 Marking the Jews' Presence. Throughout the Jewish Quarter of the Old City of Jerusalem one finds physical features marked with references to the Jews' past presence. These appear in the most ordinary spaces, as everyday reminders to those who live in the community and as noticeable signs for those who are passing or touring through. Referring to the Broad Wall, believed to have been built by King Hezekiah in the eighth century BCE in order to fortify a growing and expanding city, the sign on these stones reads: 'Estimated Height of the Wall.' In my discussions with tourists, I discovered that many believed the descriptive labels about the Broad Wall site referred to the Wailing Wall (photo from 1996).

4 Heart of the Past. These stone-paved streets and columns of 'The Cardo' were excavated and restored in the 1970s during the reconstruction of the Jewish Quarter. The area is described as 'the heart' or main district of Roman-era Jerusalem, and nowadays one may visit tourist and artisan shops in the covered section (photo from 1996).

5 Fortifying the Past. The reconstructed Jewish Quarter of the Old City of Jerusalem sits on a hill west of the Wailing Wall Plaza. Within the Jewish Quarter, a map on one of the walls represents the topography of the area as well as the 'expansion' of Jerusalem's boundaries during the First Temple Period. Those boundaries include the area now designated as the Jewish Quarter (photo from 1998).

6 Exclusions/Erasures. Street signs in Israel are required to be in Arabic and Hebrew as well as English. Here the street sign in the mixed commercial and residential area of the Jewish Quarter of the Old City, from which all Palestinians are excluded from living in by law, has been spray-painted to erase even the traces of an Arab presence (photo from 1998).

7 On Guard. Military and security personnel casually guarding the entrance/exit of the Western Wall tunnels which lead from the Wailing Wall Plaza through to the Muslim Quarter. They glance at the ID cards of those who enter and exit and look on as tourists photograph them (photo from 1997).

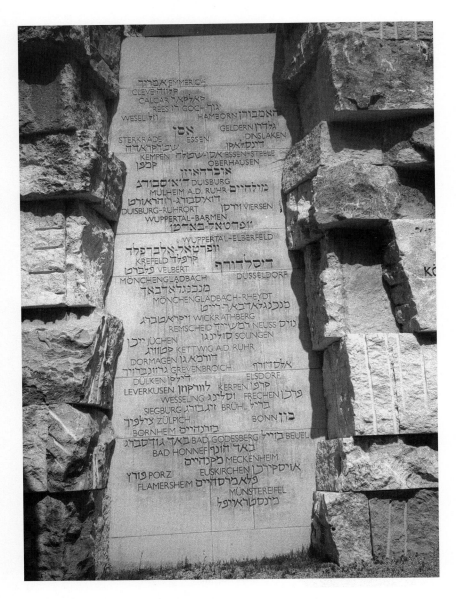

8 Monument. One walks through a walled maze that is the Valley of the Destroyed Communities at Yad Vashem, Israel's Holocaust Museum. Looking up
and around, each wall lists those communities whose Jewish populations were
expelled and which were never to be the same after the war. My grandmother's
community, Oberhausen, Germany, appears on this list (photo from 1998).

9 Golani Bunker. This site is described to us as having been used by the Syrians as a military bunker during the 1967 War with Israel. The Golan Heights area was captured by the Israelis in that war and annexed in 1981 (photo from 1998).

10 Donkey and a Bus. This Bedouin village in the Negev has been 'recognized' by the Israeli government, allowing for access to running water, sewage treatment, and gas power. We are told that while many Bedouin refuse government compensation for their lands, others use the monies received to build new homes in the village (photo from 1997).

11, 12 Before and After Zionism. For many, Israel's *kibbutzim* represent Zionism's greatest achievement and exemplify the Zionist modernist mission. At this kibbutz we are invited to look one way to see how an arid and empty land was transformed into a lush green, civilized environment (photo from 1998).

Statements like these have important political implications for Israeli and Palestinian politics. When an Israeli archaeologist declares that the Temple Mount area is much larger than first imagined, this gives strength to extremist ultranationalist Jews, who claim the entire Al Haram Al Sharif area as the site for rebuilding their Temple. It also legitimates these Jews' illegal take-over of lands in the rest of Muslim East Jerusalem.

Throughout Mr Bartock's presentation, there was never any serious discussion of the non-Jewish communities' relationships to Jerusalem.[4] In fact, the only references to other religious representatives were to 'sheikhs' who would not allow excavations on 'the Temple Mount,' and to the Christians' Church of the Holy Sepulchre as a site essential only for studying the Second Temple 'tier.' Other national communities and their historical or indigenous ties to Jerusalem vanished in this presentation. All that was presented was the reclamation of the 'City of David' as it was designed, built, and lived in by Jews in the past. Since it had been recaptured as 'Jerusalem,' Jews were justified on historical, biblical, and archaeological grounds to excavate and reconstruct it for themselves. In effect, the great imperative for every archaeological dig was to establish the site's importance to the Jews' history in order that they could proclaim their exclusive right to the area.

Dr Bartock was conceptualizing the 'ancient' land called Israel solely in terms of Jewish history and survival. Among all the 'ancients,' only the Jews could claim an ongoing relationship to the region. It is this tie and their 'chosenness' that returned them to the land.

But can Israel be the Jews' state *and* a Jewish state? This distinction may at first seem slight, yet it provides the basis for several significant debates. Underlying every such discussion is the requirement to assess the needs and wishes of community members living within and outside the state and those who identify with Israel for religious, national, or political reasons.

All the presentations took for granted that Israel is the Jews' nation-state; however, the question of whether a state can be both Jewish and democratic was often raised. At a 1996 event, Michael Levine, an elderly professor of law from one of Israel's most prestigious universities, spoke to a small public audience.

In his introduction, Mr Levine outlined how, by reflecting on the work of three important Jewish philosophers – Maimonades, Spinoza, and Mendelssohn – he would critique the debates raging within Israel and among Jewish scholars (albeit sometimes exclusively among the

Orthodox). The question at hand was this: Will Israel become a Jewish democratic state that emphasizes its democratic nature, an Israel for Israel's citizens? Or will Israel become a democratic Jewish state emphasizing the Jewishness of the state of the Jews?

Mr Levine began by noting that Orthodox Jews living in Israel today were facing an 'acute dilemma.' Many of them had 'accepted democracy,' evidenced in large part by the fact that they had institutional political representation (e.g., the Status Quo Agreement of 1951 gave the Chief Rabbinate of Israel jurisdiction over such matters as marriage, divorce, and dietary laws for the Jewish inhabitants of Israel) and also by the fact that they were participating in state elections (e.g., through their support of the National Religious Party). Yet they still found it difficult to reconcile Judaism with the realities of a modern Jewish state. The Orthodox had long taken one of two positions: There were some who denied that Israel was an authentic Jewish state, going so far as to claim that Israel was 'the deed of Satan' and 'a hindrance to redemption.' These members of the Orthodox community had excluded themselves from the state's everyday politics and, in some cases, had even worked with 'enemies' against the state (i.e., with the Palestinians). Then there were some who had a messianic understanding of the state: Israel was an authentically Jewish state, and though it had not reached its 'ideal,' it was still part of the longed-for 'return.' According to Mr Levine, most of Israel's Orthodox Jews took this latter position. Thus, they were participating in what to them was a messianic struggle for the ideal Jewish state.

Mr Levine explained that in order to fully understand and appreciate these debates, one needed to return to the foundations of modern Jewish thought itself – in particular, to three thinkers who tried to bring ideas of religion, nation, and state into line with the religious and political assumptions of the modern world. These three were Maimonides (1135–1204), who wrote *The Commandments* (*Sefer Ha-Mitzvot*), among other great works; Spinoza (1632–77), who wrote *The Treatise* (or *Tractate*); and Mendelssohn (1729–86), who wrote *Jerusalem or, On Religion, Power and Judaism*, among other works. According to Mr Levine, these philosophers had transformed concepts of the nation and of God in their discussions of the transcendent and the corporeal, and in doing so had politicized religious thought.

He summarized the significance of their ideas:

- Maimonides condemned those who believed in the 'corporeality of God.' Thus God is spirit, not body, and there should be no worship of a human messiah. One should rather follow their spiritual calling.

- Spinoza offered a secular understanding of Judaism and was the 'first secular Jew.' In his *Treatise* he had called on the Jews to 'overcome the Jewish tradition' of 'awaiting the messiah' because it 'hindered their progress.' He also called on the Jews to engage themselves with the world and to participate in human History (with a capital H). Finally, he radically transformed conceptions of the Jews' relationship to God; from a Spinozan perspective, all people had been elected by divinity. Spinoza was thus undermining the Jews' claim to chosenness. He also argued that the Jews could achieve redemption through reason rather than through prayer. Spinoza would have felt comfortable with mainstream Zionism, for it was an ideology guided by the yearning for a national and therefore secular ideal rather than a transcendent one.

- Mendelssohn had written the 'antithesis to Spinoza's claims' and in the process had also 'transformed Maimonides' claims.' He had promoted the Spinozan perspective of 'entering the Jews into history, but against Spinoza,' he felt that the Torah held 'religious and national significance' for Jews.

Returning to the situation facing modern Israel, Mr Levine argued that 'Israel is a Jewish state' with a Jewish 'religion' and that any move 'to separate state and religion was wrong' for 'neither was true to or in man's best interest.' Every person and every collective had spiritual as well as temporal concerns, and these were matters of justice and duty; thus, there was a role for both religion and state in these matters. According to Mr Levine, 'religion and state are not different in their purposes; they are different in their means.' The 'state may be coercive,' whereas coercion is the 'antithesis of faith.'

He then returned to Mendelssohn's thesis, explaining that there was 'only one time' when there was 'no tension between state and religion.' This was the period of the 'Mosaic Constitution' when 'God was King' and the administration of the 'civil arena was sacred'; any offence against religious law was also an offence against civil law, and the 'enforcement of religious law [was the] same as the enforcement of civil law.' Since that time, and up until the creation of Israel, the Jews had been compelled to practise under 'another's sovereignty' – in other words, to 'perform their duties to their own God' while living under others' administration. This Mendelssohnian theology was eventually to form the basis for Reform Judaism.

Having outlined the main points of the debate among these three philosophers, Mr Levine restated the main question for the evening: 'Can a Jewish state be a democratic state?' He dismissed Jewish religious leaders who believed that a Jewish state was impossible and that there could never be a Jewish democratic state; in his view, it was wrong to assume that Rabbinic Judaism's concepts of power fundamentally clashed with democracy. He emphasized that the rule of law (e.g., Supreme Court judgments) in Israel flowed not from *halakhic* Judaism but rather from 'cultural Jewishness' – that is, a Jewishness based in language and tradition. Thus, for him, Judaism and Jewish national identity followed Spinozan thought in their focus on secular Jewishness. Others emphasized a democracy with Jewishness 'added on' (i.e., you build a democratic state and you make it Jewish if there is something in Judaism that improves the democratic model); he, however, preferred that his audience think about the Jews' capacity to create 'a balance of both Judaism and democracy.' This approach had guided Israel's drafting of its most recent Basic Laws, which according to Mr Levine embodied 'the abstract dimensions of both Judaism and democracy.'

Furthermore, he explained, we had to understand that for Orthodox Jews it was still 'difficult to separate duty and divinity,' because to them duty and the divine were mutual considerations. The Orthodox could not accept this separation, for 'there is no single individual sphere'; to the Orthodox, 'every action is for and about the collectivity.' Thus, for them, human rights were a function not of 'individual desires' but rather of their beliefs regarding the 'metaphysical notion of mutual responsibility.' This is why, within Orthodox communities, any individual sin was thought to create the possibilities for 'collective damage.'

Mr Levine then described Israel as a secular, liberal state confronting its *halakhic* tradition, aware of the resulting contradictions and striving to 'balance' the distinctions between the private and the public. The symbolic means of identifying coexistence among religious and secular Jews were important and remained part of the pragmatic or 'complementary' approach taken by Israel's legislators and lawmakers. They recognized that the contradictions they were facing would never be resolved by denying one or the other's practices and sensibilities.

Even so, he also acknowledged that although the population was largely non-observant, all Israelis needed to cope with the Orthodox community's position. Referring to the 'who is a Jew' debate as an example, he explained that this clash of civilizations was more than merely an internal matter; it also affected Jews living outside the state. In this way, Israeli statehood was posing challenges to Jews both within and outside Israel. Even so, the debates between the secular and religious sectors of Israeli society were ages old, and rooted in Jewish philosophy. They were not a function of the peculiar circumstances facing a state that claimed to be both Jewish and democratic.

Mr Levine omitted from his main discussion the fact that the Israeli state also governed non-Jews and that the 'balance' he spoke of had no relevance to those who had no duty to Rabbinic authorities or to their faith communities. This latter point was to arise in the question-and-answer session that followed the lecture.

After Mr Levine completed his talk, an elderly Jewish man, referring to the present era as post-Zionist, asked: 'How do we respond to a Jewish generation that doesn't seem to know its own history, tradition, or identity?' The professor replied, in part: 'We cannot leave this room assuming that this is simply a post-Zionist or postmodern moment ... The Arab population has its own problems of identity with the state ... For who is an Arab in a Jewish state?' He went on to state – perhaps as a correction to the inquiry – that the 'post-Zionist concept of Israel' was one that suggested that Israel 'shouldn't be Jewish at all,' but rather should be 'a state of its citizens.' With obvious disdain for this position, he contended that the problem faced by this Jewish generation could be solved through education:

> [We] can only be hopeful that the experiment of Zionism will succeed ... There are external and internal enemies to the concept of the Jewish state. The conflict is not just about whether or not the state should be Jewish, Zionist, and democratic. The problem in a Jewish state is 'How can a non-Jew identify in an ethnically Jewish state?' and 'What happens to a Jewish Zionist state with non-Zionists in it?'

The professor ended this discussion by stating that notwithstanding the contemporary understandings of human rights and democracy, 'the Law of Return should be accepted because [Israel] is the only Jewish state ... even though it discriminates against non-Jews.'

This presentation illustrates how diaspora and Israeli Jews debated the various relationships between modern Judaism, the state, and ideas of democracy. Mr Levine was arguing that Israel had reconciled Orthodox and secular positions and had become a democratic Jewish state. Notwithstanding this position, this presentation also demonstrated that Jews do not have a simple relationship to Israel as the Jews' state. The differences are philosophical and political, and their individual and collective orientation to the state is informed by various historical trends in religious, philosophical, and political thought. Furthermore, the speaker was more or less acknowledging that within the state's borders, there were non-Jews who might not 'identify' with a state defined as Jewish or Zionist. Nevertheless, he was not arguing that this recognition should fundamentally shift the definition of democracy. In the final analysis, he defined Israel as the Jews' state; thus, the state had good reasons to struggle with the philosophical and theological foundations of Judaism and its traditions.

In these presentations, Israel was described along a more or less classical Zionist trajectory, as a nation-state whose traditions could be linked to its present formation as the Jews' state. Israel was a state confronting its ancient and traditional past, and it faced existential dilemmas such as how to reformulate Jewish traditions within the structure of a nation-state, and how, in so doing, to recreate the Jews' presence on the land.

9
Identifying (with) Israel after Zionism

One of Zionism's primary goals was to normalize the Jews, to bring them into the modern era and into History (capital H). Vital to this was the establishment of their own nation-state.[1] This partly explains why a number of community presentations focused on how Jews were confronting issues of the sort faced by other modern nation-states. These presentations were mainly about the new relationships that Jews were developing with one another (within Israel) as well as with the world (i.e., with neighbouring states). The Jews were no longer a nation without a state; now they could celebrate and meet head-on the full dimensions and challenges of living in the time of the Jews' state. As a nation-state, Israel no longer necessarily identified diaspora Jews' interests as its own; it now concerned itself mainly with the interests of its own inhabitants, especially its Jewish citizens. Diaspora Jews would have to come to terms with their new role vis-à-vis the nation-state.

In many discussions, differences between Israeli Jews' practices and those of diaspora Jews came to light. In the 1990s, the role played by Israel's religious authorities was hotly debated in the community. 'Who is a Jew?' and 'Who identifies as a Jew?' were the central questions to emerge. Also, 'How can religion and rabbinic authorities define the course of Israel's future, politically and socially?' Equally important were questions about the peace agreements with neighbouring Arab states, and about what role, if any, the Palestinians would play in Israel's future. These latter discussions were the most heated; they also inspired the most difficult questions for Israeli guests in front of diaspora audiences.

At one community event, sponsored by the local fundraising arm of Israel's most prestigious university, the Hebrew University, Dr Harold Black, an Israeli professor, was invited to speak about the relations between secular and religious Jews in Israel. The event was very well attended, with about two hundred guests congregating in a museum hall. While the audience waited for the lecture to start, they chatted over a marvellous selection of wines, cheeses, desserts, and coffee. About an hour into the reception, we were directed into a lecture hall, where we were seated in a semicircle facing a podium. After a few welcoming remarks by the presidents of the local and national Friends of the Hebrew University, the chair of a Jewish studies program in the city introduced the guest speaker. Dr Black was described as a political philosopher and as 'a voice of moderation among the modern Orthodox in Israel.' He had been invited to talk about the relationship between Orthodox and secular Jews in Israel – a relationship that was being represented that year (1997), in the local Jewish as well as in the international media, as fractious and irreconcilable.

Dr Black began the lecture by reminding us that he was bringing 'an Israeli perspective to the problem.' He asked us to recall:

> Forty-nine years ago, [author Arthur] Koestler came to visit the new-born state ... He wrote a book with some analysis of the future and had predicted that in over two generations Israeli society will become non-Jewish. [Social critic] Veblen said if Zionism succeeds to bring the Jews to Palestine, they will isolate themselves and the world would lose the Jews.

He contended that in order to understand 'who was right' and 'who was wrong,' we 'need to examine the different sections of Israeli society ... Some are totally alienated from Jewishness. On the other pole, there are those who are running to separate Zionism and Jewishness and who isolate Judaism from anything modern.'

According to Dr Black, 'there is a tremendous gap between Sabras.' He predicted that this gap would grow and that it would also intensify 'between the diaspora and Sabras and the next generations.' But, he warned, it would be dangerous to characterize this relationship simply in terms of 'polarization.'

Dr Black suggested that 'when analysed conceptually' all the tensions arising in Israel 'shouldn't be a surprise to us [because] there is a tension within Zionism itself':

> Zionism was a radical revolution, perhaps the most radical revolution ever. [It was] much more radical than any other. [In order for this revolution] to succeed [we needed] to revive the nation [that was] without terri-

tory; [to ask people to] leave a territory to settle in a new one; [and to] revive a mother tongue. Mothers had to learn the language from their children. [We needed to] create from nothing a revolution. Where do other revolutions get their myths? The future. [But] Zionism takes the past, the renaissance, the ancient homeland, and turns back and looks towards the future.

For all these reasons, Israel would always need to deal with the tensions between the past and the future. Such tensions were inherent in Zionist ideology. Furthermore:

There is no historical analogy of the revival of a spoken language; no precedent of return of people to an ancient land ... I mention this not for the sake of Zionist propaganda, but because ... on the one hand, we want to normalize and we have to go through an abnormal process to get there, both in terms of using Hebrew as our language and then [settling] in the land. There is no historical analogy to this. But this tension [is] not ... between Judaism and Israeli Zionism. It is a tension between past and present.

Nevertheless, he believed that 'the numbers' or statistics were evidence that the tension was not between Judaism and Israeli culture. He cited these polling results to prove his point:

Twenty-three per cent of Israelis say they do not turn on their radios on Shabbat; 75 to 79 per cent fast on Yom Kippur ... and say yes, when asked if they perceive themselves to be good Jews – 20 per cent say no. Fifty-seven per cent believe God gave the Bible to the Jews in Samaria. [With respect to] religious Orthodoxy and secular Orthodoxy [they are represented at] 20 per cent each. Everyone else is in between [the two extremes].

Even so, Israelis 'are always confronting both sides because "the boxes" have been written by these two groups ... There is in Israel a cultural and political clash and not necessarily a social clash.' Contradictions that had been 'managed' for more than thirty years by the 1951 Status Quo Agreement (an agreement that set the terms of Rabbinic powers vis-à-vis the state) were no longer fruitful for either side.

Dr Black contended that this agreement, which had established the terms for the relationship between religious authority and the secular state authority, had been based on 'one false common denominator':

Each side believed the other would disappear. Ben-Gurion, [always the political] pragmatist, [believed] entering into the agreement wouldn't pose any future harm to the state. [He assumed that the] Jews' Orthodox religious practices were 'a phenomenon of exile' [and that once] in Israel, the Jews [would become] normalized [and] Orthodoxy would disappear [or, at the very least, become ever more] marginalized. [It was also] perhaps for nostalgic reasons [that] he agreed to release the Orthodox [from any] military service.

Yet, for the other signatories, the Orthodox Jews, 'a secular Jew is an oxymoron.' Our speaker described how Rav Kook, Israel's first Chief Rabbi, was 'one of the most tolerant of Orthodox Jews' because he, unlike most Orthodox Jews, had believed the return of the Jews to Israel to be one 'from foreign lands to the Holy Land,' and because he had celebrated the substitution of 'the foreign tongue for the Holy tongue.' But Kook had also believed that the Jews had escaped 'from assimilation to Jewishness' and that eventually secular Jews would disappear. To Kook and his followers, the secularism of the Jews was simply a 'symptom of life in diaspora.'

According to Dr Black, until very recently each side had tolerated the other and 'the hegemony of mutual recognition' had prevailed. However, he explained, the situation in Israel had changed so much that the agreement no longer embodied the expectations of either group. He cited a number of examples. First, when the military exemption was granted to Orthodox Jews, there were 'very, very few of them.' No one expected that in the future there would be a large and politically significant Orthodox community. The 'religious Zionists,' for their part, had agreed to allow taxis to operate on the Sabbath; since so few people owned cars at the time, they assumed that the streets would 'always remain practically empty.' As a result of a series of historical misjudgments like these, each side could only perceive what they have lost rather than what they had gained through the agreement. This was the background for the tensions between these communities in the mid and late 1990s.

In his final comments, Dr Black contended that the agreement was no longer 'efficient' because Israelis were feeling more confident and no longer believed they had to rally around one another to prevent their own disappearance. Paradoxically, they no longer felt a need to fight in order to accomplish 'the simple things'; they now wanted their own ideological needs to be fulfilled. In other words, Israelis were feeling more politically secure than in the past; as a result, they felt they could express their differences as well as their desires and expectations.

Stating that he did not want to leave his audience with the impression that Israel was in a terribly fractious condition, Dr Black asserted that all of these developments were evidence of 'the accomplishments of Israel' and that they had resulted in a number of 'important cultural developments.' For one thing, he said, there had been a 'tremendous revival' in the study of classical Jewish texts among 'elite secular Israelis,' who, although not interested in religion *per se*, believed these texts embodied 'our cultural memory, and our history' and that the ultra-Orthodox were 'not capable of preserving these' cultural memories for secular Jews. Besides, the ultra-Orthodox should not hold a monopoly in these matters.

Second, Dr Black surmised that the 'conflicts over the Law of Return' and 'who is a Jew' should not have been framed as such, for the argument was not over 'who is a Jew' so much as 'who is a rabbi.' At the heart of this matter was a battle over rabbinical authority, since it was rabbis who were disagreeing over who had the right to declare who was a Jew. If the Orthodox were to maintain their monopoly over the conversion of Jews, and thus the confirmation of who is Jewish, most Jews who converted in North America – where Reform and Conservative rabbis form the majority – would be denied legitimacy. So it was not a matter of 'who is Jew,' but rather which rabbis had the authority to define someone as a Jew. Dr Black gleefully pointed out that the opponents in this battle for authority were the same people who had at one time opposed the Zionist state: Lubavitcher rabbis and Reform rabbis. In the past, neither group had conferred any legitimacy to the State of Israel, yet now 'both care very much about Israel.'

Dr Black ended his lecture on what he considered an 'optimistic note':

> The most crucial elements of Jewish identity will be [worked out] there in Israel and as a Zionist I am very happy about that ... for Zionism was not just about the revival of Israelis but also about the revival of the Jewish people. So I am very happy the tensions are being played out in Israel ... This is a question of cultural national interests in Jewish history ... This is not a religious versus secular question. It is a cultural one.

Thus, Dr Black had situated the debate between Israelis and Orthodox Jews within Israel's contemporary history and had pointed to

Zionism's founding philosophy as well as to the political and the pragmatic actions necessary for the development of the state. He had presented Israel as a country working through the always unpredictable
processes of state building and as undergoing the very normal processes of maturation and advancement.

In his presentation, Zionism's founding principles were both celebrated and critiqued. Of course, he was clearly articulating a position
that situated the Jews' cultural centre in Israel, and in so doing arguing
that the problems Israelis were confronting were crucial to the entire
Jewish nation's cultural development, not simply its spiritual or political development. His presentation looked past the damage that battles
between ultrareligious and secular Jews had done to Israeli society. He
chose to cite more positive developments, such as the recovery of and
interest in traditional practices among secular Israeli Jews. As importantly, he did not overemphasize the distress felt by North American
Jews resulting from the fact that Orthodox rabbis in Israel had the sole
right to determine who was a Jew. It was remarkable that even though
he proclaimed himself a Zionist, he presented no role for diaspora
Jews and took no time to represent or even speak to their interests.
Although he rejoiced in Zionism's success, he had presented his audience with a post-Zionist vision of Israel. From his account, one could
only assume that the existential crises associated with the Jews' survival had dissolved away, to be supplanted by the luxury of living
authentically Jewish lives in a Jewish state.

With regard to the conflict between secular and ultrareligious Israelis, a more ominous tone was set by an Israeli sociologist who attended
a weekend conference on the relationship between Israel and Canadian
Jewry. This event was hosted by a Reform temple and attended by
more than one hundred community members. The paper that Dr Amir
Tov presented at this conference rang alarm bells. He expressed grave
concern for Israel as it tried to cope with rabbinical challenges to the
state legislature. He represented religious authority as a threat to the
democratic development of Israel.

In examining the 'conflict between the rule of law, democracy, and
Rabbinic rulings' and the related issues of 'illegalism and disobedience,'
Dr Tov asked his audience to think about 'what happens when *halakha*
becomes politicized.' He argued that when 'a group of Zionist rabbis'
announced that 'no Jew' should encourage or help 'remove Jewish settlers' living in the Occupied Territories, they were asking their followers
to 'collectively disregard' what could soon 'become law.' He cited Prime

Minister Rabin's assassination as an example of an 'illegal act' that had been 'incited' and supported by 'religious nationalists' and 'religious authorities.' He noted that two weeks before Rabin's assassination, he had nearly been attacked by a Canadian audience after warning them that 'the cynical exploitation of religion' was highly dangerous. Dr Tov implied that North American Jews were naive about the role being played by religious leaders in Israeli politics. He told us that 'Israelis were dismayed' that many 'in the diaspora' had supported the 'politicization of the *halakha*.'

He acknowledged that many *halakhic* debates predated the foundation of Israel, but he added that some of the issues facing Israelis and Jews were new. In particular, 'the role of gentiles on the Land of Israel' had only become an issue 'after the 1967 War.' He blamed the current situation in Israel – what he described as 'a gap between the rabbinical rulings and the political parties' – on the 1951 Status Quo Agreement signed by Israel's first prime minister, Ben-Gurion, and the 'ultra-Orthodox religious leaders' of the time. He described how the religious parties had 'demanded' a 'heavy price' and that they had since that time consolidated their power. In fact, they now held the 'balance of power' even though they constituted no more than 15 per cent of the population. In a 'properly functioning democracy,' it would be 'inconceivable' that any 'collective' representing such a 'minority' would be allowed to 'disrupt the lives' of the general public.

He presented Israel as a state in which the legislators and most of the people had to struggle with – and sometimes against – religious authorities and rabbinical leaders. According to him, the Israeli political system suffered from a 'lack of separation' between state and religion that was distorting Israel's political structure. Rabin's assassination was only one symptom of a much deeper problem in Israel. In Dr Tov's view, democracy could not be reconciled with the power held by religious authorities.

Dr Tov was questioning the role played by religious leaders in Israeli politics. The Jewishness of the state was not the issue; the rabbis' representation of that state certainly was. Other presenters claimed that Israel was becoming more representative of its Jewish citizens and that Zionism had succeeded in redefining the relationship of Judaism and Jewishness to state politics. In contrast, Dr Tov claimed that Israel was undemocratic as a result of the very relationships that had developed between Israeli legislators and Judaism's official representatives. He considered Israel undemocratic because its religious minority had managed to grab and hold on to a great deal of political power. Until this power imbalance was resolved, violence would continue to grow.[2]

The questions that community members asked Dr Tov focused on whether any law could have prevented such heinous acts as the assassination of a prime minister. For example, he was asked, 'How can any court prevent a person from committing these acts individually or from acting on matters of conscience?' and 'If violent acts had been predicted, why were they not prevented?' In reply, Dr Tov conceded that no court could prevent people from acting individually. He added, however, that the problem in Israel was that individuals who were committing such acts were doing so as 'members of a collective' and in response to their leaders. He explained that from a strictly legal perspective, these leaders could have been charged for breaking the law – specifically, for inciting violence. However, Israeli political leaders had 'remained inactive' in order to avoid further polarizing the secular and religious groups in Israeli society. He believed that before Rabin's assassination, most Israelis had been mollified by the 'myth that no Jew would kill another Jew.' He warned that there could be more bloodshed between Jews if future agreements ordered settlers removed from the Occupied Territories. He remained sceptical that any lessons had been learned from the recent past or that any actions would be taken to prevent violence in the future. From the tone of his answers, he perceived the questioners as quite naive, as not fully appreciating or understanding the constraints within which Israeli political alliances had to be developed and maintained.

The role of religion and democracy in Israel commanded the attention of many audiences in the community. However, many lectures and discussions dealt with the prospects for peace for the region. Other aspects of Israeli life, the Israeli state, and the diaspora were represented in the discussions that followed these events. The tensions between Israeli and diaspora representations of Israel's future became most apparent during debates over the Oslo Accords and the relations between Jews and Arabs, Israelis and Palestinians. In a very real way, Israeli scholars and politicians were remapping Israel and pushing diaspora Jews to think about Israel after Zionism.

In 1996, Dr Malcolm Kramer, an Israeli geographer, came to speak about 'Israel after Rabin.' He had presented lectures at two other synagogues, one Conservative and the other Orthodox. On the night I attended, he spoke at a Reform temple. The room was filled with many of the people who had attended the previous lectures. I spoke to two elderly men, who told me they had been impressed by the earlier lectures but still had a few questions to ask our guest. About fifty people, mostly men of middle-age or older, were seated in a small lecture hall in the temple basement.

After a very brief introduction by a professor of Jewish studies, Dr Kramer, who had made *aliyah* from England, began by telling his audience that he was not seeking to

> make a sell for or against the peace process. I leave that to the politicians. [Still] I will be mixing my personal thoughts with my professional analysis on where the peace process is, where it is going, and where the elections [of 1996] may take it ... Some believe the only way forward is the peace process while others believe it is the worst thing possible ... But I do want to point out that there is less dialogue within the diaspora than even in Israel itself.

I thought at the time that this was a very defensive statement with which to introduce the evening. It was not until the question-and-answer session that it began to make sense.

Dr Kramer explained that although Prime Minister Rabin had been assassinated for 'ideological reasons,' in order to 'prevent the continuation' of the peace process, the killing had in fact 'prompted the opposite reaction.' By the time of his presentation, the second stage of the Oslo Accords had been implemented almost precisely by the deadlines set out by the signatories. He thought it strange that the first stage of the accords, or 'Oslo I,' which was 'less far reaching,' had not been implemented in time, whereas 'Oslo II,' with 'more at stake [and] more land to return,' had been implemented on time. Moving next to explain that implementation involved 'the transfer of power to the Palestinians in Gaza and the West Bank' and ensuring that Palestinian elections would take place, he said that 'the transition of power [had] taken place remarkably smoothly ... considering we [Israeli Jews] are working with two million people [the Palestinians] who don't particularly like us.'

Dr Kramer asserted that although 'many are eager to look at the negative side of the peace process, everyone needs to look at what has been achieved ... and to recognize that each party weighs the cost-benefits differently, depending on their political leanings.' As an example, he described how despite their histories of conflict, Jordan's King Hussein and Egypt's President Hosni Mubarak had attended Rabin's funeral and had even offered their condolences. 'Who would have believed that these people would arrive to say eulogies, even in a "cold" peace? ... Still, it is also ironic that it took the assassination of an Israeli prime minister by a Jew to prompt this.'

Next, Dr Kramer placed a map depicting the Oslo II agreements on an overhead projector and explained that although 'there is no logic to the map at first glance ... It looks like splatters of green, yellow, and rusty brown,' it had a rational design. In effect, the map illustrated how the Occupied Territories would be divided into 'three zones of redeployment ... Area A, Area B, and Area C.' He described the Oslo II plan:

- Area A designated areas where the 'majority of Palestinians live.' These included 'all the Palestinian towns except Hebron.' All of the towns in Area A had been 'transferred to the Palestinian Authority – for example, Ramallah, Nablus, Jenin, Bethlehem, and Jericho.'
- 'Ninety per cent of Palestinian residents who do not live in Area A, live in Area B.' This area covered the 'rural regions.' On the whole, Israel had withdrawn from these areas but still had 'some administrative control in some parts of the land.'
- Area C remained 'under Israeli control.' It was 'completely controlled by the Israelis' and included 'all Israeli settlements' and areas where 'bypass roads are being constructed' or where they would eventually be 'built to cross' through Areas A and B. The roads that had been built were 'some of the best roads ever constructed in the last thirty years' – for example, the 'Jericho bypass roads.'

He then told us that 'the map itself is postmodern. It is about exclaves and enclaves [and] disconnected territories ... It bears little relation to most maps where the boundaries are set to exclude some and include others.' And, clearly, too, it was 'not the final map.'

Dr Kramer predicted that in the final negotiations the boundaries of a 'Palestinian state' would be established. This would mean that eventually there 'will likely be two people living within those boundaries.' Noting that Oslo II had come about because 'Israelis did not want to deal with the [Jewish] settlements in the West Bank right away,' he told us he expected that 'in any case' the day would come when the settlers would 'have to be moved' and that this would be a 'traumatic event.' In other words, Israel's negotiators and politicians had only postponed the inevitable and more difficult problem of moving Israeli citizens out of the Occupied Territories. Dr Kramer stated: 'It is an Israeli problem ... and [a resolution] will come.'

He went on to explain that under Oslo II, Israel had insisted that 'no territory' in Areas B or C would ever be 'handed over' to the Palestinian Authority and that the map had been designed in this way in order to 'protect' areas where the 'settlers lived.' Even though the settlers represented 'only 10 per cent or 20 per cent' of the total population of Israel, and even though the 'new boundary will be redrawn to include 60 or 70 per cent of the settlements,' he anticipated that the Israeli government would find it hard to ignore their situation. He lamented that Rabin had 'delegitimized the settlers' concerns' by casting the future of the settlements incorrectly as a religious question. In fact, many Israeli Jews cited strategic as well as humane reasons for protecting the settlers. For this reason, Dr Kramer concluded, most Israelis were concerned that their government meet its responsibilities to those citizens.

Finally, Dr Kramer told us that the upcoming Israeli elections between the 'anti-Oslo forces of Benjamin Netanyahu' and the 'Oslo supporters' behind Shimon Peres would be 'a referendum on the peace agreements' and that they were likely to be the 'most important [elections] in Israel's history.' He ended his lecture with this anecdote:

> A year ago, I was in [this city] dealing with some difficult questions posed to me by some community members. [One of the questions came from] an individual who said he was not in support of the peace agreement. He said, 'Everyone wants peace but we are a democracy, while they on the other side are dictatorships. What will happen if we make an agreement with one of them and someone assassinates *their* leader.

Dr Kramer provided an ironic reflection on the challenges of presenting Israel to a community still caught in a pre-Oslo vision and version of Israel. Despite the fact that he had sent this clear signal, as he had at the beginning of his lecture, he was challenged on nearly every one of his points. This occurred despite the fact that he had spoken of the basis for, and the problems of, the peace agreement from an Israeli perspective, highlighting only strategic and political problems that might arise for Israel. For example, he had nothing to say about the Palestinians who continue to live under occupation in order that the 10 or 20 per cent of Israel's population who continue to live in the settlements can be protected by an army; nor did he talk about the hardships that a redesigned map of the area creates for Palestinians who are forced to find alternative routes in and out of what were once contiguous work and living spaces.

When I thought later about the passionate responses to this presentation, I realized that the geographer had done something very radical that night: he had used a map very unlike the ones provided to participants on organized tours, or in promotional literature about Israel, or at any of the other community presentations I had attended. Nearly all the maps of Israel used on the tours and in promotional literature represented an Israel that had annexed the West Bank and Gaza Strip. That is, no clear boundaries designating these areas as 'occupied territories' were ever shown. In fact, on one tour the guide had used a black marker to draw these boundaries on his map.

Dr Kramer had shown his audience perhaps the first politicized map of Israel they had ever seen, that is, a map in which different areas were designated as out of bounds to one group or another. Most importantly to this audience, he had used a map of Israel that showed the territories from which Jews were to be excluded. For many diaspora Jews this simple map emphasized the fragmentary nature of a land that they had, until that moment anyway, considered whole. Perhaps this in turn forced some audience members to consider the likelihood that the Oslo Accords would result in two national communities sharing the land. Were the passionate reactions prompted by this unusual visual cue? Dr Kramer was presenting to the audience a postmodern territoriality – he was showing them not one state and one national community but rather two national communities living both inside and outside the boundaries of a current state and a 'state in progress.' Thus, he was forcing them to envision how the territories were to be relinquished – territories that many considered part of greater Israel – as well as the transformation of those relinquished territories into a Palestinian state. In this way, he was presenting the Oslo Accords as very radical indeed.

Whatever their interpretations, many audience members were clearly upset by what Dr Kramer was telling them, and they responded with sharply emotional questions. The session quickly grew heated. Every answer the doctor provided seemed to distress the audience still more. Some of the exchanges follow:

Q: Arafat speaks a different language [depending on his audience, and the] Palestinians take what they want. Why don't we now say, 'No more!' [And] what about the Covenant?[3]

A: In practical terms, I agree with Arafat that the Covenant is irrelevant since Palestinians are as unable to push Israelis into the sea today as they were ten, twenty years ago.

Q: [Do you really think the] Arabs will be satisfied with a Green Line retreat [or will the] situation deteriorate, ruin the Israeli economy and then create insecurity for all [Israelis]? [Will this present] an opportunity for the Arabs [especially] if Israel is only nine miles wide?

A: I do not share your pessimism. I do not try to be an expert on the Arabs since I have a difficult enough time trying to figure out what Israelis and Jews want. [Just to] reiterate: Israel is not prepared to discuss the Green Line as the boundary [if only] because of the settlements. [And it is] important to note [as well that] the few extra miles [that would be] annexed are miles of elevated areas. [Note too that this] annexation of part of the West Bank is based on pragmatic, not ideological terms ... [And lastly, if] each side said what it wanted, each would say it wanted the whole without the other! [I believe that] a strong nation makes peace. [The] Palestinians are no threat and they won't be, even as a state.

In both of these questions, diaspora Jews were expressing their fear that a smaller Israel would become an insecure Israel and that the Palestinians would continue to be untrustworthy and a threat to Israel. Dr Kramer tried to allay these fears, citing the pragmatism of Israel's position. But he was generally, unsuccessful and the next few questions repeated the theme of Israel's insecurity:

Q: In Oslo I [the statement] regarding the Palestinians [was that they would gain] autonomy [and not] statehood. [Therefore] there is the basis for the nullification of all agreements because now the discussion has turned to Palestinian statehood. [Many military] generals are opposed to this agreement [saying that the] strategic answer is the only answer.

A: One can get carried away with the terminology. Remember Israel negotiated its own solutions. [To come to] people like Rabin who have created the state [and who have] made good on all of their agreements for security [and then] to refer to Oslo as though it were another Munich agreement is blasphemous. Among all generals [there will be some] disagreements [but the] generals you refer to are American generals [and those] I refer to [are the] four out of five Israeli chiefs of staff, [all of whom] support this agreement. Nothing is ever clear-cut [but] to assume you know more than these Israeli generals regarding Israeli security is foolish. Besides, on some days you say that all Americans are out to destroy Israel and on other days you quote them as our friends. Why?

Q: American security experts [say that Israel should] hold on to the territories. [Explain why we shouldn't.]

A: [There is] real ambivalence [about what] Americans have to say. [Some of] what they have to say is anti-Semitic. Don't you think Israelis know best?

Some audience members were not convinced by Dr Kramer's answers and continued to insist that the Oslo Accords would make Israel insecure, citing American generals as their sources. The geographer began to grow frustrated – the audience members were referring to outside authorities in ways that dismissed Israeli positions and integrity on these matters:

Q: [Do the] Israelis take into account [the fact that the] Palestinians of Jordan may topple King Hussein [and] take over the military? [The] Palestinians [do] form [a] majority there.

A: There is more likelihood of that happening *after* a Final Agreement, and not before. [You're right], Jordan is demographically a Palestinian state [but the] international community keeps an eye on the Palestinians [and] Hussein clamps down hard on the Palestinians, [so there is] little room for them to manoeuvre. [They] suffer in Jordan as they suffered in the West Bank. [The] military implications of any move to topple Hussein would be great. And generally speaking, Jordan is more favourable to Israel than to any Palestinians.

Q: If Arabs have written a red line in the sand, why doesn't Israel just say 'no'? [They're] getting everything they want.

A: There are different negotiations being described here than the ones I know and have been privy to. Israel has said 'no' many, many times. You just don't have a realistic perspective on these issues.

Q: Israel seeks peace and security, while the Palestinians want land and a state. What are they giving up?

A: Each side feels extraordinarily threatened by the other and yet each side continues to be surprised by the other. [The] Palestinians [are often] surprised [to hear that they are a] threat to Israel [and] they say things like we haven't got the capability to drive you out or even to get rid of you from the West Bank ... Remember, the Palestinians under Oslo get 23 per cent of what they would have had in 1948. [To them it is] a lot to give up. [This is] something we might find hard to understand.

Amazingly, the speaker was presenting the suffering not only of the Palestinians living on the West Bank but also of those living under Arab rule in Jordan. Thus, he was debunking the myth that Palestinians could identify with the Jordanian state and that they had another Arab state to go to. Also, he was presenting an alternative interpretation of what the Palestinians would gain as a result of the Oslo Accords, and in the process radically reframing the Palestinians' sense of loss as most of the audience understood it. In one answer, he had referred not to Israel and the 1967 borders but rather to the terms set in 1947–8, when the UN partitioned Palestine. He was not suggesting that the terms of the partition were now a legitimate basis for peace and reconciliation; he was, however, interpreting the Palestinians' dilemma from that perspective. This was far more radical than anything suggested by the Oslo Accords.

More than any other exchange that night, this one was the most emotional:

Q: If there had been two million Jews in the territories, would things be different?

A: Yes, the government would have to be responsible for whoever is there [because it] provided all the incentives. With all due respect, however, the two million are in the diaspora and not in Israel and if you think it is that important then it seems your answer lies in that very fact.

At this point, Dr Kramer was visibly frustrated, and his answer reflected that. He had made *aliyah,* and now he was being forced to point out to diaspora Jews who were not comfortable with an Israeli withdrawal from the Occupied Territories, basically, that they could have all the territory they desired for the state if only they would make the same commitment he had. This was a strongly Zionist argument and one that all diaspora Jews had heard before. Dr Kramer was clearly in favour of the Oslo Accords with all of their implications, and he didn't like having to defend them in front of people who were implying through their questions that Israelis did not know anything about security matters and were placing their future at risk. The geographer ended the session with this strongly emotional plea: [précis]

I want to end [by saying that] it frustrates me to find that in the diaspora there are more people against the peace agreement than even among the Israeli right wing. We may be partners but we are asymmetrical partners. It is legitimate to oppose the peace agreement but it is illegitimate to just slag the Israelis and their government. I do not mean to say that only Israelis should speak out but there is a difference. [Much of the] discourse in [this city] has gone way beyond [the bounds of reason and many] Israelis are embarrassed by the rhetoric in the diaspora. Israel is the place where over 50 per cent of the Jewish population [will eventually live] and we have to build the future around a society that has moral and ethical values. We have faced the existential crises. [But] think about what is most important for us to invest in now? ... Education, not land. [Less territory to control] may mean we have more time to devote to the Jewish people and their development, [which is] more important.

That night, Dr Kramer was presenting the Israeli state as one that was ready to move beyond its existential crises and to deal with the pragmatic concerns of everyday life. 'His' Israel was strong, secure, independent, and democratic. The coming elections would decide whether the Oslo Accords would be implemented. Israel did not need to rely on its allies for intelligence. It was deciding its own fate and ready to live in peace.

The evening ended with many of Dr Kramer's challengers approaching him for further debate. After a few more brief exchanges, his sponsors whisked him away. Many audience members still looked shaken by the presentation and continued to debate the issues among themselves as they left the hall.

The condescension and disdain expressed by diaspora Jews for Israelis and vice versa came as a surprise when I first observed it. But this reaction and counter-reaction turned out not to be so unique.

In 1997, a member of the Israeli Knesset and the daughter of one of Israel's military heroes was invited to speak as part of a year-long celebration marking one hundred years of Zionism. She gave her talk in the large lecture theatre of a Reform temple. After her talk she was confronted by a small but vocal group of people who opposed her position on the peace talks, and she was forced to defend her position vigorously. What she told us in her presentation was as radical as what she told her challengers during the question-and-answer session. I will outline the lecture portion of her talk and then examine the extraordinary question-and-answer session, during which many audience members strongly expressed their anger.

After being introduced, Shoshana Ben-Aviv took her place at the podium. She was in her mid-50s, and though slight of build, her strong, gravelly voice filled the room:

We Jews are all together. We do share a commitment and there is an ongoing connection among us, and although the topics of discussion change, we survive ... The question is no longer will there be an Israel but rather what kind of Israel will there be and what kind of dialogue can there be with the Jewish diaspora. I would like to bring us up to date ...

First I will begin with dates. Even though they are artificial, at the end of the millennium we have had one hundred years of Zionism, fifty years since Israel [was created], four years since Oslo [was signed, and] two years since the assassination of Rabin. What we are about today is about the assassination of a prime minister who tried to bring peace. But this assassin did not just assassinate the peace process, he also killed Israeli democracy ... This assassin had nothing to do with being Jewish or with being democratic but let's not say he was so marginal. We need to guard against him and people like him. Did you know that our Supreme Court judges need to be protected by bodyguards because of threats from the Orthodox? There are still lots of people who do not want the peace we are talking about. There are others like Yigal Amir, Yigal Amir supporters. But without peace and without democracy [in Israel], there is nothing to support or be proud of. And what kind of peace [do we want]? [Prime Minister Netanyahu] won the election ... But he stopped the peace, and the terror is renewed. The end of terror is never to be a precondition to peace but will be the result of peace. [Yasir] Arafat can only be strong with the support of the United States and us. He can do more the stronger he is ... I hope my government is not stupid enough to put the end of terror as a precondition. It's not a zero sum game. Bibi thinks when Arafat loses, Israel is winning. But when we win, they win. If both sides are winning there is a motivation to continue the dialogue. Otherwise, what motivation is there for the Palestinians? What kind of peace is there for the Palestinians? It is still an occupation ... seventy-five per cent of Israelis support a Palestinian state next to the State of Israel. How can we think of depriving them of this? Are we different? Are we superior? They have to buy it from us? They have a natural right like all people – they have a right to a land. The one good thing that's happened to Bibi? He's finally dealing with the end of a fantasy! There will not be a Greater Israel. There is no Likud ideology anymore. Most of the settlements are going to be left behind. We'll keep some of the settlements, and we will give the Palestinians a viable piece of land which will remove any motivation for conflict. There is nothing but despair and desperate feelings whenever another settlement and another Har Homa is built, in addition to the hunger and the closures [they suffer] ... Is that motivation ...? We don't want to live in someone else's home ... The Bible is our literature, our history, our geography, but it is not a political science diktat! ... Their ancestors are there too ... You don't go to the UN to present biblical reasons. Israel is strong not only in terms of war [and the military] but in terms of compromise. This is for us. We can't stand the immorality of the occupation. It doesn't adhere to any Jewish morality. This is the denial [to] other humans [of] their rights ... Instead of talking about the next war whether in Lebanon or Syria or against the Palestinians, Iraqis, whoever, we need to talk about the next peace. This should be presented as something of value to the world because we know what it is to be oppressed and we certainly do not want to inflict pain on others ... This strength is given to us in order to make peace not to make a place of conflict and sadness. It is in our own hands [and] we must do what is right, what is of value, of strength. We have to give up territory to get the coveted peace. When this is done with a full heart, we will do it with strength.

In this presentation, Ms Ben-Aviv managed to cross out virtually every Zionist signpost and deconstruct every Zionist myth. She presented an Israeli democracy that was threatened by an *internal* Jewish foe. She claimed that it was the strength of peace and not military strength that should hold the pride of place for Israelis. She insisted that the Palestinians were human and deserving of ethical treatment; when they were desperate or hungry, they were more likely to commit crimes, and they therefore required the Jews' support. Giving the Palestinians a state would not threaten Israel but might instead 'remove the motivation' for further conflict between the two communities. In stating that Israelis did not want to live in 'someone else's home' and that '[Palestinians'] ancestors are there too,' she was making some of the most radical public statements I was to hear during my fieldwork. Although she was recognized for her activism – especially as a feminist politician – she was not a member of any of the radical political parties in Israel. In fact, she was a member of the establishment Labour Party.

At the end of her lecture, audience members lined up behind microphones to ask questions. The room held about three hundred people, and, at first, around twenty audience members were lined up. The first question set the tone for the questions that followed. It seemed that every answer Ms Ben-Aviv gave prompted more people to line up. I have selected a number of these exchanges:[4]

Q: Why do you call this an 'occupation'? It is our land.
A: What would be your proposal? What would you do with Hebron or Gaza? Are you for annexation? Thank God even the right wing prime minister has given up on this idea. It is not ours! How many times can it be said: it is not an empty land. There are people there. They are a different people. They

have a different culture, a different language. In 1948, a lot of people questioned the right of people to self-determination. Jewishness is not only about a religion but also a nationality and Zionism was to give us a homeland ... How can we now question another people's right to a home? I don't see such a long line of people from [this city] to come. And why should you leave? I'm not saying that you should leave ... You are all big heroes [but] we just want to live! ... About the Palestinian Covenant: There is a headache about it but even Bibi has given up on it. I care what we do, not what Arafat does. Everyone is an expert these days ... But we also say terrible things including 'slaughter the Arabs.' This peace is what we want for ourselves, not for others!

Q: You are a voice of sanity and it is my pleasure to hear you speak today and I agree with you that peace is more important than real estate. But the issue is not peace or land. The Arabs have lots of land but they don't want to solve the problem. They just don't want us there. They've been waiting there in the West Bank and have had it good there for thirty years.

A: The Palestinians are not Iraqis or Saudis. They are a nation. They do not have other land. Have they ever been integrated to Jordan [or] Lebanon? It's not in our hands to give them land here or there. We have to take care of them because the situation as it is, is bad for Israel. The second part of your statement is patronizing. This racism has no place in the Jewish world. This [is an] attitude that many Israelis and Jews have that we are dealing with a primitive, uneducated people, and that they are benefiting from the occupation. There are more university graduates in the West Bank than per capita in Israel. I feel bad that I even have to say this ... My response is that they are an advanced society, an educated society, [etc.]. I will be proud to be their neighbour and share a society with them in peace.

Q: I hope you are right about the Palestinians. Remember the four girls that were killed by Palestinians because the American negotiators were on their way? And what about Hamas? They have the support of the vast majority of Palestinian Arabs and if the Palestinians get a state, and everything else, how do we protect ourselves from those who are extremists?

A: What is your answer to this? How are we going to protect ourselves? Let's say you're right. Are we going to shoot them all? Let them prove to us that they can provide security ... It is not true there is support for Hamas – it is a minority [that supports them]. And remember there is a limit to power. Not France, not even America, can control fanatic religious motivations. There is no such thing as 100 per cent prevention. We were everywhere before, for thirty years, [we were there] in order to control. We produced an *intifada*. There is a limit to this way. This limit is where the rights of the other begins.

No one can fight a guerrilla or a freedom fighter. The Palestinian cause can either motivate for peace or it can motivate others to violence. We must have a dialogue, and confidence-building ... If we weaken Arafat, how can we motivate them to fight for peace against Hamas when we have bulldozers?

Q: The amount of peace is related to the degree of our security, but if Arafat can't give us peace, why should we give him land?

A: Rabin didn't take any risks on security when it came to the Palestinians. They don't have land, nor is there any symmetry at all. This symmetry idea is ridiculous. They are all under our control in refugee camps.

At this point someone in the audience yelled, 'Who put them there?' Ms Ben-Aviv ignored the interruptions and continued:

You cannot refer to Palestinians in the same terms as you refer to the Israelis. There is a degree of exaggeration among us ... Our tendency is to perpetuate ... to see ourselves as victims. [Former prime minister] Begin did this a lot. He was part of a group that felt that there is a need for Israel because of the cohesiveness of the hatred of others. There is more to us ... than anti-Semitism. We are five-and-a-half million people in Israel. Two-and-a-half million children walk in Israel. We go to school. This paranoiac way of thinking that a Jew cannot walk in the streets [this] is not Israel ... The only solution is if we get out of this situation of occupation. No one threatens the existence of Israel.

As time began to run out, four final questions were taken together and received a joint response. Ms Ben-Aviv was asked the following (1) 'What will happen with Jerusalem?' (2) 'Why don't we hear more from enlightened Palestinians like Hanan Ashrawi?' (3) 'Why are the Palestinians demanding land and peace from us? ... They want to kick us to the sea. Why don't they ask Jordanians or Egyptians for a state? They just don't want us there, period.' (4) 'Netanyahu has taken the position that he wants Arafat to fight terror. This seems reasonable and it is part of Oslo. If you don't accept at least that, then what is peace? Of what value are those Palestinian commitments to Oslo?' Ben-Aviv responded to these questions:

[About Jerusalem.] There is a consensus among all the Israeli and Zionist parties that the annexation of East Jerusalem will continue although there are differences as to the status of the people there. They are a total of 200,000 people who live there. We can annex their land but not the people. There is a difference between annexation and confiscation and giving them their citizens' rights. We made them Israelis but we did not let them have building permits, no schools, and in a populated space, this is a temptation to evil. The negotiations will continue. No country in the world accepts this annexation of proper East Jerusalem and the 200,000 who live there ... The Palestinian capital is all part of the final agreement and it is negotiable. I hope we will be creative enough to find the solution to this.

[About other Palestinian speakers.] I don't know who you get to meet. There is Nabil Sha'ath. I've appeared with Hanan and there is no question that we speak with the same passion. Faisel Husseini too or Abu Mazen and any of these leaders would be good. We come together [and] there are some technical differences, but the passion with which we talk about the prospect of a two-state solution, and attitudes to Hamas, and attitudes to terror, are all the same. I would be delighted to bring the other side with me. I find I have to speak on their behalf but they can speak for themselves. It is not necessary that I do so.

[The Palestinians just want to get rid of us.] There are some who want to get rid of us, but we don't need the Palestinians for it. There is the entire Arab world against us. You think the Egyptians love us? ... There was never a war with the Palestinians.

A person yelled out: 'So what?' She answered:

So what? So we can go back in time or we can go forward. They know that by war you will not get rid of the Jews. They tried and they failed. You think Sadat fell in love with us? They couldn't beat us, that is all.

There was loud applause to this point. She waited for it end:

It is the same case with Asad, and the same with Arafat. The worst off of all the Arabs were the Palestinians and they had to count on other Arab countries that kept saying, 'Just wait.' Egyptians, Hussein, Saudis, Iraqis, and so on, all said this and the Palestinians waited and they finally came to terms with the reality that no one but Israel could give peace to them, and only by negotiating with Israel could there be peace ... Remember, there are also Jews who advocate transfer of a whole people from where they are across to Jordan.

[About Oslo.] We have weakened [Arafat] and we have to understand his power is limited. If we punish him it lowers his ability to control anything at all and renews [support] for Hamas. The Palestinians do not support Hamas but if we say in advance that they're not getting peace or land, then they have nothing to lose; too many people have nothing to lose ... Even the doves are not stupid people. It's *our* children, it's not only the right wing's children. If I thought for one minute that stronger demands from Arafat would save children's lives ... But the distortion of it is the problem and it is the opposite of what you say. When the Zionist Organization of America prints pictures of children injured by terrorist bombs, it is just pornographic and it is a means to incitement, especially when they write: 'Arafat supports terrorists' above the pictures. That's just what I need! Believe me, Arafat is under pressure. And this kind of support we get from American Jewry! You know all the questions that were asked here tonight were in the *New York Times* today. All of them asked today were about the covenant. Those who are for the peace, let your voice be heard.

At the end of this tense evening, Ms Ben-Aviv received only luke-warm applause. It was obvious that she had upset quite a few people in the packed hall. After the presentation, I met with a number of people whom I had come to know in the community. They all seemed some-what shocked by Ms Ben-Aviv's talk. I thought for a long time after this session about something that an Israeli artist had told me in 1999: Her preference was to call diaspora Jews simply 'Jews,' and Israelis Jews simply 'Israelis.' 'We are different,' she insisted. 'We live our lives very differently. We always have and we always will. Why would you call us Jews? We are Israelis. *They* are Jews.'

These examples reflect the typical responses that North American audiences made to Israelis who talked about the Peace Accords. How-ever, the positions these speakers took hardly reflected those of all Israelis. Some Israelis would have agreed with and argued from the same positions as the audiences took (I witnessed this on the tours). That said, most of the people I came to know in the communities as well as on the tours seemed interested in events very much like these and not other ones.

For mainstream Jews in the communities that I studied, the Peace Accords were among these most contentious of issues. The same ques-tions arose over and over again at each and every discussion of the issue. Even pro-peace community meetings, such as those sponsored by Peace Now, prompted the same kinds of questions – and, interestingly enough, similar responses from spokespeople. The audience members were most concerned about military security, trust and confidence in their peace partners, and the future of Israel as a Jewish state. At each session, I was surprised at the passion and vehemence with which audience members confronted the Israelis. From the way so many people had idealized Israelis in our discussions, I expected to see greater deference and respect.

But it was only during the discussions about peace that the Israelis challenged their diaspora audiences, not only with respect to their views on the peace process, but also with respect to their location in North America. That is, they took every opportunity to challenge diaspora Jews to make *aliyah*, asserting that one should become an Israeli if one wanted to fully and legitimately participate in the peace process. Also, the presentations about the peace agreements were very different from any other presentations about Israel because they humanized the Palestinians by describing and sometimes even explaining their position with some degree of empathy. Only during these presentations were Arabs discussed as people with histories, communities, and identities, and with political and humanistic rather than atavistic motives for their actions.

In 1997 a prominent Conservative rabbi presented his reflections on the success of Zionism, which he called a 'revolutionary' movement. The nature of this discussion was significant for it pointed to what I call the 'negation of the negation of diaspora.' Zionism assumed that the establishment of a state for the Jews would 'negate the diaspora' – that is, Jews would no longer have to live as a diaspora community because they would have their own nation-state. Their lives would become normalized once they became nationals within that state. Zionists assumed that this process of normalization would occur within the State of Israel. But how do diaspora Jews perceive the effects of Israel on Jews living outside the state? Have the grounds of identity shifted in ways that neither the classical political Zionists, nor those who founded and established Israel, such as David Ben-Gurion, could have predicted?

On the occasion of one hundred years of Zionism, Rabbi Greenfield was invited to speak at a Reform temple in a large city. The rabbi was also a Jewish historian and scholar. The meeting was very well attended. After a long introduction, the guest lecturer took the podium, where he began by telling his audience that 'there is a vast difference between those who study the text one hundred times and those who study it one hundred and one times.' He had studied Zionism for a very long time, yet he had discovered only very recently that he had been living under the 'delusion' that he actually knew what Zionism meant. He now realized that he needed to rethink his assessments of the movement. He claimed that he was 'on a journey' to gain a better understanding of 'the greatest of revolutions.'

Rabbi Greenfield asked the audience to reassess Zionism from the perspective of someone living in the 1890s. In that era, Jews had believed that 'anti-Semites were the hooligans' and that modernity would bring an end to anti-Semitism. But, he explained, it was 'the intelligentsia' who did not 'speak up against anti-Semitism ... There was no word from Tolstoy or Dostoyevsky' because all they really wanted at the time was to get rid of the Tsar of Russia. He then cited political philosopher Hannah Arendt's contention that the rise of totalitarianism, and Nazism in particular, was due to the intelligentsia's growing anti-Semitism, 'because suddenly Jews were bidding for roles in gentile society ... Nineteenth-century anti-Semitism was not directed at the Jews who were peasants but rather at the intelligentsia among the Jews.' Thus, according to the rabbi, 'Zionism arrive[d] out of a situation in which the Jewish intelligentsia [lost] hope.' The Jews were left with only two 'solutions.' One was the Bundist party, an anti-Zionist party which argued that in order for Jews to escape the situation they were in, they would have to 'radically change the system.' The other was the political Zionism articulated by Theodore Herzl, who was quoted by the rabbi as saying that 'where we are everywhere powerless, we must evacuate the Western world – we must cease being a powerless people.' The rabbi declared that the greatest success of the Zionist revolution was that the holiest place in the world was no longer the Western Wall in Jerusalem:

> Yes, I go [to the *kotel*] but I get tearful every time I walk from Ben-Gurion airport to the desk where I have to present my passport. It is the one place in the world where someone can't say, 'We don't need anymore Jews' ... Herzl knew that we could not leave the lives of other Jews in others' hands. So the customs shed in Tel Aviv is the place I cry for all those who did not have the fate to get there. That is the towering achievement in Herzlian terms ... The second achievement of Zionism is that it changed the way we stand. We no longer stand as the poor man at the door asking for favours ... The contemporary Jewish community thinks and acts not as victims but as victors, and not only in relationship to

Israel ... One of the two things that modern Zionism did was to end the otherness of the Jews.

He suggested there have been two monumental achievements that Herzl, Zionism's political founder, would himself be proud of: that there was now a safe haven for all Jews; and that as a result, all Jews now had a sense of power and pride. Moreover, because of Zionism's success there was now a role for those Jews living outside the State of Israel: diaspora Jews were the holders of tradition. In fact, it was these Jews who had restored Jewish tradition to a secularized Israeli state:

> Zionism was created by those who revolted against the Jewish past and Judaism. There were no kosher hotels in the 1950s [in Israel]. Now the hotels in Israel have become kosher because *we* come there ... The Israelis created a different culture ... The counterattack [to Israeli secularism] began in the 1960s as some claimed that this secularism had gone over-board. They decided they needed more Jewish culture and tradition ... Remember [Prime Minister] Rabin's funeral? How his son was breaking his teeth on Kaddish when he had to read the Aramaic ... He had clearly never been to synagogue. The embarrassment was too great. There is a sense that in Israel the Jewish people have been secularized – they are 'goyim [non-Jews] who speak Hebrew' ... There is a profound sense now that we cannot continue by breaking with the past but by reshaping and linking ourselves again to it.

In this way, the rabbi was inverting one of the tenets of Zionism (i.e., the rejection of life in diaspora) and suggesting that under Zionism, it was easier to lead an authentically Jewish life outside the State of Israel. He was accusing Israel's founders, in their efforts to break with the Jews' diasporic past, of going 'too far' by rejecting Judaism's roots and traditions in favour of a secular state. The rabbi's reflections were another example of a fundamental shift in perspectives, from Zionist to what I would consider one of a range of post-Zionist positionings.

In sum, the community events seemed to orient diaspora Jews to Israel in a number of ways. The historical narratives placed the Jews as a nation in the land of Israel. Many of the themes I had heard on the tours of Israel were repeated in the community. Some felt that Judaism had an important role to play in normalizing the Jewish state; others were troubled by the relationship between secular and religious authorities. Many Israeli speakers presented political agreements signed by Israel and the Palestinians as hopeful signs for peace in the Middle East. Interestingly, it was diaspora Jews who mistrusted the Arabs and Palestinians the most, and who feared that the Israelis were placing themselves in grave danger. Their concern was for the security of the Jews rather than for the territory itself, except insofar as occupying it might provide Israel with strategic security.

10

Narrating Relations for Diaspora

Anthropologist Pnina Werbner's definition of diaspora as a matter of 'co-responsibility' proves useful for understanding diaspora Jews. Studying Pakistani and Muslim migrant workers, her 'argument begins from a definition that seeks to retain a prior emphasis on the compelling nature of the obligations "diasporans" feel across space and national boundary.'[1] Her description of diaspora communities is based on an interpretation of them as 'communities of co-responsibility, recognising not simply their loyalty but their existential connection to co-diasporans elsewhere, or in a home country ... This sense of co-responsibility is expressed in tangible material gestures of charitable giving and complex forms of political mobilisation.'[2] She suggests also that in public arenas, moral and political subjectivities are formed so that 'ethnicity and nationalism emerge dialectically from a reworking and transcendence of local disputes ... and in the local negotiation of shared symbols.'[3]

Speaking at a Reform temple in the latter half of the 1990s, Jewish historian Harold Troper framed the changing relationships of Jews to Israel as corresponding to three periods. According to him, during 'the classical Zionist era' there was a great deal of support and pride in Israel's achievements. The second period, 1967 to 1982, was distinguished by the Jewish community's response to the Six Day War of 1967. Diaspora Jews celebrated Israel's victory, and Jewish community organizations began major fundraising campaigns for projects throughout Israel. Any criticism of Israel by non-Jews was characterized as anti-Semitism; Jews who uttered the same criticisms were accused of self-hatred.

The 1982 Israeli war with Lebanon, the continuing conflict with the

Palestinians, the beginnings of the 'who is a Jew' debate, and various other events and issues have all helped shift the perspectives of diaspora Jews vis-à-vis the Israeli state. A new, third era of 'fragmentation' has been ushered in. For example, Israeli peace groups like Peace Now and *Yesh Gvul* (There Is a Limit) have publicly and massively demonstrated dissent, and as a result, diaspora Jews have been forced to take notice. Many have shifted their perspectives. Troper suggests that the new generation of Jews (Jewish youth in particular) may no longer be ready to support Israel. He explains that this group is temporally removed from the crises of the Second World War and the formative years of Israel as a state struggling to survive. Moreover, not all of them have endured the anti-Semitism that their parents or grandparents experienced.[4]

The profiles I offer of diaspora Jews reflect Werbner and Troper's position. The first three profiles of Jews in diaspora – Myrna, Warren and Sarah, and Aaron – are of Jews who have identified with Israel since the founding of the state and who had visited Israel more than once. The second group of Jews in diaspora – Marlene, Lynn, Karen, and Paul – celebrated and identified with Israel's post-1967 idealism. As a result of their parents' or their community's activism, they developed a relationship with Israel by visiting it soon after 1967 and since then as well.

A third group of Diaspora Jews – Ozzy, Josie, Gillian, Hope, Ian, and Samantha – who have only recently come to know Israel (i.e., in the last decade or so) are also interesting. The first two groups of people tended to be from successive generations, whereas the last was mixed young and old. When all three groups are read together, the kaleidoscope of positions and experiences can be seen to reflect the diverse perspectives I encountered during my research but importantly, not in the context of the violence that interrupted in 2000.

These profiles do not present the stories of all the people I met during my research, but as a whole, they constitute a representation sample of diaspora Jews and their relationships to Israel. They offer a rich collage of the diversity of views, 'poached' narratives and complex creations and identifications with the nation and the state.[5] All are narratives of co-responsibility.

11
Longings

Myrna, Warren and Sarah, and Aaron all experienced Israel in its founding years. Each now identifies with and feels attached to Israel. Their personal experiences of anti-Semitism and the Second World War form the background for this relationship. All of these people had travelled to Israel at least once before I met them.

Myrna

Myrna has had a long-term relationship with Israel and Israel-related issues. In her late eighties, she was very keen to participate in my research. After only a few days on tour, she invited me to her hotel room, where she was taking an afternoon nap after a long and uncomfortable flight to Israel. She propped herself against some pillows, stretched out on her bed, and asked me to sit beside her in an upholstered chair. She then proceeded to hold my attention for almost three hours.

Myrna was born on the Lower East Side of New York City to Russian immigrants at the beginning of the last century. She described her early life:

> We were really very poor, we never had a telephone ... nothing except a newspaper to tell you what was going on in the world ... and we never went anyplace or did anything or never even left the neighbourhood for many, many years. I felt protected. It was 60 per cent of it Italian and 40 per cent Jewish.

Her parents were practising Orthodox Jews, against whom she

rebelled. She 'didn't believe in God' and when she had her own family she 'kind of dropped the ritual altogether although [they] kept the holidays and knew what it was all about. Secular is the word.'

Myrna earned a state university scholarship, graduated in January 1931, and became a social worker. Her siblings also completed postsecondary education. All of them stayed in their home neighbourhood until they found full-time jobs and married. Myrna had since lived in a number of American states, including California and Michigan.

Myrna recalled how Israel had not at all been part of her Orthodox Jewish upbringing: 'All I knew about Israel in the twenties and thirties was that we had ... a couple of *pushkas* [boxes to collect money for Israel] in the house ... and my mother would occasionally put pennies in it. They didn't get very much from us but that's what Israel was – it was a place where the *pushka* money went to. We didn't have much interest in it at all.' She explained how Israel became part of her consciousness:

> I began to have an interest after the Second World War [when] the Jews from Germany, [and] Europe began to go [there]. Then I realized that was the solution and if Israel had existed beforehand, this never would have happened ... I understand at some point Hitler offered to let the Jews out for money, [but] there was no place for them to go. So the importance of Israel became very real at that time and subsequently, when the Jews ... started going, [Israel] became the most important thing in my life.

I met Myrna on her fifth trip to Israel. Her first had been in the fall of 1959; a group interested in developing Israel's social welfare had recruited her:

> I had come with a great interest in Israel and ... left with the most extravagant admiration for the society and tremendous emotional commitment. Great, great love, great enthusiasm and such pride, such pride. I was so glad to be a Jew ... Their perceptions, their honesty, their decency, the struggle that they showed ... It was, to me, an experience I've never gotten over, never forgotten and never will. I've been dedicated to Israel ever since ... The guide was ... a young Sabra, a man, a little bit crude and coarse in his appearance but so strong in his understanding, so strong in the way he presented himself and so firm about his knowledge and convictions that I just couldn't believe it. I was so proud of him. He knew everything and he had been in the army and here he was talking about

the history that comes from the Bible. In other words, he was the best-informed person I have ever in my life met.

After 1959, she returned to Israel with her spouse for a few professional meetings and to see old friends. But, she told me, 'largely we had travelled as tourists.' Before the tour we travelled on together in 1996, her last trip to Israel had been in the early 1980s.

Myrna's commitments to Israel encompassed the unconventional. She gleefully described a moment on her visit in the early 1970s. In this story she played with one of the most significant Zionist markers: Israel is the place where Jews are everywhere doing everything:

We came to Tel Aviv and stayed there ... and we stayed on the beach in a very shabby hotel; it was shabby and inexpensive ... but that was fun because it was so casual ... It was interesting. We met a darling, darling young man ... He took our bags in ... and he and I exchanged glances and immediately I liked him and he smiled to me; he must have been about twenty. [He was] quite dark, [and] Semitic-looking. And then, we asked for water and he brought up the water and then ... the toilet was broken, so he came up and fixed the toilet and by this time we were [all] laughing ... And I was so [happy, thinking], 'Gee, it's so nice to have a Jewish boy like this' and so on. I said 'What is your name?' He said 'Mohammed'! But we stayed good friends and when we left, he kissed me. It was a charming thing.

Later, she said:

I think I told you this, [I was so proud because] everybody here was Jewish. That's why when the little boy said 'Mohammed' it was so funny. I laughed. But the first time [when] I saw people cleaning the streets, they were Jews; the policemen were Jews ... Everything. It's the only place, [and it was] the first time in my life that I felt anybody who disliked me it won't be because I'm Jewish ... Because ... I've lived under a cloud of anti-Semitism all my life.

Myrna, while playing with the 'everybody in Israel is Jewish' line, expressed her deep feelings of security and happiness at finding herself in the only state she believed could be truly free of anti-Semitism. In this way she was also signalling early in our conversation that she knew non-Jews lived and worked in Israel and that they were all around her.

Myrna had considered living in Israel 'many times' but most especially after her first visit, when she realized that in Israel 'nobody can be anti-Semitic to me anymore ... Everybody's Jewish ... [It's] so wonderful to be free of anti-Semitism.' For family and other pragmatic reasons, however, she never left the United States to live in Israel.

Myrna had long been a supporter, and board member, of such groups as the American Civil Liberties Union; however, she did not like supporting Jewish organizations, preferring to support groups that were 'more needy.' Although she had supported Israel all her life, she had never identified with or supported any Israeli funding organizations until very recently. The Israel Civil Society Fund (ICSF), which was sponsoring the tour we were on, was the first Jewish organization she felt she could support. She developed this commitment after meeting speakers at an ICSF-sponsored community event:

> [The speaker] told me ... that being a Jew or being anybody, but especially a Jew, social justice is the most important thing in the world. I think that society is a conspiracy against the poor. And nobody cares about the poor ... You don't have to have been poor like I was in order to know what poverty does to people but it helps ... I knew what it was like to be poor just as I knew what it was like to be Jewish ... That's why I was always in favour of ... equality and social justice. [And this organization] just fit into my life. It's just what I've been looking for. [This was] a way of helping Israel ... I love Israel, I would die for Israel, but I want Israel to be good, to be a wonderful country and this is my way of chipping in.

In our conversations about the Oslo Accords, Myrna reflected first on how the Israeli government, then led by Benjamin Netanyahu, was stalling the process. After that she talked about the Israeli 'extremists,' who in her view were preventing the accords from being implemented. She expressed some frustration about the entire situation, exclaiming at one point: 'I hate the people that are destroying the character that I think Jews should display.'

Throughout our discussion, Myrna talked about Israel not as a unique nation-state but as one in the family of nations: 'I think that we're going to have to take our place with every other country and just be a country and try to be the best country we can, but it will never be without troubles.' Soon after, she spoke of wanting 'a country that tries to make equality where people got enough to live on.' Reflecting on the post-Rabin era, she said that 'people kill one another for no cause' because this is the 'nature of man.' Then she warned: 'I don't see us being wiped out [because we're Jews]. I think we'll kill ourselves before Israel's wiped out.' But when I asked her if Israel was just like any other state, she reacted quite strongly: '*No* ... Israel, to me, it's special – not like anything else. I don't like any other state like I love Israel.' When I asked if she felt this way because she is Jewish, she was emphatic: '*Yes* I'd like to see anything that strengthens Israel's existence and I certainly think Jews owe it to Israel. Jews all over the world owe it to Israel. They saved us. They saved us and I don't want the Jewish presence in the world to be diminished in any way.' I asked her what she meant when she said that Israel had 'saved' the Jews:

Well what would have happened to the Jews if there was no Israel? That's changed the whole world ... It gave Jews all over the world a prominence and a presence and an identity which made them more viable. I think that Jews without a country were at a great disadvantage ... I think that we were people in the air, *Luftmenschen*, and now ... there's a place where we can be proud and happy and good and comfortable and decent and successful. [It] is a great boon to all the Jews in the world and I like to see anything that would make it better and stronger.

Myrna's position was close to Rabbi Greenfield's: Zionism had liberated all Jews, not just those living in Israel. I asked her whether travelling to Israel gave North American Jews 'a better sense of themselves as Jews':

Absolutely. Absolutely ... that's why I'd like to see the country perfect ... You know Jews have always been at a disadvantage. They do good and there are suspicions about them – they're wicked, they hurt people, they take money away from blacks, and so on and so forth. I'd like to see a proud, functioning, successful country that – not that it won't have problems – but that it will deal with the problems in ... an intelligent and righteous way, make a great contribution to the world which is certainly likely and everybody will be proud. I feel a different person now that there's an Israel. Not only that I could come here but that it's here and I'm proud to be a Jew. I always was but now ... I have a real concrete commitment to my Jewishness.

Anti-Semitism had obviously affected Myrna's life, so that the founding of Israel had changed her life. She spoke about the founding of the State of Israel at every turn and in many different contexts. She placed Israel at the centre, believing that its success accounted for the changing perspectives about Jews, both within and outside the Jewish community.

According to Myrna, a social worker and activist with liberal views, one could distinguish Israel's military forces from those of other states, and one could even be proud of their accomplishments. About the Israeli Defense Forces (IDF) she had this to say:

I always hated armies but [when I met with a general in 1959, I thought] the Israeli army was so wonderful, so democratic, and ... my impression was that it was the most constructive organization in the country. To think that ... no army could do what this army did. It ties people together. It made the nation. It educated. It took everybody who came in, including the African Jews [e.g., Moroccan, Yemenite] at that time. And the story is ... they didn't know how to use a toilet or anything and sent them out polished, educated, sophisticated in some way of making a living, and healthy, and Israeli. They came here stumbling and bumbling and having lived in a primitive life and suddenly they became Israeli citizens. It was the only educational opportunity these people ever had and they got a wonderful education. So I found myself cheering for this wonderful army. It was so different from what an army meant to me in the United States. In the United States [the army] was the dregs and they never did anything like educate them for good and ... so [the IDF] was the civilizing experience for these young people. So when I talked about the [Israeli] army, when I talked about Israel, I talked about everything they were doing right. You think the Jews are smart? Yes they are. And you know what they're doing with these unbelievable problems they have? Wonderful things. They think just the right way and they're doing the right thing. So ... with their intelligence and with their suffering, with their energy and their willingness to work like dogs, [and] to do their own thing – it was just what I thought the world ought to be. You know, you had an ideal new world. Turned out they're just like everybody else but better, on a higher level ... Adversity does that. It was being at the bottom of the well that made them strong and determined and brought out the best in them. They were not as exploitative as they could be later. I think part of that is that they were a more socialist society.

Following her own definition of Zionism, Myrna envisioned Israel as a socialist state with its own 'people's army.' Her Orientalist perspective reflected a familiar theme: Israel had 'enlightened' those Jews who had immigrated from the African nations. She also believed that Israel had once been a socialist state and that while it was, it had been fairer and less exploitative of its people. This was all part of Israel's attraction for Myrna, a highly motivated woman whose self-identity was linked to her belief that all Jews were committed to social justice. Israel, for her, was the model for what Jews could accomplish. As importantly, Israeli Jews were now safe from anti-Semitism and could begin to realize their own ideals. They were smart, powerful, and independent. But the Israel she had first known had changed. She showed an awareness of the more complex realities, when she alluded to the 'exploitation' of Palestinian and foreign labourers on Israel's farms and in its factories. Her idealism about Israel had been tarnished by this awareness.

I asked Myrna if her views about the Arabs had changed over time. She admitted that she did not know very much about them except that they were a threat to Israel: 'I didn't know how many there were, or I knew that the Grand Mufti was a friend of Hitler's. You know, he was in favour of Hitler and so on, and I knew there was great danger but I didn't know anything about their state ... It didn't have cogency ... for me.' Later, she reflected on the Oslo Accords:

> I think it's probably the success of Israel [that led to the accords]. It made the Arabs feel also that there was something there for them. If they could come to terms with Israel, their lives would be better. Of course in the meantime I think the Jews exploited them, used them as slave labour and controlled their lives for the benefit of private enterprises in this country and that troubles me very much.

Again, Myrna was identifying with Israel's successes, which she believed were critical to understanding why new relationships had developed between Israel and the Arabs. This identification shaped her assumption that the Arabs wanted something from, or a relationship to, Israel – that they too perceived Israel as a modern state that they would want to be part of. Yet she also recognized that the Jews' exploitation of the Arabs contradicted the very modes of redistribution and sharing of wealth implicit in the socialist ideals of the Israeli state. So it was interesting that even though she seemed aware of the economic exploitation of Palestinians in Israel, she never referred to the effects of militarism on this population – or indeed, on the Palestinians living in the Occupied Territories.

Throughout our discussion, Myrna exclaimed: 'I love talking about being Jewish, and I love Israel!' She would repeat this in many of our later conversations.

Warren and Sarah

I met Warren and Sarah on the Jerusalem 3000 tour of 1995. It was their second trip to Israel. Their first had been in the mid-1970s. After our tour together, I would meet them at community events. Several times they invited me over for lunch.

Warren and Sarah are retired. Both are still active in community and leisure activities. Warren writes letters to local and national newspapers as well as articles about social issues. He also maintains an active Internet listserv. Sarah golfs and paints watercolour landscapes. The two of them spend every winter in Florida. He was a trade union politician, she was an educator. Warren was raised in an Orthodox family; he rebelled in his youth and as part of this rebellion became an anti-Zionist. Sarah was raised by communist and atheist parents who had not belonged to any synagogue. They have two daughters and two sons, all of them successful now and living far from their parents.

When reflecting on their relationship to Judaism, Warren and Sarah recounted a time when they had to found a Reform temple because they did not want to attend Orthodox or Conservative services. Sarah became quite involved in Jewish education at the temple; even so, 'Israel didn't play a big role for us. I didn't know anything about Israel and I don't think there was anything on the curriculum for those early years.' In those years, Reform Judaism 'wasn't acceptable' to the Jewish religious authorities in the community, so the congregation had to meet in church basements. Warren recalled: 'A lot of my feelings about Jews ... and Jewish community life [are negative] because of the way they treated a lot of Reform people, and I have some negative feelings also about Israel now because of that. It goes back a long time.' Warren told me that despite their attempts to educate their children within the Reform movement, 'none of them feel [Jewish]' although they have asserted that identity by having their boys circumcised and by celebrating the Passover Seder.

When I asked them how their perspectives on Israel had evolved, each had a different story to tell. Warren had been

anti-Zionist at one time ... when I was very, very young ... When I could think about what Nazism [and] Fascism meant to me I equated it with

that. Nationalism and socialism to me was a very ugly thing, and I guess I
had some of the ideals [about] world government, the world unity. I saw
Zionism as the antithesis to that at one time. I don't have that same feeling
now except I do feel that the [Orthodox and nationalist] extremists [now
in Israel] represent that to me. They're Nazis.

I asked him what had changed his feelings about Zionism. He said
he had once been a 'one-world idealist' and had come only later to see
Israel as a pragmatic answer to the Jews' situation. He said of this
pragmatism: '[We needed] to have a homeland for the Jews after what
they'd gone through ... We lost a lot of my family, mainly from my
father's side, in the Holocaust, and [from] my own personal experiences with anti-Semitism in this country, [which had been] very
strong.' A significant element of Warren and Sarah's identification
with Israel was the Holocaust and its aftermath: the Jews needed a safe
haven.

Sarah became a Zionist only after a 'dear friend' of hers made *aliyah*.
For many years she had ignored her friend's advice to join groups like
Pioneer Women. Sarah had joined B'nai B'rith when she was young,
but she had avoided other Jewish organizations:

I just didn't have a feeling for Israel until war broke out and what we
knew of what was going in Nazi Germany and Austria and them killing
Jews right and left ... And then I read *Exodus*, Leon Uris's book, and then I
realised it: I'm a Jew and my family's Jewish and I have some kinship
with all these Jews that were killed and tried to flee, [who tried to] save
themselves. We really need a homeland, we really need some place of refuge, a place to go to, to call our own. That was when I ... started to give to
the Hadassah and other [Jewish] organizations ... So that became important to me. I realized that we needed homeland, we needed somewhere
where our people could go to when they weren't welcome anywhere else.
Not only were they not welcome anywhere else at the time, they were
being killed just because they were born Jewish. So that's when I became
interested in Israel. I still believe that we need an Israel, we need that
country badly and we need to support it.

While I was listening to Sarah, I noticed that she had an interesting
way of shifting her descriptions from 'they' and 'them' to 'we' and 'us'
when describing Israelis and Jews. Myrna had done the same. And yet
both had described the Jews' need for a home and a homeland, on the
basis of Jewish kinship and collective responsibility.

Warren and Sarah made their first trip to Israel in 1975. Sarah described one of their strongest memories of that journey – their visit to the Diaspora Museum in Tel Aviv. It had inspired Sarah to get 'in touch with my roots ... I found I was reading the Bible after that and reading books on Jewish history. It created a strong interest. If I hadn't gone to Israel, I don't think I would have felt that interest.' The first tour had given them 'a real feeling about what Israel was all about ... Like the history and the sites we visited which we didn't want to let go [of], like Masada ... And [it all] told us a lot about Israel.'

Warren and Sarah were attracted to the ILF tour that we participated on together in part because it was meant as a celebration of Jerusalem's three-thousandth anniversary. This tour 'brought back many memories' about their first trip; even so, they were 'astounded [with] the changes in Israel and it was like a wonderland to us. Some wonderful things that the country has done ... We were just thrilled to be there and [we felt] like we were part of it':

WARREN: It's multifaceted.
SARAH: It's a bustling, energetic country full of people who are –
WARREN: Creative energy is words that come to my mind. There's a lot of that creativity.
SARAH: A lot of high-energy activity, a lot of innovation.
WARREN: A lot of creativity.
SARAH: We went to the farms and saw [the] experimental work that they are doing. It was astounding. There is so much high energy, brainy people there. That's why it's for young people. It's a country for young people.
WARREN: Something that's very unique about Israel is the people who are making Israel what it is.

Their strongest memories were tied to two sites. Warren said that on the first tour, he and Sarah had been

moved ... most by the Masada experience ... It's not just the physical thing about the Masada but the story about ... how people ... tried to save themselves and defend themselves. ... What they had done to preserve their lives and their faith and their freedom, that is enormously impressive ... That they fought so hard to create this ... gives the lie to the idea that they killed themselves ... I can't believe they committed suicide. That I don't believe.

Sarah preferred the more common interpretation of Masada: 'They didn't want to give their enemy [the] satisfaction of killing them or making them into slaves.' But Warren insisted: 'They would have fought to their death.'

Sarah then described their second-strongest memory from their first tour, their visit to Megiddo, 'the site where Armageddon ... was going to be':

> We saw the cotton fields planted there and so on and that [is] where they believe ... there will be a great conflict or a war, that will be where [Armageddon] will be, and that will be the time in which we will have the Messiah come. Now I don't know that, [but] I couldn't believe that cotton was growing [there]. I mean, we always think of cotton growing in the Deep South of the United States, right? And you expect to see black women and children picking the cotton. We saw machines harvesting the cotton and then we found out afterwards ... on our second trip that they are irrigating. Oh, you heard him, the guide telling us how they irrigate the cotton fields and other fields with purified sewage water. Remember?

Here Sarah was naming the site in terms of its biblical significance and – presumably following the tour guide's presentation – describing it in the context of Zionist development narratives. The area she was discussing is in the Hula Valley, which on all of the tours was described as unproductive marshland prior to the Jews' arrival. Interestingly she had forgotten that our tour guide had also noted the environmental damage caused by the same cotton fields.

Warren was 'greatly impressed' by

> the building, [and] reconstructing the face of the earth. [For example,] what the Israelis are doing there in the desert. [It] is the basis of a new technological revolution. [And] if you can do what they're doing there and transfer that technology to other countries in the world, it means that more people can survive and not die of starvation ... There are possibilities of feeding more people, just because of what they're doing ... transforming Israel. It's a transformation of a whole world and they're dealing with the problem of starvation and poverty. So it's not just there for the Israelis – the Arabs and other countries maybe can benefit from this ...

Warren and Sarah revelled in Israel's development, especially in the Negev. Warren rejoiced in the Jews' accomplishments. He also emphasized the potential for these developments to foster peaceful relations with non-Jews. Sarah was less optimistic, believing that these technologies could also be the root of the Arabs' resentment toward Israel: 'I can just picture them, the people looking down on Israel from the Golan Heights, and looking at all these rich fields and wonderful pasture land, and then they look at their own land and say "Well, why not us? Why can't it be for us?"' Perhaps Sarah had only been exposed to tour narratives and popular or community narratives. That being so, she could not have known that until the closure policies were established in the mid to late 1990s the West Bank had been growing a great deal of the agricultural produce for Israel, or that the Syrians and Jordanians were highly productive farmers in their own right. It seems that few of the Jews I spoke to remembered that the entire area is often referred to as 'the Fertile Crescent.'

It left 'a big impression' on Warren that 'there was a city with nobody living there ... It was in between Jerusalem and Tel Aviv ... How they put that all together ... Fantastic.' I explained that the place he was describing was called Ma'ale Adumim and that it was one of the controversial Israeli settlements built in the Occupied Territories. Both Sarah and Warren were quite taken aback with this. In disbelief, they exclaimed: 'There's a whole city? ... Wow.' Sarah naively asked me: 'Didn't they know that when they were building it?' Warren groaned: 'A whole lot of work ... and money gone into it.' They were also surprised to hear that the area had been settled under the Labour government; at the time of our tour that party had purportedly been against the building of new settlements.

I later checked my field notes and transcripts to see what we had been told about Ma'ale Adumim on our tour. Avi, the general who had assisted our tour guide, had described the area: 'Look how a new city is being built ... One year ago, this was nothing. If you come back five years from now, it will be a beautiful city ... The Green Line was one kilometre from here. This mountain was Jordanian between 1948 and 1967. It is very, very expensive land here.' Unless one listened very carefully, it would have been easy to assume that Ma'ale Adumin was part of Israel proper. In fact, that land had been part of the Occupied Territories since 1967.

I asked Sarah and Warren how they felt about the tour and our guides. Both of them appreciated Avi sharing his military knowledge. Warren felt that Avi had given him 'useful' and 'valuable' information as well as

some insights ... when we went to look at the Golan Heights ... You know, when I saw that, that gave me a pessimistic view about the possibilities of peace in Israel. How the hell can that Golan Heights problem really be solved? ... From the defence standpoint, I don't see how the Israelis can give it up. [When] we were standing up looking down onto the Syrian encampments ... in the distance, [Avi] said ... it was a very short distance from there to Syrian bases.

Sarah added: 'It almost looked like a stone's throw.' I asked Warren to explain why he felt so pessimistic and whether this was due to Avi's framing of the conflict. Warren nodded 'yes':

But [it is] also the space, the geography ... I had a view of it on the ground ... I couldn't see how that issue could be resolved. In fact my view of it now ... is that it couldn't be resolved without having ... the United Nations or somebody occupy that ground and to make it like international ground[1] so it doesn't belong to either Syria or Israel ... maybe to neutralize it in some way. Because to have it occupied by the Syrians would be a threat to Israel, [and] having it occupied by Israel, I think the Syrians will see it legitimately as a threat to them ... So it gives you a somewhat pessimistic view, together with the other things about the whole politics of the region.

As if to soften Warren's 'pessimism,' Sarah interjected with a heroic description of Israel:

Except that they've done ... such miracles with that land up until now. The Israelis, I think, can accomplish anything they want to. Yes, I think [peace and peace in that area] can be accomplished. I'm not a strategist and I don't even know how they accomplish what they've already done ... I think what they've done is a miracle so they can create another miracle.

Warren replied ruefully: '[But] they can't even get themselves out of Lebanon.[2] Even if they wanted to, they can't. And Lebanon and Hezbollah is tied in with Syria ... The Lebanese have a real problem. How can [they] escape Syrian domination? It isn't just Jews against Arabs. It's a complicated situation.'

Warren had accepted some of the finer points of Israel's conflict with Lebanon much as they had been presented on tour. Thus, he was now tying the Lebanese conflict directly to Israel's conflict with Syria. In contrast, Sarah believed that Israel could survive such obstacles, though it might take a miracle. Warren's pessimism was based in his belief that

Israel's security was at stake in the Golan. This perspective blended the militarism and the heroism of the nationalist narratives as they were presented to us on tour and at home in community settings.

Notwithstanding his scepticism regarding the prospects for peace in the region, Warren argued forcefully that Israel's accomplishments should be considered on a global scale:

> The Jews have a lot to offer the world and the world can benefit enormously ... I think it's a pity in a way [that] what the Jews have to offer the world should be limited in the way it is right now ... Bounded by the borders, whatever they will be, of what we're going to call Israel, bounded by the chains of history, the passions of racial and religious animosities. There's so much more to be gained by co-operation and by communications if we only find a way of overcoming a lot of it ... because we have a lot to offer the world and the world still has a lot to offer to Israel in all these exchanges. When we talk about trade I don't think about it ... just in terms of a commercial basis but [with] the Arabs themselves ... They're our brothers, we have the same ancestors and I wonder how is it that a lot that we have can't be shared with our brothers and cousins – not just Arabs, but the whole world but particularly with Arabs who see themselves as our enemies and I think that there's the challenge.

This complex statement reflected Warren's layered understanding of Jews' identities and Israel's place in the world. For Warren, the Palestinian conflict was weakening the Jews' place in the world and their potential to contribute to the world. According to him, Israel needed to be tied to the Jews' potential contributions to world history. Furthermore, Israel was a place where the 'chains of history' could be broken by a universal sharing of technological knowledge. Notwithstanding Warren's technological determinism – his belief that science could solve the world's problems – his generally universalistic attitude led him also to declare that the Arabs were 'our brothers and cousins.' The implication was that they should share in the Jews' wealth and technical knowledge.

According to Sarah, not all Arabs could be trusted or even traded with. She was highly sceptical of Warren's peace plan:

> When I was there, or when we were there, I remember thinking when I was coming back to the hotel, how small [Israel is] on that map. It's such a small little country, a jewel – a jewel in rough terrain and surrounded by a

lot of hostility, hostile people. How do they manage to survive? You can't help it. This whole thing is a miracle, how it manages to survive. Not only for itself, but as a haven for other peoples, you know, other Jews around the world. If more Jews go there, where are they going to go? They're going to explode this little tiny spot on the map.

Israel was thus threatened from the outside as well as under pressure from within. After making this statement, Sarah suddenly shifted the conversation:

Do we send our children there to go and get killed in their army? ... It makes me feel a little uncomfortable ... 'cause here I am rooting for this little country to survive but what do I do other than give them money? I don't send my children there. They wouldn't go anyway and I don't go myself except, you know, I support them with whatever money we can ... I don't do anything else ... Well, sometimes I feel guilty. Like when I was there. I felt guilty about it. I did.

Warren immediately told me that he didn't share her feelings:

I can see the necessity of a Jewish homeland, I can see the legitimacy of my support in that, but I find no legitimacy being restricted to it. Like my identity as a Jew ... doesn't begin or end with Israel, nor do I feel it would be good for Jews in the world or Jews in Israel or anywhere else to have our Jewish idea ... and the Jewish identity restricted by that. I see the need for Israel to exist and I see the need for working out [what] people call ... peace ... a way of living and working together between Arabs and the Palestinians so that we can both go on and fulfil our mission to the world ... It is something that is a problem now that's restricting us from realizing our potential worth as Jews and as Palestinians.

This tension between Sarah and Warren was based on a fundamental disagreement over the role of North American Jews vis-à-vis Israel. Sarah felt that she had not contributed enough to Israel; Warren felt that Israel was only one small part of the Jews' collective mission and that the Jews' accomplishments were unrelated to their commitments to Israel. For Warren, those who insisted that Jews could only live authentic Jewish lives in Israel were restricting Jews to living in and committing to one geographical place – in essence, ghettoizing them. Those who suggested that Jewish identity was tied mainly to Israel were limiting the potential contributions that not only Jews but also Israelis, Palestinians, and Arabs could make to the world. The differences between Sarah and Warren were now tangible. Both believed that Israel had to exist for those 'who need it.' Warren, however, told me that 'I'm making my own [and we] are making our own contributions [to the world] by this. Like what our son is doing [a community care physician]. He's a Jew ... even if he doesn't feel like he's an Israeli or doesn't have any identification [with Israel or Judaism].' For Sarah, North American Jews needed to make a greater commitment to Israel:

> You know, what if there wasn't an Israel ... and another Hitler rears its ugly head? ... Where would we all run to? And ... it's very easy for another Hitler to come to be. The German Jews didn't think that there'd ever be a person, a dictator who would wipe them out, who would want to wipe them out, and they stayed on. Many of them stayed on to get killed ... I'm surprised [you feel the way you do] because I'm still, I'm still young enough to remember what happened.

To which Warren angrily retorted:

> But I'm also old enough or young [enough] to remember. I remember what happened to my parents, for instance. I'm a little kid who was on the ... streetcar and we were immigrants. I was just a little kid, [the] oldest of three, and we were going downtown to visit our relatives way out in the east end of Toronto. My parents were jabbering at each other in Yiddish and some old drunk says: 'Hey, speak English. You're in an English-speaking country or go back where you came from,' or something like that. That is important to me, right, because when I say we don't belong just in Israel, where do we Jews belong? Because we got a homeland and we belong in it? I think we belong to the world ... and I want Israel [to belong to the world] but I think we must all fight for the sense of saying we belong in Canada, too. We can belong wherever we want. A lot of these barriers are being broken down ... I like the idea of globalization, I just don't like to see a few corporations dominating that globe ... [I like] the idea that we belong, the world is our oyster. It's ours. It's for everybody. Not just for Jews. The Palestinians unfortunately, you know, I think they should have their homeland. We need our homeland but that doesn't mean that the Palestinians don't belong in Canada as much as Jews do, or anywhere else they choose to go. That is the thing that I think is worth fighting [for]. But we are ... being distracted by it and I think this is why I

said I started out with being anti-Zionist. I like the Zionist mission but not if it's going to be in terms of the idea of having a homeland. Everybody has to have a place where they can call home, right, but I'd like to be able to move where I'm not confined to our homes like they're jails. Israel is –

Sarah interjected: 'You can choose to be a Jew but ... you're still vulnerable to anti-Semitism [and] you can still be subjected to, you can still be a slave by a Nazi.' Calmly, Warren replied, 'And that will be whether there is or isn't an Israel.'

SARAH: By a dictator. You can still be wiped out. You and your people can still be wiped out.
WARREN: You know what, that's true but at the...
SARAH: At the whim of some crackpot.'
WARREN: Anti-Semitism is just one form of racism. What I'm saying is that racism will always be here ... to some degree whether there is an Israel or not. My concern is that there should be less of it and my concern is that for certain people Israel means something that is more restrictive than I would like it to be ... The racism will ... always be there but it shouldn't be the force that it is, and to many people – even Jews – to the idea of a Palestinian state they say 'Alright, that's a place for the Arabs, get them out of Israel, put them into Palestine' [and there] that goes again. ... Whether you're Jewish or Palestinians, ... Irish, Scottish, or whatever, yes, you got your homeland – you got Scotland, you got Ireland and we can all live in peace together in Ireland or wherever – but you still can go anywhere. The Irish and Scots came to Canada and prospered here and they belong here even though they can still feel that Scotland is their homeland.
SARAH: That's why I think Israel has to exist.
WARREN: Well I'm not denying that, I said yes, but not to say that it's got to be a jail for us.

Sarah and Warren disagreed over a fundamental issue that I had often heard debated among North American Jews – namely, the degree to which the Jews' place in the world should be defined by or confined to the territory of Israel. Sarah's fear was palpable. She had not been raised in a Zionist household, she had not been especially active in any Zionist organizations, and she had been an educator in Reform settings. In other words, hers was not an extremist's position by any stretch of the imagination. Yet history had taught Sarah that the Jews were endangered and it was difficult for her to imagine trusting non-Jews.

Warren, in contrast, went so far as to normalize anti-Semitism by discussing it as another form of racism. Each desired an Israel for the Jews. However, Israel for Sarah was fundamental to the Jews' survival as a nation, whereas for Warren it was one of a number of places where the Jews could claim a right to live. In fact, Warren warned against assigning any peoples to any one place; he went so far as to suggest that assigning one place for the Jews would be as dangerous as allowing them no place at all. He also recognized the danger that such assumptions posed for the Palestinians, worrying that if the logic of assigning people to one place were played out, the Palestinians might end up being forcibly transferred to a future Palestinian state. Warren stated categorically that the Palestinians had as much right to keep living in Israel as he had to choose *not* to live in Israel. (The fact that Palestinians cannot choose where they might like to live was not discussed here.)

Asked whether tours to Israel were a means of maintaining or strengthening North American Jews' identity, Warren and Sarah both told me that they feared that current extremist positions within Israel, as represented by the ultra-Orthodox and ultranationalist settlers, threatened that role. Nonetheless, Sarah believed it was good to 'send young people to Israel ... They used to work on a *kibbutz* but now they just go over there and maybe help out in the fields but they get to know other Israeli kids and I think it's a good experience. It's always good to learn how other people ... in other parts of the world live.' It surprised me that Sarah did not describe Israel as a particularly special place for Jewish youths to travel to, considering her earlier statements about the uniqueness of Israel and about the need for Jews to support the state. These statements confirmed her personal conflicts over the relationship between Jews and Israel. She seemed to long for normalcy for the Jews – they should be able to travel like any other young people – but she also held that Israel was potentially necessary as a place of refuge.

The role of the Orthodox rabbis – in particular their power to decide 'who is a Jew' – dominated the rest of our discussion. It was clear that each had thought carefully and deeply about how these policies personally affected them, and they were angry. At one point Warren explained:

There's a lot of inconsistencies and problems within the *halakhic* view of what is a Jew. And it [doesn't] fit in the modern world, [or] the ... political realities in Israel right now. For instance, one of my sons married a Japanese girl, [and] they've got two children ... Supposing they regarded themselves as Jews [and] they followed Jewish practices ... The boy had ... the circumcision ... and supposing even that they were brought up as Jewish ... Because the mother had not converted according to *halakha* ... they would not be accepted as Jews. But if it was one of my daughters who married a gentile ... and they had children and the children denied they were Jewish, they would still be Jews ... Right now ... the Orthodox refuse to examine it ... Even amongst the rabbis there couldn't be a unanimous agreement of what *halakha* means and how it's to be applied and yet they don't want to apply it in a way [which] unites the Jewish people ... So I think what they need now is to have somebody write a new *halakha*.

Warren was describing what to him seemed the irrationality of the current Israeli (Orthodox) rabbinate's position. In the process he was touching on the nature of the dilemmas. On what basis is a Jew to be defined – by nation, by culture, by religion? But even though they recognized that these religious laws affected them as Jews living outside Israel, neither Sarah nor Warren felt they had any business interfering in Israel's governance. After all they were not fully participating citizens of that state (i.e., they did not pay taxes and did not have a right to vote there). Though powerless to do anything about it, they both worried that Israel's policies would affect their own lives and those of their loved ones. To Warren and Sarah, the Orthodox rabbinate and its followers were simply fanatics expressing religious passions that were leading to unfair policies and – in the extreme – even to murder. They believed that the Orthodox had incited the hatred that led to the assassination of Prime Minister Rabin. They did not recognize Orthodox Jews' religious attachment to the land and idealization of Israel as a sacred space. For Warren and Sarah, Israel was a democratic and secular state under threat from an extremist minority.

With respect to the Oslo Accords, Warren felt that both sides needed to 'deal with extremists and the terrorists ... That to me is the key. I think the land issues are subordinate. I think the land issues and money issues can be resolved but the problems, like from my experience in labour relations, the ideologies are the problems ... The security problem is how to deal with the crazies, that's what it is.' Ever the labour negotiator, Warren suggested that the issue was simply one of reconciliation and could be resolved dispassionately. However, he did not seem to recognize that taking what he called 'the land issue' off the table would only shift the balance of the negotiations to one framed solely in terms of Israeli interests. For the Palestinians, the conflict was

precisely about their right to land. Warren seemed to believe that ideological differences were at the root of the conflict, but he was unclear
what ideological problems could be resolved without also dealing with
access to and occupation of land – especially land that Israel was
claiming as uniquely its own.

Warren and Sarah were both committed to the existence of a strong
Israel, and they interpreted its place in the world through their own
experiences of anti-Semitism and memories of the Holocaust. For
Sarah, Israel was a place of refuge, a place of history, a place that every
Jew should safeguard and feel proud of. In her own way, she suggested that Israel was unlike any other state: it was uniquely a place
for the Jews, and necessarily so because of the world's long history of
hating Jews.

Warren seemed to be normalizing the Jews' experience of anti-
Semitism; at one point he compared it to other forms of racism. However, he also cast Israel as a unique example of the Jews' contributions
to the world. Israel, for him, had the potential to become a 'light unto
all nations' and a model for all other states.

Aaron

I interviewed Aaron on a bright, warm day while sitting on a dock on
the Red Sea in front of our hotel. It was our last day on the IDF tour. I
was especially glad that Aaron had granted me an interview because
he seemed very engaged by the tour presentations and events, rival-
ling me in documenting the tour by taking hundreds of photographs.
He had also been willing to challenge Arnie, the tour guide, on several
occasions.

Aaron had immigrated from England to Canada 'after having survived the blitz and the bombing of London in the War.' His first trip to
Israel was in 1957, when he represented Canada in the Fifth Macabbean Games, the 'Jewish Olympics,' which are held annually in Israel.
He said of this present trip: 'It's been amazing. It's hard to recollect
what type of deserted place Israel was forty-one years ago, in my eyes.'

When I asked Aaron what tied him to Israel, he said, 'You're asking
very emotional questions.'[3] I was caught off guard by his response,
then told him he didn't have to answer any of my questions. But he
quickly replied, 'no', and said:

> I would say it stems from really the Holocaust. I was twelve at the start of
> the War and I have vivid, vivid memories of pictures of the camps printed

in the English newspaper. That was just heart-rending – they are printed on my mind [and] never go away. I think really that's what led me to ... really lean towards Israel. I would say that I'm not a religious Jew, I'm Jewish and I'll defend my Jewish rights. I don't go to synagogue every Saturday ... I'm not that religious, although I come really from a very religious family back in England where we used to walk on Saturdays and I couldn't use the scissors Friday night. I would always end up playing chess with my father Friday night. But now, of course, it's a little bit different. There are all sorts of fads, everything. But I'm not, well, we're not really that religious but, you know, we do believe in the state of Israel. There's no question about it ... it's just a beautiful state. To see what they've done is unbelievable ... I think a lot more people should come and see what Israel has done to itself – the way it has made oh, beautiful groves out of desert ... One angle you look at just plain dirty old desert and you turn around the other way and you've got beautiful buildings, [well maybe] not beautiful but at least a liveable situation.

Aaron's secular ties to Israel were rooted in his personal experiences of anti-Semitism and his memories of the Holocaust. He had witnessed the changes in the State of Israel, and he considered the transformation, particularly of the desert, to have been impressive. His last comment referred to a trip we had taken to a desert *kibbutz* where at one point we were told to look in one direction, where there was 'nothing,' and then to look at what had been accomplished by the *kibbutz* founders (see photos 11 and 12).

Because he had immediately identified Israel's development of the Negev, I expected him to repeat this narrative when I asked him to reflect on the tour and what he had learned. But he surprised me: 'I only had one generalization of ... the whole world [and that] is man's inhumanity to man. This is really what the whole story's about. It's trying to live in peace and let people do their own thing.' Aaron's statement that he had learned about 'man's inhumanity to man' suggested to me that he did not see the world in Zionist terms, ones that particularized the Jews' condition and presented their history as a condition of 'man's inhumanity towards all Jews.' Nevertheless, when I asked Aaron how important Israel was to North American Jews, he replied:

Well [it's] very important ... It's basically our land ... One of the things that I found very interesting forty-nine years ago ... what I couldn't believe and what made me ... feel at home was the fact that everywhere I turned – like the maid in the hotel was Jewish, the taxi driver was Jewish, the waitress was Jewish, even the lady of the night standing on the street in Dizengoff in Tel Aviv was Jewish ... I couldn't get used to it. It is a very satisfying feeling because I grew up in England and ... there was a lot of anti-Semitism there. I felt it in school. I came across it first-hand and just realized that 'Hey, it's us alone, almost, unfortunately,' and that's what I feel.

For Aaron, as for others, Israel was to be celebrated as the Jews' homeland. But Aaron's final comment struck me as curious. When he said 'almost' and 'unfortunately,' he seemed to be reluctantly conceding that the Jews had not arrived in an empty land – other people were already there. He understood this as an 'unfortunate' circumstance, because it troubled the relationships between the Jews and the others. What began as the Zionist narrative about a uniquely Jewish space turned into a description that acknowledged that the Jews were not in fact 'alone' on the land after all. This was consistent with his perspectives on Israel's settlement policy, over which he had challenged Arnie. Why did the Jews not settle in a zone that was safe, secure, and legal (i.e., inside the Green Line)? Why they were pushing into areas where the Palestinians, or non-Jews, were the majority?

But Aaron was not necessarily sympathetic to the region's Arabs. When he reflected on his decision to disregard the Canadian government's travel advisory in 1998, he compared Iraq's leader Saddam Hussein to Hitler, just as Prime Minister Netanyahu had done when we heard him speak on that tour, and just as many in the media had been doing since 1991:

> I don't trust Saddam. I think he's just another Hitler and ... when I was twelve years old, I'll never forget Neville Chamberlain coming home, getting off the plane from Munich, in his hand waving a piece of paper 'Peace in our Time' and I think the very next day Hitler walked into Czechoslovakia. And you can't let a madman have biological warfare type of chemicals, et cetera, and anthrax. I mean, if a man kills his own Kurds in his own country ... what can you think? It's like Chrétien, the Canadian prime minister, ordering all Indians to be killed in Canada. Same thing, basically. I don't know what you think, but ... we have our own problems with the Indians in Canada. It's a difficult problem.

Aaron's memories of Chamberlain's appeasement formed the background against which he interpreted any agreements between the

West and Iraq. Netanyahu's position that the Iraqi leader was an untrustworthy partner in any peace because he was also a dictator obviously resonated for Aaron. But in an interesting way, Aaron stepped back from this hard line with respect to Hussein when he acknowledged that the Kurds' separatism and nationalism were indeed a 'difficult problem' for the Iraqis. He compared the Kurds to Canada's indigenous communities. In switching from a particularistic to a universalistic model of conflict in the region, Aaron was poaching various elements of the narratives that represented Muslims as especially untrustworthy and/or violent while also acknowledging that some Muslims are worth protecting.

Aaron felt that the tours to Israel were a 'great way' to learn about Israel because they represented 'the mysticism of the country, [which] is fascinating 'cause it is a mystic place.' I asked him what he meant by the term 'mystic.' 'Because of the background,' he explained. 'From day one, you're in a country where it all started at, the old Bible, the New Testament. I remember the first time I came here, we visited Nazareth and that was unbelievable.' And what had been so 'unbelievable' about Nazareth? 'The caves.' The caves are a series of Christian sites. They include the Grotto of the Annunciation, where it is claimed that the Archangel Gabriel told Mary she would give birth to the 'son of God,' and a crypt in St Joseph's Church said to be Joseph's shop. Aaron had clearly been captivated by biblical history, both Jewish and Christian. The narratives and the land had captured another time for him – a time that is spiritually and historically important. This made Israel 'mystical.'

Although obviously engaged by the political issues raised on the tour, Aaron was surprisingly uninformed. When I asked him about the signing of the Oslo Accords between Israel and Palestine, at first he asked me when they were signed. Only after I prompted him – 'Remember the famous handshake?' – did he ask: 'What, with Arafat?' 'Yes,' I replied. He described what he had felt at the time: 'I think sceptical ... It's a problem. You know the mandate of the PLO at that time was to drive Israel into the sea. I don't think that mandate's been changed, if I recollect. Has it?' Aaron was suspicious. He did not trust the Palestinians because he believed they had not yet dealt with what he called their 'mandate,' meaning their revolutionary charter, also known as the Covenant. Still, he expressed great respect for the Israelis because they were trying to resolve the conflict. When I asked him if he was at all 'hopeful,' he shifted his position:

Oh, I'm hopeful, yes, and internally optimistic. And it seems a shame that the two can't live in peace together. I mean ... you see Arabs working in Jewish places, Jewish hotels and [they] seem to be living peacefully with each [other] ... There was an old saying from the First World War, where I lost two uncles ... They said they should put all the politicians in a field together and let them fight it out themselves, and that's about the size of it. [People] in the general public [don't] have any animosity toward the other. I mean ... you're Palestinian – half – I don't feel any animosity toward you ... You're a sweetheart of a girl ... No, really, I think it's ridiculous. As ... I've always said and I repeat it, man's inhumanity to man is just one of the tragedies of the whole world. When you see what's going on everywhere, other countries, this is just ridiculous ... They get all worked up.

Aaron's universalistic, humanistic, and generally apolitical sensibilities informed his position on the peace process. While searching for the ways that people generally get along together, he did not see the exploitation of some (e.g., the Palestinians); he did, however, see everyone's humanity. For Aaron, the politicians were the main obstacles to peace: they were interfering in the lives of people who could otherwise work well together. It is significant that although Aaron cited the Palestinians' controversial charter as an issue – something done by many in the anti-Oslo camp – the charter itself did not for him represent the basis for any understanding of the conflict. In other words, he did not interpret its existence as an expression of an eternal animosity among the peoples of the region, or indeed, among people in general toward the Jews. He also did not choose to speak in terms set by *Realpolitik* or national security. His was perhaps a naive perspective on the relationship between Palestinians and Israelis, since he did not raise the issue of any power imbalance, or the issues of occupation and the refugees. Even so, his humanitarianism led him to a fairly radical position.

Near the end of the interview, I asked him if he had ever considered living in Israel. He recounted that forty-one years earlier he had been tempted to come to live in Israel by 'a gorgeous Israeli girl.' But since then: 'I've enjoyed the material things I've had in Canada. My late uncle said come over [to Canada] when I was living in England. [I was] thinking the streets are paved with gold and I've been looking for that gold ever since!' Aaron did not seem at all conflicted about his choice to remain and make a life for himself in Canada. He took pride in Israel but he did not seem especially worried about its future. Though he

envisioned Israel as the Jews' ancestral land, and attributed its achievements to the Jews' economic and social development of the land, he
recognized that others had a history on that same land, and he was
ready to consider sharing it. He did not discuss the issues in strictly
political terms; rather, he seemed guided by a belief that people could
get along and that peace was possible. He was not interested in the
more politically driven and parochial issues, though he recognized
that politicians certainly were.

Myrna, Warren and Sarah, and Aaron had each identified with a
number of Zionist markers. All were proud of Israel's accomplishments though they differed in their emphases. Only Sarah expressed
any guilt that Israeli Jews were sacrificing their lives so that she could
have a safe and secure haven, should she need one in the future. All
were concerned about Israeli democracy and security, but none of
them resorted to militaristic or territorialist arguments for security or
against Israel's neighbours. They imagined Israel as their ancestral
homeland and they took pride in what Israeli Jews, their national kin,
had accomplished.

A Home Away from Home

Those who first visited Israel when that nation was in a euphoric mood – the first few years after Israel's victory in the Six Day War of 1967 – told very different stories from the ones told by those who had experienced the anti-Semitism of the first half of the twentieth century, including the Holocaust. Relationships developed across the diasporic divide in the 1970s which were possibly the strongest I witnessed in the research period. 'Co-responsibility' for members of this group seriously shaped their lives and relationships to Israel.

Marlene

Marlene's grandfathers came to the United States from the Ukraine in the early 1900s and settled in a mid-Atlantic city on the east coast. Her parents followed later, as young children, after the Russian Revolution, which had delayed the reunion. According to Marlene, both sides of her family were 'antireligious,' one for political reasons, the other for reasons unrelated to politics. Marlene grew up in what she called a 'radical household,' explaining that her grandfathers and her parents had been communists for a time. Their politics changed during the 1950s after they '[saw] through the lies' of communism and witnessed the dangerous rise of Senator Joseph McCarthy. A close family friend, a physician who had joined the Communist Party, died destroyed in spirit soon after McCarthy's rise. Marlene's parents were heavily involved in Israel-related activities in the late 1950s and early 1960s, and her father was an important figure in one of North American Jewry's most prominent community organizations, the United Jewish Appeal. She described herself as a 'non-observant Jew' whose 'sense of Jewish identity ... has almost nothing if not nothing to do with religion.' She added that her 'identity as a secular Jew [and] Jewish identity' were 'very important' to her.

During the tour, Marlene and I often ate together or simply chatted. I conducted a formal interview with her on our last day in Israel. Later, I visited her at her home in the United States. Marlene is a clinical social worker and is heavily involved in developing community mental health programs for inner-city children. She is also strongly committed to Jewish community organizations; for example, she has done a great deal of fundraising for her local Jewish Community Centre. She was so proud of her work in this that she took me for a tour of the building. Later, I returned to attend a lecture on Jerusalem's future in the centre's new lecture hall. After I returned home from Israel, Marlene sent me a newsletter from a Jewish feminist organization in the former Soviet Union to which she belonged. As a woman committed to social justice, Marlene had come on the Israel Civil Society Fund (ICSF) tour expecting to meet like-minded people and to learn more about the projects to which she had donated money.

I met Marlene on what she told me was her fifteenth trip to Israel. She first went there in 1972 to 'see Israel, to experience Israel,' and she had 'found it tremendously exciting ... seeing all the places that I'd only heard and read about.' After her first trip she had been 'excited enough' to get involved with the Israeli Embassy for a few years. Her family's involvement in the Jewish community had made that easy for her.

When I spoke to her about Israel and the role it might play for North American Jews, she had this to tell me:

> I think [Israel is] very important if one chooses it to be important. I think it's perfectly possible to be a North American Jew and not be deeply involved in Israel, I suppose. That's just not where I come from. There are many parts of the North American Jewish community that don't appeal to me at all.

According to Marlene, North American Jews have no duty to identify with Israel. They can choose to do so if they want, in the same way that they can support community organizations if they want. She had chosen to support Israel, but not to support all community groups.

We later discussed what Israel meant to her as a Jew:

> It's not really possible to separate it 'as a Jew' from 'as a person' and for me that's an important point ... My first trip to Israel in '72 ... was a real turn-on. I mean it was very, very exciting to see this new country because

it was still very new at that point, and things that were being created and beautiful things that existed and people who were reconstructing lives and families and so on... But after that, my next trip to Israel was 1975 ... very soon after I had become separated and divorced. For the first time, ... I was on my own, literally for the first time in my life. So the excitement of that somehow became co-mingled with the excitement of the independence here [in Israel]. I made a lot of identification that way, which is not literally Jewish ... Theoretically, I suppose I could have gone through that development equally somewhere else, but I wasn't drawn to do so. Maybe this felt safe, in some psychological sense of safe, not physical safe ... I don't in any sense mean security in its usual sense. Safe because this felt like mine to experience – what it was like to be alone, to be sure a little frightened and a little nervous and a little this, but in a basically comfortable context.

Marlene wanted me to understand from the outset that being a Jew did not set her apart in her identification with Israel. This theme arose in all our conversations. She wanted me to know that her relationship to Israel was less nationalistic than might be expected of someone with such long-term associations with the state. She described Israel as a safe and secure place, even for a woman living there on her own. She gave me the impression that for her, Israel was a cocoon – in interesting contrast to the more familiar descriptions of Israel as dangerous.

When we talked about the Oslo Accords, Marlene smiled and told me she had been 'very excited. I was on the White House lawn ... Oh it was thrilling, absolutely thrilling.' A small peace group that brings Jewish and Arab children and teens together for summer camp had invited Marlene, as one of their supporters, to the 1993 signing at the White House. She was 'delighted' to see 'a whole group of their kids, twenty-five or so ... on the White House lawn.' She had taken 'a picture of them with [Palestinian Authority Leader] Arafat.' When telling me about this event, Marlene beamed with pride at having witnessed and contributed to the ceremony. She kept a photo of Arafat with the camp's children – a sign of her openness to peace-building processes. I suspect that most of the people I met on tour would have preferred a picture of Israel's Prime Minister Rabin. Still, she felt 'reasonably cynical' about the entire process: 'Ultimately ... there will be tremendous changes ... I'm very hopeful but I won't be living [in Israel] so I am fearful, not in a personal sense but for what some people, or maybe all the people here, are going to have to process and go through in order to be part of the new Israel. It is not going to be easy.' When I asked her what the 'it' was she explained: 'Peace has become a word that's ambiguized [*sic*]. Some kind of ... peaceful coexistence, some kind of ability to live side by side in all the senses of life.' She feared that Jews in Israel and North America were not entirely prepared for what peace might in fact bring to the region. She felt close enough to some community members to know that they would be deeply affected by these changes. Throughout the tour and then again at her home, we talked about the implications of these changes.

Our conversations focused on her criticisms of Israel's Jewishness and on Israel's exclusivity as a state for Jews. Marlene often criticized other tour participants for holding on to this idea of Israel. I asked her to elaborate on those discussions:

> Yes, I mean I don't know that I can understand individual, by individual but ... If you recall, I was telling you about my mother, who has all this genuinely sophisticated background politically, and ... who still comes down to the point of saying, 'Oh my God, we've got to make sure it remains a Jewish state.' So yes, I do understand the claim to that and what I imagine to be the terror – and that may not be too strong – the terror at the contemplation that they're going to wake up one day and it's no longer going to be a Jewish state. Not because they have any idea about what that's really going to be like, but it's a perception. It's a mental experience of huge loss, whether or not it would actually work out that way.

Although critical of those who contended that Israel must be primarily the Jews' state, Marlene was close enough to community activists – even radical activists – to know that if and when this foundation shifted, they might experience it as a terrifying loss. Diaspora Jews and Israelis who held these positions frustrated her, yet she also seemed to understand why they were afraid.

I asked her to explain for me what others called the 'Jewish character of the state':

> Well, when you try to talk about the character of a state or a country or a city ... you're talking about the avowed values ... versus the actual realities. Suddenly the avowed values that add up to the Jewish character in this place are about social justice, [and] democracy ... So I can say that one of the important aspects of [this state's] character is democracy even though you and I and a lot of other people know that there are many undemocratic if not non-democratic things that happen [in Israel] all the time.

In other words, the character of any state is an idealization rather than a representation of reality. Here Marlene's cynicism about other diaspora Jews' perceptions slipped into the conversation. According to Marlene, tours like the ICSF one represent Israel as a democratic state by providing opportunities for participants to meet with Israeli journalists, feminists, and human rights lawyers. To Marlene, Jews who had for a long time described Israel simply as a Jewish state, had only now 'suddenly' begun describing it as a democratic state as well. This involved the intentional forging of links between the state's democratic institutions and its Jewish character – links that were not to be questioned. She was concerned that several, if not all, tour participants were taking the democratic nature of the state for granted instead of critically exploring to what extent Israel is at all democratic.

Marlene was generally unhappy with this tour experience because she did not 'connect' with others in the way she had hoped. She had expected to meet 'like-minded' people; instead the participants were more 'tied to the status quo ... of what Israel is, of what Israel should be, of what their lives should be' As an example, she described the participants' concerns over the power of the ultra-Orthodox in Jerusalem as disingenuous, simply 'intellectual [because] it doesn't influence anything about their religious affiliations.' As a secular Jew, Marlene did not believe that other practising Jews had any right to condemn Orthodox practices in Israel; they were religious, so there was no meaningful distinction to be made between them. According to Marlene, one was either religious or secular.

This conversation led us into a discussion of Jerusalem, which Marlene described this way:

A hideout ... It is a hideout for, and it's rather strong ... for the religious Jews who want to be on top of a mountain, who want to keep the world the way they want it to be, who do not want to make room in their lives or literally, physically, make room for anything different ... When we reached Tel Aviv, I breathed a sigh of relief ... It is the secular city and it's where the action is.

For Marlene, Jerusalem was claustrophobic, mainly because the Orthodox controlled it. She seemed to feel no sentimental ties to the place. She expressed no connection to Jerusalem's history or to the Jews' history there. For her, it was in the secular space of Tel Aviv that she could feel free and independent; she associated this freedom with the virtues of being a Jew in Israel, the Jews' state. But this was a secular freedom and one inflected with the Zionist ideals of the state. Religious insularity reflects a pre-Zionist and premodern Jewish identity, one from which Marlene distanced herself almost entirely.

Marlene and I discussed her contacts with Arabs and her exposure to their perspectives on Israel. She told me that a very close friend of hers was an Arab who was 'very astute with regards to the political scene [and who] appreciates Israel.' She added that 'he has many views of what he feels Israelis must do to make peace possible, in order to right the balance – things on the level [of] control of water.' Her friend had asked Marlene to ask tour organizers and lecturers why Israel had never officially declared its physical boundaries. She never did ask anyone this question. She told me that 'the way I get around all this sticky-wicky parts ... and this is not just getting around [the issue], it is simply to say that there ought to be a comparable Law of Return for the Palestinians, rather than debating is there such a thing as a Law of Return or should there be.' She had spoken to Arabs and Palestinians about some of the most controversial issues facing Israelis. She believed there was an imbalance between the parties and that control over resources was also an issue. In order to correct the balance, Israel would have to give 'comparable' rights to the Palestinians. She was implying that to some extent, the roots of the conflict between Israel and Palestine were related to the inability of some Palestinians to return to their homes. In suggesting a 'comparable' Law of Return for the Palestinians, she was radically reframing Israel's role in Jews' lives. For to propose a Palestinian return is to shift the very basis for the Jews' return: that return is based no longer on a Zionist framing of redemption and reclamation but rather on citizenship and human rights. This suggests that for Marlene, the issue of the Palestinians could only be solved through immigration and citizenship reforms. Interestingly, Marlene framed the possibilities for peace in terms of 'righting the balance' rather than in *Realpolitik* terms such as national security and separation. As committed as Marlene is to the Israeli state and the Jewish community, she envisions a secular and bicultural future for the state.

It was also apparent that Marlene had been exposed to different perspectives on Israel and had even internalized an alternative Israel. Her willingness to discuss such alternatives indicated to me that although Israel was important to her, she did not perceive it as sacred territory. Despite her many years of deep personal attachment to and support

for Israel, she seemed almost indifferent to its religious and territorialist roots. She was far more engaged with the effort to make it a just,
democratic and secular state, one that would represent of all of its citizens, Jews and non-Jews alike.

Marlene's relationship to Israel was emotional and personal but also
highly political. Her commitment to social justice was reflected in her
engagement with the very dilemmas that many secular and progressive
Jews identifying with Israel have faced. She had distanced herself from
the strictly nationalistic perspective on Israel, and she had thought very
deeply and carefully about what she perceived as the problematic position of those who were claiming that Israel could be both Jewish and
democratic.

Lynn

After about a year of meeting at the 'Jewish lunch'[1] in the metropolitan
community where I conducted some of my research, I was very pleased
when one group member asked me to interview her. We arranged to
conduct the interview after one such lunch. While kitchen workers and
waiters passed back and forth, clearing tables and serving others, we
set up shop. It was a thrill to be conducting an interview in this space,
for in many ways it had been our communal kitchen table.

Lynn, a woman in her forties had grown up on the Canadian prairies
but was now living in central Canada. Soon after we met, she became
curious to know all about my work, and we quickly developed an easy
relationship.

Lynn first visited Israel while in her teens; her last visit had been in
1992. Her parents had no interest in Israel, had nothing to do with 'Zionist organizations,' and had never seen Israel; even so, Lynn had always
felt that she had a 'very strong relationship' to Israel: 'I feel that in a way
it's a kind of home away from home and I feel that it's much more than
a country that I visit. There's a real kind of psychic connection.'

Lynn was sixteen when she first visited Israel with 'a Zionist group.'
She had not been a dedicated group member; she and two friends had
joined the group only six months before the tour in order to go to Israel
'because it was the cheapest trip that we could go on.' She said, laughing: 'I could not stand being part of what they called "the movement"
and in fact the only relationship I had to a movement was that we all
had diarrhea all summer. That was what I thought of as "the movement." I found the ideology and the rah-rahness actually repulsive but

we were able to do our own thing [once in Israel].' Lynne is lively, brazen, and obviously no follower. Her secure individualism affected all her experiences of Israel and her interpretations of Israeli and Jewish politics.

She recounted that once the group was in Israel, a *kibbutz* family adopted each of the teens and that they all 'became very connected to the social group there.' They also had to 'do *Gadna* in the army ... a kind of pre-army experience [in order to] get [us to] understand what the army is about ... I think with the idea of making [us] very rah rah about the army. I was not at all rah rah about the army, but I was very rah rah about the soldiers!'

Lynn also reflected on what it had meant for her as a young woman to leave her home city, where 'there were 20,000 Jews and I knew every one of them and mostly Jewish men were nothing to write home about. Well, we landed in Israel and we all went, "Oh, my God," because it was astonishing that all these gorgeous guys were Jewish and we just couldn't wait to basically drop our pants. So ... I would say it was very much an adolescent experience, okay, and that was as far as a Jewish experience as it went. The Jewish part was almost negligible.' Notwithstanding Lynn's interpretation of this experience, her reaction to the men of Israel was more complicated than that of a sex-obsessed teenager. Perhaps only subliminally, she was expressing a Zionist-inflected perception of the weakness of diaspora men and the strength of the new Jews, Israeli men. Many have written about the degree to which Zionism was very much about discarding the Jews' diasporic identity, which was associated with bookishness, pacifism and urbane intellectualism. In contrast, Israeli men – and women, to some extent – were models of strength and self-sufficiency: as soldiers defending the nation, they were pioneers and *kibbutzniks* working the land, and in the political sphere they were sovereign.[2] Of course, there was more to Marlene's experience in Israel than a newfound attraction to Jewish men:

There was a whole way of looking at the world and a whole sense of freedom ... that I had never experienced before. And I was very taken with the kind of independence that [Israeli] teenagers had, with the sorts of issues they were involved with, [and] with the politics. And I was fascinated by the fact that they had to go into the army ... [that] you needed to protect the Jewish state against people who basically wanted to destroy you. I bought into that and big time. I think the idea that we deserved a homeland ... was a kind of culmination of my Hebrew School, which I didn't pay much attention to and really couldn't care less about. But having been there, all those ideas were actually very strongly reinforced, and I came back very, very pro Israel ... I came back from a situation where in [my home city] you don't want to tell anyone your last name or admit to being Jewish, to having a sense of pride, [of] belonging to really a special group.

For Lynn, Israel symbolized Jewish strength – the men, the teens, the army – and it quickly became part of her own identification as a Jew. When she returned to Canada, she could comport herself with more pride and with a greater sense of security.

Lynn returned to Israel in 1973, only three months before the Yom Kippur War: 'For someone who came from [a Canadian Prairie city] where nothing really ever happened, to going to the middle of a war and being a part of things – it was a very exciting process. I had no fear at all. I did not really understand what was going on. Friends of mine were wounded and I thought that was pretty neat.'

However, Lynn's identification with Israel was to evolve from one of blind support – which she attributed in part to her youth and naivety – toward a more critical and mature perspective on the state and the role that it plays in Jews' lives, both in Israel and in North America. In 1979 her 'jingoism sort of started to decline rapidly,' partly because she realized that 'people were less enamoured with the whole thing. A lot of the kibbutzniks [who were her friends] had changed their opinion significantly.' A trip to Israel in 1989 was the real turning point for Lynn. This was after what she called the 'invasion of Lebanon' and during the intifada. She began to see 'the army and the whole government situation in a much, much different way. People who had been rah rah and [who] couldn't wait to go into the army [in the past] really felt it was a duty that they really couldn't stand.' As a result of these experiences, she joined Peace Now: 'Most of the people that I knew there supported it and the people who didn't support it, I felt I could barely talk to.' Even her relationship to Jerusalem had changed:

I mean Jerusalem really changed for me. [In the past] I did not feel that there was a dangerous presence at all within the city. I never felt fear before. At this point I was quite fearful. [The tour organizers] said we should not go into the shuk [the market] but I went anyway because I really wanted to see [it] and I was very upset by what I saw because ... there was a real economic decline that was visible there and people were also suffering. The whole situation was really untenable.

As Lynn's perception of Israel changed, so too did her travel experiences. Even though she had become critical of Israeli government policies, her commitment to the state remained strong. As she noted, she had chosen to support a peace group that her Israeli friends supported.

In 1992 she agreed to be a 'chaperone on a March of the Living' tour, which took a group of teenagers to Auschwitz and then to Israel. Her anger was palpable as she recounted this experience:

> I really... felt much more disconnected to this idea of a Jewish state than ever before, which is interesting because here I'd come back from seeing the Holocaust and all the horrible things that had happened to Jews and there I was in Israel. And ... they took us first thing to the Wailing Wall and I felt extremely disconnected from this whole kind of Jewish process in some way ... I guess I also reacted to the same thing that I had [in the past], like this very rah-rahism [being imposed on] the kids. I kept trying to put a damper on it and trying to say, 'Well, look at the reality of the situation.' So it was a kind of troubling trip for me in terms of the Israel part, anyway. When people talked about Israel arising from the ashes of the Holocaust, I really wanted to puke. I tried to be a kind of foil ... to that way of thinking ... There was a split among the leaders. We had Rabbis there and we had ... ultra-Zionists who ... just felt that we were right and everyone else was wrong ... We had people who I thought were quite racist, and [who said] Palestinians and Arabs were trash, and they had no value for human life and we were the good people and we were the chosen people [which] I found extremely difficult, and I did try to counteract it [because] some of the kids were quite smitten with that ... I still felt a real connection with my friends but I couldn't wait to get out of the whole Israel part of the trip and go with my friends.

Lynn was still very upset that the Holocaust had been exploited in order to pitch Zionist jingoism to a group of vulnerable teenagers. As she saw it, this tour had been used to promote an Israel she could no longer identify with. She felt compelled to retell the story of Israel's conflict with the Palestinians and Arabs in order to provide the teen participants with an interpretation of Israel from a more peace-oriented and less anti-Arab and anti-Palestinian perspective. She had been so overwhelmed with the task, and so distressed and dismayed by what she called the 'Israel part' of the tour – the more ideological orientation of the tour – that she could not wait to escape it by joining her more like-minded Israeli friends.

Lynn's understanding of Israel's militarism had influenced her thinking on the Israel–Palestine conflict and how it could be resolved:

I think there has to be a Jewish homeland but I think that the whole structure of it has to be very, very different ... My views are that there has to be a kind of just divorce. That warring parties – and I'm talking about now about Jews and non-Jews – don't have to like each other but they have to come up with a fair and just settlement. And if it means sacrificing land [so be it]. The whole idea that the land, the Occupied Territories have to be settled and the policies of the last government are just repulsive to me. So when I see people who are Jewish acting in this way, I feel very disconnected from them.

Lynn's most recent experiences in Israel and her life experience in North America had prompted her to rethink her relationship to Israel:

I guess what's interesting is – and I don't know if it's because of my age or because of the political situation – but ... I have become much more connected to Israel because of my own history and personal relationships there, but much more disconnected from the country itself. At the same time I've become much more connected to being Jewish ... I did not become religious but I became much more interested in the religion and the rituals ... I moved my daughter from one Hebrew School to another [because] I wanted her to learn more Hebrew ... I felt Hebrew is the language of access to the Torah ... So I think that I've become much more Jewishly involved and much less Israel involved.

With Israel no longer the symbol of Jewish continuity for her, Lynn had returned to the Torah, which she described as the embodiment of Jewish cultural heritage and tradition. Even Hebrew carries new meaning: it is no longer the state's language, but rather the language of the Torah.

But unlike Marlene, Lynn felt she could return to the Torah without implicating herself in the religious politics of the state. She was careful to distinguish her practice from that of Israel's ultra-Orthodox. Both she and Marlene blamed them for Israel's undemocratic behaviour. Lynn told me:

I feel much more connected to the Torah but I feel much less connected to certain forms of Judaism. But I feel total disassociation from the ultra-

Orthodox, which I did not when I first got there. When I first got there I saw, well, isn't this wonderful. They're going to keep the Jewish state alive. I don't have to keep kosher or do anything ... Right now I really ... view them as a much more significant enemy to the well-being of the state of Israel, to the well-being of Jewish people in general than, in fact, I would view ... even Saddam Hussein ... The reason is that I think ... by their behaviour, ... they have discredited the Jewish people, that they have disenfranchised a large number of ... Jewish people, both in Israel and here, and I just see them as fundamentalists who are dangerous, like any fundamentalists who are dangerous ... They have a mission and they're zealots and they're a very dangerous element and ... I'd like to see a policy to take away their power and... initiatives. But it seems to me that they've been given more and more power and more and more of a say and more and more are able to define even the questions about Judaism.

Lynn's concerns for the continuity and survival of the Jewish people had shifted from a concern for the security of the State of Israel to a concern that this state no longer embodied her ideals of Jewish practice. For these reasons, she had turned to classically diaspora practices (as the Zionists would have it) associated with and embodied by the cultural and communal practices of the Torah. It is ironic that the very same person who was first attracted to the physicality of Israel's existence was now turning away from all that the state represented in classical Zionist terms. In essence, she was making a move toward diaspora.

Yet, Lynn also told me that despite her experience on the March of the Living tour, she still believed that tours to Israel were especially important for 'bringing youth on board in terms of a Jewish identity':

I think that the only way to cement a connection with being Jewish is to visit Israel even with all of the negative things because I do think that there's a kind of *gruha* – I don't know how you say it, spirit – that is there that you can't experience in the diaspora. What that *gruha* is – I think it still is – number one, seeing a state where most people are Jewish. I think that's a phenomenal experience for anyone who lives in the diaspora, especially if they come from smaller places.

So Israel apparently was still an important place of difference for Lynn; she was holding on to the power and dynamism associated with Zionism. For this reason, she was distressed that her daughter showed no interest in Israel and felt no desire at all to visit. Lynn wanted young Jews to see and experience Israel and to be exposed to all its problems. She also wanted them to make a conscious decision about how to live as a Jew. She contended that

> seeing ... that it's basically a theocracy ... and seeing ... how difficult it is to be a secular Jew in Israel ... I think that we don't have that ability to personally choose that in the diaspora, but in Israel you can say, 'You know what? I'm going to a night-club on Friday night,' or 'I'm eating bread at Pesah [Passover],' which is something that you can't afford to do here in the same way.

'Why not?' I asked. She replied:

> You can't afford to do that because when you're ... in Israel if you eat bread on Pesah, if you travel on Shabbat, if you spit in the face of the Torah, you're still Jewish because you're there and you're in a Jewish state. You don't have to be Jewish in Israel to be Jewish. In the diaspora if you're not that then ... you can't belong ... You can't possibly be connected in a full way to Judaism, being Jewish, or the Jewish experience. It's a different kind of statement here than it is there and I think that ... young people need to understand that sort of statement, so that they can make real choices.

Lynn's description of Israel as a theocracy reflected her fear that the Orthodox community was changing the nature of Israeli society – a society that until recently she had envisioned as secular. In Israel, people once took their Jewish identity for granted because they lived in a Jewish state; ironically, this suggests the crux of the Orthodox argument in Israel: they insist that the Jewishness of the state is threatened when Jews dismiss Orthodox religious practices.

I asked Lynn what kind of youth tour she would organize if she had the opportunity:

> I think what I would try to ... meet a lot of other Israeli youth from many, many backgrounds and ... I'd have a lot more dialogue. I'd have them meet with Palestinian youth ... I think being on a kibbutz – although the kibbutz system is dying – is very, very critical because I think that they can understand ... something of ... the residual pioneering spirit ... I would focus it less Jewishly and more historically and the reason is because the

Jewishness has been usurped by the ultra-Orthodox now ... I would take them to the Wailing Wall but ... I'd talk about how you don't have the right to go to the men's section, how it's ... monitored by the ultra-Ortho-dox ... I would focus on Jerusalem as the religious capital of many religions and look at how all those religions interact. I think in terms of the physical focus that I would have the kids do *gadna*. I think that they need to be less enamoured of the army than they are, and [they need to] realize how harsh the conditions are and that just because you're in the army doesn't mean you're smart ... or even brave, and instead of looking at the weaponry I think I'd have them talk to people who had been in the army [and] what is it like to serve in the Occupied Territories and to really talk about that and the fear and all of that ... I think that the connection with the land can be forged through much of the natural beauty of the land and that I would ... walk through the *wadis* [desert valleys]. We would go and visit, like, Sde Boker [Ben-Gurion's *kibbutz* and site of his tomb], and the field school so that they had a sense of the terrain of Israel, not just the cities; do some hikes up in the north. [In the Galilee] there's history and there's beauty and there's Jewish sites and there's burial sites ... We would walk up Masada ... We would also talk about what happened there in a less ... heroic gesture and how Masada has evolved and what it means. I think I'd try to bring out a lot more controversy in the tour.

As soon as she finished outlining her own tour itinerary, she exclaimed: 'Now that I've recorded this I'm never going to get a chance to take anybody who's Jewishly funded!' Actually, Lynn had produced what was practically a summary of the itineraries generally offered by tours to Israel. She had mapped Israel using the classical Zionist sites and tropes: the land, the *kibbutzim*, the Masada, and the Galilee. But she also was insisting on a very different interpretation of these places as well as on a dialogue between Israelis – including Palestinians – and diaspora Jewry. Although she still contended that Israel's Jewish sites were meaningful, she wanted Israel to be reimagined in a more multi-faceted and less militarized manner.

When I asked Lynn why she did not move to Israel, she said she was never 'prepared to make the personal kinds of financial sacrifices that it took in order to move there ... Did I want my children in the army? No ... Could I live through the kind of personal suffering that mothers go through there? No.' In her past support of Israel, Lynn had been very active – she even described herself as 'jingoistic.' Yet not even her high level of ideological commitment could motivate her to sacrifice the comforts of life in North America. She had recently began rethinking her life in North America when a '*kibbutz* friend' came to visit her. She recounted how they had

> looked at slides of '73–'74 and talked about all the people that we knew [and] I think that I would have been very bored in Israel. I don't think that I would have found the same kind of intellectual community that I found here. I think that I would have been preoccupied so much by the daily struggles of life that life would have been pretty boring so ... no. If I was extremely wealthy I would go there for six months a year like people [who go to] Florida, but that's it.

In many respects, Lynn had shifted from a more classical, idealistic, and Zionist position toward a more critical, post-Zionist position in which both Israel's Jews and Jews living outside of Israel had a place – and even more than one place – to call their own. As critical as she had been about Israeli politics, she still imagined Israel through some of the most potent symbols of Zionism. For her, Israel was still a place with deep significance.

Karen and Paul

Karen and Paul are the life-long friends of someone I met on tour. I was introduced to them at their home in an exclusive suburb of a large American city. I was invited to their house for coffee, dessert and an interview. They were in their sixties but looked much younger. Paul had worked with labour organizations. Karen had once owned her own small business but was not employed at the time we met.

We began with a discussion of their childhood and youth. Both had heard about Israel while they were growing up. Paul had been 'indoctrinated very early on' and even remembered the 'birth of the State of Israel.' He described his parents, who had contributed 'large sums of money' to the state, as 'very active in the formation of Israel.' Since his youth he had 'followed [Israel's] events, the different wars, the changing political parties.' For Karen, Israel was always 'simply there':

> I had simply always felt a kinship, a connectedness ... And there was a period of time in fact I remember, I would say 'we' when referring to Israel and [Paul] would say, 'But it's not ['we']. You're not an Israeli,' and he's right, I'm not an Israeli and I shouldn't be referring to 'we' in terms

of nationality ... but that is what I am talking about – the connectedness – and just [how] it had always been there.

Although Israel had always been a presence in their lives, they were adults before they went to see it for themselves. That first trip, in 1983, was important to them: it marked their daughter's Bat Mitzvah, and it enabled them to share their attachment to the state with all their children. When they discussed their trips to Israel, Karen and Paul emphasized the state's economic and social development. Karen described what had impressed her on her first trip and the subsequent ones:

I guess one of the things which struck me during our trip [was] the conversion of the dry Arab piece of land into lush vegetation sitting next to more [desert], and the realization that the only reason that [there] was lush vegetation was because of [the] technical and scientific advances that simply don't exist in other parts of the world. And it was extraordinarily impressive to see [Israeli] accomplishments ... I mean it's a brand new country.

Karen had imagined Israel in classically Zionist terms: as a barren land transformed and developed into a modern, productive one by the Jews. Paul nodded his agreement while Karen spoke and then told me:

I guess I tend to talk [to friends and family] about ... the country being there as a bastion of democracy in an area where democracy is not very prevalent. And the history ... it's impossible not to go there and be overwhelmed with Jewish and Christian and Muslim history. It is all around you. Also there's a third connection in my case. I'm involved with the Labour Movement here and ... there's a powerful tie with Histadrut [the largest Labour Union Movement] in Israel ... So that's an additional connection.

Paul's more political reflections added to an already Zionist depiction of the state. He described Israel as a democratic state that had developed strong social institutions such as the Histadrut. These institutions are often associated with the vision of Israel as fair, egalitarian, and socialist – all-important descriptors to Paul, who cared deeply about labour rights and politics.

I asked Paul whether travelling to Israel had prompted him to think differently about Jews in the world:

I have a feeling of being perhaps even more impressed of the obstacles that the Israelis have overcome through the series of wars. When I ... looked from a point in Israel across a very small valley and saw Jordan, an adversary, or when we went up on to the Golan Heights and looked down on the *kibbutz*, which could be so easily shelled, I had an even greater appreciation for the dangers with which Israel had been presented ever since its formation.

Clearly, Paul and I had taken very similar tours, albeit as many as fifteen years apart. After touring these sites, Paul had come to believe that Israel is militarily insecure and that, in a remarkable way, it had overcome some of the greatest odds posed against it.

On her first trip, Karen had been especially 'struck with the fact that this was the first time that Jews around the world had a haven, had a home' after having 'been dispersed' throughout the world. As she put it: 'I knew it before, I knew it theoretically, but it was much more poignant.' Paul interjected: 'There was a feeling that "Oh, my God, I'm in the Jewish state." So there was an emotional response.' Later Karen added:

It's in the abstract for those of us who don't plan necessarily to relocate ... I would say that it's important for most Jews [that] the state of Israel continues to exist for Jews as a Jewish communal. I have no evidence to back that up. It's just our communication ... with friends, an awareness of the Jewish community in this country. It feels very strong that we have the existence of this homeland.

Both Karen and Paul described the importance of Israel in psychosocial terms. That is, they believed that Israel helped Jews develop a sense of security as well as communalism in North America. Just knowing that a Jewish state existed helped Jews forge stronger links to one another. It helped them imagine themselves as a nation and a community in North America, as well as in relation to Israel. Thus, it was all the more important to Jews that Israel be a 'strong [and] dynamic place' and 'a bastion of Western democracy.'

Karen and Paul also said that notwithstanding their Zionist attachment to Israel, they were 'living examples' of the kinds of problems facing Jews in North America. Although their identity as Jews and their commitment to Israel had been very strong, all their children had married 'out' – that is, they had married non-Jews. Their children's

Jewish upbringing had not provided their family any protection against intermarriage. They noted this, yet they did not seem upset by it. As Karen put it:

> The only way to maintain Jewish identity is to have oppression because the more oppression you have and the more ghettoization you have, the more banding together you have. But once you have a ... country that is tolerant of Judaism [like the United States], you find a greater assimilation and that is happening here and I think it's probably happening all over the world. And yet there are some families where there is no intermarriage, maybe the more Orthodox. At this point I think that's unusual.

This statement reflected Karen's nostalgia for a sense of community rather than any desire for a less tolerant North America. But Karen's comments were also important because they reinforced her own need for and association with Israel in Jewish communal and collective terms. According to Karen and Paul, this commitment needed to be extended to include the responsibility of all North American Jews to protect Israel should support for the state lag at the political level. As Paul stated later:

> I think if the time came when there were a government in this country that wasn't quite sure what its relationship with Israel was going to be, it would be helpful to Israel for American Jewry to [use] all the legitimate political pressures to say, 'Hey, don't forget Israel. She's been our friend. We still want her as our friend.'

Karen and Paul did not identify with Israel for individual reasons; they did not cite anti-Semitism or any vulnerability in their own identifications as Jews. Even their reflections on intermarriage were not framed in terms of loss but rather were informed by a pragmatism associated with their own choice to live secular lives outside of Israel and in an open society like the United States.

I asked whether either of them would ever return to Israel to live. Both immediately exclaimed: 'Never.'

KAREN: But that's not [because it is Israel]. If you [asked], 'Would you live anywhere but this country?' the answer would be 'never.' It's not that we would never go to Israel. We would never leave this country on any basis ... Why should we? I have no reason to go. There's absolutely no reason to leave a country that we have grown up in, where our parents were born, a country to which our grandparents migrated. There is no –

PAUL: And that we think is the greatest country on earth.

KAREN: Yes, there is absolutely ... no motivation [to go] whatsoever ... I would live in another country for a year ... If Paul got assigned to Switzerland or some wonderful place for a year or two, sure. But would I ever permanently leave? Absolutely not.

PAUL: As much as we have a tie to Israel the tie would never be that strong to make us to leave America and live in Israel.

KAREN: I find them very frightening, those Orthodox Jews ...

PAUL: The control they exercise, this tiny little group whom we do regard as fanatics.

KAREN: Any fanatics, it doesn't matter what religion they are.

PAUL: Fanatics and zealots shouldn't control any country, and given the very fragile conditions there now, they have a tremendous amount of power. Scary.

In their exchange, Paul and Karen shifted from reflections on the safety and security of life in the United States to the fear of what life might be like in an Israel they saw as controlled by Orthodox Jewry. Israel's modernity, development and democracy, which they had celebrated earlier, came into question and even paled in comparison to life in the United States.

Clearly, Karen and Paul's perceptions of Israel were complex. They identified with and idealized Israel in classically Zionist terms and they recognized its importance for all Jews living outside the state. But at the same time, they preferred the United States, especially in light of the rise of Orthodox power in Israel.

Regarding the Oslo Accords, both Karen and Paul had felt 'delight,' 'relief,' and 'happiness' when they were signed. But Paul did not believe that the accords themselves had changed North American Jews' perspective on the conflict. Rather, 'more recent events' had done that:

There are at least two, or maybe there are three, schools of thought ... in this country among American Jews. Number one: What else could Israel do? This Arafat always was, always will be, a terrorist. It's hopeless and it's all his fault. That's number one. Number two: What is this idiot [Prime Minister] Netanyahu doing to screw up the peace process? And then there's at least one other school, [and] I think I'm in that school, which is: I'm not sure I fully trust Arafat ... but on the other hand, we'll

never know how far the two groups can travel toward the road to peace if
the present Israeli government keeps putting roadblocks in the path ... I
guess ... from week to week, from month to month I condemn either or
both.

He turned to Karen and asked: 'What do you say about that?' She
responded:

> Well it's interesting. I agree with you ... I don't know that you necessarily
> can expect somebody to philosophically change – and I'm referring to
> Arafat now – but at the same time he can become very pragmatic as he
> recognizes that without some form of a peace process, that war is going to
> go on for another two thousand or more ... years. So [it's] not that he has
> changed but that, perhaps, his thinking is much more focused on trying
> to resolve some of the issues. Whatever [Arafat's] feelings and thinking is,
> it's Netanyahu that is a shock to us. We heard him speak at the Israeli
> Embassy when he was an underling here in this country [and] he was so
> impressive ... There was a brilliance to this man.

On one trip to Israel, Karen had wondered why there was any need
to keep the West Bank at all. She had asked herself, 'Why are we fighting over this? There are so many ways that the West Bank could be
used other than to create controversy between the Arabs and the Jews.
It could be [divided] between Israel and the Arabs ... as a homeland for
the Palestinians.' Both Karen and Paul believed that the solution to the
problem of the conflict between the Palestinians and the Israelis could
be dealt with pragmatically. Neither focused on human rights issues or
security issues or on the long-held animosity toward Israel in the
region. Rather, they cited political reasons for the ongoing conflict – in
particular, the weakness and untrustworthiness of the leadership on
both sides of the conflict.

This latter discussion led to one focused on the role played by
Rabin's assassination, at which both had felt 'shock and great sorrow.'
Paul then asked: 'What will this mean for the peace process? ... The
way things have turned out, of course, [is] to make that tragedy even
more tragic ... The lunatic that killed [Rabin] has succeeded in doing
exactly what he wanted to do.' In contrast to those whose response to
Rabin's murder was to say that they had been shocked that 'a Jew was
murdered by another Jew,' Paul's immediate reaction to the murder of
the prime minister was to wonder aloud about its ramifications for the

peace process. Neither Karen nor Paul ever spoke of military solutions to any of the conflicts in the region.

Interestingly, then, diaspora Jews who travelled to Israel in the period between the Six Day War in 1967 and the 1982 War with Lebanon emphasized their political attachment to Israel. They were proud of Israel's accomplishments, but they rarely idealized their relationship to the Jews as a nation or to the State of Israel. In fact, they were often quite critical of some things, in particular, the power of the ultra-Orthodox Jews and the ongoing conflict between Israel and the Palestinians. They were optimistic – though not in any naive way – that a just resolution to the conflict, namely, a sharing of the land, would emerge in due time.

13
Routes to Belonging

Historian Harold Troper suggested that diaspora Jews' relationship to Israel changed after 1982, the year that Israel invaded Lebanon and a peace movement began to form within Israel.[1] For some diaspora Jews, this was when they began criticizing Israel openly, its military policy in particular. Yet many North American Jews have developed relationships to Israel only since 1982, and for them the 1982 war has little or no significance. Theirs is a fairly recent attachment to the state. Some of the diaspora Jews I met on the tours were seeing Israel for the first time – an experience that would change their lives.

Ozzy

I met Ozzy on the Israel Development Fund (IDF) tour in 1998. I interviewed him near the end of the tour in a small vegetarian restaurant on a beach promenade on the Red Sea. He was born in Hungary during the Second World War, had immigrated to Canada as an adult, and was the head of a medical faculty in a large Canadian city.

It was clear to me almost immediately after we met that Ozzy was a thoughtful and engaged traveller. We soon struck up a friendship with an elderly couple who helped us understand some of the religious practices we were asked to join. Ozzy was a quiet and pleasant man, though few of the others had a chance to speak with him; he kept his distance while observing carefully and listening intently – to the participants as well as to the guides.

Ozzy is the son of Holocaust survivors. At Yad Vashem, he told tour participants the story of his family's miraculous survival and of the heroism of the righteous gentile who rescued his father. Ozzy's father and five of his brothers and brothers-in-law were press-ganged into the Hungarian Work Brigades, but only his father returned after the war. The others perished under slave labour conditions, having been sent to the Ukrainian front to [work in] the mines. His father, along with 120 others, was able to escape death at the front lines because a colonel in the Hungarian army who was a 'Hungarian aristocrat, a Christian, a gentleman' sent them to do 'menial tasks' instead. The colonel's actions were discovered and he was court-martialled and sentenced to death for his deeds, but the Soviet advance into the area saved his life. He was 'rewarded' for his courage by being demoted to night watchman in a shoe factory. Ozzy expressed deep love and respect for this man, who was responsible for his family's survival. Though he was only five or six years old at the time, he fondly remembered the colonel's visits to his parent's home after the war, and his parents' love for the man who called those he saved 'his boys.'

When we met, Ozzy was on his third trip to Israel. He had come in part to complete a 'mission' he had begun two years earlier: to finish inscribing the names of the last of the fifty-one people in his family who had perished in the Holocaust. But he also wanted to 'learn about the country, see the country ... and see some friends.' Also, he was thre to attend a board meeting for a major development organization working in Israel. His attachment to Israel was fairly new, yet he was already deeply engaged.

Ozzy told me that before his first trip to Israel in 1995, to celebrate Jerusalem's three-thousandth anniversary, he had 'basically no relationship to Israel ... Israel was a stranger to me other than the fact that there were Jewish people living here and some very distant relatives and some distant friends.' All he knew about Israel came from reading about it. He recounted how he felt after landing in Israel for the first time: 'I was getting off the plane with this very major question mark in my mind and in my heart. Who am I? How do I fit into this picture? How does this picture fit into me? What is this going to be like? And what am I really doing here?' In Israel, Ozzy began seeking answers to existential questions about his place in the world. On his second day ever in Israel, the first day of the 1995 tour, they were driving north along the coast:

As the guide started to talk about history, about things that I was comfortable with and familiar, I started relaxing. And then, as I was watching there was something that I caught out of the corner of my eye: uniforms, soldiers. And I kept on looking at their faces, these children in uniforms, these Jewish children in uniforms – who would maybe live or die, God only knows, but they had to do it – that's where I started crying, seeing those kids. That was my connection at that moment in time with what the hell I was doing here, who I was, and it was just an opening and that made the whole trip afterwards a roller coaster [of] up-and-down emotions ... It was ... from a personal perspective ... an understanding, an awakening, a fresh start.

For Ozzy, Israel was the place of his own 'awakening' or 'fresh start.' Here he might find the reasons for his family's suffering as well as for their survival. He described Israel:

It's a certain part of my own personal mosaic. I identify with things, [and the] people ... here. It allows me to forge a more secure self-identity and, based on that, exposing my children to this hopefully will allow them to get a better-balanced view of what the world is ... Basically, being a descendant of Holocaust survivors, the only identity I had was pain and my mother's denial of who we were all about and what we're all about ... Perhaps the positive things that can be happening in Jewish life, that there is a good side to being a Jew, there's things that you can be proud of, things that can be accomplished [when you] identify yourself a Jew. It was an option that has been given to me, and it's an option that I grabbed onto with two hands. I feel ... I'm more at peace with myself and [with] others.

In the past, Ozzy could only associate being Jewish with tragedy, pain, loss, and insecurity. Israel had enabled him to explore and reflect on modern Jews' accomplishments and empowerment. Although he claimed he had only begun to 'put the pieces of the mosaic together,' it was clear that by now he was strongly attracted to Israel's great potential, not only for himself but also for his children. He explained why he felt that Israel is essential:

It's not only for North American Jews but Jews all over the world. Having lived for thousands of years under other people and having to conform to everybody else's way of life, and being subjected to the more or less discriminatory practices of others – depending who they were under – the simple fact that a Jewish homeland exists [is essential]. And it's clearly not the biblical land that the Mosheah's [Hebrew for Messiah] going to come into. It's a political entity. It's a last potential place for refuge. It's a source of pride and peace; peace with the notion that if ... things will happen like they did happen to my family and other people's family ... there's a place where we can go home, where we're welcome.

Ozzy envisioned Israel as a political space where Jews were able to assert their sovereignty after centuries of subjugation. His Holocaust experience formed the background for his belief that the Jews need a safe place of refuge.

He talked about how he described Israel to friends and family:

It's the land and the people. The land is absolutely breathtaking. The land is full of history, [it holds] a lot of emotions for a lot of people in this part of the world. And ... the mosaic of people that you see here is just unbelievable, from all parts of the world, from all walks of life, from all cultural, ethnic, and religious backgrounds. It's a phenomenal place.

Ozzy did not allude to the sacredness of the land nor did he romanticize it as the Jews' territory. In fact, he recognized that the land had deep meaning for others in the region, and he seemed to appreciate the multicultural, multiethnic, multireligious mosaic. But he had also observed that there were divisions in Israeli society, especially between secular and religious Jews. He said of the intolerance he witnessed: 'The religious don't claim to be tolerant but at least some of the more secular [Jews] claim to be. [But] even within that camp there are extremists who have a hard time getting along with their brethren who practise Judaism, [or] see Judaism in a different form.'

Ozzy talked at some length about his experiences on the IDF tour. He had learned that some Israelis have difficulty separating religious narratives from secular ones. This resulted in a form of intolerance on the part of secular Jews, who either would not or could not understand that their own practices were also shaped by religion.

This tour had provided Ozzy with his first meaningful experience at the Wailing Wall. In the past, it had been difficult for him to find meaning there because he had experienced a 'very secular upbringing.' But as a parent, he had recently developed a new and pleasurable relationship to Judaism. He enjoyed learning about it. He described his experience at the Wailing Wall:

It was perhaps threatening for me to go up and see all these people [the Orthodox] with their black hats and [to see] things that I didn't understand ... Having had the explanation [by one of the tour guides who had humanized the Orthodox] [made] it a lot easier also going up to the Wall on a *Shabbat*, which I've never done before. All of a sudden hearing people singing songs where I recognized the tune and I looked at them – and these are people from all over the world – it made for a sense of commonality. It was not divisive, it was inclusive, and that's what I've been looking for on this trip ... and that has made a difference for me.

The tour of an Orthodox section of Jerusalem we had taken early on the tour had engaged and enlightened him. He felt a good deal more comfortable, no longer 'threatened' by the unknown that the Orthodox represented. As a secular man who had been searching for the roots and the meaning of his own identity as a Jew, and who had had no upbringing in Judaism, he found the Wall to be the one place where the Jews' continuity as a people was positively expressed in a communal way. The wall was meaningful for him not because of its religious power, but because the songs he heard were part of a tradition and allowed for the expression of the collective, the creation of a communal atmosphere. The Wall was no longer an intimidating space for him; it now symbolized continuity, survival, and community. It had become a meaningful place.

When Ozzy and I discussed North American Jews' relationship to Israel, he expressed his hope that Israel's dependence on North America would one day shift so that there would be 'a two-way street.' He then paraphrased a comment he heard Israeli politician Shimon Peres make on an earlier tour: 'Israeli Jews can learn a little *yiddishkeit* [Yiddish knowledge] from North American Jews and [North American Jews] can learn a little Hebrew from [Israelis].' Ozzy added, 'I believe that North American [and] world Jewry in general is very important [to Israel]. When it's lonely at the United Nations ... Israel still has to think and, hopefully the people in Israel know, that there are people out there who care.' Ozzy here was positioning Israeli government as a fairly weak player in the international arena, as needing not only political but also moral support from others. But Ozzy worried that the close relationship between North America and Israel could be blamed for Israel's recent Americanization – something he did not appreciate:

I'm a throwback, I guess, from the pioneer days. I liked the spirit this country had before Coca-Cola and McDonalds invaded, [before] the me, me, me. [I preferred] the 'let's get together [and] work together.' I guess it's the price you pay when you get out of the ghetto mentality. But I wish they would have emulated something a little bit more worthwhile ... There's nothing wrong with money but this buy, buy, buy, [it's] material- istic, [and the] spiritual loses.

Ozzy imagined Israel as a less consumerist and more communal place in the past. For him, its subsequent Americanization was a great disappointment. He was idealizing Israel's past, especially what he characterized as its 'pioneering' era. This could only emerge from a Zionist reading of Israel's beginnings, and from an even more nar- rowly conceived origin myth based almost solely on the role of the *kib- butzim*, which are often represented as austere and non-materialistic communities.

Twice while we were talking, Ozzy told me he had been watching me at different sites, hoping to gain some understanding of my per- spective. I asked him what he would tell friends and family about this tour. He replied that he would tell them he had experienced 'the plea- sure of seeing first hand the mixed emotions of individuals of mixed backgrounds and how this place affects them.' I asked him if anything he had experienced had prompted him to think differently about Palestinians:

Yes, *you* did ... because you qualified [the tour]. With this trip the simple fact is we have not had contacts with the Palestinians ... Other than the odd time in the hotel, somebody running by you whose nametag clearly [is] not found in Judaism, [or] walking by them in the markets ... there was no provision for interaction with people. There's no provision to allow [for the] exchange of ideas, opinion, and that's also very difficult because language barriers do crop up. So vicariously I had to see it through your eyes – [to see] some of the difficulties and some of the per- haps pain that has been encountered by positions taken by people or gov- ernment agencies, whatever that may be.

It interested me that Ozzy thought it important to try to gain a dif- ferent perspective on Israel, and that he assumed my perspective would be informed by my Palestinian and mixed heritage. Instead of dismissing my experience as simply 'biased' – something many others had done both on tour and in the community – he seemed genuinely curious and concerned about my perceptions and about those of others he had not had the opportunity to speak to.

When we discussed the Oslo Accords, Ozzy recalled how in 1993 he had felt a 'guarded hope.' However, the 'history of the region [and] the difficulties encountered in the past between combatants' made him cautious. I asked him, 'Do you think the Oslo Accords change North American Jews' perspectives on the Israel-Palestine conflict?' He answered, 'In essence, no,' and explained:

> The reason I say in essence no [is that] fundamentally I don't think that North American Jews or even North American Palestinians for that matter have the hands-on information that is accurate, in-depth, that reflects the true reality on the ground. You read what you read, you hear what you hear, you try to glean in between, you get whatever information that you can and then try to sort of come up with a position or an understanding ... We're not being sold the true bill of goods by anybody. We hear only a certain elite or a certain voice emanating ... Had I had the opportunity to go in to ... live with somebody on the West Bank and speak Arabic with them and live with them, them not knowing who I was, and truly get into there, that's how you'd get a totally different answer. But North American Jews, I don't think so, because they are not privy to the truth. The world is not privy to the truth.

Ozzy was highly sceptical of the representations he had been exposed to with respect to the Israel-Palestine conflict. He was suggesting that one way to get to the truth would be to experience the conflict by living among Palestinians in the West Bank. I did not ask him why he felt he could not be safe as a Jew in the West Bank. By this time, however, knowing his gift for empathy, it was a fair assumption he was not afraid of the reception he would get from the Palestinians so much as he was worried about the dangers of living in a militarized zone.

For Ozzy, Israel was an enchanting albeit complicated place. Early in the interview, he described Israel as 'a diamond – it has got a ton of faces and I'll never cover them all in a lifetime.'

Josie

When I met Josie, she was working for the Israel Civil Society Fund (ICSF) in the United States, where she coordinated social events for local donors. A few months after meeting on the ICSF tour, we met at the American office. Later still, I conducted a telephone interview with her.

Josie grew up in New York state. Her Jewish mother 'really knew Israel, [but] Israel to me was a tiny little plot on the globe that was fun to try and find when I was growing up ... Other than that I had absolutely no relationship to Israel.' She had begun 'working on and developing [her] Jewish identity as a young adult and felt ... Israel was ... the next step in that process.' When the opportunity to work for the ICSF opened up, she took it.

She visited Israel for the first time in 1993 when the ICSF held a board meeting in Israel. She described that trip as 'a very strange and disappointing experience':

> I felt, I thought I was going to have a 'click' when I got there ... I got off the plane and thought 'Ah, here I am. This is ... going to concretize the sort of Jewish things that I've been thinking about and learning about and trying to incorporate into my life.' And it didn't [happen] at all. I felt no 'click.' I felt no connection. I felt no passion. I felt really empty about the trip.

On her return, one of her childhood friends asked her, 'Well, what was it like to be in a place where everyone was Jewish?' Josie had immediately replied, 'Well, not everyone's Jewish ... There are more people who are Jewish in Brooklyn than there are in Israel.' Josie had felt completely out of place when she returned to the United States, not certain if she really belonged in a job where she would be 'working in the Jewish community where everyone just ... grew up with Israel as a mantra in their home.'

Josie stayed with the ICSF, and had what she described as a 'life-changing experience' on her second trip to Israel. She attributed this experience to the fact that she had been 'lucky enough' to join a group of 'ten incredible women' and that she was pregnant at the time, which she believed had 'furthered' her 'feelings for ... Judaism.' Also, she was becoming close friends with an Israeli who worked at the ICSF. When Josie returned from that tour, she asked her husband, 'When are we going [to Israel], when are we moving, when are we going back?':

> It was amazing and I just developed this passion that I'd never felt before for a place. I mean, I've always loved different places in my life. I loved France when I lived there and I loved places, but I never felt this. There's something about Israel that got to me inside that I had never felt about any place before, and my love for it, my connection to it, my understanding of it has deepened since then.

Yad Vashem was a turning point for Josie:

> Before that second momentous trip to Israel the Holocaust Museum
> opened ... in Washington. I went a couple of times with [my spouse] and
> the first time I went I ended the trip in the Holocaust Museum [and I had]
> the overwhelming feeling that I wanted to have children. That was like
> how I felt coming out of the museum. It was very intense understanding
> what continuity was about. And then we left and forgot about it. [I] went
> back to the museum a couple of months later and felt that again after I
> left, and [I] thought 'Oh, my God, that's what I felt the first time I was
> here.' And when I went to Israel and was actually pregnant, it kind of
> was a closure for me of that feeling. It was a sense of I understand *there*,
> [and] I understand *here*, what it really means to want to have children ...
> And [when a friend told me that the experience of the Holocaust
> Museum in Israel would be more powerful] I just didn't understand what
> that meant. And I went to Yad Vashem my first trip and said, 'Oh it's an
> old dusty museum, it's not particularly innovative and I don't under-
> stand it.' And then when we went back on the second trip, I understood
> it. I understood what it meant to be at Yad Vashem in Jerusalem versus
> being at the Holocaust Museum in Washington ... You know, we grew up
> in an age where the Holocaust was discussed, there were Holocaust
> classes at my high school and college ... So I feel like, in some ways – and
> that's how I felt when I went to Yad Vashem the first time – I've seen this,
> I've done this. And since I didn't have the sensibility of Israel, the land ...
> at that time ... it wasn't moving. I mean, it's always moving but it wasn't
> particularly moving to me. But that second time it really was. And the
> second time I went I didn't even go into the museum. We took the group
> and I sat out in one of the gardens and that was much more meaningful
> to me.

As Josie developed an attachment to Israel and came to understand
its importance for Jewish continuity, her experience of Yad Vashem
took on greater meaning. The Israeli museum's age and shabby
appearance were no longer important to her. Important instead was its
location in the place of the Jews' renewal, return, and rebirth. She had
made the connection between the Holocaust, Jewish continuity, and
Israel. At both sites, her desire for continuity was literally embodied in
her desire to become pregnant.

I asked Josie if she believed that trips to Israel were an important
means of linking North American Jews to Israel:

I think that going to Israel, going someplace and walking the streets and feeling the pavement underneath your toes and really talking to people who live there and breath[ing] it and see[ing] it every day gives you a very different perspective on what it's about and why it's important to have Israel ... Not only are you linking yourself to your history and you're linking yourself to the land ... you're linking yourself to the current-day Israel, you're linking yourself to the people you're travelling with and the people that you meet there.

Regarding the importance of Israel for North American Jews, Josie told me it 'represented ... the continuation and the continuity issues of the diaspora community. [They] look to Israel for a sense of having a homeland.' In other words, Israel embodied Jewish continuity and provided security: Jews could always know they had a place to call their own.

Because she worked for a diaspora organization, I expected that Josie would tell me it is important for Israeli and diaspora Jews to maintain strong relationships. That is just what she told me – also, that trips to Israel are among the most important tools at the disposal of organizations like hers:

Those are incredible experience and meetings ... and it makes you think about your life and their lives and what the intersections are and aren't ... It's the same thing when you meet one of our Arab grantees working in the Arab community. When you meet [a woman] up in Nazareth, think about the work that she's done to set up preschools and equivalent Head Start ... programs and to try and bridge the gap between Arab schooling and Jewish schooling in Israel and you think, 'Oh my God ... that happens in my country too.' I understand what this means now. I can see it. And ... this woman, this incredibly educated, very beautiful woman who is doing work to help the children of her community. So, I think those are the experiences that really change people's lives and views and thoughts about their relation to the world.

According to Josie, these organizations were bringing people to places where they would be able to see that their donations were being well spent. The ICSF's donors were politically liberal. They were aware of the racism and discrimination faced by American minority groups, so when they saw these things in Israel, they quickly recognized them and were happy to donate to programs that addressed them. However, the problems faced by Palestinians had to be explained to these donors in apolitical terms. That is, they had to be presented in ways that did not highlight the national struggle (e.g., no *kafiahs* in sight). Tour narratives never fully articulated the extent to which the Palestinians' asymmetrical economic and social position was due to Israel's policies, which reflected its interests as a Jewish state.

Josie's evolving relationship to Israel was interesting though not unusual. The closer her ties became to the Jewish community in the United States, the greater her attachment to Israel. It was noteworthy how often she spoke about survival, continuity, tradition, and the collective. Only after she accepted her place in the community did she come to appreciate the importance of Israel to it.

Gillian

Gillian, a nurse in her late fifties from a Canadian prairie city, was on her second trip in almost ten years when we met on the IDF tour. She agreed to be interviewed in the lounge of our hotel, a few days before we left Israel. Her father was a Jew (originally from Odessa) but she had not been 'brought up Jewish.' Just before he died, she promised him she would attend services every Yom Kippur; she remembered him telling her, 'Anybody that has an ounce of Jew in him should be in *schul* on Yom Kippur.' She claimed that it was a brother-in-law who had really sparked her interest in the IDF. Gillian brought her boyfriend, George, along for his first tour of Israel.

I asked Gillian about her reasons for coming to Israel and her relationship to Israel:

> I feel like I have roots [here]. My father is Jewish and it's something that I've just always wanted to experience ... I feel a sense of belonging. Maybe I'm being too presumptuous when I say that but I just feel like it's a part of me. [It had evolved from] a curiosity [and] grew to an interest and ... it's a passion now.

Gillian's connection to Israel was based on her imagining it as a Jewish state, and her ties to it were based on what she perceived to be its very Jewishness. This sense of belonging was what I really wanted her to talk about, so I asked her how she described Israel to others:

> [What] I always say to them is that I can't begin to describe to you the

feelings I experience when I'm over there, the emotional roller-coaster you get over there. It's just beyond words and when I talk to friends and when I talk to family and some of my family have been here, immediately they say, 'No more. We know exactly what you mean.'

I asked her to explain why it was a 'roller-coaster':

I guess the height for me is the Western Wall and I know when I was there last night, everything just overflows ... And I can't really explain it. I don't know what it is ... why I'm touched so much at that point, but I am. And it's just like I'm in my own little world and I come away with a great sense of strength, of peace, and I had that experience the first time I was here too ... I came back with a very strong sense of well-being and ... rejuvenation ... It's like a source of strength here and I wish I could explain it better but I can't. It's just an emotion that I feel and that I experience.

Gillian represented Israel – and the Western Wall in particular – as sites imbued with spiritual and even mystical though not especially religious significance. In those places she felt rooted, connected with the ancestral and collective identity of the Jews. She experienced Israel affectively and could not describe it. Interestingly, she never described the ultra-Orthodox presence at the Wall or their political role in Israel either.

Gillian was strongly impressed by the work of organizations engaged in the economic and social development of Israel. She was especially pleased to see the Canada Centre, a community centre we visited in Metulla on the Golan Heights. Implied in her comments was that Israelis depended heavily on outside funding and that diaspora Jews' fundraising was crucial to them.

Gillian seemed mostly uninterested in politics. She said she had been much 'more impressionable' on her first tour of Israel. I asked her to explain:

I think that when you're ... away from Israel, you listen to the news, you listen to people's opinions and you can become influenced so easy from the truth ... With my first trip, I really experienced the Israeli, the Jewish-Arab relationship – it became very real to me. And when I went back after my first trip, when I interacted with other people, whenever they said something about 'Oh, those poor Arabs,' I became very defensive, and I said, 'You must go and see for yourself.' 'You have to get it first-hand.'

And again [on this trip] I will come away with that. [George] has never been here ... I [tried] to impress on him – like he's often said, 'Oh, yes, sure, but there's this small piece of land and they both have the right to live here' and on and on [and] I said to him ... 'Let's talk about it after the trip. Just come down here and be open-minded and keep your eyes open, your ears open, and see. I'm going to see a change in you.' Not that he was prejudiced in any way. He was ignorant, like most people are when they haven't experienced it. And, yesterday, he said to me, 'I'm beginning to see the light.'

When I asked her what she thought might have prompted such a change in him, she beamed:

I think a lot of things [like] Prime Minister's [Netanyahu's] speech ... He's never had the greatest respect for him and where that came from I don't know but after listening to him I think he realized that yes, [Netanyahu] really does want peace, he does want a peaceful settlement. [Netanyahu would] like everybody to live in peace but he understands, I think, that peace isn't all about [the Jews'] sacrifice. I mean, the one party can't keep on sacrificing and sacrificing territory and rights and et cetera. It's got to be both ways, and I think [George] became more aware that maybe the Arab role is a little too demanding.

Gillian's interpretation of the conflict and of Netanyahu's speech was that 'the Arabs' wanted more than they deserve and that they were forcing the hand of the Israelis. From her perspective, the Arabs had at least as much power as the Israelis. She described the Palestinians as Arabs – a description that portrayed them as part of an larger, amorphous Arab population; thus, she did not recognize their national rights or their particular history in and relationship to Israel. She believed that those who did not 'see Israel for themselves' were more likely to be biased against Israel and to misrepresent the situation in favour of the Arabs. I asked her whether anything she had experienced on the tour prompted her to think differently about Palestinians or Arabs:

Well, I didn't realize that, like [at] the hotel [in Jerusalem], that the employees are 50 per cent Jewish, 50 per cent Arabs ... I didn't realize that and I understand that's a lot ... I was told they have to be 50 per cent Arab and 50 per cent Jewish ... I was very amazed at the openness demonstrated even by our tour guide [Arnie from the IDF]. Like he does not speak negatively about the Arabs at all. In fact, he's very positive. And that was ... shocking to me because I thought that there would be more of a distinction between them and us and I didn't sense that at all.

Gillian saw Israel as a tolerant state not only because Arabs could be found working in its tourist sector (mainly in hotels) but also because the tour guides did not articulate anti-Arab sentiments. This was a naive representation of the issues, to be sure, and one that highlighted her animosity toward Arabs. In her estimation, they were unmistakably Israel's enemies and the distinction between *them* and *us* needed to be made.

Gillian 'always hoped that they could live peacefully,' but she also wondered whether 'two separate identities' or nations could do so, and she felt that 'time can be stubborn and so that makes for problems.' She did not believe that signing a treaty could bring peace because 'it's a little more involved.' I asked her if the Oslo Accords had transformed her own or others' perspectives on the Palestinians conflict:

I think the prejudice [against the Palestinians] probably came out stronger. I think it's the land issue. Eventually you feel like, how much more does Israel have to give up? Like, I mean, when is it enough? When are they going to be satisfied enough and say, 'Okay, we won't make any more demands'? So when you hear that it just seems like it was never enough, so then you sort of became resentful. At least I did.

I asked her whom she resented. 'The Palestinians,' she told me. 'Although I know they have a right to be here ... I think they're too demanding.' According to her, the Palestinians had blocked any peaceful resolution by making unrealistic demands for land. She saw Israel as having to 'give up,' not return or exchange, territory. However, it is significant that Gillian never represented the Palestinians as violent, only as unreasonable. Also, she did not discuss the conflict in militaristic terms or in terms of Israeli security. Remarkably, she saw the conflict as based strictly on land issues rather than on Arabs' longstanding hatred of Jews. Here, the Palestinian negotiators would likely have agreed with her. She seemed most concerned about how the two communities could share the land, and how much the Jews might have to relinquish in order to have peace.

I asked Gillian if anything on the tour had prompted her to think differently about Jews in the world:

Yes, actually. I had heard about the Ethiopian immigration and it was starting to sink in, in a sense. Now, isn't that interesting because you don't think of Jews as being Ethiopian – which is very naive on my part – but I just felt a greater unity with other Jews in the world and I think ... they're demonstrating it with the invitation for anybody to return. Like the return law, the Laws of Return I think have become very open and liberal and that again tells me that, yes they want the people back.

Gillian represented Israel as a place that promoted the rights of the collectivity, as a 'unity.' Its Law of Return was significant for allowing Jews to return to their community in Israel. Significantly, although she clearly knew the much publicized story of the Ethiopian Jews' immigration, she did not represent Israel as a safe haven for North American Jews.

Gillian's reflections on the Israeli and the North American Jewish context revealed a certain disjuncture. Apparently, not all Jewish spaces were quite as welcoming or unifying as Israeli space. This emerged when I asked her if she had learned anything on the tours that prompted her to think differently about North American Jewry:

I think there's a big difference between the Israeli Jews and the North American Jews ... I feel it's more of a cultural thing in North America ... and here [in Israel] I feel it's very much a spiritual thing. I come away with this feeling – in attending synagogue back home – ... that it's almost a form of socializing. It's like a club ... more than an identification with the roots [of our culture].

Gillian experienced Israel as a place imbued with the spirit of the Jews' heritage, their roots. She believed there was an organicity that linked the Jews to Israel – that it was the authentic place to be Jewish. Outside of Israel, synagogues were less spiritual than social places. As such, they were no substitute for Israel – to some extent, they represented its opposite.

I asked Gillian whether Israel was important to North American Jews. 'Not important enough,' she told me, and explained that Jews must make greater efforts at 'rebuilding Israel.' She suggested that their responses were intermittent, prompted only when Israel was being 'threatened by an attack. [Then] everybody's heart pounds.' Even if Jews could 'survive without Israel ... I think Israel really does need North America. They need support from North America ... financially

and emotionally, spiritually. I've ... appreciated the expression of gratitude [shown by the Israelis] that we have chosen to come at this particular time to show support.' For Gillian, North American Jews were
secure even without Israel but Israel was still an insecure, isolated state
in need of outside political and financial support.

Despite her position with regard to the Palestinians and the Arabs in
the region, Gillian, George, and I spent quite a bit of time together
while on tour, and we developed a strong camaraderie. Our shared
experiences led me to believe that she was unhappy about how she
had been treated by other diaspora Jews on the tour. When I asked her
at the end of the interview if she had anything to add, I was not surprised to hear these comments:

> I probably would like to say this: I found that at the beginning of the tour,
> I didn't know whether it was me or whether it was my defensiveness ...
> but I felt that people were less open to me than they are at this stage of the
> game ... You put a bunch of strangers on a bus and at first it depends who
> sits around you and so I really enjoyed getting to know you, chatting with
> you, that was really nice. Now as the week progressed more people
> [were] more open. But what I found quite unusual [was that] they asked
> why did I want to go on a tour with [IDF] and they have a right to know
> ... They were very diplomatic about it and they said, 'You don't have to
> tell us.' And when they asked me [about] my religious orientation, again
> they said, 'You don't have to answer this.' 'Well,' I said, 'I have no prob-
> lems answering it.' And when I explained both [George's] and my back-
> ground, 'Well,' they said, 'that's very interesting.' They were very
> accepting of it but once I got on tour I felt there was a wall ... It was ...
> 'Why are they on our tour?' And as the word got around several people –
> in fact, as late as today – came up to me [and said], 'Oh, I understand your
> father was Jewish.' They said that to [George] too: 'Oh, I understand your
> father was Jewish.' Now all of a sudden there's an acceptance ... I almost
> feel like we qualify now.

Gillian was accurately reporting other's suspicions. A number of
people had even approached me – probably because I had been chat-
ting with Gillian and her partner – to ask why she had taken the tour
and why her partner had come along. All of this was congruent with
her experiences in the Jewish community in her home city, which she
implied was cliquish and exclusionary, as closing itself off from those
whom they perceived as outsiders.

This experience was in stark contrast to what Israel stood for, to its perception of itself as place where all Jews were accepted because, as Gillian understood it, all Jews were spiritually and historically connected. She naively believed that in Israel one's Jewishness was simply one's heritage, that there was no distinction or hierarchy among Jews – certainly not the sort of social hierarchy that she experienced in North America. In Israel, Gillian had found a place that connected her to her past, to her roots; she had found her identity in a place that she believed connected all Jews to one another. Gillian's depictions of Israel as a tolerant nation-state were linked to her perception that this state brought all Jews, regardless of their background, together to their homeland. Hers was also a nationalist imagining of Israel – one which insisted that all Jews needed to be attentive to and responsible for its needs. That is, that they should develop a diaspora relationship to Israel. Moreover, Gillian had these impressions while not at all being engaged in North American Jewish community organizations or activities.

Hope

When I met Hope, she was on her first trip to Israel. I interviewed her after breakfast in our hotel restaurant on the last day of the ICSF tour.

Hope is an experienced political consultant who lives in the northwestern United States. She described how she had 'started out being very involved in the feminist movement' and eventually became heavily involved in 'women-only organizations ... that elect women [and help women get] appointed to public office.' She had managed the political campaigns of three 'underdogs,' and all three had been elected to public office. She was involved in Affirmative Action programs and described herself as 'working to reflect the diversity of our community.' In her own work environment, she had hired 'people of colour,' and most of her staff were women. This was 'a little bit difficult on the white males that worked there but that was okay. They adjusted or they left.' She was clearly a committed liberal and activist.

Hope had never been a member of any synagogue, had never celebrated her Bat Mitzvah, and had never been affiliated with any Jewish organizations. Her family did celebrate Hanukkah and Passover, but this was 'in conjunction with Christmas and Easter.' Hope believed in 'religious pluralism,' and cared about both Christian and Jewish traditions. She maintained no tradition in particular.

As a child, Hope had not learned very much about Israel. Her father, who had planned to become a rabbi before entering medical school instead, had 'a great love for religion, and the history of religion, and the really positive aspects of religion,' and had spoken about and travelled to Israel. But instead of connecting her to Israel, he had instilled in her a 'very strong sense of family and [of] not forgetting the past.' Becoming a grandparent had changed Hope's relationship to Israel: 'Whenever you go through those major transitions [you think about] what [you] want to pass on to the next generation.' She did not believe she knew enough 'about the Promised Land or ... about Israel.' Because she was not religious, she was not interested in 'the biblical parts' but rather in 'Israel and the whole meaning of Judaism.' That is, she cared about her heritage, which was bigger than Israel.

She described Israel as 'the place that many Jews, after World War Two, came to in the hope that in the Promised Land nothing like what happened to them could possibly ever happen [again] ... It was ... like seeking nirvana, seeking a place free of discrimination.'

Hope was visiting Israel to see her relatives and to get in touch with her roots. She also wanted to gain a better understanding of issues that she had only read about. One of the most important things she discovered was that Israel was not as homogeneous as she had expected it to be: 'I can see that the spectrum in Israel among Jews and non-Jews is as wide as it is in North America.' She discovered an Israel that was more than a Jews' state.

Hope wanted very much to learn why some Jews had chosen to make Israel their home. In general, she had learned that:

> They feel like there's more they can do here, there's more opportunity to make a difference in their society. They're fully cognizant ... of the problems. They're secular Jews. But they feel – like the pioneers – that there's a chance here to make a difference whereas in the [United] States they'd just be ... like everybody else: work hard, get rich, but not really make a big difference ... Clearly it's their roots, it is their home.

Before this visit, Hope had envisioned Israel as a highly dangerous place and she could not understand why anyone would choose to leave the comforts of life in the United States. After this trip she felt that those Jews who had made *aliyah* had made more meaningful lives for themselves, in part because they had 'returned' to their 'roots,' their 'home.'

Hope compared the moment when Israel's Prime Minister Rabin was assassinated to the assassination of President John F. Kennedy:

The idea that a Jew was killing a Jew was just terrifying. I mean I just couldn't believe that it happened ... Because I had assumed that if there was an assassination it would be an Arab killing a Jew – the enemy, not from within. Yes ... it was incongruent. It was terribly sad ... I always thought of killing as something that a terrorist or a madman or an enemy would do but not someone that was one of your own.

For Hope, Rabin's assassination by another Jew was unexpected and strange. She had accepted the naive myth that all Jews support one another and that they would not hurt one of their own. Immediately after discussing Rabin's murder, she began to talk about the power of the Orthodox in Israel:

I really cannot identify at all with the ultra-Orthodox segment of Judaism. I don't understand how anybody in modern times can cling so much to the past and be blind to the positive parts of progress ... I think they're all sort of nuts ... Seeing the Hassidic Jews ... very religious Jews, praying at the Wall and then getting on their telephone ... to me that was an anachronism I'll never get over ... I just don't understand how people can believe this nonsense. It's a fable. It's a story, and why they can't see reality? And this would be true of any religion ... I mean their day, their night, their week, their clothes ... everything is connected to the past ... I have a sort of very negative, negative feeling about it.

As a secular North American, Hope could not identify with Orthodox practices. In her view, the ultra-Orthodox were ridiculous and were denying the positive aspects of modern life.

Not surprisingly, she fully identified with all the women we met on tour:

I felt much more connected to the women, both Arab and Jewish Israelis, because I do feel that women are very much the same the world over. [They are] the nurturers, the gender less willing to go to war, that will do anything to try to work things out ... I mean, they're pretty much like you and me in their hopes and their aspirations and just the way they're trying to work for change. I think the women are much more, from what I could tell, willing to try to change the patterns of the past then the men are.

Hope saw Israel as a 'young troubled country that has traditional values.' She saw it as 'working very hard at living peacefully with her neighbours.' Although she criticized some Israeli policies she also defended Israelis efforts to become a nation-state that was both democratic *and* Jewish (though not religious – a distinction she felt it was important to make):

> I think a true democracy ... and the statehood of Israel being a religious state are incongruent. It will always be a battle because a true democracy doesn't value one point of view, be it a religion or a type of state. It allows true freedom of choice and as we've seen ... there are a lot of areas where there is no freedom of choice. The right to marry or be buried ... or get an equal education are all controlled by the state, the religion. And I don't see how they're going to totally reconcile [this]. I don't think this will ever be a real democracy as long as laws of the land are embedded in a religious foundation. Until we have the separation of church and state, you're never going to have a true democracy, in my opinion. And that's troublesome. I can't reconcile it.

Hope was a committed liberal for whom the separation of religious and state institutions was of paramount importance. She referred to a number of talks we'd had about the power that religious groups, specifically Orthodox Jews, enjoyed at the state level. They were preventing non-Jewish (Russian) soldiers killed in action from being buried in national cemeteries; they were refusing to recognize marriages performed by Reform or Conservative rabbis; and their control over educational spending was so strong that many communities – mainly Palestinian – were suffering badly as a result.

Our conversation was pointing toward questions of citizenship rights. I asked her whether the state of Israel could ever come to represent all of its residents as full citizens rather than only Jews:

> That's difficult. I guess I would agree with it ... reluctantly. Yes, reluctantly. It's tough. I would rather redefine what a Jewish state is than abandon the notion of a Jewish state. I'm not comfortable just throwing it open for the person who grabs the most land regardless of nationality, regardless of religious heritage. I guess I'm not just for starting all over with an open desert and seeing who inhabits it. On the other hand, I certainly don't think that the Jews should hold all the power, and we saw how they just stomp on the Arab citizens, non-citizens. Obviously that's despicable, but I'm afraid I don't have the answer. But I sure see a problem the way it is ... I guess its because I'm Jewish ... Perhaps it's not really rational – maybe it's just more

emotional. I'm not sure that's definitely one of the things I'm contemplating and trying to figure out. I guess I do identify [more] with the Jews – emotionally now, not intellectually – than I identify with the Arabs just because that's me. On an intellectual level I see that it's absurd, but ... we all are ... products of where we came from. Both my parents were Jewish. My grandmother was killed in the concentration camp. I do have that identity and I've always said that I'm a Jew. I've always felt that I just didn't do much with it. So to suddenly just throw it all away doesn't feel right.

Hope seemed conflicted about just what kind of Israel she could identify with. Her strong belief that religious and political institutions must be separated seemed to conflict with her desire for Israel to declare itself a Jewish state. Interestingly, only now did she imply, by referring to her grandparent's death in the camps, that the Jews might again need a state as a place of refuge. In the end, for Hope the Jewish national priority took precedence over the need for a fully democratic polity. When it came to Israel's future, even a committed and activist liberal like Hope claimed the state for one nationality, even though she recognized the effects this would have on Israeli Jews who were secular and non-Orthodox as well as on, more obviously, the Palestinians.

The tour had changed Hope's life. She told me she had become much more 'emotionally and intellectually' engaged with Israel and that she planned to get more involved in a Jewish 'fellowship group' when she returned to the United States. She was somewhat fretful that this new interest might affect her marriage. Her husband was a secular Jew, and 'it's going to be a problem because on a Friday night he's going to want to go to the movies or go see our kids or do something else and I'm going to want to go to this [fellowship meeting].'

Ian and Samantha

One beautiful summer day I travelled to the suburb of a large Canadian city to meet Ian and Samantha. We had not spent much time together on the tour, but they had shown a sustained interest in the research and had written to me after our return home. They happily invited me to their home for an interview. I was somewhat nervous – this was my first formal research interview – but Ian and Samantha immediately put me at ease.

Ian and Samantha were both in their sixties. Samantha had grown up in a remote area of Canada, so 'Israel was also a remote thing. It was way out there.' Her parents would talk about Israel 'like [it was] a dream [and] something unusual,' and they would talk about Ben-Gurion with great admiration; however, she could not recall Israel having 'much meaning.' When Samantha moved away from what she described as a Christian-dominated community to one where she 'mixed with a Jewish community,' Israel began to mean something more to her. She heard more about Israel as a homeland and became attracted to it 'more and more as the time grew on ... especially ... the potential of being able to see historic sites that were centuries old.' Samantha's first real encounter with Israel came at university, when a friend brought her to a *habonim* (founders) meeting. There she met others her age who 'were interested in going to Israel and becoming pioneers, and they were quite fervent in how they spoke about it, and it was almost like ... a religious revival in the way they felt [about] what they were going to be doing.' She knew some people who had decided to make *aliyah* but she 'didn't have, at that point ... the urge to go and visit it.'

Ian was raised by a 'strong, left-wing, *yiddishkeit* family [in] not ... an anti-Zionist but an a-Zionist milieu':

> Every time someone of note came here from Israel, we would attend the lecture and learn something more about the politics, sometimes religion, the country ... And these opened up areas ... you wouldn't normally care about ... You might read [about it] but when you hear someone who's participated and been there [it's different].

Ian's identification with the Jews of Israel began in 1947, at the time of the UN Resolution on Palestine:

> [I] began to see Israel, as the years progressed [and] as it developed as any other state. [It was] somewhat different from what many of the early Zionists wanted it to be, but [it was] still a state where a lot of survivors of the Holocaust went ... and where many of the grandparents and parents of the Jews who had been pioneers and drained the swamps, [and] dreamed [about] the land, lived.

His feelings for Israel had remained fairly constant over the years. He worried about the situation in that part of the world 'not only because I'm concerned about Israeli Jews, I'm also concerned about Palestinians and Arabs as human beings in the Middle East.'

I asked Ian to discuss a comment he had made when we first discussed my research interests:

I [had] commented on the whole concept that you mentioned about Israel as 'home.' I don't consider Israel as home, I consider Canada as home. I was born here. My parents and grandparents came here early in this century to this country. There was gold along the golden land ... and that's basically what I identify with. Israel is the home of a portion of the Jewish people. It's a state. It's a state like any other state. It wasn't supposed to be a state like any other state but it is. In terms of Israel, I can identify with the early *halutzim*, the pioneers – one of whom was an uncle of mine who still lies buried somewhere in Israel, [and who] was there at the turn of the century. [He was] one of the early Zionists – I can identify with the sweat and tears that those people went through. On the other hand, I regret that in order for the state to be established another people were dispossessed, the Palestinian people. Mine is, as you know ... a minority opinion in the Jewish community, but that's what I feel, that's the way I was raised.

Here, Ian was articulating a complicated relationship to Israel: he spoke of its founders as 'pioneers' but he also recognized that its creation had led to the Palestinians' displacement. He was right, of course, to state that his was a minority position. I rarely heard any diaspora Jew claim that Israel was a state like any other or that it could be judged as such.

The ILF tour had been Ian and Samantha's first trip to Israel. I asked why they had chosen to travel in 1995. Samantha explained: 'Everybody seemed to be going to Israel [and] the price was right, which is an important factor, and ... we both decided it was time that we joined everyone else to see our origin.' Ian said he wanted to go because 'I'm ... a history buff and I wanted to see ... the first Jewish State in almost two thousand years.' Samantha was also interested in the 'historical sites ... the people, the completely different land, customs and things that ... certainly we [don't] see here.' Ian described Israel and what had impressed him there:

Well, Israel to me is *kibbutzim*. It's the only place in the world where some form of socialist experimentation is taking place which, until recently ... worked. [It is] ... an illustration of a kind of idealism which motivated the early pioneers who went to Israel and, to some extent, has been betrayed in Israel. Israel to me is the cosmopolitan areas of Tel Aviv, the historic sites in Jerusalem and Israel. Also, to me [it] is the slums of Jaffa, which [we] visited and considered to some extent an eyesore and an eyesore which, sadly enough, has been neglected by successive Israeli governments. Israel to me is ... seeing Jerusalem when we first arrived. And I don't know whether my ancestors were there nineteen hundred years ago, or two thousand years ago, where they stayed ... I really don't know, but ... I think, through conditioning, that Mount Scopus [overlooking Jerusalem] was the most touching moment of the trip as far as I'm concerned. And I can remember Rabbi Leopold getting us together, and I believe we sang the hymn to hope. That's what Israel is to me...

And ... standing at the Wall in Jerusalem and touching the stone and realizing that those stones go back to King Herod, that's King Herod's wall, King Herod's time, and you really get a sense of the history of that particular piece of real estate in the world.

Ian's descriptions defied the norm in several interesting ways. He identified with the idealism of socialist Zionism as it was represented by the Israeli *kibbutzim*; but at the same time he felt that their virtual collapse had meant that the dream – the ideals that Israel represented – had been betrayed. He was attracted to the cities, mainly to the cosmopolitanism of Tel Aviv, but he was also aware that Jaffa, just down the road, was a run-down city of Palestinians and Jews. He was not a practizing Jew, yet the rabbi's prayer on our arrival in Jerusalem moved him deeply and allowed him to reflect on his ancestral connection to the land.

I asked Ian and Samantha how they described Israel to family and friends. Ian answered:

Generally speaking, when I talk about Israel it's ... the anxiety of the situation there, a regret ... In [AD] 70 the Jews took a wrong turn. [They] revolted – a hopeless revolt – against Rome and they were crushed and there wasn't a Jewish state then for almost two thousand years. And I think what's regrettable are the Jews are missing out on a peace ... that they made a mistake of electing a government which is going to lead to another Holocaust. That's what I'm afraid of. It's going to lead to another Holocaust in the Middle East.

While seemingly distant from classical Zionist dogma, Ian and Samantha had mapped Israel in Zionist terms, identifying the importance of the first settlers and their work on the land. As Ian put it, Israelis were 'survivors of the Holocaust and the children or the grandchildren of the original pioneers who went there [and struggled]. They drained the swamps and then irrigated the land. It sounds like propaganda, but a lot of it's true.' Samantha concurred with this, adding that the pioneers had also 'started ... farming' in the region.

Thus, their recognition and 'regret' that the Palestinians had been 'dispossessed' hardly provided much of a contrast to their Zionist imaginings. However, when I asked whether the tour had prompted either of them to think differently about Israel, Ian said:

I think we're together in our feelings that when it comes to propaganda, we Jews don't take second boat to anybody ... I think ... the problem with that ... tour is if they were going to show us another reservoir – and the reservoirs are important in what they did in bringing water to the ... other parts of Israel [and] it's important in planting trees, we knew about this ... before we visited Israel – but if we were going to see another reservoir, I think I would have blown up the bus.

Yet both Samantha and Ian also said they had been impressed by 'all the plaques and things' honouring 'the people [who] have really extended themselves to help the country, to make the country greener, to help it prosper' They felt good inside knowing 'that there was some connection between ... some Jews in the diaspora and Jews living in Israel.' It was important, moreover, 'that support came through agriculture, [and] reforestation [as] these are ... the most positive aspects of the Jewish settlement.' Reforestation projects represented the positive kinds of contributions that diaspora Jews made to Israel. This was an area that seemed somehow uncontaminated by politics. They had not considered – or perhaps they did not know – that the Israelis had also planted forests over hundreds of 'abandoned' Palestinian villages.

Avi, the general who had accompanied us on the ILF tour, was the most memorable person that Ian met on the tour:

He's almost got the flavour of a Jewish peasant ... and I don't say that in a pejorative sense ... This is something which, in terms of the diaspora Jews, is a difference. Diaspora Jews are intellectuals. They're businesspeople ... You don't see very many Jewish farmers in the diaspora, but you do in Israel. And not only was he sort of a peasant but he was also a soldier. Well, he fought on Golan Heights didn't he?

Ian, like Lynn, made the Zionist distinction between diaspora and Israel: the urbane and intellectual versus the robust and resilient. Samantha was not quite as taken by the general as Ian was, and thought that '[he] had participated in something awful,' though she could not remember what it was and could only say, 'He was part of something where there was a lot of killing.' Ian explained to Samantha that Avi had been on the Golan Heights and that there had been a 'very big battle there ... in the Six Day War where the Syrians came down and came into Israel, and there was a lot of people killed, and there are still mines in that area.' Ian's understanding of the conflict on the Golan Heights corresponded with – and may even have been based solely on – Avi's presentations on tour. The general had justified the Israeli war with Syria, saying that the Syrians had invaded Israel during the Six Day War and that the state needed to defend itself. Samantha had been more attentive on this leg of the tour. Avi had indeed been part of something more controversial – the siege of Beirut after Israel's invasion of Lebanon. The discussion prompted Samantha to say that she really had mixed impressions of Talia, the principal guide on the tour:

> I can't say she impressed me but [she] represent[s] – and I've met a few others – ... Israeli women ... who are very harsh and very aggressive ... As we both understand, it's how they grew up, how they struggled, how they've fought to get where they are. Like many others, of course, she spent her time in the army and she's still an army person ... And it's sort of a personality type, and I've heard other people describe Israeli women in that way. I mean, they can't all be that way, but a significant number, I'm sure, fought their way into whatever they're doing in the country. So although we didn't like her as a tour guide, we had to think of her as a particular kind of personality.

Thus for Ian and Samantha, not only Israeli men but also Israeli women could be typed as tougher, brasher, and more assertive. Samantha believed this behaviour reflected the harshness of Israeli life, as well as the skills needed to cope with it.

Ian felt that Talia had been a 'little patronizing and insulting' when speaking to the group, especially so when she spoke about

> the war with Iraq [in 1990], when Israel was under threat and [there were] Scud missiles from Saddam Hussein ... Somebody at the front of the bus

said, 'You know we were very worried about you people, we were very worried about the people of Israel,' and she said, 'What do you know about something like that? ... What do you know about it? We were here.' In other words you had to be there, on the land, in order to appreciate what was going on there. Well, most Jews weren't in occupied Europe ... between 1939 and 1945 but many of us lost relatives there and we could identify. We didn't have to be there to know what kind of slaughter that was ... I think some of the Zionists – I don't know if Ben-Gurion was one of them – said that in order to be Jewish you really have to live in Israel. Well, that eliminates a hell of a lot of Jews. [It] certainly eliminates a lot of North American Jews because ... the *aliyah* to Israel from North America is practically nothing. It's very, very small and I think ... the formulation is you can't live a full Jewish life unless you live in Israel. Well, it depends on what you mean by living a full Jewish life. I think Samantha and I have a full Jewish life ... I'm involved in different kinds of activities, social action-wise, against the present provincial government ... and I think that's very Jewish, that's leading a full Jewish life. And when I'm a member of Peace Now, that's leading a Jewish life ... Trying to push for a more egalitarian society in Israel, that's Jewish.

Samantha agreed with Ian: 'I think social activism and participating in things like that had more meaning to me to be Jewish and to show how I felt about it than just the mere act of going to Israel or the mere act of participating with a Jewish group.' Ian and Samantha had rejected Zionism's presumptions about authenticity and the need for the 'negation of diaspora.' They believed they could appreciate the dangers that Israelis face, and that they could lead full Jewish lives by committing to the greater social welfare of all people. For them, there was a strength to the Jewish identity that was unrelated to settling in Israel or to committing themselves Zionism.

Consistent with these commitments, Samantha told me, when I asked what she had learned about Palestinians and Arabs on the tour:

The fact is we find, and we feel very strongly about, [the fact] that their living standards are so low and [they] are not properly attended to. And there's a feeling on their part about why are they [being] treated in this way. And certainly we began to think, well how can they have any great feeling for the Jews in their country or the country where they live if they're living in proximity with them but not benefiting from the same things as other people. We began to have a different perspective [on

Israel], and I think when we saw poverty in some of the areas and knew who [suffered] it ... I think this hit home very hard. We were seeing it, [though] we weren't hearing remotely [about it from the guides] and to us as Jews and ... with our focus on the social needs of people, I think it really hit hard.

As Samantha had noted, none of the guides on the ILF tour paid any attention to any of the issues that she and Ian were concerned about. Still, they had taken side trips during the time we were in Israel and had become aware of some of Israel's social problems on their own. On the very first day we were in Israel, they had spent time in and around Tel Aviv. Ian recalled:

It's interesting, anything that we saw ... that pertained to Palestinians was not part of the tour. [It was] a tour of Israel without Palestinians, and that's interesting because Herzl in his book *The Jewish State* talks about ... a country for a people, a country without people or people without a country. And of course this is [because] he'd never been to Palestine but obviously there were people living there, indigenous people living in Palestine. So the ILF tour was like the Herzlian type of thing where they [represented] a country without Palestinians.

Ian and Samantha placed the Palestinians back into the history of Israel in a way that challenged the Zionist myth of settling an empty land and that also redefined such practices as in conflict with what both identified as the Jewish principle of caring for the social welfare of all people. Recognizing that Palestinians lived on the land prior to the founding of the state and that they had suffered the consequences – but not the benefits – of that state was also a fairly radical reframing of the narratives that had been presented on the tour.

I asked them how important Israel is to North American Jews. They expressed a shared belief that, as Ian put it:

It's very important ... For many North American Jews it's about the only identification they have with Jewry. Israel is like the secular religion of the North American Jewish community. And I can understand that importance. It's important to me too because there are four million Jews [living there] and I guess a million – I don't know how many – Palestinians were there and the lives of these human beings are at risk. And I think it's important that a lasting peace be evolved there ... I think to a great extent what the Palestinians have been given is a form of ghetto type of thing and I think as Jews, because we are the more powerful party, [we] could have afforded to have ... done a bit better.

Ian and Samantha's feelings for Israel showed concern for their national kin as well as for those with whom they do not share national- ity, the Palestinians. Each believed, as well, that Israel was obligated to implement a better peace because it was the stronger of the two parties.

For this couple, Israel was important because it tied Jews to their past as well as to their kin. But it was not an extraordinarily sacred space, nor was it unique as a state except insofar as it was Jewish. Ian closed our discussion by telling me that Israel did not play a role in many areas of his personal life and that he was concerned about cer- tain issues in Canada that were unrelated to Israel. Except as he put it, for one aspect: 'The same idiot, who is the Prime Minister of Israel, [Netanyahu] ... [has as] his Gentile counterpart ... the [Conservative] premier of [this province].' That is, one connection between Israel and Canada was based on the need to resist the reactionary right-wing pol- iticians who were dominant in both places.

Among this last group of diaspora Jews, there were a range of per- spectives of Israel. Some simply rejoiced in the existence of a Jewish state, others thought it deserved more attention and support. Despite the differences among those profiled, however, there were some similari- ties, especially with respect to recognizing the state's accomplishments, especially developments in the Negev Desert. Just as importantly, they all seemed to recognize that non-Jews as well as different kinds of Jews live within the state. The language of tolerance and recognition formed part of every discussion.

14
Fielding Questions of Identity

As I entered the final stages of writing this book, I came across the work of Henry Giroux, a social critic and educator. His reflections on the need both to enter into and engage with public sphere texts spoke to my efforts and interests. He writes: 'We need to go beyond questions of literacy and textual critique to issues of politics, power, and social transformation. A new vocabulary is necessary to understand not just how to read texts critically. It is also crucial to comprehend how knowledge circulates through various circuits of power and promotes images, experiences, representations, and discourses that objectify others and create the ideological conditions for individuals to become indifferent to how violence in its diverse expressions results in human suffering.'[1]

As a result of my activism on the Israel–Palestine question, many times during my fieldwork I was asked to locate myself vis-à-vis Israel. It was quite clear to me that I was being invited to present at least one version of an alternative narrative of Israel. A year into my research, I gave a presentation at a Reform temple breakfast meeting. This event enabled me to make new contacts in the community where I had chosen to do some of my research, it also led to a number of invitations to speak to other community organizations, including a Reform temple in the United States, and to appearances on radio and television programs. Everyone asked me to reflect on what it means to be both Jewish and Palestinian. In all of these settings I talked about how my identity had been formed by the stories told to me as a child and young adult – stories about Nazi Germany, the Holocaust, and settlement in Israel; about displacement, political resistance, and Palestine. I talked about how these were stories of hope and of the betrayal of hope. These stories of nationalism and liberation focused not on primordial hatreds but rather on collective struggle; not on identity as such, but rather on the dangers of social, economic, and political powerlessness.[2] In these talks I discussed the discrimination I faced in both Jewish and Arab community and activist settings.

In many ways, I felt I had opened up to community members in these presentations. I was hoping they would sense my own vulnerabilities as a person caught between two severely polarized and often narrow-minded communities. I was not there to represent both communities; instead, I wanted to explain how each must make an effort to understand the other's experience of Israel.

I took pains to define myself as both Jewish and Palestinian; even so, I was constantly asked to locate myself on one side or the other of this divide. Some of these experiences made starkly plain to me the depth of commitment to, and the strength of, the narratives of Israel as the site of an exclusively Jewish nation; they also reminded me just how profoundly Palestinian traditions and histories had been silenced. But there were other times when the discussions led to some very interesting moments of realization and to the very dialogue I desired.

Gayatri Spivak writes of the 'subject position' in an appropriate and useful way:

> Quite often when we say 'subject position' we reduce it to a kind of confessional attitudinizing. We say, 'I'm white, I'm black, I'm a mulatto, I am male, I'm bourgeois.' A subject-position is not, in fact, a confessional self-description either in praise or in dis-praise ... This is because the position of the subject can be assigned ... and 'assigned' means, I think, that it can and must become a sign; not for the person who speaks, but for the person who listens, not for the person who writes, who can say what she likes about who she is, but for the person who reads. When, in fact, the responsible reader reads the sign that is the subject position of the speaker or the writer, it becomes the sign, let us say, of an ethno-politics, of a psycho-sexual reality, or an institutional position, and this is not under the control of the person who speaks. She cannot diagnose herself; we are given over to our readers.[3]

Through my fieldwork, I was to discover the degree to which my assignments were defined by national, cultural, and (most importantly) political terms of Middle Eastern politics. I was always introduced to Jewish community members this way: 'Jasmin is a Palestinian with a Jewish mother'; or, 'Jasmin is an Arab but she's more Jewish than some Rabbis'; or 'Jasmin's mother is Jewish, her father is an Arab.' I cannot recall ever being introduced to anyone in the community simply by my first or by my first and last names. In the beginning, I wondered why such introductions were so important to people; I feared they were signalling my difference to others. But then I asked myself, why would they want to do this? What difference could my difference make? Were people simply introducing me in order to count me in (as a Jew)? Or were they raising flags so that others would not be surprised to learn independently who I *really* am (i.e., also a Palestinian)? Was I being included or excluded by these introductions? After several conversations, I began to make note of precisely when my Jewishness was taken for granted, when it was questioned, and when it was dismissed so that I was identified only as a Palestinian. I found myself caught within politicized communities where to be a Jew or a Palestinian-Arab is to be recognized simultaneously as a nationality with an ascribed politics, personality, and, of course, bias. If my mother had married a non-Jew, that would have been one thing. But she married a Palestinian, and for many in these communities, they are the enemy, so that was quite something else. As a result, the people I met could not help but embed me in the identity politics of Israel and Palestine. A few examples follow.

I was many times taken to task for suggesting that I was serious about my multinational (Jewish, Palestinian, Canadian) identity and that I would not want to discard any one of these identities: all of them were mine. When I attended Hebrew lessons at the Zionist Council, my tutor, a Canadian Jew in his seventies who had immigrated from Russia, would always ask me, 'Why do you say you're Palestinian *and* Jewish? As far as I'm concerned, you're a Jew. You should know, you probably already know, that according to our laws, you are a Jew so you don't need to worry.' He expressed some frustration that I was denying myself what he thought of as a proper identity; he even offered advice on how I could legitimately hide that other identity if I ever felt the need. Barely concealing his Orientalist and Eurocentric biases, he worried that I would never marry properly if I continued to identify as part Palestinian, for this inferior identity is commonly associated with the Muslim Third World and is thus a 'primitive' identity. He was assuming that anyone would rather identify with their European self if given the choice.

When I was invited to speak in the community on the Israel–Palestine conflict, it was suggested to me that my access to the Jewish community was permitted only insofar as my specifically Palestinian self could be controlled by the fact that I am also a Jew. During a Jewish night-school class presentation, which the organizers framed as 'Being Jewish and

Palestinian,' I asked whether anyone in the class had ever met an Arab or a Palestinian in their travels through Israel or in their home community. All but one young woman said 'no.' One young man then turned to me to say, 'You don't think you'd be invited here to speak to us if you weren't at least half Jewish, do you?' Until that moment I had not thought about it, even though I had been giving talks to Jewish audiences for some months. He was right, of course. Few of the Jewish organizations that invited me to speak had ever invited a Palestinian or an Arab to discuss the Israel–Palestine conflict. These community settings were genuinely closed to outsiders, even to those with whom, under the Oslo Accords, a partnership was to be built.

During a lunch meeting with Bernadette, an elderly woman I had come to know quite well during my research, she admitted that after hearing me speak at her temple, she had at first been 'intrigued' about my 'background,' as she called it. We began to spend a good deal of time together, sharing meals at her home and in local restaurants and discussing personal and political issues. One of these discussion revolved around Bernadette's son, who had just announced that he was going to marry a non-Jew. Bernadette told me she was deeply concerned about the high rates of intermarriage in the Jewish community. When she asked me how I felt, I told her I opposed identity politics and community practices that would deny people the choice to share their lives with whomever they wish. I added that such politics were especially difficult for me to understand, since I had never claimed any one national identity. Also, I could remember how my mother suffered as a result of her community's exclusionary practices. Seeking to reassure me, Bernadette confided that after spending time with me she did not really believe that I was 'one of them' – meaning a Palestinian, an Arab. She told me this openly and without any hesitation. I was startled by her response, since only two months earlier on an art gallery tour we had taken together, she had said the very opposite. We were discussing Israel's settlement policy, especially around Jerusalem, and in response to her statement that Jerusalem must remain unified, I told her that Jerusalem could be unified but it would have to be shared. Correctly interpreting my refusal to accept that Jerusalem is important only for Jews, Bernadette angrily retorted: 'Jasmin, you will never know what it means to be a Jew.'

My father's nationality did not serve to open discussions of what it might mean to be a Jew who takes some fairly unorthodox positions on the Israel-Palestine conflict – such as the position that recognizes both nations' right to share the same land, or the right of compensation and return for all Palestinian refugees. Rather, his nationality seemed to overdetermine all other aspects of my experience and practice. My interlocutors dismissed the political ideas I expressed by claiming that the Palestinian in me was overshadowing the Jew. This attitude precluded any acknowledgment that my position was rooted in a progressive – some might call radical – Jewish-Israeli-left tradition, one that could also be a liberal and left Palestinian position. In this way, my positions could be discredited as simply pro-Palestinian, or worse still anti-Semitic, because they were critical of Israel in ways that were unacceptable to diaspora Jews.

These experiences, and many similar ones, opened an opportunity to think through the practices of identification. The question was not so much 'Who are you?' as 'What do you do that allows me to decide who you are?' or 'What do you do that makes you think you're a Jew?' These questions are crucial for understanding why I was perplexed at first by the strategies my interlocutors followed for identifying me, and why they were confused by my identifications. When they perceived that my attachment to Israel was not like that of other mainstream diaspora Jews, I simply became a Palestinian. Clearly, the audiences expected a 'real' Jew to know how to identify with Israel. Thus, my positions on Jerusalem, on intermarriage, and on the exclusivity of the Jewish state signalled to those with whom I spoke that I was not a Jew in the same way that they were Jewish. My mother's Jewishness conferred on me the right to call myself a Jew, but that was not enough for them. As a result, they often identified me in terms of my other self on the basis of their political understandings, all of which fit the logic of nationalist systems of identity. Rarely could they identify with my creolized or hybridized being (though I'm not singling them out for this failure); if anything, my hybrid identity generated a kind of anxiety in them and for me. More often than not, I was assigned a singular identity based on understandings of what it meant to be a diaspora Jew. When I did not respond in a way that was comprehensible in those terms, I became an outsider. Perhaps as well, I had to be identified as a Jew in those first introductory moments because the audiences would learn soon enough that I was not like them, even if I was also a Jew.

What I discovered, then, was the *strength* of their representational order. The concept of national identity was vital to these people, whom postmodern theorists would define as a 'deterritorialized' community. I wanted to insist on the possibility of multiplicity; but my audiences, from their location as diaspora Jews living in one place but with some attachment to another, insisted on an authenticity in relation to Israel.

When I insisted on the multiplicity of my location, they resisted this possibility by locating me as a member of one national group or the other.

I began to wonder whether I had been misled by the celebratory ethos of postmodernism. What if in my meditations on the postmodern ways in which identities are constructed, I had left behind how identities are constantly being reconstructed not as plural and hybrid but rather in terms of authenticity, unity, and singularity? As I thought about my fieldwork, I began to realize, as well, that ideas about hybridity failed to open spaces for sustained interpretive discussions or reinterpretations of nationalities, whatever the claims of cultural theorists and postmodern anthropologists.

One such thinker is Chantal Mouffe, who recognizes that identity is multifactoral and encourages us not to base its definition in exclusion. In an effort to theorize a way out of the antagonisms and violence of difference, she writes, 'Only if people's allegiances are multiplied and their loyalties pluralized will it be possible to create truly "agonistic pluralism." Because where identities are multiplied, passions are divided.'[4] Perhaps we cannot yet escape the antagonisms of national identity. Instead, we might want to consider how the current agonisms are determined by the extent to which deterritorialized and diaspora communities must reconfigure, reterritorialize, and relocate their national identities in order to escape the antagonism of dislocation – of being nowhere – in a world where nation-states are still the main arenas of powerful (because legitimate and organized) political representation. Perhaps Jewish diaspora nationalism points the way to an understanding of how even deterritorialized identities are locatable or situated identities. In escaping the 'antagonisms' of cultural identity founded on the unity of territory and nationality, people living as a diaspora become *re*located rather than *dis*located in ways demonstrated by diaspora Jews: they maintain a sense of their location as Jews in relation to Israel. Diaspora Jews can therefore locate themselves as members of a nation that has a history, a memory, and most recently a territory, Israel, yet they do not specifically have to territorialize that identity. That is, they believe they can live authentic lives outside the place identified as their nation-state.

Perhaps Mouffe's comment – 'where identities are multiplied, passions are divided' – should be revised to read, 'commitments must be multiplied, in order that passions can be allied.' For although I could see the hybridity among diaspora Jews, I now have to ask: What if those whom we meet and engage refuse to acknowledge the pluralities of their own locations? What if people *do not* self-identify as plural identities but rather are guided by the terms set by the modern notions of authenticity and identity? And what if this too provides openings?

Locating an Other's Israel

I want to highlight the ways that politics and dialogue can be conducted across nationally defined borders. To that end, I share one moment when being part Palestinian presented me with an opportunity to share my sense of place and the practices in place.

I met Jeremy on the Israel Development Fund (IDF) tour. He was there as the IDF's representative. He has a postgraduate degree in Jewish social studies and has been a Jewish educator and fundraiser in Canada and the United States since completing his degree. By the time we met, Jeremy had travelled to Israel five times. The first time was in 1984, when he took a leave from his university studies to work on a *kibbutz* for six months. He described his first trip as 'unbelievable. I was real excited. Everything was in bloom and I really felt like I was in Israel. It was a real exciting feeling. [My] fondest memory [was] the real sense of community that exists [on a *kibbutz*].' Jeremy lived among Israeli Jews, but he was housed with non-Jewish visitors to the *kibbutz*. Even so, he distinguished his experience from theirs, telling me that he experienced a connection to Israel that non-Jews could not:

> They saw it as another part of history, but I felt a real personal part of that history... I think it was really learning about the land ... To me the land incorporates the people, the history, the language, the land, the physical. I took a lot of classes in Jewish history and I think that by going there it sort of illuminated a lot of the things that I was studying in school. It made it a lot more tangible talking about biblical history and then also jumping into present-day Jewish history, the establishment of the State of Israel. Everything became real. It just wasn't something that was taken out of a book. I didn't have the connection before through the books but that connection became even more real ... As you're just walking around I just kept on thinking back to myself: Jews walked on this spot before I have. They fought for this land ... My first trip to Masada ... was a very moving, very emotional experience. Just thinking about the whole story that took place on top of the mountain, about Herod's palace, the Zealots that so as not to be taken captive by the Romans elected to kill themselves. To me it still represents ... captivity they shouldn't fall into. I really felt for them a connection in that space of two thousand years where they lived for their

ideals. They were born as Jews; they'll die as a Jews. This will never happen again. [And] the Wall [represents] two thousand years of history ... It represents a strong connection [for me].

Jeremy was offering a classically Zionist representation of Israel. Every site and every interpretation pointed to the Jews' place in the 'land of Israel.' Jeremy's description of Israel included the following:

Falafel ... Guns. Tension. Turmoil. Responsibility. Beauty. Hope. Future ... I think Israel is a country relative to the future, sort of placed on a pedestal. A country to respect, for the most part, to admire the way they've taken in people from around the world ... To me it represents the essence of what it means to be Jewish, and I hope that after me, these feelings will be carried on into the future. Politically people may disagree, and that's okay, but I still think that wherever you come from [it's ours].

Jeremy's relationship to Israel was strong. It was also quite typical. He had committed his life to the Jewish community, and in particular to organizations supporting the development of the State of Israel.

During the tour we had several friendly conversations. On one occasion, sensing the tour participants' great excitement at an upcoming visit to an Israeli air force base, I asked Jeremy why he thought Jews – and especially North American Jews, who are normally associated with the peace and antiwar movements – so admired the Israeli army. He laughed and told me: 'Think about it. The key word in Israel Defense Force is "defense." This is not like any other army in the world. It is defensive.' He asked me several questions about my research as well as my political position, and he seemed genuinely interested throughout the tour.

After the Friday afternoon services at the Wailing Wall, Jeremy asked me if I would walk with him through what he called the 'Arab Quarter' of the Old City on our way back to the hotel. At first I thought he was joking and laughed it off. But he became quite serious and said he really did want to walk through the area with me. He had something he wanted to ask me there. So as the sun began to set, we walked from the plaza in front of the Wall toward the Arab Quarter. As we walked, we talked about the day's events, including the visit to Yad Vashem and the presentation by Prime Minister Benjamin Netanyahu. Jeremy said he always felt angry at Yad Vashem; it was there that he had begun to appreciate Israel's importance for the Jews. When I asked

him if he really believed the Jews would always be a threatened community, especially if they did not have their own state, he replied that
he did. When I asked him why he still lived in North America if he felt
so strongly about Israel, he confided that his wife – who had many relatives in Israel who belonged to 'the peace camp' – did not want their
children to have to serve in the Israeli army. Also, she considered Israel
a dangerous place to raise a family.

As we walked through the dark alleys past closed shops, passing Palestinian teenagers and elderly men, as well as a number of uniformed
Israeli soldiers, we continued to talk, though I noticed that we were
almost whispering. Suddenly Jeremy stopped, faced me and asked,
'Okay, so how do you feel now?' I was baffled and asked, 'what do you
mean?' He explained: 'When I'm in the Jewish Quarter I feel like I
belong there, like it is home. I just want to know how *you* feel *here*, in the
Arab Quarter.' In effect, he was asking whether I, as a Palestinian, could
feel at home in a place like Jerusalem in the same way that a Jew feels at
home in Jerusalem. Disregarding the fact that he had assigned me an
exclusively Arab identity, I replied that standing here had an air of
familiarity to it, yet I could not help but 'feel the oppression of the place.'
[when] I see these Israeli soldiers walk by, I can't help but ask, "What
are they doing here?"' Jeremy looked astonished: 'You don't think we
have to give up *Jerusalem*, do you? This will *never* be a part of Palestine!'
I shot back: 'For as long as there are soldiers here it is *nobody's* place, and
for as long as it is occupied and people have to live under military rule,
there will *never* be peace.' He responded with a deafening silence, and
we continued to walk through the Old City. Just as we passed through
the Jaffa Gate into West Jerusalem, he stopped me and again spoke
about Nazi Germany and the depth of his anger toward the Germans for
the crimes they had committed. He told me he always paused when he
met an older German to wonder whether he or she had been or was
related to a Nazi, though he admitted feeling guilty about this. Jeremy
believed that as a people, the Jews had been hated throughout history,
and that the Holocaust had been one moment – perhaps the culmination
– of a long history of atrocities committed against them. I listened carefully as he spoke. Then, still standing at the Jaffa Gate, I asked him if he
believed that hatred toward the Jews was of some theological significance or a matter of natural law or if it was learned: 'Do you believe that
the Germans had to learn to be Nazis?' 'Yes,' he told me, and added that
all people have to learn to hate, that one is not born to hate. At that
moment I came up with a daring idea. I asked him if he had ever met an

Arab or Palestinian family. When he replied, that he hadn't I was not surprised. I asked him whether he would accept the 'challenge' of putting a face to the 'enemy,' so to speak, and come to visit my family. He hesitated, but then he accepted. We began walking toward the hotel again.

As we walked, Jeremy became more and more excited, telling me that such a visit was exactly what he wanted and urging me to telephone my uncle immediately to arrange for a visit the next day, since we had no activities scheduled on our tour. At this point I began to wonder if I was making a mistake by placing my family in a position I myself had been placed in over the years, of having to share the painful experience of being an Arab, or a Palestinian, in Israel. Nonetheless, I telephoned my uncle and told him what had transpired between Jeremy and me that day, and that Jeremy was a fundraiser for a major Jewish organization. I asked if he would mind meeting him. As I expected, he was delighted to be asked, if only because it was another opportunity to spend time with me. We agreed to meet the next evening at the hotel in Jerusalem.

On the Saturday, my uncle, a building contractor in his late fifties, and my cousin, a college student in her early twenties, came to pick us up. After a few brief introductions, my uncle sized up Jeremy, at one point rubbing Jeremy's chin and asking why he had not shaved for the occasion – the formality of the Palestinian up against the informality of the North American. Then we climbed into my uncle's rusting gray Citroen. We puttered along in the pouring rain, with windows rolled up and gas fumes filling the interior. My uncle, who speaks English quite well, told us he thought it would be interesting to show Jeremy the 'new state of Palestine.' When I asked Jeremy if that was okay, he bravely said 'sure' (he later confided that he was quite nervous about it all). The discussions about Palestine and Israel began soon after we were on our way. My uncle wanted to establish, early on, that he and Jeremy would get along just fine as long as Jeremy treated him with the respect he showed to others: 'As long as you agree we are both human, we will get along. I don't care who you are as long as you come to me as a human being first, then we will be able to judge, to talk, to agree and to disagree. But only as human beings first.' We drove through Jerusalem, passed through the Israeli military checkpoint and the Palestinian Authority checkpoint, and then entered Ramallah in the West Bank. We hit Ramallah literally with a bang as we bounced in and out of deep potholes. When Jeremy commented that these roads were very unlike the roads we had travelled on in Israel, my uncle turned to him and smiled knowingly. We drove around the central square, where people were avoiding the pouring rain by ducking in and out cafes and shops. Jeremy took in the sights, commenting on the beauty of the new buildings alongside the old and dilapidated ones. When we passed a group of Palestinian police standing in a circle at a corner, Jeremy asked my uncle if they were the 'security police.' My uncle replied, 'They're just police.' My uncle pointed to a neighbourhood where he and my aunt had lived for a time in the 1970s. Soon after, he stopped the car, hopped out and climbed a steep set of stone stairs to a home at the top. He conferred with an older woman there and then signalled for us to come up. We were being welcomed to visit a family friend.

At the door, a woman in her nineties, Im-Tawfik, and her middle-aged daughter-in-law, Leila, greeted us. The older woman was expecting her son, Tawfik, to join us at any time. We were shown to two old sofas and offered cold drinks and cookies. While we sat, Jeremy looked around, noted that the television in the room was set on CNN, and seemed to relax. My uncle introduced Jeremy, telling the family he was a member of a Jewish organization from North America. And the discussion began. Im-Tawfik told us her son was also an American citizen; even so, while working in the West Bank he had to carry his Palestinian ID card and he was not allowed to travel with his American agency's car. Jeremy immediately tried to set the record straight, telling us that in his view, such 'oppression is wrong.' At that point he launched into a discussion about how wrong it was that the people did not accept the Jewish state in 1947, and how things might have been different if everyone had accepted the state at that time. To this, my uncle immediately replied: 'Why did you come here and take my land? What did I do to you? Why couldn't you come here and live with us instead of taking the land from us and asking us to live with you?' Im-Tawfik broke into the discussion to say that the situation in the area was much more complicated than whether or not the Palestinians should have agreed to any settlement in 1947. She pointed to the furniture we were sitting on and told us it was furniture she had lost in her house in Ramle (now an Israeli city) in 1948 and that she got it back only after Israel occupied 'the rest of Palestine' in 1967. She told us that nothing much had changed since 1947; she was still living under occupation.

Soon after, the quiet discussion grew heated. Jeremy's interjections ranged from 'How could your people murder innocent people in a market or on a bus?' to 'Why didn't you stand up for those innocents?'

My uncle, the women, and the son, who arrived later, responded: 'Wait a minute, not all Palestinians are doing this' ... 'Why do you think that Arabs are less human than you?' When do you stand up for us?' At one point, when it seemed as if everyone had exhausted their arguments, Jeremy said, 'This is such an emotional issue and there is no truth, only perspective.' To this, my uncle responded, 'This is politics, not psychology.' When my uncle and Tawfik argued that without an end to military occupation and the return of the refugees or compensation for the land there would never be peace, Jeremy seemed almost cowed into an agreement. But then he quickly added that although the occupation should end, return was probably impossible. There was no response. Silence.

After about an hour of watching Jeremy come close to tears as he argued his position, and watching my uncle and his friends shake their heads in disbelief, I felt completely drained. And hungry. I signalled to my uncle and told him I did not want to overstay our welcome. We thanked our hosts and left. My uncle then invited us to a dinner at a nice grill restaurant in Ramallah. Inside, we were greeted by the owner, who seemed to know my uncle, and were seated at a table for four. The conversation resumed where it had left off at the house, although there was less tension now; Jeremy and my uncle were even able to joke about it. Everyone was now more relaxed and at the same time ready to discuss serious issues and disagreements. After an excellent meal – the best Jeremy and I had eaten in all our time in Israel – we travelled back to Jerusalem. On the way back, we saw no Israeli soldiers at the military checkpoints. I asked Jeremy what he thought about that in light of all the fear that had been instilled in the Israeli people and all we had been hearing at the time about the 'infiltration of terrorists from the West Bank.' We had just passed through what was, for all intents and purposes, an 'open border' between Ramallah and Jerusalem, between what was then an autonomous region of Palestine and Israel. Jeremy replied that it frightened him and that he could not believe it. My heart sank.

Since that day, Jeremy and I have stayed friends. We have met whenever he comes to town, and we often chat on the phone about Israel, Jewish politics, American politics, personal relationships, and just about everything else. Jeremy often tells me how much he appreciated the opportunity to speak to my family and their friends. He tells me it was hard for him to listen to what they had to say, but he knows it must also have been hard for them to listen to him. I was pleased he had made the effort to meet them and to confront the issues he felt so strongly about with people who had experienced the ramifications of policies whereby only Jews had full rights in Israel.

During a post-tour interview, I asked Jeremy what he remembered most about our tour. He recounted our visit to the West Bank as follows:

> [I met this woman]. She still has a lot of family on both sides, mother's side and father's side, and when we were in Israel I was invited to join her together with all the different relatives and I believe it was the highlight out of all the trips I've ever been in Israel. [They were] Palestinian Arabs who knew that I was Jewish, who knew my passion for the land and the people ... It was very, very meaningful, because I could see that by being invited into their home, not that anybody noticed, they were people just like myself and my family who wanted to [live normally]. And just by being in their homes ... It was so crazy, why can't two people coexist with one another? We're all different. They can go their way, we can go our way but still get up in the morning without [everyone] fearing for their lives, for no reason whatsoever. It was, again, it was a very emotional experience for me to think that. I think there is hope for peace between the Arabs and Jews. We have to actively change [our] attitude toward each other and I think it won't happen overnight, but it has to happen.

By locating Israel in the lives of Palestinians, Jeremy had come to appreciate that something other than a 'one nation, one land' model might one day be possible. He had rethought his earlier position, switching from separation to sharing, and he had humanized the Palestinians. This was a small step, of course, and many other people have taken much larger ones. Here was a man who was committed to Zionism – he was the only person I met during my research who wanted to make *aliyah* – yet he was reconsidering the effects of the politics of dispossession, and he was speaking about the possibilities for coexistence between Jews and Palestinians.

Jeremy, like Lynn and Marlene, had set out to discover all he could about the conflict with the Palestinians. Lynn believed that more contact with Palestinians would lead to greater understanding between Jews and Palestinians. Marlene promoted and supported such contacts in both Israel and North America. All of them were, in their own ways, reconsidering their relationship to the state without diminishing their commitment to Israel, Jews, or Jewishness.[5]

15

Diaspora Belonging

A complex array of power relations can be seen in every diaspora's attempt to make sense of the nationalist narratives it is presented with – power relations that compel it to see and act in particular ways. During my fieldwork, I found that power was involved not only in the relationship between the audiences and the narratives, but also in my relationship as the ethnographer to the rules, assumptions, and practices that defined my life. Understanding these interpretations is useful anthropological work. It is also useful political work.

The tours generally presented exclusivist, territorialist, Zionist narratives about the Jews' place in Israel; yet the narratives presented at community events sometimes complicated these narratives by pointing to the drawbacks of exclusivist politics (e.g., this happened during the geographer's presentation and the politician's). All of the positions elicited a response from tour participants and audience members and signalled their awareness of the classical Zionist narratives – and, to a lesser extent, non-Zionist or post-Zionist narratives, though these may not have been recognized as such.

The profiles of diaspora Jews I have offered represent the many possible identifications with and to the state of Israel. The relationships I have explored, while quite diverse, are not the only ones found among diaspora Jews living in North America. That said, I have good reason to believe they are very common.

Whether those I interviewed had visited Israel for the first time in their lives or for the fifteenth, most had poached (in de Certeau's sense) the majority of Zionist narratives presented to them: they situated the Jews' ancestral, biblical heritage in Israel; they expressed the need for a national state of refuge for all Jews; and they proudly envisioned Israel as a modern and democratic state. Included in these reflections was enormous pride in Israel's development practices – for example, its agricultural, reforestation, and water redistribution programs.

Yet holding these views did not preclude the research participants from raising questions about citizenship, equality, democracy and (surprisingly) security, as issues that Israel must confront not just in Zionist or *Realpolitik* terms but also in terms of human needs and rights. The same people who imagined Israel in Zionist-historical terms also had the capacity to reflect on Israel as a normal state (i.e., not a uniquely Jewish state). Their concerns focused on the governance and security of Israel's population, rather than on the land *per se*. This was my first indication that the diaspora's ties to Israel were based on national rather than territorial bonds.

Many of those I interviewed – and not just those presented in this book – were quite troubled by the power wielded in Israel by the Orthodox minority. Some feared their antimodernizing tendencies and characterized them as premodern yet powerful enough to push Israel 'into the past.' Some interviewees worried out loud that if the political power of the Orthodox continued to grow, the state would eventually become disassociated from its role as the primary symbol of modern Jews' accomplishments.

The diaspora Jews' reflections on the extraordinary power held by the Orthodox must be understood in the context of other issues, including the assassination of Prime Minister Rabin by an Orthodox Jew and the 'Who is a Jew?' debate that was raging at the time. With respect to the latter issue, many diaspora Jews represented the Orthodox as having the potential to determine their lives even beyond the geographic borders of the State of Israel. Thus, the responses of diaspora interviewees to the Orthodox reflected not so much their desire to see a secular Israel (which was the framing of the argument within Israel) as their understanding of Orthodox principles, which many saw as forcing antimodernizing, undemocratic policies onto Israeli society.

Some interviewees told me their trip to Israel led them to connect with Judaism and the Torah. One tour participant told me that she had done so as a consequence of her own lack of identification with Israel; for her, it no longer completely fulfilled her desire for Jewish authenticity. Her return to 'the Word,' as some put it, rather than to the land of Israel, was a diasporic, deterritorialized gesture. This suggests that diaspora Jews can develop their identity and maintain their traditions without living in the territory they claim is their state. After all, they have being doing just that for many centuries.[1]

Yet often, diaspora Jews' knowledge of Israel was not always simply associated with their ancestral, spiritual, historical and traditional ties. All participants knew that Israel was a contested territory, although their degree of knowledge about this issue varied, from very deep to very superficial. Both at community events and while on tour, many diaspora Jews used the language of peace and coexistence when discussing the possible terms of engagement between Palestinians (and other Arabs) and Jews. Militaristic narratives led some participants to perceive Israel as a tiny country under siege, but even these people expressed their doubts that military violence could resolve the conflict. Some participants represented Israel in celebratory Zionist terms but in their next breath recognized the plight of the Palestinians, especially those living in the Occupied Territories. Often, however, they were unaware of the structural reasons for such inequalities. Overall, the interviewees seemed less concerned about any threat from the Arabs and more concerned about building a good Israel, an Israel that could be true to the ideals of democracy, equality, and peace.

Generational differences in identifications with and perceptions of Israel were also crucial. Those who had experienced anti-Semitism in their youth, and who remembered the time before there was a State of Israel, imagined the new state as their refuge, but also as a model of all the good things that liberated Jews could offer the world.

Among those who remembered Israel's time of glory in the 1970s, celebratory remembrances began to be displaced during the controversial 1980s. Their critical awareness was raised after Israel invaded Lebanon. At this point they also began to understand that the Six Day War of 1967, although it had 'reunited Jerusalem,' also meant that Israel was now an occupying force in lands that had belonged to the Palestinians. Some of these interviewees yearned for the idealized Israel of pre-1967 times and were disappointed that Israel had lost the potential to be all it could be. Many interviewees believed that the Arab–Israeli conflict could be resolved through meaningful co-operation and the recognition that coexistence was necessary.

Those who had recently begun identifying with Israel had formed a range of relationships with it. Some had decided to take more responsibility for Israeli state building by becoming more active in Jewish organizations. Others had turned their attention to Jewish practices in North America and simply celebrated the progress and security of the state. Many in this group did not trust Arabs, but the militaristic language they used was tame compared to that of some tour guides and hosts. They described coexistence and cooperation among Israelis, Palestinians, and Arabs as a possibility, and they desired it.

Those diaspora Jews who had travelled to Israel several times held relatively complex understandings not only of Israeli politics but also of the regional conflicts. In other words, those who had long identified with and committed themselves to the state – usually starting in their youth – were also the most critically aware of the state's complex realities and the most committed to peaceful coexistence.

Consistent with other researchers' findings,[2] very few diaspora Jews had considered making *aliyah*. In fact, I never encountered anyone who wanted to immigrate to Israel; the only exception said he wanted to go but could not. All offered pragmatic reasons for staying in North America, and very few felt guilty about it. No one expressed any regrets. Everyone seemed to tolerate quite easily their identity as a diaspora Jew. No one expressed any sense of living in exile, somehow out of place, and their attachment to Israel did not manifest itself as a desire to become Israeli. Israel was the way they derived a sense of their place in the larger world of Jewry.

The biggest concern expressed by diaspora Jews was that they might not be able to continue identifying with a nation-state that no longer represented their ideals, especially with respect to democracy. Within an ethnic or national framing (i.e., 'We are all Jews') Israel held pride of place, but this did not extend to cultural politics. Diaspora Jews felt they were living authentically Jewish lives, or that it was possible to do so in North America, and they did not yearn to become Israelis. This hardly meshed with classical Zionist political theories, which deny that Jews can live full, safe, and secure lives outside their nation-state, Israel.

Some readers of the profiles in this book may read *Zionism* where I read *diasporicism* because many of the diaspora Jews I spoke to used Zionist symbols, tropes, and markers to describe Israel. But the diaspora Jews' sometimes ambivalent relationships with Israel were rarely expressed in terms of belonging or not belonging, nor did these individuals describe Israel in territorialist terms. Moreover, when I compared the responses of diaspora Jews who had a more distant relationship to Israel (i.e., who had visited only once or twice and who were not involved in development organizations), to the responses of diaspora Jews who were most committed to Israel (i.e., who had visited often or were involved in fundraising), I noticed that the latter were more strongly committed to a non-violent, non-military resolution of the Israel–Palestine and Israeli–Arab conflict. This difference is not one that I have seen explored by those who suggest that travelling to Israel strengthens Jewish identification with Israel. It seems that a better understanding of the region's political complexities emerges over time, allowing for the development of more nuanced perspectives. This point deserves much more attention.

Liebman and Cohen's findings (noted in the Introduction) that Jews who identify strongly with Israel are pro-Israel turns out to be a misrepresentation: it does not account for those diaspora Jews who are deeply attached to Israel while also highly critical of its politics. These individuals cannot easily be described on such limited terms. By simply calling diaspora Jews 'pro-Israel,' Cohen and Cohen and Liebman[3] miss the opportunity to explore what in fact it means to these Jews that they have developed any relationship to Israel at all. The importance of Israel to the interviewees was not simply about the founding of a state for the Jews; or the creation of 'the new Jew'; or the bringing of development, redemption, modernization and democracy to a place of 'chaos and primitivism.' In all the interviews, discussions, and exchanges, I consistently found that for diaspora Jews, Israel was the unifying symbol of the Jews' survival as a community, of the Jews as a nation – a nation within both diaspora and Zionist frameworks. Thus, when diaspora Jews imagined Israel they were also reflecting on their collective history and the continuity of their community, the nation of Jews.

Diaspora Jews took up some but not all of Zionism's tenets. Furthermore, and in important ways, they reformulated nationalist longings not as a simple territorial belonging but as a diasporicist belonging on the basis of kin and co-responsibility. Anthropologist Pnina Werbner points out much the same thing in her insightful analysis of the practices of diaspora communities. It seems that for the diaspora Jews I spoke to, exclusive territoriality was contradictory – they were able to experience and maintain an authentic national identity through a diasporic relationship to Israel. The territory itself meant less to them than the survival of their kin, the Israeli Jews. Thus, their concern was for a secure, fair, and democratic state. This post-Zionist shift, from imagining Israel exclusively for the nation to imagining Israel as a normal state, opened up opportunities for the kinds of discussions and debates I witnessed.

I call these imaginings 'diaspora nationalism' because they underscore how the security of the national community is no longer necessarily guaranteed by a territorial imperative – for example, in the form of the commitment to living in Israel. Jews are able to commit themselves to their community in other ways than by supporting and identifying with Israel. A post-Zionist understanding does not shift the emphasis away from kin and responsibility to the nation; it does, however, shift the basis for that relationship away from territorial state-building toward addressing the entire nation's survival needs. This is why diaspora Jews could criticize those who were territorialist (e.g., the settlers, and the Netanyahu government), and claim that communal meaning could be found in religious and traditional practices. The rise of Orthodox power in Israel also made people nervous because they perceived it as a shift away from the normalization of the state. This return was a return to the fold, to tradition, rather than to Israel.

Diaspora Jews' personal histories and experiences became an important factor in understanding diaspora nationalism as a form of taking up one's obligations as kin, for such support would ordinarily be understood as personal rather than political. For example, several interviewees noted that my questions delved into the deeply personal and elicited emotional responses. Soon enough, I realized that what I thought were political questions were in fact questions that forced participants to reflect on their place in the world – on their often tragic family histories and on the commitments or sacrifices they were making to their community. The nationalism literature, moored as it is within a politico-institutional framework, had affected my thinking about these questions. At moments like these, I also noticed my own biases. I had mistakenly conceived of diaspora Jews as mainly a political community, especially in the context of the Israel-Palestine conflict; thus, I was unprepared for the strength of their emotional commitments to one another as Jews, as a collectivity. Moreover, Zionist narratives likely resonated strongly for North American Jews in part because most of them were, or were descendants of, Jews from the areas in Europe most affected by the Holocaust. These origins contributed to feelings of responsibility for the nation's survival, to the sense that Israel was the safe haven that the Jews of Europe were denied. This may also be why most diaspora Jews referred to and identified with the survivalist narratives at Jerusalem, Masada, and the military sites.

All of these factors point to the emergence of a diasporicist ideology that can only be understood in terms of the development of post-Zionism.[4] Post-Zionism should not be confused with anti-Zionism or non-Zionism. Post-Zionism is, like postmodernism's relationship to modernism, a reflexive ideology that neither fully transcends nor fully rejects Zionist conceptions of history or praxis.[5] It critiques and looks beyond the current state of affairs; it seeks to reappraise Zionist myths, models, and suppositions.

With the rise of Zionism came the concept of the need to 'negate the diaspora' – that is, to return to a territory that would be the Jews' own – in order to normalize the nation of Jews. It was presumed that once a Jewish state was established in Israel, there would no longer need to be a diaspora population. No longer would Jews be out of place, without a state to call their own.[6] This concept formed the background to endless debates and discussions about the survival of the Jews in diaspora and the roles that Israel, and *aliyah*, should play in modern Jewish life. In contrast, the discussions among diaspora Jews seemed to focus on both locations: on the permanence of Israel as the Jews' state *and* on the permanence of life for those Jews who chose to live outside that state. This was reflected in the discussions I had with interviewees who did not yearn to change their diasporic status, and who instead expressed an awareness of and appreciation for the permanence of diaspora. The post-Zionist era has opened up opportunities for diaspora Jews to identify with Israel, even while locating an authentic Jewishness outside the state.

At community events, when *aliyah* became a point of contention between Israeli Jews and their North American audiences, it seemed that both sides – diaspora Jews and Israeli Jews – came to these encounters from positions of strength. Paradoxically, then, it seems that a territorial nationalism, Zionism, may have achieved the security not only of a Jewish homeland but also of a deterritorialized, diaspora nationalism. As a result, a new politics of North American Jews' locations seems to have emerged. There have been countless critical and celebratory analyses of Zionism,[7] but none of them has specifically addressed how Zionism may have contributed to the diaspora Jews' sense of achievement and rootedness in communities ouside Israel. Rabbi Greenfield only hinted at the latter phenomenon in his discussion on Zionism.

Some readers may wonder whether the interviewees were shielding me from their deepest feelings about Arabs and Palestinians. That may have happened sometimes. But I don't think it happened often, in part because the interviewees seemed honest and forthcoming and were often critical of Palestinian and Arab practices. Also, if people had very strong feelings, I surely would have heard them expressed during the tours or in community settings. In any participant-observation fieldwork, the researcher is clearly part of the research situation; even so, I do not believe I affected *all* of the practices of those with whom I worked *all* of the time.

Some readers might contend that the people with whom I engaged most were the ones most likely to hold post-Zionist attitudes. Is it possible that I only spoke to Jews who were willing to speak to a Palestinian? My answer to this cannot be unequivocal. Some tour participants warned me – sometimes obliquely, sometimes not – to stay away from certain other tourists. On one occasion I was told that one of the tourists did not think I 'looked Jewish' and that I should probably stay away from her. On another occasion, two tourists told another that the research effort was 'bothering' them; then another participant told me that she believed those two simply didn't like Arabs, and that I should ignore them. Some people in the community shunned me. I never did approach or reach out to those few whom I had been warned to stay away from, since I wanted the research process to develop on the basis of trust and reciprocity. So it can be said that I did not try to interview those whom I suspected had strong negative feelings about Palestinians, and that I didn't talk to them much.

Many of the tourists and community members with whom I developed long-term relationships were at least sympathetic to a peace agreement between the Palestinians and the Israelis; that said, it is significant that I did not and could not know about their sympathies before meeting them. I must note that only a few of the people were engaged with these issues to the extent that we could discuss in depth the debates about the alternative or new history, or the Palestinian and non-Zionist counter-narratives of the founding of the state of Israel. Furthermore, not everyone with whom I became acquainted was at all sympathetic. Especially important, too, is that most people I spoke with were neither activists nor on the front lines of peace-building practices between Jews or Israelis and Palestinians.

The Other Israel

Details of Israel's discriminatory policies toward and maltreatment of the Palestinians were available to diaspora Jews; yet they interpreted and understood these policies in limited ways. In no small measure, this was because the narratives they were presented overwhelmingly described Israel as a glorious, democratic, fair, pioneering, and heroic but also tiny and threatened state. As well, tour participants and community members had few if any opportunities to meet Palestinians or other Arabs. This limited diaspora Jews' personal exposure to other people's narratives.

Among those I interviewed, discussions about democracy in Israel were limited to the threat the ultra-Orthodox posed to Israeli-Jewish democracy. Unfortunately, this analysis never extended to include the implications for non-Jews – an especially important issue when one considers that many ultra-Orthodox Jews openly lobby against any peace with the Palestinians and promote the building of settlements in Jerusalem and in the West Bank.

Also, most diaspora Jews who expressed some sympathy with the Palestinians' plight did so only on the premise that Jews and Palestinians would have to be separated into two distinct states. Land and some sovereign status would be granted to each community. However, Palestinians in Israel would live as second-class citizens, and would continue to do so as long as Israel remained legislatively defined as a Jewish state. Under these conditions, Palestinians would not be treated as nationals in a Jewish state; they would be citizens but with limited rights. Land, education, military, and social policies would all favour Israelis who are Jews.[8] As Warren, one of the tour participants profiled earlier, hinted: limiting Israel to the Jews could effectively limit Jews' and other people's opportunities for living wherever they wish, should they have the choice.

In general, there were few tour participants or community members with whom I was able to discuss Israel's land policies. On occasion, I suggested that Israel is a state defined by 'demographic denial.' That is, in areas where the Palestinians continue to be the majority, or where Israelis believe that one day Palestinians will form a majority, Israeli land and settlement policies are being used to change, or deny (in Freudian terms), the region's demographic profile.[9] When I expressed this point of view, I was treated with either hostility or incomprehension. Moreover, reactions to my suggestion that we begin to re-envision Israel on binational terms ranged from surprise to anger. These ideas were dismissed as 'impractical' or 'impossible' (because 'no state has ever been bi-national'), or as 'racist' or 'anti-Semitic' (because it denied Jews their own nation-state).

Diaspora Jews imagined Israel in the context of a Eurocentric ideal. That is, nations can only realize themselves as territorial nation-states: to each nation, its own state. This perspective denies the realities of the histories of peoples in the Middle East (and in many other regions as well). As a consequence, even religious practices are now becoming burdened with national importance. In this way, Druze, Christians, Bedouins, and Jews are, by virtue of their different cultural or religious or political practices, transformed and divided into different bounded communities or nations in ways that deny their shared geographies and histories. This perspective creates a distorted sense of the Middle East as a messy space of mixed peoples (e.g., the way that Lebanon was represented on tour), and is contrasted with the ideal and pure nation-state, the Jews' state, that Israel either already is or should become. Ironically, Europe's once-fascist states were the most frequently cited models: Germany for Germans, France for the French, and Italy for the Italians. Curiously, even though all of the participants were from the United States and Canada, these counties were never referred to as ideal states. Even more startling was that multiculturalism – a concept that many participants understood and supported through their community organizations – was never once mentioned in these contexts.

It is also true, of course, that the tours and community presentations did not show the extent to which the people of Israel-Palestine live alongside and among one another. Even the Oslo Accords called for the construction of 'bypass roads' so that Israeli Jews (mainly) could bypass non-Jewish communities. Israel's maps are nothing if not reifications. They do not illustrate the lived realities and daily interactions of those who live in Israel or in the Occupied Territories; or the fact that Israeli Jews and Palestinians must endure the impacts of each other's politics and economic and social policies no matter how many roads or fences crisscross the same territory. The histories of all of the peoples in the region are, as they always have been, bound together not only by conflicts but also by daily interactions in the marketplace, at work, in the streets of Israel, and of course, in those areas which have been militarily occupied. Lack of awareness of these rich and sometimes dangerous encounters, or of difficulties of sustaining separations in everyday domains, limits diaspora Jews' understandings and experiences of Israel. This lack of awareness may also be why Israelis and diaspora Jews often seemed to be talking over each other's heads in community settings. For example, when Israeli Jews proposed peace, North American Jews held to impractical and idealistic hopes, imagining that Israel would not need to come to some agreement with the Palestinians, especially with respect to returning land and disengaging the army from the Occupied Territories.

I have set out the many differences, disappointments, and constraints within the conceptualizations of community, nation, territory, and the past that I encountered in my discussions with community members. Yet there were also many moments of sharing.

During my fieldwork, it became clear to me that nations are narrated and imagined, but they are also open to challenge and reinterpretation. The interviewees repeatedly poached certain narratives (e.g., biblical heritage, national refuge, modern state), but not others (e.g., democracy is coincident with a Jewish state, militarism is essential). This indicated clearly that certain narratives were more powerful than others. Indeed, each of the points of resistance was tied closely to personal experience, or to liberal North American principles such as separation of church and state, multiculturalism, peace building, and human security.

As de Certeau makes clear, there is always the possibility of innovating against the rules – the *possibility* of creating by bending or breaking convention, of drawing on other rules from other arenas of life. These possibilities depend on the existence of conventions, although they are not entirely constrained by conventions. Such practices and resistances may or may not have profound consequences, but the fact that it is possible to resist, reinterpret, and select, and that the consequences of such practices are not determined by a single set of conventions, allows more freedom than attributing these practices to a top-down, ideological power would suggest. Thus people, readers, consumers, and tourists are not located in a single ideological or power convention – rather, they are located in several. It is not clear that de Certeau has this particular approach in mind when he describes the practices of poaching.

Diaspora Belonging

Anthropologists face questions arising from a postmodern moment in a global world that describes identities as hybridized, creolized, diasporicized, exiled, migrant, and deterritorialized. This research reveals how some of the most explosive political and cultural questions facing North American Jewry in today's world emerge from a deterritorialized politics and identification with a homeland. Much of the postmodern and diaspora literature points to the potential for the nation-state to be displaced as the basis for collective identity and politics; in the context of this book, diaspora Jews' relationships to Israel are complexly intertwined with imagining the nation *and* the nation-state. All of that being said, relationships and attachments are much more complicated than the anthropological and cultural studies literature on diaspora would have us think.

Other researchers have explored some of the possibilities opened up by the study of the changing relationships of Jews to Israel,[10] but their work either is non-ethnographic or has described other settings. Of particular interest are those scholars who have shown that there are many elements in Jewish tradition that can be drawn from in order to recast diaspora politics and Israel-diaspora relationships so as to include a non-exclusivist, non-territorialist perspective on Israel. For example, in 'an alternative story of Israel,' anthropologist Jonathan Boyarin and cultural theorist Daniel Boyarin call into question the idea that a people must have a land in order to be a people. Citing biblical scholar Thomas Davies, they argue that in fact, 'the Land of Israel was not the birthplace of the Jewish people. Israel was born in exile. Abraham had to leave his own land to get to the Promised Land: the father of Jewry was deterritorialized.'[11] With such deterritorialized beginnings, the Jews' survival has been attributed to dialectical tensions they had to endure as a people defined in national, genealogical, and religious terms. The Boyarins argue that a people can 'maintain its distinctive culture, its difference, without controlling land, *a fortiori* without controlling other people or developing a need to dispossess them of their lands.'[12] Moreover, 'diasporic cultural identity teaches us that cultures are not preserved by being protected from "mixing" but probably can only continue to exist as a product of such mixing.'[13] Thus, they reconceptualize in confident terms the Jews' existence without a territorial state and suggest that the Jews' survival is predicated on their continual 'wanderings' rather than on settling in one place.

The Boyarins' attempt to reconceptualize diaspora for contemporary Jews is an important theoretical move. Although not an accurate reflection of how diaspora Jews I spoke to envisioned their relationships or identifications with Israel, some of what the Boyarins point to does take us in the same direction; primarily, they recognize the possibilities and celebrations of a deterritorialized Jewry. The Boyarins advocate a spiritual rather than a national identification with Israel, mainly because they identify nationalism with territoriality, as do most nationalist theories, including Zionism. But by assuming that nationalism is territorially based, the Boyarins miss the point that the relationship of diaspora Jews to Israel is *not* specifically limited to territory and that it is already about Jewish heritage or tradition – their relationship to a people from the 'Land of Israel.' Equally important, this attachment seems to be about maintaining the survival of Jewry and is consequently linked to a sense of communal obligation for one another, for other Jews.

The concept of post-Zionism, which has been applied by some scholars to describe Israeli Jews' renegotiated relationships to Israel,[14] might also apply to diaspora Jews, since they too seem to have shifted from a Zionist territorial identification with Israel to one defined by a strongly diasporicist or deterritorialized imagining. This is 'diaspora nationalism.' In doing so, diaspora Jews were not themselves identifying as outsiders; rather, they were redefining their relationship to homeland in national instead of spiritual terms. Such a definition was fundamentally structured by their identification with the nation as Jews, rather than by any territorial imperative or by the need to make *aliyah*.

These practices focus on a reterritorialized homeland insofar as it is an ancestral land; however, diaspora Jews are not tied to its territory so much as to its population – its Jewish population – as members of the same nation and kinship collectivity. This diasporicist identification with Israel is based mainly on the practices of 'co-responsibility' to others of the nation.[15] In contrast to the problematic that Zionists had grappled with before the founding of Israel, these Jews envision their relationship to Israel from a secure position outside the state.

It must be said, as well, that the narratives and practices reported on have existed during a complex and changing historical moment in which many were rethinking ideas that have dominated the past century. It was also a moment when there was unprecedented success and security among Jews in North America as well as in Israel. And it was a time when the Oslo Accords had initiated new contacts and hope for peace in the Middle East.

The end of this study in 1999 also marked the end of a decade of hope. Soon after, in September 2000 (one year before that fateful day in 2001), a new cycle of violence began, laying waste to the hope for peace that had been developing, and decimating the lives and livelihoods of the Palestinians, and, although to a much lesser extent, also changing the lives of Israelis. At this writing, a 'Road Map to Peace' has been unveiled, but the path to peace seems nowhere in sight. Militarism predominates, and the policies of separation continue to inform political leaders and their platforms. However, the constrained openings discussed throughout this text are still relevant, and now more than ever they must become part of an active process of rethinking and social action in and about a new Middle East. Building greater awareness of the ongoing dangers and the increased loss of liberty to all – but especially for Palestinians – must begin, and the projects of coexistence that began more than a decade ago must resume, both here and there.

Imagining New Practices in Place

> I would like ... to imagine a place in which humans can live. A place more
> desirable than the failure which we presently inhabit. This failure which,
> we fear, cannot be defeated. I will admit that my purpose is utopian if
> that won't mean that my purpose is laughable. To be sure it's not, then,
> let's be sober about our utopia. Let's understand by it the simple notion
> that there are ideas as yet unrealized which if realized would transcend
> our present reality ... Let me put it this way, I'm after a real nowhere. A
> realizable illusion.[16]

I begin and end this book with utopian reflections: first, Hannah
Arendt's call for each of us to be able to be and experience in another's
place in order to judge appropriately, and here author Curtis White's
desire for a 'real nowhere' – a play on imaginary realities and illusory
places and the place of utopias in our imaginings. Both quotations
speak to my desire and ambivalence regarding the nature of positing
utopian possibilities for practical identities and geographies. I have
claimed that locations and nations in the world are imagined and that
such imaginings have social – that is, real – consequences for people's
lives. But I hope I have also shown that these imaginings are defined
by their fluidity, their constructed forms. Everyday actions and imaginings are a means of making both places and local identities. By
engaging with others, we transform the world, making it into a world
of places. To say 'nation' is not to limit it to location. Nations are
named, they are experienced, and they are practices in place.

Caught as I am between and among the named and imagined places,
nations, and identities of Israel, Palestine, and Canada, I long for a time
when others might feel caught as well. At such a time we will have
shifted our limited frameworks of putting people in place, to explore
the messy locations of the hybrids we all are. The question remains:
How do we find a collective practice in place?

Appendix:
Interview Questions/Guideline

1 Was this your first trip to Israel? If yes, why did you choose to travel now? If no, how may times have you travelled to Israel in the past? What were your reasons for coming to Israel in the past? What was your reason this time?

   or

   When was your first trip to Israel? Why did you choose to travel then? How many times have you travelled to Israel? What were your reasons for travelling back to Israel?

2 Can you say something about your relationship to Israel? Has it evolved over the years? How/why?

3 Describe Israel to me.

4 When you speak to your friends and family about Israel, what do you emphasize?

5 Was there any event/personality/place visited on a tour to Israel that prompted you to think differently about Israel? about Jews in the world? about Jewish identity? about North American Jewry? about Palestinians? about Arabs?

6 In your opinion, how important is Israel to North American Jews? In what way is it an important place? In what way is it irrelevant, if any?

7 Similarly, in your opinion, how important are North American Jews to Israel? to Israeli Jews? In what ways are they irrelevant, if at all?

8 Do you believe that tours to Israel are an important means of linking North American Jews to the State of Israel? to Israelis? to other Jews? If yes, how so? If no, why not?

9 How do you feel about the Oslo Peace Accords signed between Israel and the Palestinians? Do you think this agreement has transformed North American Jewish perspectives on the Israel-Palestine conflict? If yes, how? If no, why not?
10 Do you think you will return to Israel? Why?/Why not?

Notes

Introduction

1 For example, Anderson 1991; Giddens 1987; Hutchinson and Smith 1994; Smith 1991.

2 For a diverse though not comprehensive set of 'pro-Israel' perspectives, see Dershowitz 2003; Fackenheim 1978; Grosby 1999; Karetzky and Frankel 1989; Laqueur and Rubin 1985; Safran 1978; Schoenbaum 1993.

3 For a diverse though not comprehensive set of 'pro-Palestinian' perspectives, see Abdo and Lentin 2002; Abdo-Zubi 1987; Abu-Lughod 1971; Avinery 1971; Beinin 1994; Brand, 1990; Chomsky 1984; Dimbleby 1980; Farsoun 1997; Graham-Brown 1980; Kanaana 1992; Khalidi 1997, 1998; Khalidi 1984; Lilienthal 1953; Palumbo 1990; Rodinson 1973; Said 1978, 1980, 1994a, 1994b, 1996; Salt 1997; Swedenburg 2003; Zureik 1995.

4 Although I was exposed to both German and Yiddish, I learned only Hebrew and Arabic as a child and maintain that level of competence now. While I was growing up in Canada, I was exposed to the Arab and Israeli communities and only rarely to the North American Jewish one. This is one reason why I chose to investigate this community's relationship to Israel.

5 Political philosopher Hannah Arendt 1993, 241 and 223; see also Marchessault 1995.

6 Brodbar-Nemzer et al. 1993; Cohen 1983; Liebman and Cohen 1990; Sheffer 1996.

7 Kugelmass 1988, 13.

8 Rich 1986.

9 I agreed to keep the identities of all who participated in this research confidential. This included declining to identify the communities in which I conducted the research.

10 I decided not to travel on religious tours. I wanted to go on tours that anyone in the Jewish community – Orthodox or non-Orthodox – could and
often did take. During the fieldwork, I met only one person who had participated in a religious tour, and he was a rabbi. Furthermore, taking a religious tours would have meant studying a very different kind of trip – more
pilgrimage than ethnic tour. It could be said that the tours I participated on
had elements of pilgrimage (especially in Jerusalem); even so, the tours
were not defined as such, and the tourists never defined themselves in
those terms. See Badone 1995; Bowman 1991; Eade and Sallnow 1991.

I also chose not to study the 'March of the Living.' These tours take travellers to European cities and Holocaust sites and then on to Israel. There are
several reasons I chose not to take part on these. According to several tour
organizers, as well as community informants, the March of the Living tours
are among the least popular tours, perhaps because they are newer than
most, and perhaps also because many of them are designed for teenagers,
not adults. Also, these tours are designed to celebrate Jewish survival and
sometimes the survival of European communities after the Holocaust.
These tours focus on Jewish communities outside of Israel, but they are not
primarily interested in the role that Israel might play in diaspora consciousness, which was the focus of my research.

11 Conservative Judaism is a North American movement, founded in the
nineteenth century, that advocates more traditional Jewish values than
Reform Judaism but is more modern than the Orthodox. The traditional
separation of men and women in synagogue has been maintained by Conservative Jews; however, women may be ordained as rabbis. Although
there are some Conservative synagogues in Israel, Conservative Judaism is
not recognized as a legitimate representative of the Jewish religion by the
Orthodox Rabbinical Authority there. Reform Judaism is an Enlightenment
movement, founded in Germany in the eighteenth century. It rejects a
number of basic traditional beliefs and practices. The synagogue is called a
temple; there is mixed seating, and the services are performed in the vernacular language of the community. Beliefs rejected include dietary laws.
Women may be ordained as rabbis. There are Reform temples in Israel;
however, Reform rabbis and Reform practices are not recognized as legitimately Jewish by the Orthodox Rabbinical Authority there. The Reform
movement is also distinguished by its debate on the role of Zionism in
modern Jewish life. It was anti-Zionist at the beginning of the last century,
but changed in the 1960s. Orthodox groups include the ultra-Orthodox and
the modern Orthodox. The modern Orthodox reject efforts to modernize
halakha (or religious law), but they maintain a modern lifestyle, believe in

secular education, and hold vernacular ceremonies. The ultra-Orthodox reject some of the values of modernity. They are often distinguished by their traditional clothing and ghetto lifestyles. In the State of Israel only the Orthodox are officially recognized as authoritative on Jewish laws and practices; this, even though there are ultra-Orthodox who are anti-Zionist. Reconstruction Judaism is a breakaway from Conservative Judaism. It was founded in North America in the twentieth century and is distinguished by its focus on Judaism as a cultural tradition. Members of this branch do not hold the belief that the Jews are the Chosen People, nor do they believe in the Messiah. They strongly emphasize fairness and equity.

12 Government of Israel 1993.

13 Clifford 1997.

14 Chaliard and Rageau 1995, xvi.

15 For example, Appadurai 1988, 1990; Clifford 1992, 1997; Clifford and Marcus 1986; Coombe 1991; Featherstone 1990; Foster 1991; Gupta and Ferguson 1997; Hannerz 1996; Lavie and Swedenburg 1996; Knauft 1996; Malkki 1995; Massey 1994; Olwig 1997; Olwig and Hastrup 1997; Robertson et al. 1994; Rodman 1992; Said 1994a; Smith and Katz 1993; Strathern 1991.

16 Lavie and Swedenburg 1996, 14.

17 Clifford 1997.

18 Smith and Katz 1993, 78, citing Clifford 1999, 10.

19 Appadurai 1991, 191.

20 For example, the work on refugees by Liisa Malkki is different. It investigates the very meanings people make and their shifting identities in response to being defined as refugees and confined to living in refugee camps. They are nationals at one time, refugees at another, the enemy at another. This work not only situates people within a bounded place, but also illustrates how they make meanings of another place as well as their own place in response to being bounded geographically as well as by the identities that they are given – by, for example, humanitarian agencies – and that they 'take' as 'refugees' (1995; 1997). Compare this to Lavie (1996), who writes about Palestinian Arab authors' experiences in Israel as 'exiles.' Because some authors write in Hebrew, not their native language of Arabic, Lavie has designated them 'exiled' in the 'borderzone' that is Israel. But is this appropriate? Why exile them even metaphorically (she titles one subsection of her piece 'History of Home as Exile') when they are indeed at home, as the title of her article indicates? Why not speak in terms of their resistance to the discriminatory practices of the Israeli state? I have no argument with her contention that Palestinian and Arab writers are discriminated against and face enormous difficulties as writers. But labelling

Palestinians who live in the State of Israel as 'exiles' is doing exactly what we must be very careful *not* to do: name people in place, or out of place, for the sake of a new scholarly metaphor such as 'diaspora' or 'exile.' The Palestinians in Israel are not out of place. They are not exiles. They are second-class citizens in a state that defines them mainly as outsiders – as non-Jews in a Jewish state. Palestinian *refugees* are living in exile. See also Bisharat 1997.

21 For example, Boyarin and Boyarin 1993; Brown 1998; Clifford 1997; Gilroy 1996.
22 See Olwig 1997.
23 Wagner 1981; see also Preston 1999.
24 See Anderson 1991.
25 Ibid., 6.
26 Hobsbawm and Ranger 1984.
27 Anderson, 135.
28 For example, Hanson 1989; Hobsbawm and Ranger 1984; Keesing 1989, 1991.
29 For example, Badone 1991; Trask 1991; Linnekin 1991.
30 Barthes 1972.
31 Ibid., 155.
32 Ibid.
33 Ibid., 156.
34 Ibid.
35 Alonso 1988, 40.
36 Ibid., 40–1.
37 Ibid., 44–5.
38 Ibid., 45.
39 Ibid.
40 Handelman 1990, 233.
41 Ibid., 16.
42 Ibid., 12.
43 Ibid., 233.
44 Ibid., 231.
45 Ibid.
46 Ibid., 19.
47 Paine 1989, 123.
48 Ibid., 130.
49 Ibid.
50 De Certeau 1984, 1986.
51 Ibid., 48.

52 See also Allen 1992; Fiske 1992, 1993; Jenkins 1992; Morris 1992; Nightingale 1996. These scholars use de Certeau to examine popular cultural forms such as television programs.

53 Giroux 2000, 60.

1. Zionism, Diaspora, and Israel

1 Note that Simon Dubnow, a Jewish historian, wrote against this Zionist representation of diaspora in the late 1800s and up until 1941, when he was murdered. On the American Council for Judaism's anti-Zionist position during the prestate period, see Kolsky 1991. See also, for example, Biale 1986, 1992; Boyarin and Boyarin 1993; Eisen 1986; Evron 1995; D. Goldberg 1996; Hertzberg 1976; Wheatcroft 1996.

2 For example, Theodor Herzl [1896] 1976.

3 For example, A.D. Gordon [1911] 1976.

4 For example, Rabbi Isaac Kook [1930] 1976.

5 For example, Ahad Ha'am [1909] 1976.

6 Ahad Ha'am ([1897] 1976; [1909] 1976).

7 Ahad Ha'am [1897] 1976.

8 'Aliya,' *Encyclopedia of Israel and Zionism*, 53; D. Goldberg 1996.

9 Abella and Troper 2000.

10 Eisenstadt 1992; D. Goldberg 1996; Laqueur and Rubin 1985; Teveth 1987; Wheatcroft 1996.

11 Israel's new historians have challenged the Zionist framings of the founding of Israel. See, for example, Benvenisti 1996; Evron 1995; Flapan 1987, Kimmerling and Migdal 1993; Morris 1987, 1998; Morris with Rubenstein 1995; Pappe 1992; Segev 1986; and Sternhall 1998. See also Azoulay 1994; Mahler 1997. Accounts by Palestinians that serve to counter official Zionist history of the founding of the state include Abdo and Lentin 2002; Abdo-Zubi 1987, Doumani 1995, Farsoun 1997, Kanaana 1992; R. Khalidi 1997, 1998; Khalidi 1984; Said 1978,1980, 1994; Said and Hitchens 1988; Swedenburg 2003.

12 'The Declaration of Independence Pamphlet,' Independence Hall, Eretz Israel Museum, n.d.

13 The Hebrew word *oleh* comes from the word *aliyah*.

14 Israel Ministry of Foreign Affairs, Basic Laws Document, n.d.; see also Laqueur and Rubin 1985, 128.

15 See, for example, Abu El-Haj 1998, 2001; Azoulay 1994; Bauman 1995; Ben-David 1997; Ben-Ze'ev and Ben-Ari 1996; Friedlander and Seligman 1994; Golden 1996; Gurevitch and Aran 1994; Katriel 1997; Selwyn 1995, 1996;

Shenhav-Keller 1993; Shohat 1989; Silberman 1990, 1995, 1997; Steiner 1995; Zerubavel 1995a, 1995b

16 Levy 1997; Safran 1978; Safty 1992.

17 Note that Palestinians have very different names and designations for the same battles. As an example, Palestinians know Israel's 1948 War of Independence as Al Naqba, or 'the catastrophe.'

18 Levy 1997; Said 1996; Shlaim 1994.

19 D. Goldberg 1996; Kaufman 1996; Livni 1995.

20 Sheffer 1996, 63.

21 Azria 1998; Brodbar-Memzer et al., 1993; Heilman 1999; Liebman 1999.

22 S. Cohen 1983; Liebman and Cohen 1990.

23 Brodbar-Memzer et al. 1993.

24 Cohen 1983, 34.

25 Golda Meir writes: 'We have always believed ... that the foundation of Zionism is more than geographical independence ... I believe that there is no Jew in the *galut* creating as a free man and as a free Jew. Only a Jew in Israel can do so ... Whoever talks himself into the belief that the Jewish people in the diaspora can exist as it would in Israel, and that it has a lasting chance of survival there, is deeply mistaken ... The more people taken out of any diaspora community, the richer that community becomes. This is paradoxical but true. A Jewish community from which there is no *aliyah* becomes spiritually impoverished ... No real bond can exist between Israel and the Jews of the free countries without a great immigration to Israel' (1986, 301–3).

26 Other measurements include, for example, lighting candles every Friday night to celebrate the holy day of Shabbat; fasting on the high holidays of Yom Kippur; and lighting candles for Hanukkah.

27 Liebman and Cohen 1990, 84–5.

28 For example, Flapan 1987; Morris 1987; Pappe 1992; Segev 1986.

29 Segev 1993.

30 Shohat 1988, 1989.

31 For an overview, see Cohen 1995; Evron 1995; Silberstein 1999.

2. Touring Israel

1 The names of the guides and of the organizations sponsoring the tours have been changed to protect their identities. Each has been given a pseudonym. Where appropriate, I have highlighted their fundraising niches and roles in community building. Such details are important in some contexts.

2 See also, for example, Cohen 1985, 1995; Fine and Speer 1985; MacCannell 1992; Selwyn 1995, 1996a 1996b; Urry 1990.

3. Celebrating Return: One Nation, One Land

1 Of course, it is not unusual for archaeologists to narrate the past in order to identify it with a particular people's history. See Jones 1997; Kohl and Fawcett 1995; Silberman 1990. Archaeologist Keith Whitelam (1996) argues that Israel's history is limited by the biblical archaeological discourse. Writers like Neil Asher Silberman 1990, 1992, 1995, 1997, Amos Elon 1997, and Nadia Abu El-Haj 1998, 2001, demonstrate the nationalist agenda for the archaeological preoccupations of Israelis.
2 Boyarin and Boyarin 1993.
3 Abdo-Zubi 1987; Doumani 1995; Kimmerling and Migdal 1993.
4 Bruner and Gorfain 1991; Kedar 1982; Lewis 1975; Maranz 1994; Zerubavel 1995a.
5 Important as Masada is, not only to Israel's but also in Jews' and non-Jews' popular imagination of Israel – partly because of its popularization with the movie 'Masada,' partly because it is used in advertisements for travel to Israel – this site was only once on the itinerary of a tour I accompanied. In all other cases, however, the tour organizations had optional tours to Masada available, and all the tourists who had never been to Masada took these tours. In this way, even though Masada was not on all of the official itineraries, Masada generated many discussions among the tourists on all of the tours.
6 West and East do not truly designate their geographical locations, but it seems to me worth mentioning that West Jerusalem is Israeli and associated with modernism whereas East Jerusalem is Palestinian and associated with underdevelopment.
7 A 1981 Israeli Supreme Court ruling prohibits non-Jews from buying property in the Jewish Quarter of the Old City.
8 See also Armstrong 1996; Benvenisti 1996; Goldberger 1995.
9 I expect, though I cannot be certain, that a religious tour would highlight the religious significance of these sites and include scriptural readings by the guides.
10 On Holocaust museums, see Young 1993.
11 See also Liebman and Cohen 1990.
12 Goldhagen 1996. A discussion of the centrality of the role of anti-Semitism in the Holocaust arose in 1996 with the publication of Goldhagen's *Hitler's Willing Executioners*. For a discussion of this debate see also Goldhagen 1998; Riemer and Markovitz 1998; Shatz 1997.

13 See especially Marrus 1987, 18–25, on the role that uniqueness plays in debates over Holocaust historiography. On its role in American history, see Novick 1999.

14 See, for example, Dawidowicz 1986; Goldhagen 1996, 1998.

15 See, for example, Browning 1992; Herf 1987; Hilberg 1985.

16 Handelman and Shamgar-Handelman 1997. See also Lambek 1996 who writes: 'Memory ... is less a completely private yet potentially objective phenomenon stored *within* the mind and capable of remaining there than it is activated implicitly or explicitly *between* people, a confirmation of the sense of continuity (caring) and discontinuity (mourning) that each person experiences in their relations with others.' p. 239.

4. Development and Democracy

1 On Ben-Gurion and the Negev, see for example Teveth 1987; Tzahor 1995.

2 Katriel 1997; see also Daniel Boyarin 1995, 1997 on Zionism and the Jewish body; see also Shohat (1989) on the role of the Negev in Jewish narratives of nation, especially Israeli film.

3 The Sephardim and Oriental Jews were also settled in development towns in northern Israel. See the Kiryat Shmona narrative embedded in the story of the Lebanon conflict, below. On Sephardic Jewish experiences in Israel, see especially Shohat 1988.

4 Lavie 1993; Mohanty 1984; Shohat 1988, 1989.

5 See also Kennedy 1989 and Tarabieh 1995 on Druze resistance in the Golan Heights.

6 For example, Lavie 1996; Peled 1992, 1995; Shalev 1989, 1992.

7 For example, Halper 1998; Rabinowitz 1997.

5. Settling the Nation, Defending the State

1 Note that the settlement movement in the West Bank in particular uses the same logic. Often referred to as 'outposts,' these areas are nothing more than lands that settlers claim as their own simply by putting up tents or trailers and then naming them in order to designate them as new settlements.

2 See Segev 1986.

3 As in the Negev narratives, it is non-European Jews who are remade.

4 For more on this issue, see Champion 1997; Lustick 1988, 1996.

5 See Rabinowitz 1997; Yiftachel 1991.

6. The Politics of Securing Peace

1 Government of Israel 1993; Said 1994b; 1996.
2 On the Israel Civil Society Fund Tour we were taken into Jericho, where we were greeted by a spokesperson for the Palestinian Authority. See Habib 2000.

7. Representing Israel

1 Because I maintained contact with people who lived outside my research area (e.g., with some of the people I met on tour), I discovered that often the same speaker had travelled to their area. I attended many of these events on my own, although when I was invited to join community members, I did so. Note that all presenters have been given pseudonyms.
2 Though it should be noted that the public presentations examined here are also representative of the range of articles in periodicals and newspapers written for and by Jews, especially in such Jewish-oriented publications as the *Canadian Jewish News, Tikkun, Commentary, Jerusalem Report*, and *Jewish Forward*.
3 In the greater metropolitan area where I conducted my research, except for the high-holiday periods, there was at least one Israel-focused event to attend per week. At times there were as many as three events in one night. In the smaller city, there were fewer events.
4 See, for example, Brym, Shaffir, and Weinfeld 1993; Heilman 1999; Liebman 1999; Lipset 1990; Shaffir 1983.
5 In addition, these events were community events and not necessarily Israeli state-sponsored events. So, for example, synagogue and community centre talks were funded by internal budgets allotted for public speakers; in some cases they were endowed lectures. University programs – for example, Jewish studies programs – typically sponsored university-based lectures. Other community events were sponsored by organizations that support projects and universities in Israel. So, for example, Israeli peace organizations such as Peace Now, and universities such as the Hebrew University of Jerusalem have fundraising arms in North America called 'Friends of Peace Now,' 'Friends of the Hebrew University,' and so on. Each of these organizations seeks 'friends' or members who support their work in Israel. By becoming a student member of some of these organizations during the fieldwork period, I was able to receive notices of upcoming events as well as letters appealing for continued financial support.

These events were also advertised in the *Canadian Jewish News* or local newspapers and synagogue newsletters; the same ads appealed to both friends and the wider public to attend. Each of these organizations used the ads to raise awareness about Israel and the organization's good works. And of course they appealed for new members.

8. Identifying (with) Israel, Zionism and the State

1 See for example, Alcalay 1993, who seeks to uncover such intermixing and proposes that we study the region in cultural terms that define the area as Levantine, not simply in nationalist or religious terms.
2 For extended discussions of nationalist and biblical scholars' use and distortions of archaeological evidence, see especially Abu El-Haj 1999, 2001; Silberman 1992; Silberman and Small 1997; and Whitelam 1996.
3 He earlier named the three periods: (1) the 'Medieval Jewish' period; (2) the 'Christian' period; and (3) the 'time of the Jews.'
4 See especially Benvenisti (1996), who describes how Jerusalem's history has been written and represented, in local and national museums, without any recognition of others' experiences.

9. Identifying (with) Israel after Zionism

1 D. Goldberg 1996; Hertzberg 1976; Wheatcroft 1996.
2 See also Champion 1997; Lustick 1988.
3 Refers to the founding charter of the Palestine Liberation Organization, which in essence denied the legitimacy of Israel. The charter outlined the character of the struggle against Israel as anticolonial and revolutionary.
4 I skip the usual preambles and present only the questions.

10. Narrating Relations for Diaspora

1 Werbner 1998, 12.
2 Ibid.
3 Ibid., 14.
4 Troper 1996. See Bourne 1987, Falbel, Klepfisz, and Neve 1990, Lerner 1994, and Plaskow 1991 as representative of these shifts in the United States. See also Heilman 1999 and Liebman 1999 on American Jewry's changing perspectives on Israel.
5 These interviews were conducted in people's homes and workplaces, at meetings we arranged in restaurants, and – while on tour – in hotel rooms

and cafes, and at outdoor sites. Only two interviews were conducted over the telephone, and both were with tour planners and fund organizers, with whom I had had at least one personal visit after the tour they had helped organize. Some interviews were conducted with both spouses at the same time – which was their preference. Other couples agreed to be interviewed separately (although those interviews are not included in this book). A list of the general questions used for the interviews can be found in the appendix to this book. Some of the questions were similar to those Cohen used in his study of 'pro-Israelism' in *Jewish Identity and Modernity*. The questions were designed to elicit Israel's significance in people's lives. The emphasis was not only on Israel, but also on the Jewish community and Jewish identity and how Israel might play a role in Jewish lives in North America. I did not use the term *diaspora* in the questions, nor did I ever ask any questions about Zionism directly. I wanted each interviewee to raise these terms if and when he or she thought it was appropriate. At that time I would explore its context and saliency. Similarly, I also avoided defining diaspora or Zionism in advance or outside of the interview context.

11. Longings

1 The UN has a peacekeeping force separating the Israelis and the Syrians on the Golan Heights. This fact was never raised on any of the tours.
2 Israel has since withdrawn its forces from Lebanon.
3 Aaron's comment was not at all unusual, though each time it came up, I wondered why a question that I thought was political would be interpreted as emotional. On reflection, and with each answer and encounter, I realized that I was asking some people to locate themselves within their personal life histories. These histories were often marked by experiences of anti-Semitism or the Holocaust or by memories of such experiences told by family or friends. All of this transformed what I initially thought was a simple political question into one that was experienced as an emotional one.

12. A Home Away from Home

1 I did not ask any lunchmates for interviews. Though I learned a great deal from them all, lunch was not a research site *per se*, nor was it a place for subject searches.
2 Cultural theorist David Biale (1992) writes in 'Zionism as an Erotic Revolution': 'One of the central claims of Zionism was that the Jews lived a disembodied existence in exile and that only a healthy national life could restore

a necessary measure of physicality and materiality ... This political ideology was not only based on the body as metaphor but, in addition, also sought to transform the Jewish body itself, and especially the sexual body ... Zionism promised an erotic revolution for the Jews: the creation of a virile New Hebrew Man as well as rejection of the inequality of women in traditional Judaism in favour of full equality between the sexes in all spheres of life. Among the socialist pioneers, a new sexual ethic opposed bourgeois marriage and affirmed a healthy sensuality' (283–4). Novelist Philip Roth satirizes this relationship in *The Counterlife*, in which an Israeli Jew exclaims: 'The American Jews get a big thrill from the guns. They see Jews walking around with guns and they think they're in paradise. Reasonable people with a civilized repugnance for violence and blood, they come on tour from America, and they see guns and they see the beards, and they take leave of their senses. The beards to remind them of saintly Yiddish weakness and the guns to reassure them of heroic Hebrew force' (75). See also Breines, 1990; Biale 1986. On the gendered aspects of Zionist ideology, see Biale 1992; D. Boyarin 1995, 1997.

13. Routes to Belonging

1 Troper 1996.

14. Fielding Questions of Identity

1 Giroux 2001, 77–8.
2 One version of this talk was published in *Reform Judaism*. See Habib, 1999.
3 Spivak 1992, 10.
4 Mouffe 1994, 111.
5 I would add that the implications of such thinking about identity and ties to home and homeland are profound when we turn to examine the relationships of migrant workers and refugees to their homelands. This topic is beyond the scope of my research but it is an area to which I hope to turn in future research.

15. Diaspora Belonging

1 Biale 1986, 1992; Boyarin and Boyarin 1993; for a pre-Zionist perspective, see Dubnow 1961.
2 For example, Cohen 1983; Heilman 1999; Levitt and Shaffir 1993; Liebman 1999; Liebman and Cohen 1990; Shusterman 1993.

3 Cohen 1983 and Liebman and Cohen 1990, respectively.

4 Cohen 1995; Evron 1995; Silberstein 1999.

5 On postmodernism, see Collins 1989; Hutcheon 1988, 1989; Rose 1991.

6 Meir 1986; Yehoshua 1986.

7 See, for example, D. Goldberg 1996; Wheatcroft 1996.

8 See Halper 1998; Peled 1992, 1995; Rabinowitz 1997; Shalev 1989, 1992.

9 The Judaization of the Galilee region; the 'Greater Jerusalem' program; and even within the framework of the peace plans, the prevention of any contiguous Palestinian areas that might 'threaten' the Jews' majority.

10 See, for example, Heilman 1999; Liebman 1999.

11 Davies as cited in Boyarin and Boyarin 1993, 718.

12 Boyarin and Boyarin 1993, 723.

13 Ibid.

14 Cohen 1985; Silberstein 1996, 1999; Sternhall 1998.

15 Werbner 1998.

16 White 1992, 9–10.

Bibliography

Abdo, Nahla, and Ronit Lentin, eds. 2002. *Women and the Politics of Military Confrontation: Palestinian and Israeli Gendered Narratives of Dislocation*. New York: Berghahn.

Abdo-Zubi, Nahla. 1987. *Family, Women and Social Change in the Middle East: The Palestinian Case*. Toronto: Canadian Scholars' Press.

Abella, Irving, and Harold Troper. 2000. *None Is Too Many: Canada and the Jews of Europe, 1933–1948*. 3rd ed. Toronto: Key Porter.

Abu El-Haj, Nadia. 1998. 'Translating Truths: Nationalism, the Practice of Archaeology, and the Remaking of Past and Present in Contemporary Jerusalem.' *American Ethnologist* 25: 166–88.

– 2001. *Facts on the Ground: Archaeological Practice and Territorial Self-Fashioning in Israeli Society*. Chicago: University of Chicago Press.

Abu-Lughod, Ibrahim, ed. 1971. *The Transformation of Palestine: Essays on the Origin and Development of the Arab-Israeli Conflict*. Evanston, IL: Northwestern University Press.

Abu-Lughod, Lila. 1986. *Veiled Sentiments: Honor and Poetry in a Bedouin Society*. Berkeley: University of California Press.

Ahad Ha'am. [1897] 1976. 'The Jewish State and the Jewish Problem.' Pp. 262–9 in Arthur Hertzberg, ed. *The Zionist Idea*. New York: Atheneum.

– [1909] 1976. 'Negation of the Diaspora.' Pp. 270–7 in Arthur Hertzberg, ed., *The Zionist Idea*. New York: Atheneum.

Alcalay, Amiel. 1993. *After Jews and Arabs: Remaking Levantine Culture*. Minneapolis: University of Minnesota Press.

Allen, Robert C. 1992. 'Audience-Oriented Criticism and Television.' Pp. 101–37 in *Channels of Discourse*. Chapel Hill: University of North Carolina Press.

Alonso, Ana Maria. 1988. 'The Effects of Truth: Re-Presentation of the Past and the Imagining of Community.' *Journal of Historical Society* 1(1): 33–57.

Anderson, Benedict. 1991. *Imagined Communities: Reflections on the Origin and Spread of Nationalism*. Rev. ed. London: Verso.

Appadurai, Arjun. 1990. 'Disjuncture and Difference in the Global Cultural Economy.' Pp. 295–310 in Mike Featherstone, ed. *Global Culture: Nationalism Globalization and Modernity*. London: Sage.

– 1991. 'Global Ethnoscapes: Notes and Queries for a Transnational Anthropology.' Pp. 191–210 in R.G. Fox, ed. *Recapturing Anthropology: Working in the Present*. Santa Fe: School of American Research.

Arendt, Hannah. 1993. *Between Past and Present*. London: Penguin.

Armstrong, Karen. 1996. *Jerusalem: One City, Three Faiths*. New York: Alfred A. Knopf.

Asad, Talal, ed. 1973. *Anthropology and the Colonial Encounter*. London: Ithaca Press.

Avinery, Uri. 1971. *Israel without Zionism: A Plan for Peace in the Middle East*. New York: Collier Books.

Azoulay, Ariella. 1994. 'With Open Doors: Museums and Historical Narratives in Israel's Public Space.' Pp. 85–112. in Daniel J. Sherman and Irit Rogoff, eds., *Museum Culture*. Minneapolis: University of Minnesota Press.

Azoulay, Ariella, and Adi Ophir. 1998. '100 Years of Zionism: 50 Years of a Jewish State.' *Tikkun* 13(2): 68–71.

Azoulay, Katya Gibel. 1997. *Black, Jewish and Interracial: It's Not the Color of Your Skin but the Race of Your Kin and Other Myths of Identity*. Durham: Duke University Press.

Azria, Regine. 1998. 'The Diaspora-Community-Tradition Paradigms of Jewish Identity: A Reappraisal.' Pp. 21–32 in Ernest Krausz and Gitta Tulea, eds., *Jewish Survival: The Identity Problem at the Close of the Twentieth Century*. New Brunswick, NJ: Transaction Publishers.

Badone, Ellen. 1991. 'Ethnography, Fiction, and the Meanings of the Past in Brittany.' *American Ethnologist* 18(3): 518–545.

– 1992. 'The Construction of National Identity in Brittany and Quebec.' *American Ethnologist* 19(4): 806–17.

– 1995. 'Anthropological Perspectives on Pilgrimage.' Paper prepared for Religious Studies Departmental Colloquium on Pilgrimage in Diverse Religious Traditions. McMaster University. 23–4 March.

Baer, Yitzhak F. 1947. *Galut*. New York: Shocken Books.

Barthes, Roland. 1972. *Mythologies*. London: Paladin.

Battaglia, Deborah, ed. 1995. *The Rhetorics of Self-Making*. Berkeley: University of California Press.

Bauman, Joel. 1995. 'Designer Heritage: Israeli National Parks and the Politics of Historical Representation.' *Middle East Report* 25: 20–3.

Beinin, Joel. 1994. 'Israel at Forty: The Political Economy / Political Culture of Constant Conflict.' *Arab Studies Quarterly* 10(4): 433–56.

Ben-David, Orit. 1997. 'Tiyul (Hike) as an Act of Consecration of Space.' in Pp. 129–146, Eyal Ben-Ari and Yoram Bilu, eds. *Grasping Land: Space and Place in Contemporary Israeli Discourse and Experience*. Albany: State University of New York Press.

Benvenisti, Meron. 1996. *City of Stone: The Hidden History of Jerusalem*. Berkeley: University of California Press.

Ben-Ze'ev, Efrat and Eyal Ben-Ari. 1996. 'Imposing Politics: Failed Attempts at Creating a Museum of "Co-existence" in Jerusalem.' *Anthropology Today* 12(6): 7–13.

Biale, David. 1986. *Power and Powerlessness in Jewish History*. New York: Schocken Books.

– 1992. 'Zionism as an Erotic Revolution.' Pp. 283–308 in Howard Eilberg-Schwartz, ed. *People of the Body*. Albany: State University of New York Press.

Bisharat, George E. 1997. 'Exile to Compatriot: Transformations in the Social Identity of Palestinian Refugees in the West Bank.' Pp. 203–33 in Akhil Gupta and James Ferguson, eds., *Culture, Power, Place: Explorations in Critical Anthropology*. Durham: Duke University Press.

Black, Jeremy. 1997. *Maps and Politics*. Chicago: University of Chicago Press.

Bourne, Jenny. 1987. 'Homelands of the Mind: Jewish Feminism and Identity Politics.' *Race and Class* 29(1): 1–23.

Bowman, Glenn. 1991. 'Christian Ideology and the Image of the Holy Land: The Place of Jerusalem Pilgrimage in the Various Christianities.' Pp. 98–121 in John Eade and Michael J. Sallnow, eds., *Contesting the Sacred: The Anthropology of Christian Pilgrimage*. London: Routledge.

Boyarin, Daniel. 1995. *Carnal Israel*. Berkeley: University of California Press.

– 1997. *Unheroic Conduct: The Rise of Heterosexuality and the Invention of Jewish Man*. Berkeley: University of California Press.

Boyarin, Daniel, and Jonathan Boyarin. 1993. 'Diaspora: Generation and the Ground of Jewish Identity.' *Critical Inquiry* 19(9): 693–725.

Boyarin, Jonathan. 1992. *Storm from Paradise: The Politics of Jewish Memory*. Minneapolis: University of Minnesota Press.

– 1996. *Palestine and Jewish History*. Minneapolis: University of Minnesota Press.

– ed. 1994. *Remapping Memory*. Minneapolis: University of Minnesota Press.

Brand, Laurie. 1990. *Palestinians in the Arab World: Institution Building and the Search for a State*. New York: Columbia University Press.

Breines, Paul. 1990. *Tough Jews*. New York: Basic Books.

Brodbar-Nemzer, Jay, Steven M. Cohen, Allan Reitzes, Charles Shahar, and

Gary Tobin. 1993. 'An Overview of the Canadian Jewish Community.' Pp. 39–72 in Robert J. Brym, ed., *Jews in Canada*. Toronto: Oxford University Press.

Brown, Jacqueline Nassy. 1998. 'Black Liverpool, Black America, and the Gendering of Diasporic Space.' *Cultural Anthropology* 13(3): 291–325.

Browning, Christopher R. 1992. *Ordinary Men: Reserve Police Battalion 101 and the Final Solution in Poland*. New York: Harper Colths.

Bruner, Edward W., and Phyllis Gorfain. 1991. 'Dialogic Narration and Paradoxes of Masada.' Pp. 177–206 in Ivan Brady, ed., *Anthropological Poetics*. Savage, MD: Rowman and Littlefield.

Brym, Robert J. 1993. 'The Rise and Decline of Canadian Jewry? A Socio-Demographic Profile.' Pp. 37–51 in Edmond Y. Lipsitz, ed. *Canadian Jewry Today: Who's Who in Canadian Jewry*. Downsview, ON: J.E.S.L. Educational Products.

Brym, Robert J., William Shaffir, and Morton Weinfeld. 1993. *The Jews in Canada*. Toronto: Oxford University Press.

Butler, Judith, and Joan Scott, eds. 1992. *Feminists Theorise the Political*. New York: Routledge.

Canadian Jewish News. 1997. 'Zionism after 100 Years.' Special Insert. 1 October (67 pages).

Chaliand, Gerard and Jean-Pierre Rageau. 1995. *The Penguin Atlas of Diasporas*. New York: Viking.

Champion, Daryl. 1997. 'Religious Fundamentalism: A Threat to the State of Israel?' Pp. 297–335 in Paul J. White and William S. Logan, eds., *Remaking the Middle East*. Oxford: Berg.

Chomsky, Noam. 1984. *The Fateful Triangle: Israel, the United States, and the Palestinians*. Montreal: Black Rose Books.

Clifford, James. 1992. 'Travelling Cultures.' Pp. 96–112 in Lawrence Grossberg, Cary Nelson, and Paula A. Treichler, eds., *Cultural Studies*. New York: Routledge.

– 1997. *Routes*. Cambridge: Harvard University Press.

Clifford, James, and George E. Marcus, eds. 1986. *Writing Culture: The Poetics and Politics of Ethnography*. Berkeley: University of California Press.

Cohen, Eric. 1985. 'The Tourist Guide: The Origins, Structure and Dynamics of a Role.' *Annals of Tourism Research* 12: 5–29.

– 1995. 'Israel as Post-Zionist Society.' Pp. 203–214 in Robert Wistrich and David Ohana, eds., *The Shaping of Israeli Identity: Myth, Memory and Trauma*.

Cohen, Steven M. 1983. *American Modernity and Jewish Identity*. New York and London: Tavistock Publishers.

Collins, Jim. 1989. *Uncommon Cultures*. New York: Routledge.

Coombe, Rosemary J. 1991. 'Encountering the Postmodern: New Directions in Cultural Anthropology.' *Canadian Review of Sociology and Anthropology* 28: 188–205.

Cooper, Alan. 1996. *Philip Roth and the Jews.* Albany: State University of New York Press.

Cruikshank, Julie. 1995. 'Imperfect Translations: Rethinking Objects of Ethnographic Collections.' *Museum Anthropology* 19(1): 25–38.

Davids, Leo. 1983. 'The Canadian Jewish Population Picture: Today and Tomorrow.' Pp. 52–9 in Edmund Y. Lipsitz ed., *Canadian Jewry Today: Who's Who in Canadian Jewry.* Downsview, ON: J.E.S.L Educational Products.

Dawidowicz, Lucy S. 1986. *The War against the Jews, 1933–1945.* New York: Bantom.

De Certeau, Michel. 1984. *The Practice of Everyday Life.* Berkeley: University of California Press.

– 1986. *Heterologies.* Minneapolis: University of Minnesota Press.

Dershowitz, Alan. 2003. *The Case For Israel.* New York: Wiley.

Dimbleby, Jonathan. 1980. *The Palestinians.* London: Quartet Books.

Doleve-Gandelman, Tsili. 1987. 'The Symbolic Inscription of Zionist Ideology in the Space of Eretz Israel: Why the Native Israeli Is Called Tsabar.' Pp. 257–84 in *Judaism Viewed from Within and from Without.* New York: State University of New York Press.

Dominguez, V.R. 1989. *People as Subject, People as Object: Selfhood and Peoplehood in Contemporary Israel.* Madison: University of Wisconsin Press.

Doumani, Beshara. 1995. *Rediscovering Palestine: Merchants and Peasants in Jabal, Nablus, 1700–1900.* Berkeley: University of California Press.

Dubnow, Simon. 1961. *Nationalism and History: Essays on Old and New Judaism.* Ed. and trans. Koppel S. Pinson. New York: Meridien Books.

Eade, John, and Michael J. Sallnow, eds. 1991. *Contesting the Sacred: The Anthropology of Christian Pilgrimage.* London: Routledge.

The Economist. 1998. 'Survey Israel at 50: After Zionism.' 25 April. Special Insert.

Eilberg-Schwartz, Howard, ed. 1992. *People of the Body.* Albany: State University of New York Press.

Eisen, Arnold. 1986. *Galut: Modern Jewish Reflections on Homelessnesss and Homecoming.* Indianapolis: Indiana University Press.

Eisenstadt, S.N. 1992. *Jewish Civilization: The Jewish Historical Experience in Historical Perspective.* Albany: State University of New York Press.

Elon, Amos. 1997. 'Politics and Archaeology,' Pp. 34–7 in Neil Asher Silberman and David Small, eds., *The Archaeology of Israel: Reconstructing the Past, Interpreting the Present.* Sheffield: Sheffield Academic Press.

Eriksen, Anne. 1997. 'Memory, History, and National Identity.' *Ethnologia Europaea* 27(2): 129–37.

Evron, Boas. 1995. *Jewish State or Israeli Nation*. Bloomington: Indiana University Press.

Ezrahi, Sidra DeKoven. 1996. 'The Grapes of Roth: "Diasporism" between Portnoy and Shylock.' Pp. 149–58 in Ezra Mendelsohn, ed., *Literary Strategies: Jewish Texts and Contexts. Studies in Contemporary Jewry* , vol. 12 New York: Oxford University Press.

Fabian, Johannes. 1983. *Time and the Other*. New York: Columbia University Press.

Fackenheim, Emil. 1978. *The Jewish Return into History: Reflections in the Age of Auschwitz and a New Jerusalem*. New York: Schocken Books.

Falbel, Rita, Irena Klepfisz, and Donna Neve. 1990. *Jewish Women's Call for Peace: A Handbook for Jewish Women on the Israeli/Palestinian Conflict*. Ithaca, NY: Firebrand Books.

Farsoun, Samih K., with Christina E. Zacharia. 1997. *Palestine and the Palestinians*. Boulder, CO: Westview Press.

Featherstone, Mike, ed. 1990. *Global Culture: Nationalism Globalization and Modernity*. London: Sage.

Fine, Elizabeth C., and Jean Haskell Speer. 1985. "Tour Guide Performances as Sight Sacralization." *Annals of Tourism Research* 12: 73–95.

Fisk, Robert. 1992. *Pity The Nation: Lelsan on at War*. Oxford: Oxford University Press.

Fiske, John. 1992. 'Cultural Studies and the Culture of Everyday Life,' Pp. 154–64 in Lawrence Grossberg, Cary Nelson, and Paula A. Treichler, eds., *Cultural Studies*. London: Routledge.

– 1993. *Power Plays, Power Works*. London: Verso.

Flapan, Simcha. 1987. *The Birth of Israel: Myths and Realities*. New York: Pantheon.

Foster, Robert. 1991. 'Making National Cultures in the Global Ecumene.' *Annual Review of Anthropology* 20: 235–60.

Foucault, Michel. 1979. *Discipline and Punish: The Birth of the Prison*. Trans. Alan Sheridan. New York: Vintage/Random House.

Frankel, Glenn. 1994. *Beyond the Promised Land: Jews and Arabs and the Hard Road to Peace*. New York: Simon and Schuster.

Friedlander, Saul, and Adam B. Seligman. 1994. 'The Israeli Memory of the Shoah: On Symbols, Rituals, and Ideological Polarization.' Pp. 356–71 in Roger Friedland and Deirdre Boden, eds., *Space, Time and Modernity*. Berkeley: University of California Press.

Furman, Andrew. 1997. *Israel through the Jewish-American Imagination: A Survey of Jewish-American Literature on Israel, 1928–1995.* Albany: State University of New York Press.

Gellner, Ernest. 1983. *Nations and Nationalism.* Ithaca: Cornell University Press.

Gerner, Deborah J. 1991. *One Land, Two Peoples.* Boulder: Westview Press.

Giannou, Chris. 1990. *Besieged: A Doctor's Story of Life and Death in Beirut.* Toronto: Key Porter.

Giddens, Anthony. 1987. *The Nation-State and Violence.* Berkeley: University of California Press.

Gilroy, Paul. 1996. 'Route Work: The Black Atlantic and the Politics of Exile.' Pp. 17–29 in Iain Chambers and Lidia Curti, eds., *The Post-colonial Question: Common Skies, Divided Horizons.* London: Routledge.

Ginsberg, Elaine K. 1996. 'Introduction: The Politics of Passing.' Pp. 1–18 in Elaine K. Ginsberg, ed., *Passing and the Fictions of Identity.* Durham: Duke University Press.

Giroux, Henry. 2000. *Impure Acts: The Practical Politics of Cultural Studies.* New York: Routledge.

− 2001. *Public Spaces, Private Lives: Beyond the Culture of Cynicism.* Lanham, MD: Rowman & Littlefield.

Goldberg, D.J. 1996. *To the Promised Land: A History of Zionist Thought.* London: Penguin.

Goldberg, Harvey, ed. 1987. *Judaism Viewed from Within and Without.* Albany: State University of New York Press.

Goldberg, J.J. 1996. *Jewish Power: Inside the American Jewish Establishment.* Reading, MA: Addison-Wesley.

Goldberger, Paul. 1995. 'Passions Set in Stone.' *New York Times Magazine,* 10 September 42–7 ff.

Golden, Deborah. 1996. 'The Museum of the Jewish Diaspora Tells a Story.' Pp. 223–50 in Tom Selwyn, ed., *The Tourist Image: Myth and Myth Making in Tourism.* Sussex: John Wiley and Sons.

Goldhagen, Daniel Jonah. 1996. *Hitler's Willing Executioners: Ordinary Germans and the Holocaust.* New York: Alfred A. Knopf.

− 1998. 'The Paradigm Challenged.' *Tikkun* 13(2): 40–7.

Goldstein, Yaacov. 1991. 'The Settlement Ethos in the Jewish and Zionist Thought.' Pp. 80–92. in Menachem Mor ed., *Eretz Israel, Israel and the Jewish Diaspora Mutual Relations.* Lanham, MD: University Press of America.

Gordon, Aaron David. [1911] 1976. 'People and Labour,' Pp. 372–4 in Arthur Hertzberg ed. *The Zionist Idea.* New York: Atheneum.

Gorny, Yosef. 1991. 'David Ben-Gurion: From the Zionist Movement to the Jewish People.' Pp. 222–8 in Menachem Mor, ed., *Eretz Israel, Israel and the Jewish Diaspora Mutual Relations.* Lanham: University Press of America.

Government of Israel. 1993. *Declaration of Principles on Interim Self-Government Arrangements*. Jerusalem: Ministry of Foreign Affairs (September).

Graham-Brown, Sarah. 1980. *Palestinians and Their Society, 1880–1946*. London: Quartet Books.

Grosby, Steven. 1999. 'The Chosen People of Ancient Israel and the Occident: Why Does Nationality Exist and Survive?' *Nations and Nationalism* 5(3): 357–80.

Gupta, Akhil, and James Ferguson. eds. 1997. *Culture, Power, Place: Explorations in Critical Anthropology*. Durham: Duke University Press.

Gurevitch, Zali, and Gideon Aran. 1994. 'The Land of Israel: Myth and Phenomenon.' Pp. 195–210 in Jonathan Frankel, ed., *Reshaping the Past: Jewish History and the Historians*. Studies in Contemporary Jewry, vol. 10. New York: Oxford University Press.

Habib, Jasmin. 1997. 'Jewish and Palestinian: The Challenge of In-Between-Ness' *Reform Judaism* 51 (Spring): 51–2.

– 2000. *Imagining Israel Belonging in Diaspora: North American Jews' Envisioning of Israel as Homeland, Nation and Nation-State*. PhD dissertations, McMaster University.

Halper, Jeff. 1998. 'Israel's War on the Palestinians: The Campaign of House Demolitions.' *Tikkun* 13(3): 56–9.

Handelman, Don. 1990. *Models and Mirrors: The Anthropology of Public Events*. Cambridge: Cambridge University Press.

Handelman, Don, and Lea Shamgar-Handelman. 1997. 'The Presence of Absence: The Memorialism of National Death in Israel,' Pp. 85–128 in Eyal Ben-Ari and Yoram Bilu, eds., *Grasping Land: Space and Place in Contemporary Israeli Discourse and Experience*. Albany: State University of New York Press.

Handler, Richard. 1988. *Nationalism and the Politics of Culture in Quebec*. Madison: University of Wisconsin Press.

Hannerz, Ulf. 1996. *Transnational Connections*. London: Routledge.

Hanson, Allan. 1989. 'The Making of the Maori: Cultural Invention and Its Logic.' *American Anthropologist* 91: 890–902.

Haraway, Donna. 1988. 'Situated Knowledges: The Science Question in Feminism as a Site of Discourse on the Privilege of Partial Perspective.' *Feminist Studies* 14: 575–99.

Heilman, Samuel. 1999. 'Separated but Not Divorced.' *Society* 36(4): 8–14.

Herf, Jeffrey. 1984. *Reactionary Modernism: Technology, Culture, and Politics in Weimar and The Third Reich*. Cambridge: Cambridge University Press.

Hertzberg, Arthur, ed. 1976. *The Zionist Idea*. New York: Atheneum.

Herzl, Theodor. [1896] 1976. 'The Jewish State.' Pp. 204–25 in Arthur Hertzberg, ed., *The Zionist Idea*. New York: Atheneum.

Hilberg, Raul. 1985. *The Destruction of the European Jews*. New York: Holmes and Heier.

Hobsbawm, Eric. 1990. *Nations and Nationalism since 1780: Programme, Myth, Reality*. Cambridge: Cambridge University Press.

Hobsbawm, Eric, and Terence Ranger, eds. 1984. *The Invention of Tradition*. Cambridge: University of Cambridge Press.

Hutcheon, Linda. 1988. *Poetics of Postmodernism: History, Theory, Fiction*. New York: Routledge.

– 1989. *The Politics of Postmodernism*. New York: Routledge.

Hutchinson, John. 1994. *Modern Nationalism*. London: Fontana Press.

Hutchinson, John, and Anthony D. Smith, eds. 1994. *Nationalism*. New York: Oxford University Press.

Israel Ministry of Foreign Affairs. n.d. 'Law of Return.' Basic Laws Document. www.israel.org/mfa/go.asp?MFAOOhg0

Jackson, Anthony, ed. 1987. *Anthropology at Home*. ASA Monograph 25. London: Tavistock Publications.

Jenkins, Henry. 1992. *Textual Poachers: Television Fans and Participatory Culture*. New York: Routledge.

Jones, Sian. 1997. *The Archaeology of Ethnicity*. London: Routledge.

Josephus, Flavius. 1981. *The Jewish War*. Trans. G.A. Williamson. New York: Penguin.

Kanaana, Sharif. 1992. *Still On Vacation!* Jerusalem: Jerusalem International Centre for Palestinian Studies.

Karetzky, Stephen, and Norman Frankel, eds. 1989. *The Media's Coverage of the Arab-Israeli Conflict*. New York: Shapolski.

Karp, Ivan, and Steven D. Lavine, ed. 1991. *Exhibiting Cultures: The Poetics and Politics of Museum Display*. Washington: Smithsonian Institution Press.

Katriel, Tamar. 1997. 'Remaking Place: Cultural Production in Israeli Pioneer Settlement Museums.' Pp. 147–76 in Eyal Ben-Ari and Yoram Bilu, eds., *Grasping Land: Space and Place in Contemporary Israeli Discourse and Experience*. Albany: State University of New York Press.

Katz, S. 1985. 'The Israeli Teacher-guide.' *Annals of Tourism Research* 12: 49–72.

Kaufman, Menahem. 1996. 'Envisaging Israel: The Case of the United Jewish Appeal.' Pp. 219–53. in Allon Gal, ed., *Envisioning Israel: The Changing Ideals and Images of North American Jews*. Jerusalem: Magnus Press.

Kedar, Benjamin Z. 1982. 'Masada: The Myth and the Complex.' *Jerusalem Quarterly* 24: 57–63.

Keesing, R. 1989. 'Creating the Past: Custom and Identity in the Contemporary Pacific.' *Contemporary Pacific* 1: 19–42.

– 1991. 'Reply to Trask.' *Contemporary Pacific* 3: 168–71.

Kennedy, R. Scott. 1989. 'The Druze of the Golan: A Case of Non-Violent Resistance.' *Journal of Palestine Studies* 13(2): 48–64.

Khaladi, Rashid. 1997. *Palestinian Identity*. New York: Columbia University Press.

– 1998. 'A Universal Jubilee? Palestinians 50 Years after 1958.' *Tikkun* 13(2): 53–6.

– 1999. 'Why This "Peace Process" Will Not Lead to Peace.' *Tikkun* 4(1): 11–14.

Khalidi, Walid. 1984. *Before Their Diaspora: A Photographic History of the Palestinians, 1876–1948*. Boston: Thomas Todd Company.

Kimmerling, Baruch, and Joel Migdal, eds. 1993. *Palestinians: The Making of a People*. New York: Free Press.

Klausner, Samuel Z. 1991. 'Diaspora in Comparative Perspective.' Pp. 194–221 in Menachem Mor, ed., *Eretz Israel, Israel and the Jewish Diaspora Mutual Relations*. Lanham, MD: University Press of America.

Knauft, Bruce M. 1996. *Genealogies for the Present in Cultural Anthropology*. New York: Routledge.

Kohl, Philip L. and Clare Fawcett. 1995. 'Archaeology in the Service of the State: Theoretical Considerations,' Pp. 99–119 in Philip L. Kohl and Clare Fawcett, eds., *Nationalism, Politics, and the Practice of Archaeology*. Cambridge: Cambridge University Press.

Kolsky, Thomas A. 1991. 'The American Council for Judaism's Opposition to Zionism, 1942–1948: An Assessment.' Pp. 129–50 in Menachem Mor, ed., *Eretz Israel, Israel and the Jewish Diaspora Mutual Relations*. Lanham, MD: University Press of America.

Kook, Rabbi Abraham Isaac. 1976a. 'The Land of Israel.' Pp. 419–21 in Arthur Hertzberg, ed., *The Zionist Idea*. New York: Atheneum.

– 1976b. 'The Rebirth of Israel.' Pp. 424–6 in Arthur Hertzberg, ed., *The Zionist Idea*. New York: Atheneum.

Kriesberg, Louis. 1992. *International Conflict Resolution: The U.S.–U.S.S.R. and Middle East Cases*. New Haven: Yale University Press.

Kugelmass, Jack. 1988. 'Introduction.' Pp. 1–29 in Jack Kugelmass, ed., *Between Two Worlds: Ethnographic Essays on American Jewry*. Ithaca: Cornell University Press.

– ed. 1988. *Between Two Worlds: Ethnographic Essays on American Jewry*. Ithaca: Cornell University Press.

Lambek, Michael. 1996. The Past Imperfect: Remembering As Moral Practice.' Pp. 235–54 in Paul Antze and Michael Lambek, eds., *Tense Past: Cultural Essays in Trauma and Memory*. New York: Routledge.

Laqueur, Walter, and Barry Rubin, eds. 1985. *The Israel–Arab Reader: A Documentary History of the Middle East Conflict*. New York: Penguin.

Lavie, Smadar. 1993. '"The One Who Writes Us": Political Allegory and the Experience of Occupation among the Mezeina Bedouin.' Pp. 153–83 in Smadar Lavie, Kirin Narayan and Renato Rosaldo, eds. *Creativity/Anthropology*. Ithaca: Cornell University Press.

– 1996. 'Blowups in the Borderzones: Third World Israeli Authors' Gropings for Home.' Pp. 55–96 in Smadar Lavie and Ted Swedenburg, eds., *Displacement, Diaspora, and Geographies of Identity*. Durham, NC: Duke University Press.

Lavie, Smadar and Ted Swedenburg, eds. 1996. 'Introduction.' Pp. 1–25 in Smadar Lavie and Ted Swedenburg, eds., *Displacement, Diaspora, and Geographies of Identity*. Durham, NC: Duke University Press.

Lerner, Michael. 1994. *Jewish Renewal: Path to Healing and Transformation*. New York: Putnam.

Levine, Etan. 1986. 'Confronting the Aliyah Option.' Pp. 353–63 in Etan Levine, ed., *Diaspora: Exile and the Contemporary Jewish Condition*. New York: Steimatzky.

Levitt, Cyril, and William Shaffir. 1993. 'Aliyah and Return Migration of Canadian Jews: Personal Accounts of Incentives and Disappointed Hopes.' Pp. 421–432 in Robert Brym, William Shaffir, and Morton Weinfeld, eds., *Jews in Canada*. Toronto: Oxford University Press.

Levy, Yagil. 1997. *Trial and Error: Israel's Route from War to De-Escalation*. Albany: State University of New York Press.

Lewis, Bernard. 1975. *Masada: History Remembered, Recovered, Invented*. New York: Simon and Schuster.

Liebman, Charles S. 1999. 'Has the Romance Ended?' *Society* 36(4): 15–20.

Liebman, Charles S., and Steven M. Cohen. 1990. *Two Worlds of Judaism: The Israeli and American Experiences*. New Haven: Yale University Press.

Lilienthal, Alfred M. 1953. *What Price Israel?* Chicago: Henry Regnery Company.

Linenthal, Edward T. 1997. *Preserving Memory*. New York: Penguin.

Linnekin 1991. 'Cultural Invention and the Dilemma of Authenticity.' *American Anthropologist* 93: 446–9.

Lipset, Seymour Martin, ed. 1990. *American Pluralism and the Jewish Community*. New Brunswick, NJ: Transaction Publishers.

Livni, Michael. 1995. 'A Rationale and Program for Reform Zionism.' *ARZA: Journal of Reform Judaism* 2: 43–7.

Lowenthal, David. 1985. *The Past Is a Foreign Country*. Cambridge: University of Cambridge Press.

Lustick, Ian S. 1988. *For the Land and the Lord: Jewish Fundamentalism in Israel*. New York: Council on Foreign Relations.

– 1996. 'The Fetish of Jerusalem: A Hegemonic Analysis.' Pp. 143–72 in

Michael N. Barnett, ed., *Israel in Comparative Perspective: Challenging the Conventional Wisdom*. Albany: State University of New York Press.

MacCannell, Dean. 1992. *Empty Meeting Grounds*. London: Routledge.

Mahler, Jonathan. 1997. 'Uprooting the Past: Israel's New Historians Take a Hard Look at Their Nation's Origins.' *Lingua Franca* (August) (pp. 24–32).

Malkki, Liisa H. 1995. 'Refugees and Exile: From "Refugee Studies" to the National Order of Things.' *Annual Review of Anthropology* 24: 495–523.

– 1997. 'Speechless Emissaries: Refugees, Humanitarianism, and Dehistoricization.' Pp. 223–54 in Karen Fog Olwig and Kirsten Hastrup, eds., *Siting Culture: The Shifting Anthropological Object*.

Maranz, Felice. 1994. 'The Fall of Masada.' *Jerusalem Report*, 16 June, 42–4.

Marchessault, Janine. 1995. 'On Hannah Arendt: "Thinking in My Identity Where Actually I Am Not.' *Public* 12: 14–27.

Marrus, Michael R. 1987. *The Holocaust in History*. Toronto: Lester and Orpen Dennys.

Massey, Doreen. 1994. *Space, Place and Gender*. Cambridge: Polity Press.

McDowall, David. 1989. *Palestine and Israel: The Uprising and Beyond*. Berkeley: University of California Press.

Meir, Golda. 1986. 'What We Want of the Diaspora.' Pp. 297–305 in Etan Levine, ed., *Diaspora: Exile and the Contemporary Jewish Condition*. New York: Steimatzky.

Mohanty, Chandra. 1984. 'Under Western Eyes: Feminist Scholarship and Colonial Discourse.' *Boundary 2*. 2/3(12/13): 333–58.

Morris, Benny. 1987. *The Birth of the Palestinian Refugee Problem, 1947–1949*. Cambridge: University of Cambridge Press.

– 1998. 'Looking Back: A Personal Assessment of the Zionist Experience.' *Tikkun* 13(2): 40–9.

Morris, Benny, with Danny Rubenstein. 1995. 'The Palestinian Exodus 1948.' *Palestine-Israel Journal of Politics, Economics and Culture*. 2(4): 46–52.

Morris, Meaghen. 1992. '"On the Beach."' Pp. 450–72 in Lawrence Grossberg, Cary Nelson, and Paula A. Treichler, eds., *Cultural Studies*. New York: Routledge.

Mouffe, Chantal. 1994. 'For a Politics of Nomadic Identity.' Pp. 105–13 in George Robertson et al., eds., *Traveller's Tales: Narratives of Home and Displacement*. New York: Routledge.

Myerhoff, Barbara. 1978. *Number Our Days*. New York: Simon and Schuster.

Narayan, Kirin. 1997. 'How Native Is a "Native" Anthropologist?' Pp. 23–41 in Louise Lamphere, Helena Ragone, and Patricia Zavella, eds., *Situated Lives: Gender and Culture in Everyday Life*. New York: Routledge.

Nightingale, Virginia. 1996. *Studying Audiences*. London: Routledge.

Novick, Peter. 1999. *The Holocaust in American Life*. Boston: Horghton Mifflin.

Olwig, Karen Fog. 1997. 'Cultural Sites: Sustaining a Home in a Deterritorialized World.' Pp. 17–38 in Karen Fog Olwig and Kirsten Hastrup, eds., *Siting Culture: The Shifting Anthropological Object*. New York: Routledge.

Olwig, Karen Fog and Kirsten Hastrup, eds., 1997. *Siting Culture: The Shifting Anthropological Object*. New York: Routledge.

Paine, Robert. 1989. 'Israel: Jewish Identity and Competition Over "Tradition".' Pp. 121–36 in Elizabeth Tonkin, Maryon McDonald, and Malcolm Chapman, eds., *History and Ethnicity*. London: Routledge.

– 1995. 'Our "Event-Full" World: The Challenge to an Anthropologist.' *Culture* 15(2): 105–16.

Palumbo, Michael. 1990. *Imperial Israel*. London: Bloomsbury.

Pappe, Ilan. 1992. *The Making of the Arab-Israeli Conflict, 1947–1951*. London: I.B. Tauris.

Peled, Yoav. 1992. 'Ethnic Democracy and the Legal Construction of Citizenship: Arab Citizens of the Jewish State.' *American Political Science Review* 86(2): 432–43.

– 1995. 'From Zionism to Capitalism: The Political Economy of Israel's Decolonization of the Occupied Territories.' *Middle East Report* 194/5: 13–17.

Plaskow, Judith. 1991. *Standing Again at Sinai: Judaism from a Feminist Perspective*. San Francisco: Harper Collins.

Preston, Richard. 1999. 'Reflections on Culture, History, and Authenticity,' Pp. 150–62 in Lisa Philips Valentine and Regna Darnell eds., *Theorizing the Americanist Tradition*. Toronto: University of Toronto Press.

Rabinowitz, Dan. 1997. *Overlooking Nazareth*. Cambridge: Cambridge University Press.

Rich, Adrienne. 1986. 'Notes Toward a Politics of Location.' Pp. 210–31 in *Blood, Bread and Poetry: Selected Prose, 1979–1985*. New York: W.W. Norton.

Riemer, Jeremiah M., and Andrei S. Markovits. 1998. 'The Goldhagen Controversy.' Tikkun. 13(2): 48–9.

Robertson, George, Melinda Mash, Lisa Tickner, Jon Bird, Barry Curtis and Tim Putnam, eds. 1994. *Traveller's Tales*. London: Routledge.

Rodinson, Maxime. 1973. *Israel: A Colonial-Settler State?* New York: Monad.

Rodman, Margaret. 1992. 'Empowering Place: Multilocality and Multivocality.' *American Anthropologist* 94: 640–56.

Rosaldo, Renato. 1989. *Culture and Truth: The Remaking of Social Analysis*. Boston: Beacon Press.

Rose, Margaret A. 1991. *The Post-Modern and the Post-Industrial*. Cambridge: Cambridge University Press.

Roth, Philip. 1986. *The Counterlife*. New York: Penguin.

– 1993. *Operation Shylock*. New York: Simon and Shuster.

Rubinoff, Lionel. 1993. 'Jewish Identity and the Challenge of Auschwitz.' In David Theo Goldberg and Michael Krausz, eds., *Jewish Identity*. Philadelphia: Temple University Press.

Ruether, Rosemary Radford, and Marc H. Ellis. 1990. *Beyond Occupation*. Boston: Beacon Press.

Safran, Nadav. 1978. *Israel: The Embattled Ally*. Cambridge: Belknap Press.

Safty, Adel. 1992. *From Camp David to the Gulf*. Montreal: Black Rose Books.

Said, Edward W. 1978. *Orientalism*. New York: Pantheon.

– 1980. *The Question of Palestine*. New York: Vintage.

– 1994a. *Culture and Imperialism*. New York: Vintage.

– 1994b. *The Politics of Dispossession*. New York: Pantheon.

– 1996. *Peace and Its Discontents*. New York: Vintage.

– 1998. 'Israel–Palestine: A Third Way.' *Guardian Weekly*, 20 September, 6–7.

Said, Edward, and Christopher Hitchens, eds. 1988. *Blaming the Victims*. London: Verso.

Salt, Jeremy. 1997. 'History and the Meaning of the Disaster: Arab and Palestinian Politics, 1948–1993.' Pp. 275–96 in Paul J. White and William S. Logan, eds., *Remaking the Middle East*. Oxford: Berg.

Schoenbaum, David. 1993. *The United States and the State of Israel*. New York: Oxford University Press.

Segev, Tom. 1986. *1949: The First Israelis*. New York: Free Press.

– 1993. *The Seventh Million: The Israelis and the Holocaust*. New York: Hill and Wang.

Seliktar, Ofira. 1997. 'Water in the Arab-Israeli Struggle: Conflict or Cooperation?' Pp. 9–29 in Walter P. Zenner and Kevin Avruch, eds., *Critical Essays on Israeli Society, Religion, and Government*. Albany: State University of New York Press.

Selwyn, Tom. 1995. 'Landscapes of Liberation and Imprisonment: Towards an Anthropology of the Israeli Landscape.' Pp. 114–34 in Eric Hirsch and Michael O'Hanlon, eds., *The Anthropology of Landscape: Perspectives on Place and Space*. London: Clarendon Press.

– 1996a. 'Atmospheric Notes from the Fields: Reflections on Myth-collecting Tours.' Pp. 147–62 in Tom Selwyn, ed., *The Tourist Image: Myth and Myth Making in Tourism*. Sussex: John Wiley and Sons.

– 1996b. *The Tourist Image: Myth and Myth Making in Tourism*. Sussex: John Wiley and Sons.

Shaffir, William. 1983. 'Canadian Jewry: Some Sociological Observations.' Pp. 3–11 in Edmond Y. Lipsitz ed., *Canadian Jewry Today: Who's Who in Canadian Jewry*. Downsview, ON: J.E.S.L. Educational Products.

Shalev, Michael. 1989. 'Jewish Organised Labour and the Palestinians: A Study of State/Society Relations in Israel.' Pp. 93–133 in Baruch Kimmerling, ed., *The Israeli State and Society: Boundaries and Frontiers*. Albany: State University of New York Press.

— 1992. *Labour and the Political Economy in Israel*. Oxford: Oxford University Press.

Sharabi, Hisham, ed. 1990. *Theory, Politics and the Arab World: Critical Responses*. New York: Routledge.

Sharoni, Simona. 1995. *Gender and the Israeli-Palestinian Conflict: Politics of Women's Resistance*. Syracuse: Syracuse University Press.

Shatz, Adam. 1997. 'Browning's Version: A Mild-Mannered Historian's Quest to Understand the Perpetrators of the Holocaust.' *Lingua Franca* (February), 48–57.

Sheffer, Gabriel. 1996. 'Israel Diaspora Relations in Comparative Perspective.' Pp. 53–84 in Michael N. Barnett, ed., *Israel in Comparative Perspective: Challenging Conventional Wisdom*. Albany: State University of New York Press.

Shenhav-Keller, Shelly. 1993. 'The Israeli Souvenir: Its Text and Context.' *Annals of Tourism Research* 20: 182–96.

Shlaim, Avi. 1994. *War and Peace in the Middle East: A Critique of American Policy*. New York: Penguin.

Shohat, Ella. 1988. 'Sephardim in Israel: Zionism from the Standpoint of Its Jewish Victims.' *Social Text* 19/20: 1–34.

— 1989. *Israeli Cinema: East/West and the Politics of Representation*. Austin: University of Texas Press.

Shusterman, Richard. 1993. 'Next Year in Jerusalem? Postmodern Jewish Identity and the Myth of Return.' Pp. 291–308 in David Theo Goldberg and Michael Krausz, eds., *Jewish Identity*. Philadelphia: Temple University Press.

Silberman, Neil Asher. 1990. *Between Past and Present: Archaeology, Ideology, and Nationalism in the Modern Middle East*. New York: Doubleday.

— 1992. 'Who Were the Israelites?' *Archaeology* 45(2): 22–30.

— 1995. 'Promised Lands and Chosen Peoples: the Politics and Poetics of Archaeological Narrative.' Pp. 249–87 in Philip L. Kohl and Clare Fawcett, eds., *Nationalism, Politics, and the Practice of Archaeology*. Cambridge: Cambridge University Press.

— 1997. 'Structuring the Past: Israelis, Palestinians, and the Symbolic Authority of Archaeological Monuments,' Pp. 62–81 in Neil Asher Silberman and David Small, eds., *The Archaeology of Israel: Reconstructing the Past, Interpreting the Present*. Sheffield, UK: Sheffield Academic Press.

Silberman, Neil Asher, and David Small, eds. 1997. *The Archaeology of Israel:*

Constructing the Past, Interpreting the Present. Sheffield, U.K.: Sheffield Academic Press.

Silberstein, Laurence J. 1996. 'Cultural Criticism, Ideology, and the Interpretation of Zionism: Toward a Post-Zionist Discourse.' Pp. 325–58 in Steven Kepnes, ed. *Interpreting Judaism in a Postmodern Age*. New York: New York University Press.

– 1999. *The Postzionism Debates*. New York: Routledge.

Sklare, Marshall. 1982. *American Jews: A Reader*. New York: Behrman House.

Smart, Barry. 1983. *Foucault, Marxism and Critique*. London: Routledge and Kegan Paul.

Smith, Anthony. 1986. *The Ethnic Origins of Nations*. Oxford: Blackwell Publishers.

– 1991. *National Identity*. Reno: University of Nevada Press.

– 1999. 'Ethnic Election and National Destiny: Some Religious Origins of Nationalist Ideals.' *Nations and Nationalism* 5(3): 331–55.

Smith, Neil, and Cindi Katz. 1993. 'Grounding Metaphor: Towards a Spatialized Politics.' Pp. 67–83 in Michael Keith and Steve Pile, eds., *Place and the Politics of Identity*. London: Routledge.

Spivak, Gayatri C. 1988. 'Can The Subaltern Speak?' Pp. 271–316 in Cary Nelson and Lawrence Grossberg, eds., *Marxism and the Interpretation of Culture*. Urbana: University of Illinois Press.

– 1992. 'Asked to Talk About Myself.' *Third Text* 10 (Summer): 9–18.

Steiner, Christopher B. 1995. Special Issue on 'Museums and the Politics of Nationalism.' *Museum Anthropology* 19(2).

Sternhall, Ze'ev. 1998. 'A New Zionism for an Open Society.' *Tikkun* 13(3): 51–5.

Storper-Perez, Danielle, and Harvey E. Goldberg. 1994. 'The Kotel: Toward an Ethnographic Portrait.' *Religion* 24: 309–32.

Strathern, Marilyn. 1991. *Partial Connections*. Savage, MD: Rowman and Littlefield.

Swedenburg, Ted. 2003. *Memories of Revolt: The 1936–1939 Rebellion and the Palestinian National Post*. Fayetleville: University of Arkansaw Press.

Syrkin, Nahman. [1898] 1976. 'The Jewish Problem and the Socialist-Jewish State.' Pp. 330–51 in Arthur Hertzberg, ed., *The Zionist Idea*. New York: Atheneum.

Tarabieh, Bashar. 1995. 'Education, Control and Resistance in the Golan Heights.' *Middle East Report* 194/5: 43–7.

Taras, David, and Morton Weinfeld. 1993. 'Continuity and Criticism: North American Jews and Israel,' Pp. 293–310 in Robert Brym, William Shaffir, Morton Weinfeld, eds., *Jews in Canada*. Toronto: Oxford University Press.

Teveth, Shabtai. 1987. *Ben Gurion*. Boston: Houghton and Mifflin.

Trask, H.K. 1991. 'Natives and Anthropologists: A Colonial Struggle.' *Contemporary Pacific* 3: 159–67.

Trinh T. Min-ha. 1986. *Woman, Native, Other: Writing Postcoloniality and Feminism*. Bloomington: University of Indiana Press.

– 1991. *When The Moon Waxes Red*. London: Routledge.

Troper, Harold. 1996. 'Two Perspectives on the Relationship between Israel and Canadian Jewry.' Lecture at the Canada, Israel, and the New Middle East Conference held at Temple Anshe Shalom, Hamilton, Ontario. 28 April 1996.

Tulchinsky, Gerald. 1992. *Taking Root: The Origins of the Canadian Jewish Community*. Toronto.

Tzahor, Ze'ev. 1995. 'Ben-Gurion's Mythopoetics.' Pp. 61–84 in Robert Wistrich and David Ohana, eds., *The Shaping of Israeli Identity: Myth, Memory and Trauma*. London: Frank Cass and Company.

Urry, J. 1990. *The Tourist Gaze: Leisure and Travel in Contemporary Societies*. London: Sage.

Verdery, Katherine. 1996. 'Whither "Nation" and "Nationalism"?' Pp. 226–34 in Gopal Balakrishnan, ed., *Mapping the Nation*. London: Verso.

Wagner, Roy. 1981. *The Invention of Culture*. Chicago: University of Chicago Press.

Weitz, Yechiam. 1997. 'Political Dimensions of Holocaust Memory in Israel.' Pp. 129–145 in Wistrich Robert and David Ohana, eds., *The Shaping of Israeli Identity: Myth, Memory and Trauma*. London: Frank Cass and Company.

Werbner, Pnina. 1998. 'Diasporic Political Imaginaries: A Sphere of Freedom or a Sphere of Illusions?' *Communal/Plural* 6(1): 11–31.

Wheatcroft, Geoffrey. 1996. *The Controversy of Zion: Jewish Nationalism, the Jewish State, and the Unresolved Jewish Dilemma*. Reading, MA: Addison-Wesley.

White, Curtis. 1992. *The Idea of Home*. Los Angeles: Sun and Moon Press.

White, Geoffrey M., ed. 1997. Special Issue on 'Public History and National Narratives.' *Museum Anthropology* 21(1).

Whitelam, Keith W. 1996. *The Invention of Ancient Israel*. London: Routledge.

Wistrich, Robert. 1995. 'Theodor Herzl: Zionist Icon, Myth-Maker, and Social Utopian.' Pp. 1–37 in Robert Wistrich and David Ohana, eds., *The Shaping of Israeli Identity: Myth, Memory and Trauma*. London: Frank Cass and Company.

Yehoshua, A.B. 1986. 'Exile as a Neurotic Solution.' Pp. 15–35 in Etan Levine, ed., *Diaspora: Exile and the Contemporary Jewish Condition*. New York: Steimatzky.

Yiftachel, O. 1991. 'State Policies, Land Control, and an Ethnic Minority: The Arabs in the Galilee Region, Israel.' *Environment and Planning D: Society and Space* 9: 329–62.

Young, James E. 1993. *The Texture of Memory: Holocaust Memorials and Meaning*. New Haven: Yale University Press.

Zenner, Walter P. ed. 1988. *Persistence and Flexibility: Anthropological Perspectives on the American Jewish Experience*. Albany: State University of New York Press.

Zerubavel, Yael. 1995a. 'The Multivocality of a National Myth: Memory and Counter-Memories of Masada." Pp. 110–28 in Robert Wistrich and David Ohana, eds., *The Shaping of Israeli Identity: Myth, Memory and Trauma*. London: Frank Cass and Company.

– 1995b. *Recovered Roots: Collective Memory and the Making of Israeli National Tradition*. Chicago: University of Chicago Press.

Zuriek, Elia. 1995. 'Palestinian Refugees and the Right of Return.' *Palestine-Israel Journal of Politics, Economics and Culture* 2(4): 35–40.

Encyclopedia References

'Aliyah.' 1994. *The New Encyclopedia of Israel and Zionism*. Vol. 1. Geoffrey Wigoder, editor in chief. Toronto: Associated University Press.

'Zionism, History of.' 1994. *The New Encyclopedia of Israel and Zionism*. Vol. 1. Geoffrey Wigoder, editor in chief. Toronto: Associated University Press.

Index

Aaron (pseudonym). *See* profiles; tour participants, on-site resistance

Abu Ghoneim, 116. *See also* Har Homa

Abu Mazen, 159

activism, 8, 195, 229, 239, 242

agriculture: development tropes 65, 68, 70, 72, 207; greenhouses, 124; Palestinian labour, 71, 83, 117. *See also* Fertile Crescent; Green Revolution; modernization

Ahad Ha'am, 29

Al Haram Al Sharif, 133

al nakba, 6

Algeria, 12, 71

aliyah, 27, 29, 33, 34, 39–40, 45, 67, 147, 153, 161, 175, 230, 239, 254, 258, 261, 267, 275n13, 276n25

Alonso, Ana Maria, 20–1, 25

Amir, Yigal, 130, 155. *See also* Orthodox Jews; Rabin, Yitzhak

Ammunition Hill, 53, 87; State Memorial Site and Museum, 91

Anderson, Benedict, 18–20, 25

anthropology: approach to diaspora, 10–18, 35, 165, 259, 265–6

anti-Semitism, 5, 28, 60, 66, 151, 158, 162, 165, 167, 170–1, 173, 175, 183–4, 186–7, 192, 209, 246, 257, 263, 277n12, 281n3

Appadurai, Arjun, 15

Arab–Israeli conflict, 10, 257. *See also* Palestinian–Israeli conflict

Arabs, 5, 6, 12, 26, 253; and Declaration of Independence, 30–2; diaspora reflections on relationships with, 177, 180–1, 194, 197, 211, 234, 239, 254, 257–8, 261; Israeli living conditions, 73, 201, 239; and Nazis, 110, 188; North American representations of, 125–6, 164, 173, 224–6; and the Oslo Peace Accords, 33, 146–53, 157–60; representation on tour, 44, 54, 71–83; 84, 86, 87, 88–90; writers in exile, 273–4n20

Arafat, Yasir, 107, 150, 155, 157–60, 189, 194, 210–11

Arava Valley, 66–8

archaeological sites, 32, 38, 42–4, 47–9, 54, 128, 130, 277n1. *See also* Dead Sea Scrolls; Jerusalem; Masada; Sepphoris; Solomonic Gates

Arendt, Hannah, 8, 162, 268

Arnie (pseudonym). *See* tour guides

Ashkenaz Jews, 12, 35, 64, 72

Ashrawi, Hanan, 158, 159

Auschwitz, 58, 201. *See also* Holocaust; Yad Vashem

authenticity, 4, 7, 19, 239, 247–8, 256

Avi (pseudonym). *See* tour presenters

Bakka Valley, 95. *See also* Lebanon; Operation Peace for Galilee

Balfour Declaration, 29

Bar Ilan University, Friends of, 11

Barthes, Roland, 19–21, 25

Bartok, Yuval (pseudonym). *See* community presenters

Basic Laws, 32, 136. *See also* Declaration of the State of Israel; Law of Return

Bedouins, 69, 86, 264; North American representations, 125–6; representations on tour, 73–9; role in Israeli army, 74, 93

Beer Sheva, 69

Begin, Menachem, 158

Beirut, 32, 100, 238

Beisan, 7

Beit She'an. *See* Beisan

Ben-Aviv, Shoshana (pseudonym). *See* community presenters

Ben-Gurion, David, 66–7, 105, 142, 145, 161, 166, 205, 234, 239

Bethlehem, 104, 148; as a holy site, 51

Bezen, Naftali, 61

Biale, David, 281n2

Bible. *See* biblical

biblical, 40, 141, 155, 176; Abraham, 126; archaeology 128, 131–3; Book of Psalms, 52; gardens 44–7, 215; heritage, 265; history, 64, 127, 248; Joshua, 50; justification, 133; New Testament, 189; prophecies, 5; scholarship 266; sites, 42

binational state, 263. *See also* coexistence; Jerusalem, Greater; mapping; Oslo Peace Accords; peace

Bir Zeit, 76

Black, Harold (pseudonym). *See* community presenters

B'nai B'rith, 175

Boyarin, Daniel, 266

Boyarin, Jonathan, 266

British, 29, 32, 43, 50, 85, 132; White Paper, 85. *See also* England; Mandate British Palestine; United Kingdom

Bundist, 162

Burma Road, Battle of, 89

Byzantine period, 43, 55, 126

bypass roads, 107, 148. *See also* Oslo Peace Accords

Cambodia, 59

Camp David Accords, 33

Canaanites, 43–4, 52

Canada, 4, 7, 33, 109, 112, 146, 186, 198, 200, 213, 223, 233, 248, 268; Canada Centre, 224; funding for Israel, 81; Holocaust museums, 58; as home, 182, 190, 235; indigenous communities, 188–9; Jewish communities, 10–11, 34; as multicultural 264; and Palestinian refugees 114; right-wing governments, 241

Canadian. *See* Canada

Castel, battle of, 87–9, 112–13

ceremony, 22, 50; and Oslo Peace Accords, 194

Chaliand, Gerard, 14

Chamberlain, Neville, 188
checkpoints: Israeli military 253; Palestinian Authority, 251
Children's Holocaust Memorial, 58, 60
chosen people, 28, 31, 44, 60, 133, 201, 273n11
Chrétien, Jean, 188
Christian: art, 126; in Canada, 234; Church of the Holy Sepulchre, 132–3; era, 84; in Israel, 264; Maronites of Lebanon, 99–102; Quarter, 54; Righteous Gentile, 214; scholarship, 127; significance of Jerusalem, 51; sites, 189; tradition, 229
Christianity, 127–8
citizenship, Israeli, 7, 39; Arab, 31, 32, 79, 232; critique, 256; equal, 198; Palestinian, 263, 274n20
City of David. See Jerusalem, archaeology
Clifford, James, 14–15
closure. See Palestinian labour
coexistence, 257–8, 267
Cohen, Eric, 259
Cohen, Steven, 34–5, 259
Communist, 174; Party, 192
community, 3, 26; anthropological analyses of, 14–19, 246; Arab, 81–2, 242; centres, 9–11, 120, 165, 192–3, 224, 279n5; events, 8, 10–11, 14, 25, 27, 31, 41, 119–20, 123, 127, 170, 174, 257, 279n5; Jewish, 34, 335, 60, 63, 89, 208, 220, 223, 229, 242, 276n25, 281n5; North American Jewish, 4, 9, 10–13, 34–5
community presenters (pseudonyms): Bartok, Yuval, 121–33; Ben-Aviv, Shoshana, 154–60;

Black, Harold, 139–43; Greenfield, Rabbi, 161–2, 171, 261; Kramer, Malcolm, 146–54; Levine, Michael, 133–7; Scheck, Avraham, 127–30; Tov, Amir, 144–6. See also Troper, Harold
Conservative Jews, 12, 129, 131, 143, 146, 161, 174, 232, 272–3n11
co-responsibility, 165, 192. See also diaspora; Werbner, Pnina
Covenant, of the Palestinian Liberation Organization, 150, 157, 189
Cyprus, 7
Czechoslovakia, 188

Damascus, 93–4
Dan, Ori (pseudonym). See tour presenters
Davies, Thomas, 266
Dawidowicz, Deborah Lucy S., 60
Day of the Land, 106
de Certeau, Michel, 23–5, 255, 265, 275n47
Dead Sea, 47
Dead Sea Scrolls, 127–30. See also community presenters, Avraham Scheck
Declaration of Independence, Israeli. See Declaration of State of Israel
Declaration of Principles, 13, 33, 107. See also Oslo Peace Accords
Declaration of State of Israel, 7, 30, 32, 84, 87
democracy, Israeli, 5, 39–40, 64, 83, 111, 121, 154–5, 198, 208, 210; critique of, 102, 255–8, 262–3, 265; democratization projects, 37; as Jewish character, 195–6; in relation to Judaism, 134–7, 223; in relation to Orthodox, 133–7, 139–44, 144–6;

rights of Palestinians, 79; undemocratic, 40, 145, 195, 202
'demographic denial,' 263. *See also*
Jerusalem, Greater; Judaization
Desert Storm, 33
development towns, 71–2. *See also*
Kiryat Shmona; Oriental Jews;
Sephardic Jews
diaspora, 3–4, 10, 13–18, 22, 28, 165,
247, 274n20; as co-responsibility,
165, 259
diaspora Jews: as distinguished from
North American Jews, 4; opposed
to Oslo Peace Accords, 108, 147,
150–4, 156–60; relationship to
Israelis, 164, 199, 222, 237. *See also*
diaspora nationalism; Zionism
Diaspora Museum, Tel Aviv, 63,
176
diaspora nationalism, 4, 10, 18, 25,
65, 259–61, 267
diaspora Palestinians, 5
diasporicism, 258
Dostoyevsky, 162
Druze, in Israel, 73, 77–9, 99, 101,
264; in Israeli military, 78, 93; loyalty to Israel, 78–9; North American representations, 126
Dubnow, Simon, 275n1

education, in Israel: Arab vs Jewish,
222; Bedouin, 75–7; Jewish, 154,
174; Palestinian 80
education, in North America: Jewish
schools, 9, 10, 199, 202, 244; Jewish
Studies, 9, 11, 147, 248, 279n5
Egypt, 30, 32, 33, 45, 78, 86, 90, 96–7,
110, 147, 158, 159
England, 7, 147, 186–8. *See also* British; United Kingdom

Eretz Israel, 3, 87
essentialism, 4, 9
Ethiopia, 227
Eurocentrism, 244, 263
Europe, 5–7, 27, 29–30, 53, 57–60, 168,
239, 260, 272n10; anti-Semitism,
66; Eastern, 27; fascism, 264; identity, 244; Israeli agricultural
imports, 124
European Jews, 28–9, 56, 72, 85, 110,
260. *See also* Germany; Holocaust
expansionism, 6. *See also* settlers;
settler-colonial state

Faye (pseudonym). *See* tour partici-
pants, on-site resistance
feminist, 14, 156, 229; Adrienne Rich,
9
Fertile Crescent, 178
First World War, 190
Foucault, Michel, 24
France, 7, 28, 220, 264

Gabriel (pseudonym). *See* tour participants, on-site resistance
Gadna, 199
Galilee, 7, 12, 38, 43–4, 73, 92, 96, 101,
105–6, 125, 129, 205, 283n9;
Bedouins, 74; *kibbutzim*, 29; Sea of,
96; security corridor, 103; upper,
40
galut, 34, 276n25
Gaza Strip, 5, 13, 32–3, 78, 82, 111,
117, 147, 150, 156
Gentiles, 28, 145, 162, 241; Avenue of
the Righteous Gentiles, 57, 59;
Oscar Schindler, 59
German Jews, 182; and Reform Judaism, 272n11
Germany, 28, 264; anti-Semitism, 60;

Nazism 62, 64, 168, 175, 188, 242, 250
Gillian (pseudonym). *See* profiles
Ginsberg, Asher Zvi. *See* Ahad Ha'am
Giroux, Henry, 25–6, 242
globalization, 4, 15, 19
Golan Heights, 38, 78, 83, 92–7, 117, 178–80, 208, 224, 237–8; Israeli occupation of, 32
Goldhagen, Daniel Jonah, 277n12
Good Fence, the, 98. *See also* Lebanon
Green Line, 50, 108, 115–16, 150–1, 178, 188
Green Revolution, 71, 177, 207. *See also* agriculture; Fertile Crescent
Greenfield, Rabbi (pseudonym). *See* community presenters
guides. *See* tour guides
Gulf War. *See* Desert Storm

Hadassah, 175
Haganah, 85, 87
Haifa, 7, 75
halakha, 128, 136, 144–5, 184–5
halutzim. *See* pioneers
Hamas, 157–60
Handelman, Don, 21–2, 25; 'presence of absence,' 63
Hanukkah, 3, 229
Har Homa, 116, 166, 155
Hassidic Jews, 231
Hebrew University, 29, 51, 139; Friends of, 11, 140, 279n5
Hebron, 86, 156
Heidi (pseudonym). *See* tour presenters
Herzl, Theodore, 57, 162–3, 240
historians, new, 35. *See also* post-Zionist

history, 85, 135, 139, 205, 248; in relation to myth, 20; in relation to Zionism: *See* post-Zionist; Zionism
Hitler, Adolph, 64, 168, 173, 182, 188, 277n12
Hobsbawm, Eric, 18
Holocaust, 5–7, 29–31, 35, 42; 110, 119, 175, 186–7, 213–16, 221, 236–7, 250, 260, 272n10, 277n12, 281n3; exploitation by Zionists, 201; Holocaust Education Week, 11, 120; Holocaust Remembrance Day (Israel), 22, 63; memorialization, 56–64; Western guilt, 6. *See also* March of the Living; Second World War; Yad Vashem
Holy Land, 28–9, 142
homeland, Jewish, 3–7, 10, 16–19, 29–30, 183, 191, 199, 208, 215, 229, 234, 261, 265, 267, 282n5; biblical, 52; refuge 181, 202. *See also* Holy Land; Israel; Promised Land; refuge; Zionism
Hope (pseudonym). *See* profiles
Hula Valley, 92, 177
Hungary, 213–14
Hussein, King of Jordan, 100, 147, 152, 159. *See also* Jordan
Hussein, Saddam, 49, 110, 188–9, 203, 238. *See also* Desert Storm; Iraq
Husseini, Faisel, 159
hybridity, 4, 14, 17–18, 246–7

Ian (pseudonym). *See* profiles
identity, 3–19, 248, 266, 282n5; Arab, 161; Jewish, 9–10, 22–3, 34–5, 40, 136, 184, 192–3, 215, 239, 281n5; multicultural, 3–4. *See also* diaspora; hybridity; multicultural-

ism; reflexivity; who is a Jew, debate

immigrants: as category of analysis, 14–16, 265; and homecoming, 7; North American Jews as, 165, 167, 182, 244. *See also* diaspora; Werbner, Pnina

immigration: to Israel, as *aliya*, 31–2, 40, 57, 258, 276n25; of non-European Jews, 72, 227; *oleh*, 32, 275n13; policy, 114; support for immigrants, 37, 40

Independence Day, Israel, 22

intifada, 108, 157, 200

Iraq, 33, 71–2, 109–110, 156–9, 188–9, 238

Israel: Americanization of, 217–18; boundaries, 50, 107, 115–16, 138, 146–54, 197 (*see also* Green Line; Oslo Peace Accords; Palestine); as dangerous, 194, 250; development, 68, 154, 177, 207, 210, 237, 256 (*see also* agriculture; Negev Desert; water); diaspora reflections, 167–242 (*see also* diaspora nationalism); exclusivity, 117, 169, 195–6, 246 (*see also* Law of Return); fiftieth birthday, 11, 39, 123, 155; financial investment in, 34, 37, 124, 165, 206, 227, 237, 251; founding of, 5–6, 27, 65, 85, 171, 206, 267, 275n11 (*see also al nakba*; post-Zionist; Zionism); government, 41, 46, 53, 91, 93, 149, 200, 258; pro-, 5–6, 259, 281n5; as a model, 186; as mystical, 189, 224; representations in community presentations, 119–164; representations on tour, 37–118; as tolerant, 226, 229

Israel Defense Forces. *See* military

Israel-Palestine, 5, 6, 8, 11, 84, 264. *See also* Israel

Israel–Palestine conflict, 127, 197, 202, 212, 219, 244–5, 259–60. *See also al nakba*; Israel; military; Oslo Peace Accords; post-Zionist; Zionism

Israeli Arabs, 106, 231

Israeli Embassy, 193, 211

Israeli Jews, 37–8, 53–4, 61, 63, 71, 74, 78–80, 93, 106, 122, 137, 147, 205, 231, 234, 237, 248, 259, 261, 264, 267; compared to diaspora Jews, 154, 161, 164, 199, 237–8 (*see also* post-Zionist; Zionism); relationships with North American Jews, 222; pro-peace, 108 *See also* Peace Now

Israelites, 42

Italy, 264

Itmar, Yacov (pseudonym). *See* tour presenters

Jaffa, 236

Jaffa Gate, 250. *See also* Jerusalem

Jenan (pseudonym). *See* tour presenters

Jenin, 148

Jericho, 70, 82, 148, 279n2

Jerusalem: annexation of East Jerusalem, 158–9, 250; archaeology, 43, 131–3; East Jerusalem, 51, 105, 116, 133, 277n. 6; Jewish Quarter, 54–6; Mount Herzl, 56 (*see also* Yad Vashem); Mufti of, 113; narrative, 65, 260; Old City, 38, 51, 54, 56, 91, 247–50, 277n7 (*see also* Jerusalem, Greater; Wailing Wall; Western Wall tunnels); and Oslo Peace Accords, 13, 107, 158–9; Palestinian hotel labour, 225; reunification of, 32, 53–4, 87–8, 91–2, 257 (*see also* Ammunition Hill); as spiritual centre, 5, 51–3, 162, 196; three-thousandth birthday, 11, 38, 53–5, 91, 123–4, 214; tour itinerary, 51; West Jerusalem, 38, 51, 250, 277n6

Jerusalem, Greater, 104–5, 115–16, 155, 263, 283n9; as security corridors, 40, 87–90, 103, 111, 116

Jesus, 51, 54; as a Jew, 130

Jewish Agency, 29, 85–6

Jewish National Fund, 11

Jordan, 30–3, 53, 71, 89, 91, 101, 103, 110, 147, 152, 157–9, 178, 208. *See also* Ammunition Hill; Hussein, King of Jordan

Jordan River, 96

Jordan Valley, 38, 40, 71, 117; as security corridor, 103

Josephus, 130

Josie (pseudonym). *See* profiles

Judaism, 23, 55, 127, 145, 163, 174, 204, 209, 216–18, 220, 230–1, 256; contemporary, 128; and democracy, 134–8; foundation of, 138; practices, 129, 138. *See also* Orthodox Jews; Rabin, Yitzhak

Judaization, 105–6, 283n9

Judea, 44, 82, 111; desert, 74; mountains, 44, 110

Kaddish, 63

Kahalani, Victor, 97, 116–7

Karen (pseudonym). *See* profiles

Karla (pseudonym). *See* tour guides

Katz, Cindi, 15

Kennedy, John F., 230

kibbutzim, 29, 38, 83, 86–7, 92–5, 184, 187, 199–200, 204–8, 218, 235–6, 248;

Ben-Gurion, 67, 84, 100; Negev, 65–8; North American representation of, 124. *See also* Revivim; Sde Boker.

Kirschner (pseudonym). *See* tour presenters

Kiryat Shmona, 98–100

Kissinger, Henry, 97

Koestler, Arthur, 140

Kotel. See Wailing Wall

Kramer, Malcolm (pseudonym). *See* community presenters

Kugelmass, Jack, 9

Kuneitra, 93, 96–7

Kurdistan, 51

Kuwait, 33

labour, Palestinian, 71, 79, 83, 225; closure policy, 117

Labour Party, Israel's, 81, 112, 156, 178

Lambeck, Michael, 278n16

'land for peace,' 108. *See* Peace Now

Laurie (pseudonym). *See* tour presenters

Lavie, Smadar, 15, 273n20

Law of Return, 6, 32, 15, 114, 137, 143, 197, 227. *See also aliyah*; Basic Laws; immigration; settlers

Lebanon, 7, 32, 40, 74, 78, 95, 117, 156, 157, 179, 200, 213, 238, 257; conflict with Israel, 98–102, 107, 165; Hezbollah, 102. *See also* Kiryat Shmona; Operation Peace for Galilee War

Leopold, Rabbi (pseudonym). *See* tour participants, on-site presentation

Levine, Michael (pseudonym). *See* community presenters

Liebman, Charles, 34, 35, 259

Likud Party, Israel's, 155
location, 9, 14–5, 17, 242, 246–7; Adrienne Rich, 9
Lubavitcher Jews, 143. *See also* Orthodox Jews
Lynn (pseudonym). *See* profiles

Ma'ale Adumim, 104–5, 178
Maccabbean, 47, 132
Maccabee, 50
Maimonades, 133–5
Malkki, Liisa, 273n20
Mandate British Palestine, 7, 66, 87
mapping, 147–50, 264
March of the Living tour, 201–3, 272n10. *See also* Holocaust; tours
Marlene (pseudonym). *See* profiles
marriage: inter-, 119, 208–9, 246; recognition of, 133, 232. *See also* who is a Jew, debate
Masada, 176, 205, 248; movie, 277n5; myth, 47–9, 125, 129; narrative, 260; North American display, 124–5
McCarthy, Joseph, 129
Megiddo, 177
Meir, Golda, 276n25
memorials. *See* Children's Holocaust Memorial; Holocaust, memorialization; museums; Yad Vashem
Mendelssohn, Moses, 133–5
Messiah, 177, 215, 273n11
messianism, 128
Metulla, 224
Middle East, 5, 13, 31, 35, 66, 77–9, 109, 128, 164, 234, 236, 243, 263–4, 267
migrant labour: in Israel, 71
military, Arab, 30, 90; Egyptian, 97; Lebanese, 98–100; Syrian, 93–7

military, Israeli, 5, 6, 26, 32, 50–4, 73–4, 84–7, 91, 94–103, 111, 118, 141, 202, 249–50, 257, 264–7; checkpoint, 253; critique of 181, 200, 205, 215; and Lebanese militia, 99; romanticized, 172, 199; withdrawal as a result of Oslo Peace Accords, 107, 151. *See also* Ammunition Hill; Burma Road, Battle of; Castel, Battle of; Haganah; Israel-Palestine conflict; Jerusalem; Operation Peace for Galilee War; Oslo Peace Accords; Revivim; Six-Day War; War of Independence; Yom Kippur War
Mishna, 132
modernization, of Israel, 40, 64, 72–3, 83, 122, 207, 210, 255–6, 265; anti-, 256; of Bedouins, 75; development, 124; in relation to postmodernism, 260. *See also* agriculture, development tropes; Orthodox Jews
Mohammed, 51
Morocco, 12, 51, 71–2, 172
moshavim, 65, 93, 95. *See also* kibbutzim
Mouffe, Chantal, 247
Mount Scopus, 52–3; 236
Mubarak, Hosni, 147. *See also* Egypt
multicultural, 4, 25, 264; Israel as, 216, 230; threat of, 102. *See also* authenticity; diaspora; hybridity; identity, multicultural
Munich agreement, 110, 151, 188
museums, 32, 51–8, 61–4, 85, 280n4; Revivim, 86; Washington, 221. *See also* Holocaust, memorialization; Yad Vashem
Muslims, 44, 51, 54–6, 90; immigrants, 165; in Lebanon, 100; sepa-

ration from Israel, 104; Sunni, 99–101. *See also* Bedouin; Druze; Palestinians

Myrna (pseudonym). *See* profiles

myths: and Roland Barthes, 19–20; about Dead Sea Scrolls, 127; of Israel and Zionism, 47, 85, 156, 218, 240; of Masada, 49, 125, 129; military, 58

Nablus, 148

narratives, 4, 9, 14, 18, 20, 25, 29, 32, 40–1, 87, 89; alternative Israeli, 247; of belonging, 40; community, 178; counter-, 42, 262; encoding, 22; Golan, 96; heroism and resistance, 62; Israel, official, 9; Jerusalem, 65, 260; Masada, 260; military, 50, 92; nation-building, 64, 73; national, 21–3, 25, 26, 31, 37, 40, 42, 44, 118, 180; nationalist, 255; Negev, 66, 73, 166; non-Zionist, 255; post-Zionist, 35, 123, 255; presented by tourists, 112; presented to North American Jews, 119, 122–3; production, 24; redemption, 72; religious and secular, 216; resistance to, 24; of siege and defence, 87–9; as told by guides, 37; water, 70; Zionist, 26, 123, 188, 155; Zionist development, 177. *See also* post-Zionist; Zionism

nation: as abstract idea, 4; boundaries, 15; cultural practices of, 3; Jewish, 27, 31, 37, 40, 50, 56, 58, 64, 121, 196–7, 201, 204, 208, 243, 246, 274n20; through myth, 20. *See also* diaspora; diaspora nationalism; narratives; nationalism; post-Zionist; Zionism

nation-state, 4, 16, 25, 28, 32, 40, 54, 139, 247

national holidays, Israeli, 22, 45, 53, 55, 63

nationalism, 4, 13, 18–19, 22–5, 165, 266; and the Negev, 66; Zionism, 5–6, 27. *See also* Zionism

Nazereth, 51, 126, 189, 222

Nazis, 30, 57, 59–62, 110, 162, 174–5, 153, 242, 250. *See also* Holocaust

negation of the diaspora, 161

Negev Desert, 38, 40, 50, 65, 71, 84–6, 90, 105–6, 177, 187, 241, 278n3; *kibbutzim*, 29; North American display of, 124–5. *See also* agriculture; Ben-Gurion; modernization; Revivim

Neot Kedumim, 45

Netanyahu, Benjamin, 109–12; 149, 155, 157–8, 170, 188–9, 210–11, 225, 241, 249, 260

New York, 10, 38, 109, 167, 220

Nixon, Richard, 97

non-governmental organizations, 37, 77

Occupied Territories, 22, 105, 107, 144, 146, 148, 153, 173, 178, 202, 205, 257, 264. *See also* East Jerusalem; Gaza Strip; Palestine; Six-Day War; West Bank

Odessa, 223

Ofakim, 64

oil, 6, 66

oleh. See immigration

olive oil, 45–7; 68

Operation Peace for Galilee War, 32, 84, 98, 100–2, 212–13. *See also* Lebanon; military

Oriental Jews, 12, 35, 71–2, 278n3

Orientalism, 244. *See also* Eurocentrism

Orthodox Jews, 12–13, 56, 120, 129, 134, 136, 140, 142, 144, 146, 155, 167–8, 174–5, 185, 196, 204, 209–10, 216, 231–3, 272–3n11; as antimodernizing, 256; and democracy, 133–8, 139–44, 144–6; as displayed in North America, 127; ultra-, 120, 143, 184, 196, 202–5, 212, 224, 231, 263, 273n11. *See also* democracy; Judaism; marriage; Zionism

Oslo Peace Accords, 13, 33, 39, 107–8, 111–12, 146–7, 150–5, 158, 160, 170, 173, 185, 189, 194, 210, 219, 226, 245, 264, 267; anti-, 108, 149, 153–4, 190; Oslo I, 147; Oslo II, 147–9. *See also* Israel–Palestine conflict; mapping; Palestinians

Ottoman Turks, 29, 86, 132

Ozzy (pseudonym). *See* profiles; tour participants, on-site presentation

Paine, Robert, 22–5

Palestine, 5, 7, 10, 13, 28–33, 85–6, 250–1, 268; autonomous zone, 105, 112, 150–1, 156; partition of, 29, 89, 153; as a state, 148, 155. *See also al nakba*; Israel; Israel–Palestine conflict; Mandate British Palestine; Oslo Peace Accords; Palestinians; War of Independence

Palestine Authority, 13, 104, 107, 111, 148–9, 279n2; checkpoint, 251. *See also* Palestinian Liberation Organization

Palestinian Liberation Organization, 32, 107, 189, 194, 280n3. *See also* Palestine Authority

Palestinians: and border closure, 117;

compared to Bedouin and Druze, 73–4, 78; compared to Israelis, 146, 155, 253, 263, 277n. 6; diaspora, 82, 219; disappearance and displacement, 5–6, 44, 71, 92, 235, 237, 242–3; homeland, 5, 211; identity, 26, 152, 225, 241; land ownership, 103, 116, 132–3, 156; North American representations of, 126–7, 173, 201, 205, 257–8, 261; and Oslo, 33, 151–3, 156, 157, 164–5, 189, 226; police, 82, 252; politics, 133, 139; pre-Israel, 46, 275n11; pro-, 246; problems of, 149, 153, 223, 267; representation on tour, 51, 54, 78–84, 89, 204, 218–19, 240; resistance, 106, 242, 276n17; right of return, 13, 107, 197; as a threat, 100–12, 134, 156, 159–60, 252, 283n9; and Western Wall tunnels, 56; writers in exile, 273–4n20. *See also al nakba*, binational state; Gaza Strip; Hamas; *intifada*; Israel–Palestine conflict; Jericho; labour; Occupied Territories; Oslo Peace Accords; Palestine; Palestine Liberation Organization; refugees; West Bank

Pappe, Ilan, 35

Partition of Palestine. *See* United Nations Partition Plan of 1947

Passover, 45, 51, 174, 204, 229

Paul (pseudonym). *See* profiles

peace, 6, 33, 53, 56, 103, 123, 201, 216, 225, 226, 249–50, 257–58, 265; accords, 13, 33, 39, 110, 111,153, 160, 194–5; between Jews, 128; process, 122, 210, 212. *See also* Oslo Peace Accords

Peace Now, 11, 101, 117, 160, 166, 200, 239; Friends of, 279n. 5

Peras, Shimon, 149, 217
Pinhas (pseudonym). *See* tour presenters
pioneers, 235. *See also* profiles, Ian and Samantha; Revivim
poach (de Certeau), 23, 25, 166
pogroms, 5
Poland, 51, 58
postmodern, 4, 14, 16, 265; ethos, 246–7; map, 148–50; relationship to modernism, 260
post-Zionist, 27, 123, 137, 144, 206, 255, 259–62, 267
'practices in place,' 17, 248, 268
profiles (pseudonyms): Aaron, 186–91; Gillian, 223–9; Hope, 229–33; Ian and Samantha, 233–41; Jeremy, 248–54; Josie, 219–23; Karen and Paul, 206–12; Lynn, 198–206, 254; Marlene, 192–8, 254; Myrna, 167–74; Ozzy, 213–19; Warren and Sarah, 174–86
pro-Israel: 5, 34–5
Promised Land, 230, 266. *See also* Bible; Holy Land; Homeland; Israel
pushed into the ocean/sea, 113, 118, 150, 189
pushkas, 168

Qumran. *See* Dead Sea Scrolls

Rabin, Yitzhak, 13, 93, 104, 149, 151, 158, 194; after, 170; Amir, Yigal (assassin), 146, 231; assassination, 122, 145–6, 155, 185, 211, 230–1, 256; funeral, 147, 163. *See also* Oslo Peace Accords
racism, 5, 157, 183, 184, 196, 201, 242; in Israel, 114, 262, 274n20; Israel

free from, 242; toward North American immigrants, 182. *See also* anti-Semitism; Eurocentrism; Orientalism
Rageau, Jean Pierre, 14
Ramallah, 148, 251, 253
Ramle, 252
Ranger, Terence, 18
Realpolitik, 190, 197, 256
Reconstructionist Jews, 12, 273n11
Red Sea, 186, 213
reflexivity, 242–54
Reform Jews, 12, 129, 135, 143, 144, 146, 154, 161, 174, 183, 232, 242, 272n11
Refuge, Israel as, 6, 7, 168, 182, 215, 216, 233, 265
refugees, 16–17, 273n19, 273–4n20, 282n5; Palestinian, 5, 30, 102, 107, 113–14, 158, 246, 253. *See also* diaspora; Israel; Oslo Peace Accords; Palestinians
Remembrance Hill. *See* Yad Vashem
resistance: and the Holocaust, 62; Masada, 49; Palestinian, 106–9, 242. *See also* de Certeau; Holocaust, memorialization; *intifada*
Revivim, 85–87. *See also kibbutzim*; Negev Desert; War of Independence
Rich, Adrienne, 9, 25
Right of Return, Palestinian, 13, 197. *See also* Israel–Palestine conflict; Law of Return; Oslo Peace Accords; Palestine; Palestinians; refugees
Roman: era, 84, 126, 128, 129, 132, 236
Romania, 72
Romans: 43, 52, 84, 130; and Masada, 47–9, 124, 125, 248. *See also* Masada

Roth, Philip, 282n2
Russia, 28, 51, 59, 93, 162, 167, 192, 193, 214, 232, 244
Rwanda, 59

Sadat, Anwar, 159. *See also* Camp David Accords, Egypt
Sadducees, 128. *See also* Dead Sea Scrolls
Samantha (pseudonym). *See* profiles
Samaria, 82; mountains, 110–11, 141
Sarah (pseudonym). *See* profiles
Saudi Arabia, 51, 157, 159
Scheck, Avraham (pseudonym). *See* community presenters
Sde Boker, 67. *See also* Ben-Gurion
Second World War, 5, 29, 59, 60, 119, 160, 168, 213, 230. *See also* Holocaust
secular: heritage, 127; Israelis, 129, 163; Jews, 135, 140, 192, 196, 197, 216, 230, 233; vs Orthodox Jews in Israel, 142, 174, 198, 256
security corridors. *See* Jerusalem, Greater; Jordan Valley; Netanyahu, Benjamin
Segev, Tom, 35
Sephardic Jews, 12, 71, 72, 278n3
Sepphoris, 125. *See also* archaeological sites
settlements, 35, 40, 47, 65, 69, 85–8, 92, 103–6, 108, 115, 117, 149–51, 155, 188, 237
settlers, Israeli, 22, 35, 56, 65, 149, 184, 260, 263, 278n1. *See also* Ma'ale Adumim; Oslo Peace Accords
settler-colonial state, 6
Sha'ath, Nabil, 159
Shamgar-Handelman, Lea, 63
Sharon, Ariel, 102

Sheffer, Gabriel, 33
Shelley (pseudonym). *See* tour participants, on-site resistance
Shlaim, Avi, 35
Sinai: occupation of, 32; return to Egypt, 33. *See also* Camp David Peace Accords; Egypt
Sivan (pseudonym). *See* tour guides
Six-Day War, 32, 40, 50, 53, 84, 91–6, 100, 107, 109, 115, 145, 165, 192, 212, 238, 257. *See also* Egypt; Gaza Strip; Jerusalem; Jordan; military; Occupied Territories; Syria; West Bank
Smith, Neil, 15
Solomonic Gates, 43–4. *See also* archaeological sites
Soviet Union. *See* Russia
Spain, 12
Spinoza, Baruch, 133–5
Spivak, Gayatri, 243
Status Quo Agreement, 134, 141, 145. *See also* Orthodox Jews
Stephanie (pseudonym). *See* tour presenters
Sternhall, Zvi, 35
Suez Canal, 96
Sweden, 51
Swedenburg, Ted, 15
synagogues, 9, 10–11, 48, 55, 120, 131, 174, 227, 279n5; Reform, 146, 154, 161, 174, 242; reproduction, 124–6
Syria, 30, 32, 40, 78–9, 92–7, 101–2, 107, 117, 156, 179, 238. *See also* Kuneitra; military; Yom Kippur War

Talia (pseudonym). *See* tour guides
Tel Aviv, 29, 38, 63, 66, 69, 80, 108, 162, 176, 178, 188, 196, 236, 240

Temple Mount: archaeology, 131–3; First Temple, 42–3, 47, 53–5, 128, 131

temples. *See* synagogues

terrorism, 32, 101–2, 160, 185, 253; Israeli response to, 108

Tolstoy, 162

Torah, 130, 135, 202–4, 256

Toronto, 10, 38, 182

tour guides: about, 37–8, 41, 42, 43–4, 46, 51, 55, 56, 59–61, 65, 84, 107, 121, 130, 150, 214; Israel Civil Society Fund guides (pseudonyms), Karla, 80–3; Israel Development Fund guide (pseudonym), Arnie, 43, 47–50, 51–4, 57–9, 66–8, 72, 73–5, 78, 79, 87–9, 96, 104, 113–16, 186, 217, 225–6; Israel Land Fund guides (pseudonyms), Talia, 50, 57, 61, 65–6, 68, 70, 71, 77, 78, 87, 89–90, 96, 98–101, 104, 108, 177, 238, 240; Sivan, 43, 63, 68, 70–1, 82, 96, 103. *See also* tour presenters; tours

tour participants (pseudonyms): Faye, 113–14; Gabriel, 117; on-site presentation, Ozzy, 59; on-site resistance, Aaron, 115–16; Shelley, 117; Wolfe, 117

tour presenters (pseudonyms): Avi, 100–1, 178, 237–8; Dov Kirschner, 68; Heidi, 77; Jenan, 75–7; Laurie, 45–7; Ori Dan, 69; Pinhas, 93–6; Stephanie, 84; Yacov Itmar, 83. *See also* Kahalani, Victor; Netanyahu, Benjamin

tours, 7, 8, 11–12, 14, 25, 27, 31, 37–9, 40–1, 42, 44, 51, 54–5, 56, 63, 65, 73, 112, 124, 127, 130, 150, 160, 184, 198, 203, 208, 214, 257, 272n11,

276n. 1, 277n5, 277n9; Israel Civil Society Fund (pseudonym), 38–9, 63, 68, 70–1, 75, 77, 79–83, 90, 103, 116, 123, 170, 192–7, 219–23, 229, 279n2, Israel Development Fund (pseudonym), 39, 43, 47, 51, 57–9, 66–8, 73–5, 78, 79, 87–9, 96, 104, 109, 113–16, 125, 186, 213, 216, 223, 228, 248; Israel Land Fund (pseudonym), 38–9, 44, 51, 57, 62, 65–6, 68, 70, 71, 75, 77, 79, 87, 89, 96, 100, 104, 108, 176, 235, 237, 239. *See also* March of the Living

Tov, Amir (pseudonym). *See* community presenters

Treblinka, 60

Troper, Harold, 165–6, 213

tunnels, of the Western Wall. *See* Wailing Wall

Turks, 50, 54. *See also* Ottoman Turks

Ukraine, 192, 214

ultranationalists, 120, 133, 175, 184. *See also* Greater Jerusalem; settler-colonial; settlers; Zionism

United Israel Appeal. *See* United Jewish Appeal

United Jewish Appeal, 11, 192

United Kingdom, 33, 81. *See also* British; England

United Nations, 7, 30, 85, 96, 109, 114, 155, 179, 217

United Nations Partition Plan of 1947, 7, 29–30, 32, 84, 87, 153, 234. *See also* al nakba; Battle of Castel; Declaration of State of Israel; Palestine; Palestinians

United States, 4, 6, 10, 29, 33–5, 57, 80, 81, 86, 170, 172, 177, 192, 193, 209–10, 219, 220, 223, 229, 230, 233,

242, 248, 253, 264; Americanization, 217–18; military advice, 151–
2; military aid, 97; support, 155
Uris, Leon, 175

Valley of Ayalon, 50
Valley of Tears, 97
Valley of the Destroyed Communi-
ties, 57, 62, 63. *See also* Yad Vashem

Wailing Wall, 52, 54, 55, 91, 131, 162,
201, 216, 217, 224, 236, 249; tunnels, 55–6, 118, 131–2. *See also*
Jerusalem; Temple Mount
War of Independence, 32, 40, 50, 55,
84, 87–90, 113, 276n17. *See also al
nakba*; Battle of Burma Road; Battle of Castel; Declaration of the
State of Israel; military; Revivim;
United Nations Partition Plan of
1947
Warren (pseudonym). *See* profiles
Warsaw Ghetto Plaza, 57–8, 61. *See
also* Yad Vashem
Warsaw Ghetto, 62
water: development projects, 39;
Golan, 95–6; irrigation, 69, 71, 124–
5, 177; and modernization of
Israel, 72; narratives, 70; Negev,
66; and peace, 197; as propaganda,
85, 237. *See also* agriculture; mod-
ernization; Negev Desert
Werbner, Pnina, 165, 259
West Bank, 5, 13, 32, 33, 78, 82, 111,
117, 147–8, 150–2, 157, 178, 211,
219, 252–4, 263, 278n1. *See also*
Occupied Territories
West, the, 6, 189
Western Wall tunnels. *See* Wailing
Wall

Western: analyses of 'native' people,
15; democracy, 208; guilt over the
Holocaust, 6; oriented Israel, 5, 64,
102; world, 162
White House, 193
White, Curtis, 268
who is a Jew, debate, 129, 136, 139,
143, 165, 184. *See also* marriage;
Orthodox Jews
Wolfe (pseudonym). *See* tour participants, on-site resistance

Yad Vashem, 57, 58, 59, 60, 62, 63, 64,
213, 221, 249. *See also* Holocaust;
museums
Yemen, 51, 71, 72, 172
Yesh Gvul, 166. *See also* peace
Yom Kippur, 141, 223
Yom Kippur War, 32, 84, 92, 96–7,
200, 276n26. *See also* Syria; military
Yugoslavia, 101

Zealots, Jewish, 125
Zionism, 5–6, 10, 22, 28–9, 32–4, 57,
118, 137, 139, 149, 143, 172, 203,
254, 258–9, 261, 276n25, 281n5,
281n2, 282n2; anti-, 175, 234, 239;
one-hundredth anniversary, 11,
123, 154–5, 161; principles of, 144;
successes of, 145, 161–3; versus
Judaism, 141. *See also* post-Zionist;
Zionist
Zionist, 27–8, 31–6, 58, 121, 123, 126,
138, 143, 156, 183, 187, 208, 218,
234–7, 255–60, 267, 275n1, 275n11;
and annexation, 158; anti-, 174,
183, 272n12, 273n11, 275n1; classic,
34, 161, 165, 203, 207, 210, 249;
European ideology, 51; Israeli, 34,
141; markers, 169, 191; and

national identity, 4, 267; non-, 137, 255, 260, 262; political, 28, 161–2; relation to North American Jews, 5, 153; religious, 28, 142; socialist, 28, 236. *See also* Ahad Ha'am; post-Zionist; Theodor Herzl; Zionism

Zionist Organization of America, 160

CULTURAL SPACES

Cultural Spaces explores the rapidly changing temporal, spatial, and theoretical boundaries of contemporary cultural studies. Culture has long been understood as the force that defines and delimits societies in fixed spaces. The recent intensification of globalizing processes, however, has meant that it is no longer possible – if it ever was – to imagine the world as a collection of autonomous, monadic spaces, whether these are imagined as localities, nations, regions within nations, or cultures demarcated by region or nation. One of the major challenges of studying contemporary culture is to understand the new relationships of culture to space that are produced today. The aim of this series is to publish bold new analyses and theories of spaces of culture, as well as investigations of the historical construction of those cultural spaces that have influenced the shape of the contemporary world.

Series Editors
Richard Cavell, University of British Columbia
Imre Szeman, McMaster University

Editorial Advisory Board
Lauren Berlant, University of Chicago
Homi K. Bhabha, Harvard University
Hazel V. Carby, Yale University
Richard Day, Queen's University
Christopher Gittings, University of Western Ontario
Lawrence Grossberg, University of North Caroling
Mark Kingwell, University of Toronto
Heather Murray, University of Toronto
Elspeth Probyn, University of Sydney
Rinaldo Walcott, OISE/University of Toronto

Books in the Series
Peter Ives, *Gramsci's Politics of Language: Engaging the Bakhtin Circle and the Frankfurt School*
Sarah Brophy, *Witnessing AIDS: Writing, Testimony, and the Work of Mourning*
Shane Gunster, *Capitalizing on Culture: Critical Theory for Cultural Studies*
Jasmin Habib, *Israel, Diaspora, and the Routes of National Belonging*